S0-BQW-517

Escape Routes

Escape Routes: Contemporary Perspectives on Life After Punishment addresses the reasons why people stop offending, and the processes by which they are rehabilitated or resettled back into the community. Engaging with, and building upon, renewed criminological interest in this area, *Escape Routes* nevertheless broadens and enlivens the current debate. First, its scope goes beyond a narrowly defined notion of crime and includes, for example, essays on religious redemption, the lives of ex-war criminals, and the relationship between ethnicity and desistance from crime. Second, contributors to this volume draw upon a number of areas of contemporary research, including urban studies, philosophy, history, religious studies, and ethics, as well as criminology. Examining new theoretical work in the study of desistance and exploring the experiences of a number of groups whose experiences of life after punishment do not usually attract much attention, *Escape Routes* provides new insights about the processes associated with reform, resettlement and forgiveness. Intended to drive our understanding of life after punishment forward, its rich array of theoretical and substantive papers will be of considerable interest to criminologists, lawyers, and sociologists.

Professor Stephen Farrall is Professor of Criminology at the School of Law, Sheffield University and Director of the Centre for Criminological Research in the School of Law.

Professor Mike Hough is Director of the Institute for Criminal Policy Research, London.

Professor Shadd Maruna is the Director of the Institute of Criminology and Criminal Justice at the School of Law, Queen's University Belfast.

Professor Richard Sparks is Professor of Criminology at the University of Edinburgh and Co-Director of the Scottish Centre for Crime and Justice Research.

Escape Routes

Contemporary Perspectives on Life After Punishment

Edited by
Stephen Farrall, Mike Hough, Shadd Maruna and Richard Sparks

Routledge
Taylor & Francis Group
a GlassHouse book

First published 2011
by Routledge
2 Park Square, Milton Park, Abingdon, Oxon, OX14 4RN

Simultaneously published in the USA and Canada
by Routledge
270 Madison Avenue, New York, NY 10016

A GlassHouse book

Routledge is an imprint of the Taylor & Francis Group, an informa business

Typeset in Times New Roman by
Glyph International

Printed and bound in Great Britain by
CPI Antony Rowe, Chippenham, Wiltshire

British Library Cataloguing in Publication Data
A catalogue record for this book is available from the British Library

Library of Congress Cataloging in Publication Data
Escape routes : contemporary perspectives on life after punishment/ edited by Stephen Farrall ... [et al.].
p. cm.
ISBN 978-0-415-55034-5 (hbk) -- ISBN 978-0-203-83588-3 (ebk) 1. Criminals--Rehabilitation. 2. Redemption. I. Farrall, Stephen.
HV9276.E83 2011
365'.66--dc22 2010023228

ISBN13: 978-0-415-55034-5 (hbk)
ISBN13: 978-0-203-83588-3(ebk)

Contents

Contributors

Anette Ballinger is a lecturer at Keele University. She is the author of the award-winning book *Dead Woman Walking: Executed Women in England & Wales 1900–1955* (Ashgate: 2000) (Hart Socio-Legal Prize 2001), and has written several book chapters and journal articles on the subject of gender and punishment in modern history. She is currently working on a book entitled *Capitalising on Punishment: State Power, Gender and Women Who Kill*, to be published by Ashgate.

Mechthild Bereswill, Dr. phil., Professor of Sociology, University of Kassel (Department of Social Work). Studies in Sociology, Social Psychology and Political Sciences at the University of Hanover; 1998–2007: Senior Researcher in the Criminological Research Institute of Lower Saxony (KFN). Fields of research: sociology of social control; gender studies; qualitative methodologies.

Anthony Bottoms is Emeritus Wolfson Professor of Criminology at the University of Cambridge and Honorary Professor of Criminology at the University of Sheffield. He is also a Fellow of the British Academy.

Adam Calverley is a lecturer in Criminology at the Department of Social Sciences at the University of Hull and is the co-author, with Stephen Farrall, of *Understanding Desistance from Crime* (London: Open University Press, 2006) and a co-author of the Home Office Research Study, *Black and Asian Offenders on Probation*. His research interests include ethnicity, crime and criminal justice, emotions and their implications for desistance.

Christopher Deacy is Senior Lecturer in Applied Theology at the University of Kent. His publications are in the field of theology and film, with specific reference to the relationship between film and the Christian category of redemption. He is currently writing a book for Routledge on cinematic treatments of the afterlife.

Stephen Farrall is Professor of Criminology at the School of Law, Sheffield University and Director of the Centre for Criminological Research in the

School of Law. He has been studying desistance from crime since the early 1990s, and between 2010 and 2012 is conducting further interviews with a cohort of ex-probationers originally interviewed in 1997–1999.

Mike Hough is Director of the Institute for Criminal Policy Research. Mike has published on a range of criminological topics including probation work, youth justice, policing, crime prevention and community safety, anti-social behaviour, probation and drugs. Current studies includes research on sentencing, on youth justice and on public trust in justice.

Ben Hunter is a Research Associate at the University of Sheffield where he is currently involved in the project *Tracking Progress on Probation: Long Term Patterns of Desistance*, due to end in April 2012. His main research interests are white-collar crime, desistance from crime and resettlement after conviction and punishment.

Susanne Karstedt is Professor of Criminology and Criminal Justice at the Centre for Criminal Justice Studies, University of Leeds. She has widely researched and published on transitional justice. Other research interests and publications include: cross-cultural and comparative studies on democracy, crime and justice, middle class crime and the prevention of mass atrocities.

Shadd Maruna is the Director of the Institute of Criminology and Criminal Justice at the School of Law, Queen's University Belfast. His other books include *Making Good: How Ex-Convicts Reform and Rebuild Their Lives* (Washington, DC: American Psychological Association Books, 2001), *Rehabilitation: Beyond the Risk Paradigm* (London, Routledge, 2007, with Tony Ward), and *Fifty Key Thinkers in Criminology* (London: Routledge, 2010, edited with Keith Hayward and Jayne Mooney).

Anne-Marie McAlinden is Lecturer in the School of Law at Queen's University Belfast. Her first book, *The Shaming of Sexual Offenders* (Oxford: Hart Publishing, 2007) was awarded the British Society of Criminology Book Prize for 2008. She is currently working on a second monograph on sexual grooming to be published by Oxford University Press in 2012.

Lesley McAra holds the Chair of Penology in the Centre for Law and Society, University of Edinburgh and is co-director of the Edinburgh Study of Youth Transitions and Crime. She writes and teaches in the fields of youth crime and justice, comparative criminal justice, and the impact of multi-level governance on crime control and penal process.

Robert MacDonald is Professor of Sociology at Teesside University. He has researched and written about young people and youth issues for many years and wrote, with Jane Marsh, *Disconnected Youth? Growing up in Britain's Poor Neighbourhoods* (Houndmills: Palgrave, 2005). Recent research focuses on work, worklessness and welfare.

Susan McVie is Professor of Quantitative Criminology in the School of Law at the University of Edinburgh. She is Co-Director of the Edinburgh Study of Youth Transitions and Crime and has published widely in areas including youth crime and justice, gangs and knife crime, youth marginalisation and racism, and victimisation.

Joanna Shapland is Professor of Criminal Justice and Head of the School of Law at the University of Sheffield, UK. She has researched extensively into victimology, restorative justice and criminal justice and is Executive Editor of the *International Review of Victimology*.

Tracy Shildrick is Professor in Sociology at Teesside University. She is Deputy Editor of the *Journal of Youth Studies* and leads the European Sociological Association's Youth and Generation network. She has published widely on youth exclusion, poverty and worklessness including as co-editor, *Young People, Class and Place* (Houndmills: Palgrave, 2010).

Mark Simpson is the Dean of the School of Social Sciences & Law at Teesside University. His research interests focus on drug use and criminal careers. Along with colleagues, he edited *Drugs in Britain* (Houndmills: Palgrave, 2007) and his most recent research focuses on drug patterns across Europe.

Richard Sparks is Professor of Criminology at the University of Edinburgh and Co-Director of the Scottish Centre for Crime and Justice Research.

Colin Webster is Reader in Criminology at Leeds Metropolitan University. He has written extensively about youth transitions, criminal careers, social exclusion and social cohesion, and ethnicity and crime. His most recent book is *Understanding Race and Crime* (Milton Keynes: Open University Press, 2007).

Introduction

Life after punishment

Identifying new strands in the research agenda

Stephen Farrall, Mike Hough, Shadd Maruna and Richard Sparks

For the past few years, the four of us have been fortunate enough to have been involved in the organisation of a series of seminars devoted, in one way or another, to the consideration of the lives of some of those people who have found themselves caught up in the criminal justice system. The first two of the seminars were held at Keele University and were paid for by the Department of Criminology there.[1] A subsequent six seminars were funded by the Economic and Social Research Council (ESRC) as part of a seminar series devoted to the exploration of 'life after punishment'.[2] These six seminars have now resulted in two collections of essays; one of which is this volume.[3] A further seminar, devoted to a review of criminal careers research in Europe was also held in Keele.[4]

In this introduction, we will not only introduce the essays selected for inclusion in the current volume (which is of course only right and proper for such a venture), but we also want to take this opportunity to summarise what we feel we learnt about life after punishment[5] from our involvement in these seminars. Of course, it would be quite impossible to summarise and distil all that was said in over 40 presentations (not counting the formal responses made by discussants) or the discussions generated amongst attendees, and so we will have to content ourselves with 'cherry-picking' the highlights and key messages which came out from both specific papers and from across the discussions we held.

In this respect, we highlight three key areas for consideration. These are: (a) dissecting the processes associated with desistance and rehabilitation; (b) the role of the criminal justice system and similar bodies in these processes; and, finally, (c) new and previously under-researched areas of enquiry into desistance that are emerging.

The processes associated with desistance

One of the most difficult tasks facing those wishing to leave behind a criminal past is proving to those around them that they are 'more than just the sum of their crimes'. This observation was made at the very outset of the series by Shadd Maruna. Somewhat unusually for a seminar series on 'life after punishment', Maruna's opening lecture focused on the life of Tookie Williams who, as a victim of California's death row, never had the opportunity to experience life after prison. Maruna argued, however, that Williams's efforts to prove to the state of California and in particular to Governor Arnold Schwarzenegger that his life was worth preserving provided a hugely useful lesson in the challenge of developing a 'redemption script' for oneself after involvement in notorious criminal activities. Indeed, in many ways, this theme set the tone for contributions throughout the series as a whole. The topic was most poignantly returned to by Monica Barry in a later seminar in recounting the death of a young man she had worked with in a social work capacity who took his own life the night before he was due to be released from prison. Feeling that he would only ever be seen for the crimes he had committed rather than the person he was trying to become, Willy MacDonald hung himself.

In his opening presentation (and more generally, see Maruna 2001), Maruna argued that individuals like Williams or MacDonald need to find ways of re-narrating their past lives in order to make those histories consistent with who they are in the present and want to be in the future. This led to discussions about the role that apologies and other expressions of remorse play in the rehabilitation process and the extent to which elements of what can be described as 'creative self deception' are compatible with genuine reform. Taking responsibility for past actions (which is perhaps what is at the heart of an apology) appears at first glance to be at odds with some forms of re-biographing described by Maruna and others (see Maruna and Copes 2005; Maruna and Mann 2006). Yet, somehow, ex-offenders need to find a way of walking this knife-edge; like a performance artiste on a tightrope, they have to find a way of taking responsibility for (at least some of) their past actions and yet find a way of doing this without damaging too greatly their sense of themselves as someone worthy of having a future. Failure to achieve this – in extreme cases – may lead to outcomes similar to those of Willy MacDonald.

For Maruna, the answer here was to separate 'passive responsibility' from 'active responsibility' (see e.g. Bovens 1998; Braithwaite and Roche 2001). Whereby the former is about holding people accountable for what they have done in the past, the latter is about expecting them to make things right in the future. Maruna argued that ex-offenders could resist some of the pressures of passive responsibility by focusing on active efforts to 'make good' in the present. Tookie Williams's efforts to negotiate a gang peace in southern California and the series of books he wrote for young people to try to discourage their involvement in criminal behaviour typify precisely this approach to 'apologise' through one's actions rather than just words. However, these efforts (portrayed in the HBO movie *Redemption* in 2004) were clearly not enough to persuade that other Hollywood figure, Governor Schwarzenegger, who argued that Williams's plea of innocence for his crimes showed that he refused to take responsibility (i.e. passive responsibility) for what he had done.

Indeed, Hollywood's role in promoting or discouraging support for ex-prisoners was a theme that emerged numerous times over the seminar series. We found ourselves returning to a tension between films about prisons and ex-offenders (which typically present positive and sympathetic images of ex-cons in leading roles), and the wider media hostility toward prisoner release. Two papers during our series touched on ex-prisoners in film; one, by Chris Deacy is included in this volume; the other, by Mike Nellis, was published in the special edition of *Theoretical Criminology*, (2009) 13(1), that emerged from the series. Both papers demonstrate that some of the most popular films in cinema history have often portrayed ex-convicts in positive ways. Often, as Nellis notes (2009: 142) such films invite viewers to focus on the resolution of the private moral agonies associated with release and reform. Many of the heroes and heroines of these films come to realise that although there is nothing they can do about the past, they can make the future better (although this may require the use of self-destructive violence, as is the case in *Sling Blade*, 1996). One particularly interesting aspect of Nellis's paper was the divide between the portrayal of how black and white ex-prisoners forge paths away from crime. For instance, he argues that for black ex-prisoners, popular films typically emphasise individual, rather than social or collective, processes of reform and help (see also Calverley 2009, described below).

Although our seminar series took place entirely in the UK, we were very fortunate to be able to draw upon the expertise of those scholars who were visiting the UK during the lifespan of our project, such as Denis Bracken. Along with colleagues in Canada, Bracken has been involved in an evaluation of a programme aimed at intervening with Aboriginal gang members living in Manitoba (see Bracken *et al* 2009). This research is of considerable interest as it is one of the few programmes to explore ways of working with First Nationals who have become embroiled in crime. Bracken and his colleagues have had to grapple with how structural, cultural and biographical processes of both criminalisation and reform need to be addressed in such circumstances. Moreover, because of the emphasis on ceremonies placed by both wider Aboriginal cultures and by the programme they helped to evaluate, Bracken and colleagues have illustrated how de-criminalisation rituals may work in practice (see also Braithwaite and Roche 2001; Maruna 2001). Bracken and his colleagues address the question of how the desisting aboriginal offender overcomes the 'double problem' of building up the various forms of social capital necessary to support the decision to desist, within a society which not only does not provide significant support, but actively reinforces negative identities through racism and stigmatization.

These issues of cultural conflict were centre stage at one of our seminars – devoted to the consideration of special populations of ex-prisoners – hosted by Queen's University in Belfast, Northern Ireland. The Belfast seminar afforded the opportunity to learn (often first hand) about those men and women released from prison under the Good Friday Agreement as well as other groups of politically motivated former prisoners. Several papers were devoted to this topic (see McEvoy and Shirlow 2009, for one published example), including a presentation by former prisoners Rosena Brown and Rosie McCorley (Irish Republicans who served time for politically motivated activities). What these presentations brought to the fore was a very timely and considered discussion of the ways in which ex-political prisoners were uniquely positioned to be able to assist in the peace-making process and the building of a new, post-conflict society. Such prisoners were amongst the very best-placed to be able to articulate arguments which, to put it crudely, favoured the ballot box over the gun. As McEvoy and Shirlow argue, far from being a burden on society, politically motivated former prisoners have been at the forefront of progressive change in Northern Ireland. The political leadership of ex-combatants from the Northern Ireland conflict stands in stark contrast to media images of both convicted 'terrorists' and of ex-prisoners and suggests a re-examination of both labels.

In a sense, the experiences emerging from Northern Ireland provide an entirely different answer to the question, so frequently asked in terms of ex-prisoner reintegration, of 'What works?' – regardless of what the word 'works' might mean in this context (and leaving aside the matter of the question mark slowly going a.w.o.l. from the 'What works?' label, giving the impression that matters of effectiveness have now been settled in the literature). In their seminar presentation, Beth Weaver and Fergus McNeill pointed out that the 'What works?' question has been asked more often than the equally important question 'Is it just?'. Such a normative issue may at first glance appear to be a rather 'academic' one (using 'academic' in a somewhat dismissive manner, of course); however, issues relating to justness (or fairness, to use a rather less clumsy formulation of these concerns) have started to gain prominence in recent years. If sentences are recognised as fair or just by whatever measure on the part of both those sentenced and the wider community, compliance may be increased in the long term (see Bottoms 2002; Robinson and McNeill 2008). There are clear connections to be made between desistance perspectives on support for offenders and procedural justice theories, now most closely associated with Tom Tyler (cf. Tyler and Huo 2002; Tyler 2003; Tyler 2007). Procedural justice theories propose specific relationships between:

- the treatment people receive at the hand of officials in the criminal justice systems;
- the resultant trust that people have in institutions of justice;
- the legitimacy people confer, as a consequence of this trust, on institutions of justice;
- the authority that these institutions can command if they are regarded as legitimate; and,
- people's consequent preparedness to comply with the law and cooperate with justice systems.

Procedural justice thinking has been applied most often within criminology to relations between the police and public. However the analyses of prison regimes by Sparks *et al* (1996) and Liebling (2004) establish convincingly that prisoners are equally sensitive to the quality of treatment they receive at the hands of prison staff: fair and respectful treatment is a key ingredient in successful regimes. Although equivalent research on probation work with offenders has yet to be done, it seems likely that probation staff who are trusted, and who can command legitimacy from those they supervise, will have the greatest chance of securing compliance (Bottoms 2002; Robinson and McNeill 2008).

Relating to wider social contexts, a number of the papers presented during the seminars hinted at subtle variations in the processes associated with desistance and reform. Frequently, these were related to the wider social and economic contexts in which processes of reform were played out. For instance, in their study of desistance amongst offenders in the late nineteenth and early twentieth centuries, Stephen Farrall, Barry Godfrey and colleagues argued that desistance for males requires, in part, a strong, empowered female constituency in democratic society who are able to, for want of a better term, 'police' males (Farrall *et al* 2009; see also Godfrey *et al* 2007). That is, in times when gender inequalities are less pronounced than they were in the late nineteenth and early twentieth centuries, females are able to exert (willingly or otherwise) a greater degree of control over partners and husbands (and for that matter, maybe over their fathers and brothers too). Several studies have suggested that many Victorian and Edwardian marriages involved tension, violence, distrust and dislike, rather than (or as well as) romantic love (D'Cruze 1998; Hammerton 1992). Marriage today (with the increased emphasis upon romantic love) may act as a mechanism for reforming men who wish to please or win approval from their spouses. However, in the period Godfrey and colleagues studied, when economic need arguably played the key role in relationship formation, many wives' ability to control or influence the behaviour of their husbands may have been severely limited. It must be remembered that, despite any inequalities in pay that exist in contemporary society, many women in the late nineteenth and early twentieth centuries were in a far worse position; few had access for very long periods of their lives to independent sources of income, those who refrained from marriage were often dealt with suspicion and *none* had the vote until 1918. Until the 1880s women did not have the right to control their own property or wages and could be imprisoned for refusing sexual intercourse (Smith 1989: 19). Women's employment was downgraded during the industrial revolution, and many were prevented from working by trade unions, saw their work 'feminised' into low prestige jobs, and found themselves at the bottom of the class/gender hierarchy coping with a culture of female subordination to males.

As such, Godfrey and colleagues conclude that marriage in the late nineteenth and early twentieth centuries may not have acted as quite the brake on male offending that it does today. Women's position in society changed considerably after the extension of the right to vote in 1928 and after the Second World War (Smith 1989). In the era they studied, few women had the vote and few worked after marriage; after changes in legislation and the social upheavals brought about by mass war, females were in a stronger position in society than they had been previously and were in a better position to informally control males, which in turn increased their ability to support desistance (see e.g. Sampson and Laub 1993). As such it appears that male desistance, at some level, requires female emancipation in order for females to have (in male eyes) a warrantable voice and therefore be able to sway the behaviours of the men in their lives. In this respect, structures and values which enable female emancipation assist male desistance, including welfare state provision, access to birth control and political rights (all of which did much to advance the position of females of course, see Smith 1989). Male desistance, therefore, occurs through mechanisms of informal social control (*à la* Sampson and Laub 1993), but these rest on a bedrock of *formal* institutions and institutionalised values – such as greater levels of gender equality.

Whether one agrees or not with the mechanisms offered by Godfrey *et al*, others have also found that the precise role of marriage and employment differs according to national context. In Finland (where cohabitation between couples for several years prior to marriage is common), Savoleinen (2009: 300–01) suggests that Finnish women who live with an ex-prisoner even without marrying him may act as effective handlers in the process of cognitive re-orientations away from crime. Similarly, MacDonald *et al* (Chapter 5 of this volume) have argued that the lives and biographies of the young men and women which they have studied were hugely influenced by the arrival of heroin on Teesside in the mid-1990s following the collapse of working class employment opportunities in that area and the traditions which such employment maintained. As they write below:

> This sharp decline in previously established working-class routes to adulthood, in this place at this time, we believe, offers the best clue as to why criminality and dependent drug use became more likely for some, and why *purposeless* activity emerged from collapsed opportunity, aspiration and direction for many.

Such changes, of course, influenced those routes away from crime, both in terms of their timing and their nature. However, respondents in their samples did not appear to recognise these contingencies:

> To us, as researchers, the conditions of history, place and class are critical in understanding the biographies of our informants and the stories they told us. This 'sociological imagination', this placing of biographies in social and historical context, was, however, strikingly absent from our interviews. Time and time again interviewees refused to seek explanations of their criminal careers that went beyond their own personal failings and mistakes. Whilst in retrospect, in making sense of their lives, they might point to critical moments, contingencies and pressures that presaged criminality or drug use, overall a discourse of individual responsibility ruled.

These studies demonstrate the importance of locating respondents' lives historically and socially. It is highly unlikely that the processes involved in desistance are universal, transcending time and space. Although there may be important commonalities, cross-cultural and cross-situational differences are equally important.

The role of the criminal justice system

In exploring life after punishment, one is inevitably forced to consider the impacts of the criminal justice system itself. Numerous contributors to the seminar series (but by no means all of them) suggested that, on the basis of their data analyses, the criminal justice system's most immediate impact was on hindering desistance from crime, retaining people within the criminal justice system for longer than might otherwise have been the case and delaying the commencement of life after punishment for them. McAra and McVie (using data from the Edinburgh Study of Youth Transitions and Crime) found evidence that early interventions appeared to encourage young people to continue offending, rather than encouraging them to desist. Their analysis suggests that rather than this simply being the case that frequent offenders start earlier and offend at a high rate, it would appear that criminal justice interventions may serve to make further offending more likely (see also Farrington 1977; Farrington *et al* 1978). Other contributors to the seminar series (e.g. Alan France, Emily Gray and Simon Merrington, Paul Turnbull and Martin Frisher) similarly reported data which suggested that interventions in themselves may be criminalising. Frisher, when discussing the psychology of desistance from drug use, noted how, in experimental conditions, penalising past bad behaviour was not nearly as effective at preventing future transgressions as rewarding and modelling good behaviour.

Similarly, others (most notably Beth Weaver and Fergus McNeill) argued that models of work with offenders that emphasised 'risk' may serve only to damage chances of desistance as they left some people 'marked out' and stigmatised. Helen Beckett and others argued that risk models can also contribute to a one-sided view of individuals as deficits or burdens to society, rather than as resources capable of future good works (see also Maruna 2001; Farrall and Calverley 2006; Chapter 8 of this volume). Echoing this, Christine Knott (formerly of the National Offender Management Service) questioned whether current criminal justice systems did not focus too much on public protection at the expense of developing good and effective working relationships between probation officers and probationers. In this respect, some participants suggested that one way forward might be to develop a better understanding and approach to relapses in criminality and drug-use during periods of supervision. Fergus McNeill, for instance, pointed to the differences in which relapses are approached by the criminal justice system compared to the addiction recovery environment, where relapses are expected, tolerated and treated as an opportunity for learning. This is a far cry from the world of criminal justice where desistance is expected very quickly. In this respect, support of up to six years may be needed for some groups (e.g. ex-sex workers, as argued by Maggie O'Neill). Similarly, seminar participants like Juliet

Lyons argued for breach guidelines to allow a greater degree of discretion on the part of probation officers.

One of the most interesting papers from the seminar series, by Adrian Grounds, documented the post-prison experiences of a largely forgotten group – those men and women who have been wrongfully convicted of a crime (see also Grounds 2004, 2005). There have been very few accounts of the experience of being wrongfully convicted (Campbell and Denov 2004: 140). Despite this, a number of experiences have been highlighted, all related to the fact that almost all decisions within the criminal process following conviction take for granted the guilt of the convicted. For obvious reasons, the wrongfully convicted prisoner is inhibited from expressing remorse for the crimes for which they have been found guilty and such refusals can be interpreted as denial or hostility toward the crime's victims (Weisman 2004). Because the wrongfully convicted often maintain their innocence for much or all of their entire prison sentence, they are unlikely to be seen by the criminal justice system as having taken their 'first step' along the road to rehabilitation: namely admission of wrong-doing and remorse (Weisman 2004: 127; see also Campbell and Denov 2004: 152). As such, these individuals come to be treated as if they presented a greater risk of harm to others, and are, in terms of institutional cultures, unlikely to be able to create the identity of someone who is ready to be returned to the community. Such treatment creates troubling emotions for the wrongfully convicted and can enhance the psychological pains of imprisonment (Grounds 2004: 170). Additional stress arises from the uncertainty over their release date (and the general lack of preparedness for it), and concerns about criminal appeals processes (Campbell and Denov 2004: 140). The wrongfully convicted person's unwillingness to admit to an offence also often makes a person ineligible for early release or parole schemes. This perhaps goes some of the way to accounting for the psychiatric problems identified amongst this group of prisoners (Grounds 2004); depression, self-harm and attempts to kill themselves are all common (Campbell and Denov 2004: 148).

Grounds's studies of a number of long-term, wrongfully convicted prisoners have suggested that they experience enduring personality changes and other psychiatric problems (Grounds 2004: 168–70). These problems include always feeling 'on edge' or 'panicky', vividly re-experiencing the events surrounding their trial or experiences in prison, substance use, insomnia, and emotional problems. As with ordinary prisoners (see e.g. Meisenhelder 1985; Jose-Kampfner 1995), many of the wrongfully convicted report emotional troubles associated with visits from their family members (Grounds 2004: 170) at times arguing that sometimes *not* having such visits can be easier. Grounds also found that many of the wrongfully convicted, like other long-term prisoners, had lost practical or social skills by the time they were released. Many also experienced difficulties with their relationships with family members (who had often learned to live without the wrongfully convicted individual present, either physically or emotionally). In short, their life-courses were altered dramatically and in a way which was hard to undo. Grounds concluded that the wrongfully convicted bore more resemblance to soldiers returning from combat then they did to ordinary ex-offenders or ex-prisoners.

Grounds's work also introduces the concept of an 'assumptive world' – which refers to those beliefs which ground, stabilise or orientate people, and which accordingly give them a sense of purpose and meaning to their lives, as well as providing feelings of belonging and connection to others (Beder 2004; Kauffman 2002a, 2002b) – and the ways in which this fragile construct can be damaged by wrongful conviction. Wrongful convictions bring to the fore the discontinuous nature of many people's biographies. As is well documented (Kauffman 2002b: 209) many people who have had their assumptive worlds 'shattered' feel that their sense of self has become discontinuous, and hence seek to therefore establish a sense of coherence through a process of 're-biographing' (Maruna 2001). However, with the wrongfully convicted this process is made much more complex. We see something of the reverse: instead of a 'bad', former self being abandoned we observe amongst the wrongfully convicted a 'good', former self being not so much abandoned but remaining unobtainable (see Farrall 2009: 188–89). Still, a similar process is in operation, although with differing causal elements, of course, and with quite opposite outcomes. Re-biographing has only taken place once with the wrongfully convicted: they have had their old ('good') selves obliterated and a new ('bad') self imposed upon them through the courts and the internalisation of external messaging. What is required, post release, is a further re-biographing to occur.

New areas of research

A particular focus of the seminar series was on 'new directions' in research on desistance, especially studies involving groups that were often ignored by previous, well-known studies of desistance and prisoner resettlement. Of these we have already referred to McEvoy and Shirlow's study of former political prisoners. Another paper (by Susanne Karstedt) focused on the experiences of ex-Nazis. Karstedt reported that former members of the Nazi Party and SS guards were tried immediately after the end of the Second World War, and started to be released from prison during the 1950s. The church played a large part in the processes of their rehabilitation, offering them work in their bureaucracies. However, after Adolf Eichmann's trial in the early 1960s, attitudes towards former war criminals changed sharply, and such individuals began to be barred from occupations they had previously held. Such an analysis, albeit of an extreme group, demonstrates the ways in which far wider social and political attitudes engulfing a society can help to shape the subsequent life trajectories of those found guilty of crimes (see also Godfrey *et al* 2007; Green 2006, 2008).

Another paper which dealt with the subtle variations associated with different groups' experiences of desistance from crime was presented by Adam Calverley, who studied the ways in which members of some of the UK's largest ethnic minorities ceased offending. Calverley's consideration of the experiences of desistance among those British based interviewees identifying as Indian,

Bangladeshi, and black in ethnicity demonstrated that, although they had much in common, the differences that did exist between these groups had significant implications for their desistance from crime. Desistance mechanisms which were reported across all three ethnic groups included establishing a viable pro-social identity, having their efforts towards desistance recognised and certified by others, and the importance of the availability of 'hooks for change' in their environment to provide appropriate 'blueprints' for change that they could act on. Similarly, the universal importance of factors such as relationship formation and motivation was the same regardless of ethnicity. However, when the experiences of desistance were analysed for each of the three ethnic groups, important ethnic differences became apparent. Structural and cultural differences between the respective ethnic groups had implications for how they stopped offending. Calverley's analysis reveals that ethnic differences in terms of family and community, in particular, had implications for processes of desistance (Calverley 2009). These differences were responsible for shaping the environment where desistance took place and the means and opportunities available to do so. This, in turn, determined the understanding individual ex-offenders gave to their decisions and actions (see also Braken *et al* 2009).

The next phase of research into desistance from crime, then, might usefully involve the exploration of different patterns in desistance, based on ethnicity and gender, but also types of crime, culture, historical time period and other factors. By utilising those 'naturally' occurring social, cultural and economic variations which are related to (for example) ethnicity or gender, one is able to explore in greater detail the ways in which structures (represented by the wider social and cultural values) and individual agency are interwoven in processes of reform. A conclusion of the seminar series was that fascinating lessons for understanding life after prison might be learned from seemingly unusual groups – former Nazis, the wrongfully convicted, former political prisoners, even death-row prisoners.

Life after punishment: introducing this volume

Turning now to the chapters collected herein, this volume opens with Chris Deacy's exploration of the relationship between Christian models of redemption and life after punishment. Deacy develops ideas held amongst some criminologists that it is possible to develop a new, secular, ideal of redemption, and in so doing attend to the context of the role of confession, repentance and forgiveness among habitual criminal offenders outside of a religious context. Is such vocabulary appropriate in a secular society? Through his explorations, Deacy highlights the multitude of models of redemption which Christian theologians have adopted, highlighting those which have emphasised the individual agency of the person being redeemed. As Deacy notes:

> Redemption is not a trite or comfortable process, but involves a deep and acute awareness of what it means to be human, which in traditional

> Christian terms means facing up to, rather than running away from, our capacity to create harm and to destroy as well as to do good.

In this way – but perhaps not only in this way – Deacy views the role of the criminologist and that of the theologian as being sufficiently related. He argues that there are several points at which each can learn from the other, not least of all as (a point which Deacy is at pains to emphasise) notions of redemption in Christian thought have evolved over time. Whatever shape and character redemption adopts, it is never a stable concept. Our ideas of what redemption 'is' changes over time; as does, of course, our understanding of both what crime is and how it ought to be treated. A well known example of this is society's understanding of homosexual behaviour. In passages which would, by today's more tolerant standards, cause both offence and embarrassment, social scientific studies of the past century routinely refer to gays and lesbians as 'freaks' (see West 1955: 57) who cause social problems but could be 'treated' or 'cured' of their 'affliction' (see West 1955: Chapter 10 'Treatment for the Individual'). Such changes in social mores underscore Deacy's point that changes in what is considered redeemable and the processes by which such redemption may be achieved are likely to shift over time as much as they are likely to retain a stable core of meaning.

Following on from Deacy's discussion of redemption in theory, we move to several chapters examining the process of redemption (or at least desistance from crime) in practice. One of the most recently initiated studies of desistance from crime in the UK is that led by Tony Bottoms and Joanna Shapland. This study (based in Sheffield) is just starting to produce findings following several years of fieldwork. We are delighted that the co-directors of this project have chosen this volume as one of the first outlets for findings from this study. Their chapter reports on the 'headline news' from this research study, which suggests that even amongst their sample of repeat offenders (all males and all aged between 19–22 years old), the vast majority wanted to stop offending although not all believed this would be possible, at least in the initial interviews. In keeping with similar studies (Burnett 1992; Farrall 2002), however, as research participants aged, an increasing proportion started to believe that desistance was possible for them. Re-offending, of course, was common, yet over time the members of the Sheffield sample did take 'steps towards desistance'. Interestingly, and at the most basic of levels in keeping with Moffitt's thesis (1993), there is a growing polarisation between high-rate and low-rate offenders by the end of the study, yet as the authors note, there is no clear divide between 'life-course persistent' and 'adolescence-limited' offenders (see also Ezell and Cohen 2005).

The third chapter focuses on another UK-based longitudinal study of involvement in crime based in Edinburgh. The Edinburgh Study of Youth Transitions and Crime has followed a younger cohort of people than those in the Sheffield study. The researchers recruited a sample of over 4,000 children aged 12 at enrolment in secondary schools in Edinburgh in 1998, and have produced some of the best evidence about youth transitions and crime in the UK. In their chapter (originally published in the European Journal of Criminology), Lesley MacAra and Susan McVie examine the extent to which labelling processes within criminal justice agency working cultures 'serve to recycle certain categories of children into the youth justice system, whilst other serious offenders escape the tutelage of the formal system altogether'. Their findings suggest that the further a child is drawn into the criminal justice system, the less likely they are to be able to escape from it and hence desist from crime. They conclude by arguing that the key to reducing offending lies in minimal intervention and maximum diversion. However, as the closing section of their chapter notes, doing less rather than more to reduce crime and delinquency requires political courage and determination that is not in abundance at present.

Nonetheless Anette Ballinger's chapter reminds us that, whatever the failings of contemporary European criminal justice systems, almost all are at least fortunate to no longer feature state executions with all of their inherent risks. In Europe's recent past, however, some individuals were not given the opportunity to experience 'life after punishment' (see also Crawley and Sparks 2006). Ballinger's sensitive reconstructing of the story of Louie Calvert (based on her own autobiography, recently released by the National Archives, and the other official records relating to her) illustrates the vast gulf between official state accounts of crime and punishment and the experiences recalled by the accused themselves. In the battle for the truth, what the state wishes to say about the guilty, how best to account for their behaviours and how best to 'treat' them is almost inevitably going to swamp what the guilty wish to say about themselves, their crimes and the state. In one sense, none of this ought to be news to anyone; but at another level altogether, what Ballinger has done – albeit in an indirect way – is to remind us that studies based on data collated from official sources have certain biases built into them from the outset and may not be as accurate as advocates of 'what works' initiatives may claim. In modern criminology, we assess the validity of what offenders tell us by comparing this against official records, as if somehow the latter represent some external criterion of truth. Ironically, such comparisons often find that offenders report more crimes than the official 'truth' knew of (see Farrall 2005, Table 1). This underscores one of the key lessons of research into desistance from crime; listening to ex-offenders about their experiences of what helped them stop offending is often more valuable than reading government-funded research and statistics into the effectiveness of the machinery they control and run. When a more critical approach is taken, the key processes in desistance are understood afresh, and often the criminal justice system is no longer cast in terms of levels of effectiveness but rather levels of harm (see MacAra and McVie: Chapter 3 of this volume) or inefficiency (see Halsey 2008).

One of the recent trends – and very welcome it is too – in recent studies of criminal careers in general and desistance in particular, has been the efforts made to understand how processes of desistance unfold in particular contexts. Whilst there is much mileage to be gained from generic models of desistance (such as that promoted by Sampson and Laub 1993) some recent studies have sought to challenge such models by exploring contextual factors that may lead to differences in desistance patterns (see Saloveinen 2009; Skardhamar and Galloway 2010, forthcoming; Godfrey *et al* 2007). The Teesside-based research on offending over time, described in Chapter 5 of this volume, is better placed than many to chart how wider social and economic processes have affected young peoples' engagement in and escape from crime. Drawing on the numerous studies the team has undertaken in Teesside since the late 1990s, MacDonald and his colleagues conclude that:

> For our working-class informants, growing up during the 1980s and '90s amongst the economic wreckage of one of the most de-industrialised places in Britain, the conditions of their lives allowed criminal 'solutions' for some and alternative, newly economically marginal ones for many. For us, group conditions as well as individual life circumstances must form the basis of criminal career research, so that studies can grasp how the *collective* conditions and 'public issues of social structure' set the frame of possibilities for individual biographies and their attendant 'private troubles'; showing how possibilities for desistance from, or persistence in, crime are socially, economically and historically structured as well as individually made.

As such, MacDonald *et al* are able to draw connections between the nature and shape of the distribution of wealth and opportunity in a society and the character of the lives led by some of those individuals most caught up in changes to these structures. Their work is reminiscent of that of Jay Macleod (1995) who observed that 'social structures reach into the minds and even the hearts of individuals to shape their attitudes, motivations and worldviews' (Macleod 1995: 255).

The second half of our volume focuses less on broad approaches to the study of desistance, and more on the specific processes and dynamics of desistance for specific sub-populations of desisters (wannabes and actual). As such, some of those themes raised by the first five of the chapters are touched upon, developed and illustrated afresh by our final five chapters. This is not to suggest for one moment that one group of chapters is somehow subservient to the other in terms of thinking or dependent on the other for data, for all of our contributors have immersed themselves fully in both theories and data. Rather, our explicit recognition of the development of themes indentified in the first half of the volume by those writing in the second speaks to one of the clear messages of research into desistance. This is that, by and large, the main reasons why people stop offending have been identified. Even in cases which have explored these processes using specific groups of offenders (see for example, Calverley 2009) we find very similar accounts, but with subtle variations being played out. Such an observation may lead one to (incorrectly) deduce that sub-populations of offenders (categorised by gender, age, ethnicity or type of career) are of little interest to criminologists. This would be wrong, however. For by exploring these specific groups of offenders and ex-offenders one is confronted with another of the key lessons to be learnt from research into desistance from crime: namely that social structures shape the processes by which individuals cease offending and move away from crime. Variables such as age, historical period, ethnicity or type of criminal career, represent not simply facets of individuals' lives, but rather index wider social, economic, legal and cultural structures (see, for example, Godfrey *et al* 2007; Calverley 2009: Chapter 7 of this volume; MacDonald *et al*: Chapter 5 of this volume).

Chapter 6 by Anne-Marie McAlinden illustrates this well. By focusing on a group that is rarely included in desistance research – those accused of sexual offences – McAlinden uncovers both unique challenges faced by this group – in particular how intensely some aspects of the work of the criminal justice system have changed over the course of the past 30 or so years – but also shines new light on problems of stigma faced by all former offenders (but see also Robinson 2002 for an important reminder that however omnipresent 'risk' may appear to be, it has not quite obliterated all notions like 'rehabilition' or 'need'). The individuals described in McAlinden's research have found themselves portrayed as social pariahs, ensnared in increasingly punitive legislative frameworks putting tight controls on where they can live, who they can socialise with, and where they can work. In these structural contexts, and echoing the findings of MacAra and McVie (Chapter 3 of this volume), the criminal justice system would appear to have made it harder for this population to move away from their past offending. McAlinden makes the case that these structural constraints may ironically impede efforts at achieving reintegration and desistance by increasing the social isolation of this group. The 'upside' of this, one might argue, is that the system has simultaneously made it harder for sex offenders to re-offend. However, as McAlinden illustrates, an alternative model of working with sex offenders (namely circles of support) offers the possibility of both control and supervision with a commitment to supporting those practices more concordant with findings from desistance and reintegration following offending.

Calverley's chapter explores the processes of desistance from crime amongst one of the UK's poorest ethnic minorities. Although his wider study also included Indian and black-British ex-offenders, Calverley has chosen for this contribution to focus on the Bangladeshi ex-offenders from his sample. As he notes in his review of the socio-economic position of this community in the UK, recent examinations suggest that this group is very poorly situated with regards to access to employment, school achievement, housing and many other indicators of general social well-being. Despite this general disadvantage, the men Calverley interviewed for his study were still able to make the break away from involvement in crime. This was due in large part to the roles played by their families – the vast majority of which were intact – and the development of a series of joint projects between the families and their troubled sons. Rather than socially shunning their sons in trouble with the law, Bangladeshi families appeared to pull together, taking every opportunity to support them whilst they were in prison and after their release. Another key lesson to come from this chapter – and here we invite readers to explore Deacy's and Calverley's chapters side by side – concerns the role of religion and desistance. Although research into the relationship between desistance and religiosity is still embryonic, social bonds theory (Sampson and Laub, 1993) might suggest that religiosity supports desistance as it brings about a change in social circles with an additional set of values which, for the most part, are incompatible with offending. Calverley's respondents certainly suggest that these processes were in operation when they desisted. Yet, unlike other accounts of religious conversion (or 're-awakening') which one encounters in the desistance literature (which have been largely concerned with Christianity), the explainations given by the men Calverley interviewed appear to go much deeper than simply social support, suggesting a more acompassing transformation. This begs the question; are some religions better placed than others to assist in those sorts of personal, interpersonal and social processes associated with desistance? Part of the answer is to be found in Calverley's consideration of the other ethnic groups in his sample, where religion appeared to play little or no part in the accounts of desistance given by Indians, black-Africans or black Caribbeans.

Psycho-analytic models of desistance are a comparatively recent phenomenon (see Maruna 2001; Gadd and Farrall 2004; Gadd 2006). However, it is precisely this body of work (alongside more traditional theorising on imprisonment) which has informed the thinking of our next chapter, that by Mechthild Bereswill. Like MacDonald *et al*, Bereswill employs qualitative longitudinal research (QLR) methodologies to good effect with an in-depth case analysis of two German ex-prisoners. Reinforcing some of the findings regarding imprisonment made by Calverley with regards to his sample of Bangladeshi ex-offenders, Bereswill finds that one of the two men she uses as case studies had found imprisonment to be the key to helping him stop offending but perhaps not in the way that prison supporters may hope. Crucially – and we must always bear in mind that Bereswill's data comes from Germany – 'What works?' for one of her case studies is that 'nothing worked'; he is, in Sartre's terms, *condamné à être libre* by a system unable and unwilling to help and with all of the inner conflicts which this entailed. In other words, for Lukas Meier what worked was that the system was incapable of assisting him, so he learnt that he needed to take the initiative for desistance himself. This finding is a salutary one for those engaged in the seemingly never-ending pursuit of 'What works?'. Maybe a system which cannot deliver terribly much encourages individuals to take matters relating to their future engagement in crime into their own hands. This finding suggests that rather than trying to coerce change upon others, criminal justice systems might be better served by empowering prisoners to take responsibility (and ownership) of their own individualised process of self-change – the outcomes are the same in either situation of course. Radical non-interventionism aside, the pursuit of a criminal justice system which *could* account for all of the variation in successful desistance (which is at times it appears what the 'What works?' movement is committed to producing) in any case leaves ex-offenders with little direct ownership of their own desistance. Why feel pleased about having successfully desisted from crime when the criminal justice system is going to claim that its own policies and procedures were what 'worked' in securing your rehabilitation? One of the few things which some ex-offenders have to say about their own lives which *is* positive, is that despite it all, it was *they* who put an end to their offending. Despite the obvious falsehood of this (parents, probation officers and many others *do* all help, wittingly or otherwise), at least *feeling* that you've accomplished something yourself is an important psychological resource – especially for those who may have little or nothing to show from their schooling experiences or attempts to engage with the labour market. Any system which claims (or even unwittingly implies) that it alone changed you may not be helping matters. Lukas Meier's case reminds us that any social system needs to permit and encourage individual creativity – and perhaps nowhere is this more keenly felt than in processes of compliance with the law.

One author for whom Sartre's insights will certainly not be news, is Ben Hunter. In his chapter on the anxieties associated with the anticipation of release, Hunter focuses on the existential aspects of release from prison for those convicted of white collar offences. Feeling that they were in control of their destinies and believing that they had been masters of the changes they had undergone, some in his sample looked forward to their release. Again, following Calverley and Bereswill, imprisonment did not seem to have damaged these individuals, rather it had helped them to forge new identities to look forward to when they were released. For an equal number of prisoners, however, prison had damaged their sense of who they were and made them pessimistic about the futures which awaited them. Such prisoners had experienced a huge discontinuity in their lives, but one which they felt had been forced upon them and which they did not feel that they 'owned' (Farrall 2009 similarly discusses the problems associated with discontinuous pasts from an existential perspective, in his case using the experiences of the wrongfully convicted). The bottom line, therefore, in re-biographing or coming to terms with a discontinuous personal narrative, is that the important factor in all this is how the individuals concerned feel about the 'old self' that they are leaving behind. For those who wanted to leave their former selves behind, the processes associated with re-biographising were to be welcomed; for those who still wanted to be 'themselves' before their convictions, the past was a dream which they would be very lucky ever to reclaim.

Finally the chapter by Susanne Karstedt deals with the lives of former Nazi was criminals – some party members, other guards and doctors. As mentioned above, Karstedt notes how the period during which these individuals were tried, punished and released effected the nature of the possible lives after punishment left open to them. She concludes with the observation that the lives after punishment of former-Nazi war criminals were shaped as much by the wider nature of German society in the 40 or so years after the end of the Second World War as they were by their activities leading up to 1945. Such observations remind us that the nature of rehabilitation (and hence the meaning and processes associated with desistance) can and do change over time and in line with wider social and political values.

Distilling some lessons for the future of the criminal justice system

Research into life after punishment and desistance from crime, although fascinating in its own right, clearly has important implications for criminal justice policy. The chapters in this volume and those delivered as part of the ESRC seminar series are no exception in that regard. Below, we outline some of the broad, overarching themes that we see emerging from this research on desistance from crime in regard to criminal justice policy.

'First, do no harm', to coin a phrase. The research presented in this volume all points to the conclusion, described well by the Howard League's (2010) new mantra 'Do better, do less'. That is, promoting desistance almost certainly means reducing the reliance on imprisonment as a penalty for all but the most serious of offenders. In interview-based research with former prisoners, very few will credit their time in prison with triggering or supporting their efforts to desist from crime; far more common are those who will blame their time in prison for difficulties they had trying to desist. Prison may not always be harmful (often it is mundanely dull or boring), but all else being equal it is often associated with delayed desistance rather than accelerated desistance.

A further implication from the studies in this volume is that any system of criminal justice needs somehow to allow sufficient 'room' for people to 'own' the changes in their lives and engagement in crime. That is to say that a criminal justice system which does not recognise offenders and ex-offenders as active agents in their own change and which does not allow them to claim credit for what they did will not produce desistance as readily as one which does. For meaningful desistance (that is desistance which is sustained permanently, rather than temporary lulls in offending), the desisting individual usually feels that this is a change which they have been an active participant in and in which they have invested emotionally.

In this respect the work of Beth Weaver and Fergus McNeill (Weaver and McNeill 2007) suggests a number of key principles for encouraging and supporting desistance within the criminal justice system. Their first point is that the criminal justice system needs to be more realistic about what is achievable with those who have been involved in offending for significant periods of time. In short this is a call to recognise that relapses are common and that change takes time. Hence breaches and/or prison recalls on the basis of minor offences or (more commonly) breaking the conditions of one's licence (e.g., missing appointments or breaking curfews) may serve only to prolong an individual's offending. Such minor relapses could be reframed as opportunities for learning and theraputic intervention. Weaver and McNeill also recommend informal interventions over formal ones, on the basis that formal interventions can stigmatise the individuals involved. Again, several of the presentations made during the seminars supported both the contention that formal interventions can stigmatise and suggested new ways of approaching interventions which are less formal but not less successful. Along these lines Weaver and McNeill call for more efforts to avoid imprisonment, and we support this general principle. The notion that 'one size fits all' and that interventions can be designed from afar without reference to the need of the individual concerned is another recent approach to the supervision of offenders which Weaver and McNeill criticise. In order for individuals being supervised to feel that the criminal justice system is responding to their needs (and hence is willing and able to support their efforts to desist) interventions need to be individualised. Punishments, also, at some point have to end for individuals to be able to 'move on'.

Weaver and McNeill rightly note that social contexts are as important as individual contexts (again see several of the chapters in this volume). This implies working not just with individuals, but also with communities, and recognising that these communities (be they based on ethnicity, culture or geography) may be differentially resourced and orientated to those values and goals held more widely. In short, desistance may be achieved by some communities through routes which are unexpected (see Calverley 2009).

Based on both these general principles and the insights we have gained, we support those interventions which have been described as being 'strengths based' (Maruna and LeBel 2003). Such approaches emphasise the strengths which ex-offenders and/or those who are currently sentenced may possess, and are often contrasted with 'needs based' or 'deficits' models, which instead emphasise the 'failings' of such individuals. One of the central aims of this approach is that individuals are able to 'earn their way back into society' via engagement in works that support the community or specific individuals in it. Such approaches therefore allow ex-offenders to demonstrate their 'true' inner character, and transform the traditional receivers of help into givers of help thereby altering their self-conceptions. Approaches based on these principles communicate to the community that the ex-offender is worthy of support, and that they have something to offer to others. It is our hope that the chapters in this volume and the dialogue which they are engaged in may help to foster the greater adoption of such initiatives.

Notes

1 The proceedings were published as a special edition of *Criminology & Criminal Justice*, (2006) 6(1).
2 ESRC Award RES-451–25–4078.
3 The other is a special edition of *Theoretical Criminology*, (2009) 13(1).
4 Funded under the auspices of the FP6 CRIMPREV project, papers from this seminar will appear as a special edition of the *European Journal of Criminology*, (2010) 7(6).

5 And by extension, matters relating to desistance, rehabilitation, redemption and reform taken in their broadest senses.

References

Beder, J. (2004) 'Loss of the Assumptive World – how we deal with death and loss', *OMEGA: Journal of Death and Dying*, 50(4): 255–65.

Bottoms, A. E. (2002) 'Compliance and Community Penalties', in Bottoms, T., Gelsthorpe, L. and Rex, S. (eds) *Community Penalties*. Cullompton: Willan Publishing.

Bovens, M. (1998) *The quest for responsibility*. Cambridge: Cambridge University Press.

Bracken, D., Deane, L. and Morrissette, L. (2009) 'Desistance and Social marginalisation', *Theoretical Criminology*, 13(1): 61–78.

Braithwaite, J. and Roche, D. (2001) 'Responsibility and restorative justice', in Bazemore, G. and Schiff, M. (eds) *Restorative community justice: Repairing harm and transforming communities*. Cincinnati, OH: Anderson Publishing Co.

Burnett, R. (1992) *The Dynamics of Recidivism*. Oxford: Centre for Criminological Research, University of Oxford.

Calverley, A. (2009) 'An exploratory investigation into the processes of desistance amongst minority ethnic offenders', unpublished PhD thesis, Keele University, Keele.

Campbell, K. and Denov, M. (2004) 'The Burden of Innocence: Coping with a Wrongful Imprisonment', *Canadian Journal of Criminology & Criminal Justice*, 46(2): 139–63.

Crawley, E. and Sparks, R. (2006) 'Is there life after Punishment?', *Criminology & Criminal Justice*, 6(1): 63–82.

D'Cruze, S. (1998) *Crimes of Outrage: Sex, violence and Victorian working women*. London: University College Press.

Ezell, M. and Cohen, L. (2005) *Desisting From Crime*. Oxford: Oxford University Press.

Farrall, S. (2002) *Rethinking What Works With Offenders*. Cullompton: Willan Publishing.

Farrall, S. (2005) 'Officially Recorded Convictions for Probationers: The Relationship With Self-Report and Supervisory Observations', *Legal & Criminological Psychology*, 10(1): 121–31.

Farrall, S. (2009) '"We Just Live Day-to-Day": A Case Study of Life After Release Following Wrongful Conviction', in Lippens, R. and Crewe, D. (eds) *Existentialist Criminology*. London: Routledge, pp 169–96.

Farrall, S. and Calverley, A. (2006) *Understanding Desistance from Crime*, Crime and Justice Series. London: Open University Press.

Farrall, S., Godfrey, B. and Cox, D. (2009) 'The Role of Historically-Embedded Structures in Processes of Criminal Reform: A Structural Criminology of Desistance', *Theoretical Criminology*, 13(1): 79–104.

Farrington, D. (1977) 'The Effects of Public Labelling', *British Journal of Criminology*, 17(2): 112–25.

Farrington, D. *et al* (1978) 'The Persistence of Labelling Effects', *British Journal of Criminology*, 18(3): 277–84.

Gadd, D. (2006) 'The role of recognition in the desistance process: A case analysis of a former far-right activist', *Theoretical Criminology*, 10(2): 179–202.

Gadd, D. and Farrall, S. (2004) 'Criminal Careers, Desistance and Subjectivity', *Theoretical Criminology*, 8(2): 123–55.

Godfrey, B., Cox, D. and Farrall, S. (2007) *Criminal Lives: Family Life, Employment and Offending*, Clarendon Studies in Criminology. Oxford: Oxford University Press.

Green, D. (2006) 'Public Opinion Versus Public Judgement About Crime', *British Journal of Criminology*, 46: 131–54.

Green, D. (2008) 'Political Culture and Incentives to Penal Populism', in Kury, H. (ed.) *Fear of Crime – Punitivity: New Developments in Theory and Research*. Bochum: Univiversitatsverlag Brockmeyer, pp 251–76.

Grounds, A. (2004) 'Psychological Consequences of Wrongful Conviction & Imprisonment', *Canadian Journal of Criminology & Criminal Justice*, 46(2): 166–82.

Grounds, A. (2005) 'Understanding the Effects of Wrongful Imprisonment', in Tonry, M. (ed.) *Crime and Justice: A Review of Research*, vol. 32. Chicago, IL: University of Chicago Press, pp 1–58.

Halsey, M. (2008) 'Assembling Recidivism', *Journal of Criminal Law and Criminology*, 97(4): 1209–60.

Hammerton, A. J. (1992) *Cruelty & Companionship: Conflict in 19th Century Married Life*. London: Routledge.

Howard League for Penal Reform (2010) *Do Better, Do Less: The Report of the Commission on English Prisons Today*. London: The Howard League.

Kauffman, J. (2002a) 'Introduction', in Kauffman, J. (ed.) *Loss of the Assumptive World: A Theory of Traumatic Loss*. New York, NY: Brunner-Routledge.

Kauffman, J. (2002b) 'Safety and the Assumptive World', in Kauffman, J. (ed.) *Loss of the Assumptive World: A Theory of Traumatic Loss*. New York, NY: Brunner-Routledge.

Jose-Kampfner, C. (1995) 'Coming to Terms With Existential Death: An Analysis of Women's Adaptation to Life in Prison', *Social Justice*, 17(2): 110–25.

Liebling, Alison (2004) *Prisons and their Moral Performance: A Study of Values, Quality and Prison Life*. Oxford: Clarendon Press.

MacLeod, J. (1995) *Ain't No Makin' It*. Oxford: Westview Press.

Maruna, S. (2001) *Making Good: How Ex-Convicts Reform and Rebuild their Lives*. Washington, DC: American Psychological Association Books.

Maruna, S. and Copes, H. (2005) 'What Have We Learned in Five Decades of Neutralization Research?', in Tonry, M. (ed.) *Crime and Justice: A Review of Research*, vol. 32. Chicago, IL: University of Chicago Press, pp 221–320.

Maruna, S. and Lebel, T. (2003) 'Welcome Home?', *Western Criminology Review*, 393: 1–37.

Maruna, S. and Mann, R. (2006) 'Fundamental Attribution Errors? Re-thinking Cognitive Distortions', *Legal and Criminological Psychology*, 11: 155–77.

McEvoy, K. and Shirlow, P. (2009) 'Re-Imagining DDR', *Theoretical Criminology*, 13(1): 31–59.

Meisenhelder, T. (1985) 'An Essay on Time and the Phenomenology of Imprisonment', *Deviant Behaviour*, 6: 39–56.

Moffitt, T. (1993) 'Life-Course Persistent and Adolescent-Limited Antisocial Behaviour: A Developmental Taxonomy', *Psychological Review*, 100: 674–701.

Nellis, M. (2009) 'The Aesthetics of Redemption', *Theoretical Criminology*, 13(1): 129–46.

Robinson, G. (2002) 'Exploring Risk Management in Probation Practice', *Punishment and Society*, 4(1): 5–25.

Robinson, G. and McNeill, F. (2008) 'Exploring the dynamics of compliance with community penalties', *Theoretical Criminology*, 12(4): 431–49.

Sampson, R. J. and Laub, J. H. (1993) *Crime in the Making: Pathways and Turning Points Through Life*. London: Harvard University Press.
Savolainen, J. (2009) 'Work, family and criminal desistance', *British Journal of Criminology*, 49: 285–304.
Skardhammer, T. and Galloway, T. A. (2010, forthcoming) 'Does parental income matter for onset of offending?', *European Journal of Criminology*.
Smith, B. G. (1989) *Changing Lives: Women in History Since 1700*. Toronto: D. C. Heath & Co.
Sparks, R., Bottoms, A. E. and Hay, W. (1996) *Prison and the Problem of Order: Prison and the Problem of Order*. Oxford: Clarendon Press.
Tyler, T. R. (2003) 'Procedural justice, legitimacy, and the effective rule of law', in Tonry, M. (ed.) *Crime and Justice: A Review of Research*, vol. 30. Chicago, IL: University of Chicago Press, pp 431–505.
Tyler, T. R. (2007) *Legitimacy and Criminal Justice*. New York, NY: Russell Sage Foundation.
Tyler, T. R. and Huo, Y. J. (2002) *Trust in the law: Encouraging public cooperation with the police and courts*. New York, NY: Russell Sage Foundation.
Weaver, B. and McNeill, F. (2007) *Giving Up Crime: Directions for Policy*. Edinburgh: Scottish Consortium on Crime and Criminal Justice.
Weisman, R. (2004) 'Showing Remorse: Reflections on the Gap between Expression and Attribution in Cases of Wrongful Conviction', *Canadian Journal of Criminology & Criminal Justice*, 46(2): 121–38.
West, D. (1955) *Homosexuality*. London: Penguin Books.

Chapter 1

Applying redemption through film

Challenging the sacred-secular divide

Christopher Deacy

Introduction

The aim of this chapter is to explore the extent to which the language of redemption may be found to possess any viability outside the traditionally demarcated religious sphere and be appropriated in a secular context. As an applied theologian who works at the interface between theology and film, I was delighted to be invited to participate in the ESRC Life after Punishment conference that took place in Belfast in November 2006, where many of the same underlying questions which arise in theological circles concerning the remit of redemption came to the fore. How exclusive, autonomous and doctrinally specific is the concept of redemption? Do attempts by theologians to break down barriers between 'redemption' in theology and 'redemption' in film—assuming, of course, that any sort of clear line of demarcation can be drawn between the sacred and the secular in the first place—not overlook the possibility that theological themes are simply being 'read into' films, whose religious or theological underpinning may be no more than coincidental and, even, unintentional on the part of film-makers? How susceptible are theologians to the charge of misrepresentation? Although the term 'redemption' has undeniable theological connotations and, in Clive Marsh's words, "forges an obvious link to theological discussion" (Marsh 1998: para 21), why should it automatically follow that a 'religious' reading of a film such as (to give an obvious and, as we shall see, much cited example) *The Shawshank Redemption* (1994) can simply fall into place? After all, does not religion only exist in concrete and particular forms, such that even within Christianity itself there are to be found a whole plethora of different types and varieties of 'redemptions', rather than any universal, objective and monolithic brand in relation to which a straightforward dialogue may accrue? As Marsh puts it, "unless it be claimed that scholars of religion … are somehow able to transcend the concreteness of religious particularity and the detail of human living, it is necessary to attend to the specifics of what religions … actually claim and promote" (Marsh 1998: para 11). With this in mind, if, as is believed to be the case among many criminologists, it is possible to develop a new, secular argument in favour of the ideal of redemption, such as in the context of the role of confession, repentance and forgiveness among habitual criminal offenders, then some attention needs to be paid to the appropriateness of the vocabulary that is being used in view of the origins of the term 'redemption' in a Christian context, where it is inextricably bound up with Christian thought, faith and practice.

What I will be suggesting, however, is that the way in which Christian theologians have sought to interpret redemption over the centuries has varied extensively, to the point that there are, in actuality, close and theologically defensible parallels between some of the processes at work in secular fields, such as film and criminology, and a number of insights which have come to prominence in recent Christian theology. In particular, attention will be given to those models of redemption in Christianity that accord a prominent emphasis to the role of the human individual in the redemptive schema at the expense of any readings which stipulate the need for a direct encounter with God or the placating of any external, divine agencies in order for redemption to be accomplished. Revisiting some of my own work in the field of theology and film as a template, it will be argued here that a key analogy can be drawn between the Christian story of redemption and the meaning, function and *telos* of redemption as understood in secularity, with the result that fertile cross-disciplinary work between theology and criminology can be undertaken.

The specificity of redemption

At first sight, it would appear that there is a certain rigidity and specificity to what theologians mean when they invoke the language of 'redemption'. Indeed, in the case of Christianity, there is a very clear and precise remit to what redemption entails, which shares precious little common ground with the use of the term in the context of criminology. Criminologists may appropriate the same language, but it would be foolish to overlook the fact that vast, and potentially irreconcilable, differences exist between the form of redemptive possibility that has the capacity to function in secularity and the nature of redemption within Christianity, where the process carries specific religious, historical, cultural and doctrinal connotations. To what extent is 'redemption' thus being 'read into' an academic discipline whose religious underpinning is far from readily apparent? To paraphrase Chris Arthur, who is writing in the context of misguided attempts within the study of religion to draw parallels between *Maitreya*—that is, "the name given by Buddhists to a figure they believe to be the future Buddha"—and the Judaeo-Christian understanding of *Messiah*: "just because one can draw out certain themes which may appear similar when laid side by side, this does not necessarily mean that they possess the same valency within that complex metallurgy of history, practice and belief which constitutes a religion" (Arthur 1997: 44). Whereas, for instance, in Christianity the messiah is the historical figure Jesus of Nazareth who lived and died in Palestine some 2000 years ago, in Buddhism buddhas "are a regular phenomenon, repeated over the vast aeons of time which are mapped by Buddhist cosmology, rather than a single never-to-be-repeated instance of one particular individual biography" (Arthur 1997: 48). If, then, *Maitreya* is to be construed as 'the Buddhist messiah', then, counsels Arthur, it is "important to recognize that he is a messiah who is not unique and who will not bring time to an end", as is traditionally supposed in the Christian schema, but will act, rather, "as a punctuation mark in the great cycles of time" in which all beings are believed to be embroiled, "and from which, according to Buddhist soteriology, they ought to seek release in the form of nirvana" (Arthur 1997: 49). Ultimately, therefore, in attempting to outline how (and whether) the category of redemption can be appropriated in a modern context, we must guard against not only oversimplification but misrepresentation (cf. Arthur 1997: 46). From the very outset, we have to ensure that "our descriptive categories are sensitively malleable and open to the revision and nuance which their application to new subjects may suggest" (Arthur 1997: 44). Before even going down the path of seeking a criminologically coherent account of redemption, we must consider that—to put it starkly—if Christianity is what one source refers to as "the religion of redemption par excellence" (Ferm 1976: 640), criminology (or, in the context of my own research, film) may at best be merely bearing witness to ideas which have a basis in Christian thought, and in what is, at root, a 'secular' discipline (or medium).

As we see in the New Testament, there is an inextricable relationship between redemption and the Resurrection of Christ, inasmuch as the traditional expectation is that, in the words of Hebrews 9:15, Christ "is the mediator of a new covenant, so that those who are called may receive the promised eternal inheritance, since a death has occurred which redeems them from the[ir] transgressions". The thinking here is that, since Christ has been raised from the dead, so the believer will be resurrected and judged at the end of history, and can expect heavenly reward if he or she has been redeemed through Christ's atoning death on the Cross. Rather than a catch-all process, the Bible identifies a number of very specific phenomena from which Christ's redemptive work is understood to be operative. For example, we learn from Hebrews 2:3 that what one is redeemed from is divine wrath, while redemption is from bondage to demonic powers or the Devil himself according to Galatians 4:8 and Colossians 1:13. Underlying all accounts is the understanding that, due to Original Sin, humankind is in a fallen and depraved condition, from which redemption is sought. According to St Paul in Romans 5, "Therefore as sin came into the world through one man and death through sin … so death spread to all men because all men sinned … death reigned from Adam to Moses … one man's trespass led to condemnation for all men". Despite the fact that future generations did not directly participate in the Fall—indeed, they were as yet unborn—Augustine believed that all human beings are corporately implicated in Adam's transgression, and that it was through sexual desire, or 'concupiscence', that Adam's sin and guilt is passed down through the generations. Christ's role here is pivotal, as he is, in effect, performing the role of the 'second Adam', by reversing Adam's original act of disobedience, thereby enabling those who believe in him to share in his salvific power.

Rather than a process which can be straightforwardly applied to the present day pursuit of criminology, there is thus much more to redemption in early Christianity than a mere matter of seeking the forgiveness and/or transformation of habitual criminal offenders. The non-negotiable starting-point is a recognition that the Divinely created design has been spoiled, whereupon redemption amounts to the restoration of the torn fabric of personal relationships between Creator and creation. In Ephesians 1, we learn that the specific medium of redemption is the blood of Christ, a position also adopted by Augustine in the early fifth century, as evinced in the following petition in his *Confessions*: "You know how weak I am and how inadequate is my knowledge: teach me and heal my frailty. Your only Son … has redeemed me with his blood. Save me from the scorn of my enemies, for the price of my redemption is always in my thoughts" (Augustine 1961: 251–52). Augustine may not actually refer in this passage to whom the price of redemption is to be paid, but the traditional assumption is that it is to be paid to the Devil—not a position that modern appropriators of the term redemption in criminology may be all that keen to adopt!

In the modern day, of course, we are used to encountering the term 'redemption' in supermarkets and high-street stores when we wish to take points off a customer loyalty card against the value of a product. If we wish to buy a book or a bottle of perfume for, say, £30, and have accrued £20 in points awarded for regularly patronizing the store or chain concerned, then, as a reward for loyalty, it may be possible to 'redeem' some or all of the points, thereby purchasing a £30 product for, say, a third of the price. Again, though, the language is quite distinct from its basis in theology where 'redemption' is bound up with release (see Luke 2:38), ransom (Mark 10:45) and the payment of a price to set free (or 'redeem') a prisoner or slave (1 Peter 1:18–21) (see Reed 2004: 226–27). In the Old Testament, also, the term is used 132 times, principally in the context of money payments for the recovery of property (Leviticus 25:25f.), for the firstborn (Numbers 3:44–51), and from slavery (Exodus 21:7–8). In such contexts, the word means 'deliverance', and the 'redeemer' was an adult male relative who would buy back, or 'redeem', servants, animals, land, prisoners of war, debts or even, as in the case of Ruth 2:20, the wife of a deceased relative (see Mitchell 2007: 189). As Mitchell indicates, God is seen as the ultimate redeemer/rescuer, whether from slavery in Egypt or Exile in Babylon, or, as expounded in the Psalms, from violence and oppression (see e.g. Ps. 72:12–14) (Mitchell 2007: 190). Such ideas can also be found in the New Testament, albeit less frequently. In Mitchell's words, "several of the New Testament authors develop both themes found in the Hebrew Bible of God redeeming and rescuing his people and slaves having their freedom bought for them", and he cites the examples of Paul in Galatians 3:13 that "Christ redeemed us from the curse of the law" and Galatians 4:1–7 which speaks of God sending his Son to redeem people from slavery to the "elemental spirits of the universe" so that they may become God's children (Mitchell 2007: 190). There is nothing in such language that is generic or readily transferable to present debates in criminology or film. Rather, in Mitchell's words:

> In the New Testament redemption is not being used in a general sense, where God delivers his people from character deficiencies or general troubles. For the earliest Christians, and especially those used to hearing in synagogue worship about God's redemption of his people or actually seeing slaves being bought and set free in the market-place, it was an easily understandable metaphor. In our current age, lacking such concrete examples and where slavery has become a far more furtive industry, it is no surprise that the word has lost its original vividness
>
> (Mitchell 2007: 191)

Every indication is that redemption is anything but a universal process, but one which is actually unintelligible when cut loose from the categories of Christian doctrine. Some of the eagerness among theologians and criminologists to use the language of redemption needs therefore to be qualified, as in embracing and harnessing the term it is clear that no appeal is being made to Jesus's death as expiation or satisfaction for the sins of humanity, as encapsulated in article 15 of the 39 articles of the Church of England, which attests that Christ "came to be the Lamb without spot, Who, by sacrifice of himself once made, should take away the sins of the world" (cited in Gibson 1902: 439). While an atonement theory of redemption has a widespread usage in the history of the Christian Church, the difficulty for the scholar is that it is very far from readily amenable to contemporary discourse in either criminology or theology, posing as it does serious ethical difficulties. For the criminologist who seeks the rehabilitation of habitual offenders, is it necessarily helpful to invoke language which, in its Pauline and Augustinian manifestations, categorizes humanity as depraved and corrupt, to the point that God requires the sacrifice of an innocent human being for his satisfaction—and the redemption of the human race—to be attained? The problem with such a rendering is that Christ only becomes Redeemer by taking on the sins that someone else—Adam—has committed, on behalf of the whole human race. In Paul Badham's words, "It has been asked in what sense the death of an innocent person can take away the guilt of sinners, whose conscience should be still further troubled by the notion of an innocent suffering in their place" (Badham and Badham 1984: 58). Back in the second century, Origen held that by our sins we had sold our souls to the Devil, and that, in Alan Richardson's words, "God had re-purchased man for himself by paying to the devil the ransom of Christ's life" (Richardson 1986: 99). But, our modern legal system has moved on a long way from this, and, as Richardson puts it, never does it occur to Origen "that the Ransom Theory is unworthy of the Christian conception of God" (Richardson 1986: 100). It is doubtful that any criminologist would want to seek common ground with a theory which emphasizes that the shedding of the blood of an innocent victim has healing properties, not to mention what Reed refers to as "the supposed idealization of victimhood, victory through violent death, and traditional associations with the satisfaction of male honor" (Reed 2004: 227).

Redemption as a more malleable concept

So, where do we go from here? Is there really no bridge between such an ostensibly archaic theological doctrine as redemption and its more recent secular manifestations in theology and film and in criminology? One such approach in Christian theology is to take the line that, instead of overplaying the distinction between the divine and the human, with all of the connotations of there being an unbridgeable gulf between Creator and creation, redemption is a rather more inclusive and bi-lateral process. Indeed, Marsh makes the point that redemption is not just a story about God but about God's relationship with humanity (see Marsh 2007: 106), and, in his words, what makes Jesus's story a redemptive story is that it is "inhabited in the act of following by those who are so impressed that they want to imitate the actions of Jesus" (Marsh 2007: 107). Following this line of thinking, for many theologians today, the focus in accounts of redemption is not simply on the sacrificial role performed by Christ for the sins of humanity but on the role of those who have been redeemed—that is, the *recipients* of Christ's redemptive act. Without disputing that there is something innately God-centred, or Christological, about the redemptive process, those individuals whose lives have been variously touched and transformed by Christ's redemptive work, and who have subsequently sought to model their lives after him, are categorized, in effect, as Christ-figures (see Deacy 2001: 70). As St. Paul wrote in his first letter to the Corinthians, the challenge is for all Christians to become followers, or models, of Christ, in line with his own behaviour—"Be imitators of me, as I am of Christ" (1 Corinthians 11:1). Accordingly, redemption necessarily has a human-oriented—indeed, anthropocentric—dimension, which ties in with post-Enlightenment thinking more generally, whereby, in Paul Fiddes's words, "there was a widespread suspicion of any notion that help was available from beyond the human mind" (Fiddes 1989: 10). For a number of Protestants after the Reformation, including Methodists and Quakers (Lutherans and Calvinists were notable exceptions since, for them, the orbit of redemption lies entirely within God's hands), what particularly mattered was the character of each individual human person in the redemptive journey. Within Roman Catholicism, also, it was held that, in contrast to the Lutheran idea of justification by faith alone, it was possible for one to play a part in earning his or her own passage to salvation, to the point that, in Peter Stanford's words, "If you hit carefully drawn-up targets in life—the Eucharist on nine first Fridays, for example, was said to be a guarantee of a happy death—you would have saved up enough tokens to get into heaven" (Stanford 2002: 213).

Redemption is thus something that one is able to achieve on one's own, with Jesus the inspiration or model behind the process. As the second century theologian Irenaeus put it, life comprises "a divinely intended opportunity, given to us both individually and as a race, to grow towards the realization of the potentialities of our own nature and so to become fully human" (quoted in Hick 1973: 152). Having been created in an imperfect state, yet endowed with free will, Irenaeus held that we are capable of *self*-improvement and of *ourselves* becoming 'children of God'. As Augustine's rival, Pelagius, in the early fifth century, likewise saw it, it is possible to attain salvation without the need for divine grace, namely, by our own efforts and self-reliance. For Pelagius, the human will is not predisposed towards sin; rather, even in this sinful world, we have the full power to choose whether to do the right thing or not. Any other view was, he maintained, an insult to God the Creator (see Kelly 1980: 357). Similar sentiments are evinced in the present day by Greg Garrett, who, writing from a Christian evangelical point of view, makes the instructive point that, however it comes, "salvation changes our sinful natures so that we may aspire to be more like Christ and less like our fallen human nature, and so that our actions might begin to reflect our new creation" (Garrett 2007: 85). What is more, this more anthropocentric orientation of redemption has even been employed in a recent criminology article by Mike Nellis, who notes that redemption stories in American film and literature—and specifically those involving prisoners who have been released into 'mainstream society', along the lines of Jean Valjean in Victor Hugo's *Les Miserables* (1862)—"emphasise the importance of taking individual responsibility for personal change", in which the characters "have to transcend their limitations on their own" (Nellis 2009: 143). Nellis also defines redemption "as a moral quest to become a good person" and writes about the steps, or "elements", involved in the redemptive journey, which include acquiring "a new sense of responsibility" and the realization that, while it may be impossible to undo the past, "they can make the future better, if only in limited, practical ways" (Nellis 2009: 142). There may even, he writes, be a sacrificial component involved whereby "the protagonists die doing good" (Nellis 2009: 143), but, here, there is no talk of atonement, penal substitution or of an innocent victim dying in order to placate or satisfy the justice of an intransigent deity who seeks reparation for his violated honour. Rather, the emphasis is on what Nellis calls "the quasi-theological issue of redemption" in which what matters is whether or not one is capable of putting "the past behind them", making "suitable amends" and taking "responsibility for their futures" (Nellis 2009: 129). This all sounds much more positive than the traditional language of redemption, which, as we have already seen, entailed seeing the whole human race as having been born guilty.

There are certainly dangers with such an approach. As Marsh sees it, there is a risk for Christians that instead of seeing God as "the centre and focus" of their religion, it is "the impact of the presence and action of God on religious people which takes precedence", to the point that God "slips off the scene" (Marsh 2007: 94). In any theology-film conversation, it is thus pivotal that what Marsh calls "the human interest angle" (Marsh 2007: 94) is not allowed to dominate. However, the fact that there is, in theological terms, a universal dimension to redemption—the entire human race is believed to be enmeshed in sin and Christ's redemption thus has potential consequences for everyone—makes it difficult to argue that the contours of redemption can be restricted to Christianity alone. A persuasive case was made by the German Lutheran theologian, Dietrich Bonhoeffer, before his execution by the Nazis in 1945 in a German prison camp for attempting to remove Hitler from power, that there is no more than an artificial distinction between the sacred and the secular, the 'Church' and the 'world', since the Incarnation of Christ meant that the transcendent was now immanent and any barrier between the sacred and the secular had dissolved. Due to the union of the divine and human spheres, Bonhoeffer even thought that there was no incompatibility or line of demarcation that could be drawn between living a secular life and sharing in God's suffering: "It is not some religious act which makes a Christian what he is, but participation in the suffering of God in the life of the world" (Bonhoeffer 1963: 123). The transcendent and the immanent cannot be separated on this reading, prompting Harvey Cox, one of Bonhoeffer's staunchest supporters, to ask: "how can we speak in a secular fashion of God?" (Cox 1975). Following through Bonhoeffer's thinking, it is clear that the criminologist is no more presupposing the Christian faith when he or she draws upon the language of redemption than the film-maker who, in the manner of Frank Darabont, chooses to make a film with the word 'Redemption' in the title.

Redemption in film

Of course, theological purists may be dismissive of any attempt at forging a precise correlation between Christian and cinematic or criminological forms of redemption, but the fact that redemption need not have an overtly Christian frame of reference does suggest that there is scope for dialogue between theologians, film-makers, criminologists and others over the appropriation of redemptive terminology. The fact that, as Marsh sees it, redemption is "a preoccupation of many Western films" (Marsh 2007: 94) is precisely something the theologian should dismiss at his or her peril. In my own case, the rationale behind my decision to pursue doctoral work in the area of religion and film back in the 1990s was because I was so accustomed to seeing the same vocabulary being expounded in such widely different contexts that I wanted to see whether any sort of conversation could be facilitated between them. In the words of American theologian David Kelsey:

> as an assiduous reader of reviews of fiction, plays and movies, I have been impressed by the frequency with which reviewers comment on the presence or absence of a 'redemptive' note or theme in the work under review or debate whether there might be such a note. Sometimes the presence of a redemptive note seems to count in favor of the work and its absence to count against it. Although I am often unable to tell just what the reviewer means

> by 'redemption' or 'redemptive,' it is clear that the words are used in the context of certain practices that help make up Western cultural life
>
> (quoted in Marsh 2007: 94)

This is very much my experience, too, and a brief survey of some recent theology publications will show that theologians themselves are happy to employ redemptive language when referring to films which bear little or no direct relation to traditional Christian doctrine. In his 2007 publication *The Gospel According to Hollywood*, Garrett writes, for example, that the perennial Christmas favourite *It's a Wonderful Life* (1946) presents a powerful cinematic picture of redemption, in that the protagonist, George Bailey (James Stewart), "undergoes a conversion that convinces him that life is worth living and that, more importantly, *his* life is worth living" (Garrett 2007: 85). Similarly, with respect to Paul Thomas Anderson's *Magnolia* (1999)—an audacious exploration of dysfunctional family relationships within a set of characters connected in some way with the TV industry in the San Fernando Valley—Garrett notes that the neurotic and abused Claudia (Melora Walters) cannot imagine that anyone would love her as she is, but who finds in John C. Reilly's sensitive police officer, Jim, a soul-mate. Accordingly, out of a "swirling miasma of sin and suffering—out of the everyday complications of life—comes the possibility for redemption" (Garrett 2007: 106–07). In her 1999 book *Finding Meaning at the Movies*, American theologian Sara Anson Vaux goes down a similar path when she writes in relation to *Ulee's Gold* (1997)—a remarkably affecting film in which Oscar-nominated Peter Fonda plays a Vietnam veteran whose trip to visit his son in prison "turns into a massive, life-transforming journey for him and Jimmy, and for all the persons whose lives touch theirs" (Vaux 1999: 163–64)—that this is "a film about redemption" (Vaux 1999: 163). This is not a film in which redemption comes about as the result of the work of any external saviour who, in the manner of the quintessential Hollywood superhero, is "marked by extraordinary capabilities for moral discernment and physical strength" and who wields "extra-human powers to punish evil-doers while protecting the innocent" (Jewett and Lawrence 2009: 385), but is grounded in a realistic and everyday milieu. In Vaux's words, "Redemption in this movie comes unexpectedly, through loving the ones who love you", and where Ulee's redemptive journey "has been to care for his wounded family and to find that their care and love is both the trip and the goal" (Vaux 1999: 166).

What such examples show is that films provide fruitful territory for the theologian who is amenable to looking for theologically rich material, albeit in unconventional places. In keeping with Bonhoeffer's erosion of the sacred-secular duality, it is apparent that, beyond the specific categories of Augustinian theology, the medium of film is a fertile site of redemptive activity. Not only can a film invoke the specific vocabulary of redemption, but, as Conrad Ostwalt has pertinently argued, it "also functions religiously" if, as he thinks is the case in Robert Benton's Depression-era drama *Places in the Heart* (1984), "it translates religious concepts such as forgiveness and evil for contemporary audiences" (Ostwalt 2003: 147). In other words, if a film "raises religious questions for the audience", such as the hunger for redemption—which, in the words of Oscar-nominated American screenwriter Richard LaGravenese, who wrote *The Fisher King* (1991), *The Bridges of Madison County* (1995) and *The Horse Whisperer* (1998) is "the only subject" (quoted in Ostwalt 2003: 147) for a contemporary American movie—then the film concerned is of importance to the theologian "because it challenges contemporary audiences to grapple with theological questions" (Ostwalt 2003: 147). There need be nothing pro-Christian about such films, nor must there even be a consonance between the redemptive interpretation that the film is believed to yield and what the Bible has to say on the subject. No matter how far removed the vocabulary used in such cinematic discourse is from that of traditional Christian thinking, the scholar should not dismiss it out of hand, as it is saying something vital about the way in which redemption is being expressed and appropriated in the modern world. Indeed, acknowledging the difference that in films redemption tends to be something that human beings can attain of their own volition, without needing to invoke God or any supernatural, divine agencies, whereas in traditional theological accounts God is central to the redemptive schema, Lyden is right in his assertion that "though less than ultimate from a Christian point of view, it is not intrinsically bad to have self-confidence and courage or to believe that humans can truly love each other" (Lyden 2007: 217). Do not theologians have a responsibility to avoid enforcing pre-established interpretations on to a cinematic text and to take the testimony of those who work in other disciplines seriously—and even be prepared to revisit their methodologies if and when competing paradigms are encountered?

Moreover, instead of privileging scriptural or Augustinian understandings of redemption, there is scope, as I have written elsewhere, for going down the path proposed in their 2002 publication *Screening Scripture: Intertextual Connections Between Scripture and Film* by George Aichele and Richard Walsh, in which the claim is made that readings from outside biblical scholarship—including positions not identified with traditional Christianity or Judaism or even any religious position at all—"have offered rich insights into biblical texts" (Walsh and Aichele 2002: vii). Everyone interprets a text from their own particular cultural and ideological vantage points and, in a post-modern sense, no-one has privileged access to authoritative interpretation. Indeed, as Walsh and Aichele put it, "There is no proper or correct *exegesis* of any text. All readings are eisegeses, biased expressions of one ideology or another, and the conflict of readings is often a conflict of ideologies" (Walsh and Aichele 2002: vii–viii). This can be compared to Marsh's assertion that it is a misnomer to suppose that "theological meaning is *in* a film simply awaiting the discovery of trained theological interpreters"; rather, he makes the more credible claim that "theological meaning is brought almost exclusively *to* a film" (Marsh 2004: 110). I wholly subscribe to Walsh and Aichele's desire to bring biblical and filmic texts "into a genuine exchange that will open up illuminating connections between them", thereby facilitating the two-fold process of opening "new insights into ancient Scriptures" while at the same time "providing cross-cultural illumination of popular film and contemporary culture" (Walsh and Aichele 2002: ix). Gordon Lynch makes the similarly judicious claim that there needs to be "a complex conversation between the questions and insights of both religious tradition and popular culture", one that allows, moreover, "for the possibility that both religious tradition and popular culture can be usefully challenged and transformed through this process" (Lynch 2005: 105). The fact that a film does not bear witness to what, say, Augustine meant by redemption does not therefore mean to say that any 'redemption' on display in a filmic or criminological context is without value. The criminologist, when using the language of redemption, may not be urging the sinful and depraved human individual to believe in the victorious gospel of Christ's death for their transgressions and in Christ's subsequent resurrection from the dead, but, as Kelsey sees it, any "extra-Christian" uses of the term 'redemption', as in the case of the points he makes with regard to the medium of film, "doubtless shape" the way in which they are used "in the context of the common life of Christian faith communities, and vice versa" (quoted in Marsh 2007: 95). There is, therefore, an interweaving—a two-way dialogue and exchange—between Christian and non-Christian interpretations.

When, in a recent article for the *Journal of Religion and Popular Culture*, Matthew Anderson thus writes that the Charlie Kaufman-scribed comedy *Adaptation* (2002) "mines the familiar territory of the personal search for redemption", but "does this in language at times oddly familiar to the Christian exegete or theologian" (Anderson 2006: para 27), or Simon Taylor writes with respect to Abel Farrara's *Bad Lieutenant* that the film—which raises "serious questions concerning the nature of the salvation that Lt and the boys achieve in the narrative" (Taylor 2003: para 8)—"calls for a fuller articulation of the role of the resurrection in Christian soteriology" (Taylor 2003: para 15), we see how and where just such a dialogue can be fostered. Even when, in a persuasive argument by Jolyon Mitchell, in his recent *Media Violence and Christian Ethics*, the claim is adduced that "if in many movies characters are portrayed as struggling to find some sort of redemption or societies are apparently 'redeemed' through the use of violence, the nature of the redemption is significantly different from how it was used and understood by biblical authors" (Mitchell 2007: 189), there is clearly still scope for a two-way conversation. In the specific context of films which address questions of genocide—such as *Hotel Rwanda* (2004) and *Shooting Dogs* (2005)—where there is an implicit questioning of whether there exists a God "who redeems or rescues" (Mitchell 2007: 190), Mitchell writes that "by bringing these media texts into dialogue with such claims the moral landscape of both the film and the Bible can be reconsidered" (Mitchell 2007: 190). Redemption may well have taken on a wide variety of different meanings when appropriated in film—in Mitchell's words, it "can be used to refer to redemption or deliverance from the attacks of enemies, the destructive forces of habitual vices, the isolation of loneliness, the guilt of betrayal, the alienation of community or the shadows of private heartbreak" (Mitchell 2007: 191)—but there is no reason why such models cannot challenge theologians in their own interpretation of the language concerned. Taylor's critique of *Bad Lieutenant* is especially germane in this regard, since it raises wider questions about how the film's "impoverished" (Taylor 2003: para 13) treatment of redemption may query or subvert Christianity's own approach to the topic. In both the film and in traditional Christian theology, Taylor suggests that there is too great an emphasis on *individual* salvation at the expense of "the wider ecology of relationships in which that individual is placed" (Taylor 2003: para 13). In his conclusion, Taylor writes that despite what he sees in the film as an "inadequate narrative and theology of salvation", we should nevertheless still see the film "as a serious and important contribution to the theological task of articulating salvation" (Taylor 2003: para 14). Rather than critique a film because its theology is deemed to be inadequate, something much more reciprocal is thus envisaged. Indeed, as Taylor puts it, "It is a real virtue of *Bad Lieutenant* that it enables us to articulate a fault-line that the film shares with much Christian theology" (Taylor 2003: para 14).

The danger with any attempts that see the scriptural interpretation of redemption as pre-eminent and primary is that they do not allow for the possibility that there are occasions in which one may wish to re-visit, or even reject, such readings, on the grounds that they may be deficient (or, as the earlier discussion concerning the morality of the atonement in the Victorian era has highlighted, morally abhorrent). It may be tempting for the theologian to be critical of, say, the way in which we are alleged to be increasingly desensitized to violence in Hollywood—to the point, for example, that Bryan Stone has argued that so bombarded are we with the spectacle of violence that we are as a society less and less able to associate on-screen violence with anything other than entertainment value (Stone 1999)—but this is to overlook the possibility that violent films can themselves generate a serious debate about the efficacy of violence as a redeeming or redemptive force that lies at the very kernel of Christianity itself. As John Lyden sees it, the message of many Westerns or action films may be that "violence is legitimate and necessary, whereas the message of Christianity is that violence is no longer needed since the sinless one has died to end the power of all sin and violence" (Lyden 2007: 214). But, at the same time, "Christians do not all tend to be pacifists, suggesting that they are already beholden to the theology of the Western/action film, and that the biblical message has been muted in their own religious practice" (Lyden 2007: 215). In times of war, for instance, it is quite possible for some Christians to be inclined to endorse the use of violence, as George W. Bush and Tony Blair's 'war on terror' would suggest, and, indeed, there is a case for arguing that "the conservative Christians who approved of the ultraviolent portrayal of Jesus's crucifixion in Mel Gibson's *The Passion of the Christ* also tended to be extremely supportive of the U.S. attacks on Afghanistan and Iraq" (Lyden 2008: 215). As Lyden puts it, though, this is "not necessarily because people are seeing too many Westerns or action movies, but rather because the values of these films have already been internalized by Christians in spite of their apparent disconnect from the values of biblical Christianity" (Lyden 2007: 215). I would be inclined to go even further than Lyden on this, moreover, and attest that there is an inextricable link between violence and Christianity, at the heart of which lies the explicitly violent symbol of the Cross. Rather than some sort of external 'other' that stands in stark opposition to the intrinsically 'non-violent' nature of Christianity, I have made the case elsewhere that redeeming violence is, rather, an inescapable part of Christianity's origins (Deacy 2008: 141).

An over-emphasis on the claim that Stone and others profess that there is nothing redemptive about violence should thus be qualified. Mitchell writes, for example, that to focus solely "on the violence of any of the three *Godfather* films misses their proven ability to help audiences explore issues such as loyalty, revenge and redemption", and he makes the pertinent point that in "many reviews it was the narratives, characterisation and cinematography that attracted more critical attention than the violence" (Mitchell 2007: 178). In spite, therefore, of the tendency among conservative media commentators, such as Michael Medved in the United States, to affirm that the "academic connection between violence in real life and violence in the media is a stronger connection than that between smoking and lung cancer", and that what you see in violent movies "is basically a reflection of nothing other than people's warped imagination" (quoted in Deacy 2008: 129), a more nuanced—indeed, sophisticated—picture can be found in Mitchell's claim that in "the midst of the violent worlds" which such 'violent' films as *Tsotsi* (2005) and *City of God* (2002) reflect, "it is not redemptive violence but acts of compassion, such as the return of a stolen baby or tending the wounds of a friend, which stand out as points of hope in the midst of tragedy" (Mitchell 2007: 184). He also refers to how an Asian film, *Bangkok Dangerous* (2000):

> ... is a good example of how in many movies the perpetrators of violence are ultimately interrogated by the violence they themselves have initiated. The all-conquering quasi-messianic figure from *Rambo*-like films is replaced in *Bangkok Dangerous* by a fallen, explicitly fallible character who discovers that those 'who live by the gun die by the gun', and that the apparent strength of violent force is doomed to failure
>
> (Mitchell 2007: 184)

Despite being redolent in violence, such films also therefore "interrogate its value" (Mitchell 2007: 184).

A similar critique can be found in the way 'redemption' is believed to operate in the case of *The Shawshank Redemption*. According to the Pauline scholar Robert Jewett, there is an ontological difference between the type of 'redemption' on offer in Darabont's prison escape drama from 1994 and what St Paul in the New Testament has to say on the subject. Despite drawing on biblical motifs in the film—not least the image of the small rock hammer that is hidden within the bible of the protagonist, Andy Dufresne (Tim Robbins), which is meant to show how 'Salvation lies within'—and presenting audiences with a narrative in which an innocent person, falsely accused of murdering his wife, is ultimately redeemed (see Jewett 1999: 163–64), Jewett has a problem with the physical nature of the redemptive portrayal on offer in this film, in which Dufresne escapes from incarceration at the end in a very literal and material sense. This is because when St Paul talks about the term 'redemption' in his epistle to the Romans, there is a marked sense in which those who have been redeemed are not thereby physically freed from adversity. In Romans 8:24–5, for example, there is a presupposition of a situation of ongoing vulnerability for those who have been redeemed inasmuch as the "slaves and former slaves who made up the bulk of the Roman Churches could not entirely overcome exploitation by their masters and patrons" (Jewett 1999: 164). There is much more to redemption, therefore, on this reading, than mere change of (physical) circumstance. For Jewett, indeed, redemption is not about escaping from present conditions of adversity but is all about the overcoming of shame "in the present moment by God's love poured into the heart in the context of the new community" (Jewett 1999: 165). The film is quite antithetical to a traditional redemptive reading on this account. In his words:

> A new form of salvation is clearly being offered in this film, one that replaces the intervention of Yahweh at the Exodus and of Christ on the Cross. Salvation now comes through the little rock hammer in the hands of an intelligent and determined person who refuses to give up hope in his own capacity to achieve freedom against all the odds. We see in this and other films the unexamined results of a process of secular derivation that remains critical of biblical religion while continuing to use its redemptive language
>
> (Jewett 1999: 181)

That there is an inescapably physical and this-worldly dimension to the type of redemption on display in *The Shawshank Redemption* is not in doubt, but it does not necessarily follow that this is as devoid of redemptive value as Jewett's critique would seem to suggest. As debates within Christianity concerning 'realized eschatology' have shown, "Most early Christians seem to have expected a dramatic consummation of history very soon, but there were also early moves to shift the emphasis from dates and times onto the person of Jesus Christ as the one who was seen as the 'alpha and omega', the clue to the beginning and end of history" (Ford 1999: 107). On such a view, there is, to paraphrase Karl Rahner, no other sphere of operation than this physical universe and world (see Hick 1976: 231), and it has been common from as far back as Greco-Roman texts and images—in other words, from even before the New Testament period—for heaven to be seen as a garden and a pastoral landscape or a group of idyllic islands (see Russell 1997: 21). From the time of Homer in the ninth century B.C.E., poets have described a land of music, dancing, sunny meadows, flowers, fountains and sweet refreshment and repose in shady groves, in which death and disease have no dominion and no one lacks anything (see Russell 1997: 21). Is this really so distinct from the apotheosis of an earthly paradise that is presented at the end of *The Shawshank Redemption* in the fishing village of Zihuatanejo on the Mexican coast? There are many instances also within Christianity of correlating heaven with an earthly paradise, as typified by an anonymous English writer who said of Brazil in 1554 that:

> All who have gone there agree that the best and greenest fields and countrysides in the entire world are to be found there, the most pleasant mountains, covered with trees and fruits of every kind, the most beautiful valleys, the most delicious rivers of fresh water, filled with an endless variety of fishes, the thickest forests, always green and laden with fruits
>
> (Delumeau 2000: 111)

Accordingly, for this spellbound writer, "it is now thought that the earthly paradise can only be located on the equinoctial line close to it, for the only perfect spot on earth has its spot there" (Delumeau 2000: 111). Jean Delumeau refers to a similar letter written in 1560 by Rui Pereira that "If there is a paradise on earth, I would say it exists presently in Brazil … Anyone who wants to live in the earthly paradise has no choice but to live in Brazil" (Delumeau 2000: 111). The concept of an earthly paradise is also integral to the thinking of a number of the early Church Fathers, such as Justin Martyr, Irenaeus and Tertullian, who envisaged the coming of an earthly kingdom of Christ that would follow his second coming and last for the period of one thousand years (see Collins 1999: 409).

To dismiss the picture of redemption that appears in *The Shawshank Redemption* as being too mundane and limited is thus to overlook the diversity of images of redemption that have been on display throughout Christian history. Andy Dufresne may not get to experience a Christian paradise or heaven as such at the end of the film, when we see him fishing on the coast of Zihuatenejo, but there is clearly much of redemptive value in this last scene of the film that theologians should be willing to take on board. As Adele Reinhartz has indicated in her *Scripture on the Silver Screen*, there may be differences between the film and a Pauline interpretation of redemption, but there is much more to the film than the mere living of a "good life on a Pacific beach" (Reinhartz 2003: 138). Indeed, she says that "The 'redemption' in *The Shawshank Redemption* is not only Andy's patient and daring escape to freedom but also the redemption that he attempts to provide for his fellow inmates by nurturing those parts of them that the prison system and its guidelines cannot touch", as when he helps his fellow prisoners to study for their examinations and enables the expression of human dignity and self-development in an otherwise rigidly authoritarian, corrupt and institutionalized regime. In her words, "hope, dignity, music, and all other pleasures of the mind and soul are the salvation that lies within the human spirit while the human body is confined behind bars" (Reinhartz 2003: 142). What the film thus shows is that "the Bible can be a source for themes, language, and images about fundamental things, even for people who do not necessarily identify with the religious institutions and communities that hold the Bible as sacred canon" (Reinhartz 2003: 142).

Towards a criminologically and theologically fertile model of redemption

Accordingly, even if one does not subscribe to Christianity as a belief system, there is plenty in what both film-makers and criminologists, for example, are presently doing with the vocabulary of redemption that allows for a creative and interdisciplinary exchange of ideas. The fact that *Theoretical Criminology* published an article in February 2009 about how films which examine the attempted re-entry of released prisoners into mainstream society ask "searching questions about the nature of rehabilitation, redemption and public forgiveness" (Nellis 2009: 129) suggests that such a conversation has already started. When Nellis thus writes that a film such as *Sling Blade* (Billy Bob Thornton, 1996), which he sees as "arguably the first of a series of movies which quite explicitly placed personal redemption at the heart of the released prisoner narrative" (Nellis 2009: 136), can facilitate "an amorphous public conversation about crime, punishment and resettlement which is largely outside the boundaries of academic criminology" (Nellis 2009: 129), it is clear that there is plenty of mileage for just such a dialogue. What this further shows, of course, is that it is not only theologians who control or dictate the parameters of any discourse involving redemption and the use of redemptive language. When Nellis continues that redemption is being transmuted "from a theological into a social concept" and is being construed as "a viable and meaningful *secular option*, which can be achieved without recourse to God's grace, or indeed any reference to spirituality" (Nellis 2009: 143), this is not really incompatible with the aforementioned more anthropocentric and individualistic demeanour of much post-Enlightenment theology.

If the net result of such exchanges is that boundaries are more malleable, then this is no bad thing. Indeed, on close inspection it is not self-evident even within theology that redemption is a homogeneous or monolithic process. There is a very fine line between 'redemption' and such other theological categories as 'salvation', 'deliverance', 'liberation', 'freedom', 'peace', 'enlightenment', 'bliss', and even 'health'. David Ford has argued that the root meaning of 'salvation' is 'health', which can take "physical, social, political, economical, environmental, mental, spiritual and moral" (Ford 1999: 101) forms, and that 'redemption', 'atonement' and 'sacrifice' are related terms which come under the umbrella term 'soteriology'. The doctrine of redemption may have a Christian foundation, but throughout Christian history it is curious that this doctrinally-specific concept has been open to a rich, and not entirely consistent, assortment of expressions. Indeed, speaking with specific reference to 'salvation', it is notable that Ford calls it "a striking fact about Christianity that, in its mainstream forms, it has never officially defined one doctrine of salvation" but has lived, rather, "with a diversity of approaches" (Ford 1999: 102). Although in the first five centuries of the Christian Church many "individuals attempted to think out the mode" in which redemption was to be understood, Richardson makes the case that "the Church as a whole embraced no theory" (Richardson 1986: 95). Moreover, in the specific case of the second century apologist, Origen, it is significant that although the Redemption wrought by Christ is integral to his Christology and theology, scholars "have often found Origen's thoughts on the redemption complex to the point of being mutually irreconcilable, and have been hard put to it to discover a unifying theme in them" (Kelly 1980: 186). To this, we can add the consideration that redemption is at one and the same time something that is *self*-involving, *God*-involving and *world*-involving (cf. Ford 1999: 101, though note he is speaking specifically about salvation), and as the reference to 'realized' expressions of redemption has already shown, salvation is not only future in scope but something which is happening now. As St Paul writes in 1 Corinthians 1:18, "For the word of the cross is folly to those who are perishing, but to us *who are being saved* it is the power of God" (emphasis added). The suggestion, here, is that redemption is a continuous and present-oriented process which cannot simply be relegated to the distant future.

Crucially for our present discussion, Ford notes that what he calls the "unsummarizable richness is increased by the strongly practical dimensions of salvation, which mean that it is constantly being adapted to different settings and cultures" (Ford 1999: 101). It is possible to extrapolate from this that when filmmakers or criminologists draw upon the rich heritage of the term 'redemption', they are, in a positive sense, adding to and enhancing the manifold ways in which, as part of a two-way, bi-lateral process, the term is constantly able to be interpreted and re-interpreted. Neither the theologian, the film-maker nor the criminologist has privileged or exclusive access to the sphere of redemption, of course, but there is still much scope for agreement between practitioners in the various fields. In my own work in theology and film, for example, one of my areas of focus has been on the redemptive significance of gangster films, in which, as testimony has shown, audiences have often found the criminally minded protagonists of such 1930s films as *Little Caesar* (1931), *The Public Enemy* (1931) and *Scarface* (1932) to be "so much more appealing than the characters opposed to [them]" that they found themselves rooting for them "in spite of themselves" (quoted in Christianson 2005: 112). Despite the fact that they were on the 'wrong' side of the law or died for violating society's code (Deacy 2001: 98), I have argued that it is the intrinsically flawed, fallible and human nature of such film characters that makes it possible for theologians to draw parallels with Christian teaching. Indeed, in delineating quintessentially human protagonists—and gangster films, as well as *film noir*, are a particularly rich genre for exploring the underside of human life—a case can be made that such films have theological provenance, inasmuch as a correlation can be drawn with one of the schools of thought in the early Church (the Antiochene tradition, which addressed the question of Christ's humanity), according to which only a tainted and sinful individual can speak to, and be in a position to address the needs of, a tainted and sinful humanity. For Theodore of Mopsuestia (350–428 C.E.), a leading representative of this school of thought, Christ is not only fully divine but, significantly, also perfectly and completely human in nature. Without the human side, Christ could not have been the Redeemer of the human race—only by undergoing fully what it means to be human is Christ able to redeem. In Theodore's words, "Let the character of the natures stand without confusion" (quoted in Norris 1980: 113), it being clear to him that "the notion of 'mixture' is both exceptionally unsuitable and incongruous, since each of the natures remains indissolubly in itself" (quoted in Norris 1980: 120). If human nature, with all of its defects, is not therefore excluded from the orb of redemption, then films where the activities of criminals are at the heart of the narrative and whose actions are "brutally, vividly and even sympathetically portrayed" (Christianson 2005: 112) could be said to comprise a particularly pivotal site of redemptive significance. Regarding the end of *The Godfather*, for example, Mitchell writes that "Instead of finding him a morally repugnant character", many viewers "were attracted to Al Pacino's strong portrayal and his exertion of ruthless power through violence" (Mitchell 2007: 178). Eric Christianson has similarly written that, in portraying the life of Italian Americans "with some dignity and realism", and in its depiction of a "united, convivial and cosy Mafia family", Francis Ford Coppola has "created an inviting aura around criminal life" (Christianson 2005: 114), and which, moreover, is not all that far removed from the world of the Bible. Indeed, as Garrett sees it, King David was a savage warrior, adulterer and bad parent, and he refers to "those bickering patriarchs and matriarchs in Genesis whose lust-filled dysfunctional families make the ones in *Peyton Place, East of Eden, Home for the Holidays,* or *One True Thing* look like the Brady Bunch" (Garrett 2007: xix). He further identifies:

> that appalling episode in the book of Judges where a crowd of men in the city of Gibeah wants to gang-rape a Levite, a holy man, and so to protect himself he shoves his mistress into the street so that they can rape and beat her instead, and after he collects her dead body the next morning, he cuts her into pieces … and sends messengers bearing the pieces of her mutilated carcass to each tribe of Israel to protest the way he (he!) was dishonored by the people of Gibeah
>
> (Garrett 2007: xix–xx)

Despite the reservations, therefore, of more traditional theologians who may find film a far from fecund repository of redemption, Christianson pertinently asks whether, with respect to, say, *The Godfather*'s Michael Corleone (Al Pacino), we are being offered "a man that we want to be, or that we can't help being" (Christianson 2005: 118). My own position is that the more authentically human the film protagonist, the more authentic and fertile the possibility of redemptive activity (see Deacy 2001: 98). While many gangsters and *noir* 'heroes' die at the end of films without exactly being whiter-than-white role models, they do, nevertheless, embody humankind at its most fragile, fragmentary and at its most hungry for redemption. There is more than a grain of truth in what Paul Giles refers to as "that old Catholic paradox whereby the rank black sinner, the person who is horribly aware of the awful potential of damnation, can be closer to redemptive grace than the honest citizen who has never troubled himself about anything beyond his or her own domestic affairs" (Giles 1992: 332). In other words, redemption is not a trite or comfortable process, but involves a deep and acute awareness of what it means to be human, which in traditional Christian terms means facing up to, rather than running away from, our capacity to create harm and to destroy as well as to do good. Aside from the somewhat distracting debate, as posed by Augustine and Pelagius, concerning our proclivity towards sin (Are we born guilty or do we ourselves possess the ability to choose evil over good?) the very absence of celestial beings and supernatural phenomena in the present debate actually makes redemption more, rather than less, significant. As I have written elsewhere, "it is the *noir* protagonist's intrinsic feasibility and authenticity, even when—or, perhaps, especially when—that entails the delineation of human existence lived out as its most *sub*human, at its most brutal, oppressive and capricious, that makes a redemptive reading so pertinent" (Deacy 2001: 102). In the real world, as in *film noir*, something more profound has the capacity to take place than we can expect to find in works of cinematic escapism and fantasy, where there can be no more than a fleeting and transitory reprieve from the discontinuities and tensions of life (see e.g. Deacy 2005: 26). Using *noir* and an Antiochene Christology as our starting-point, perhaps, therefore, the role of the theologian and the role of the criminologist may not be all that far removed, to the point that this chapter has, hopefully, comprised a useful starting-point from which further cross-disciplinary interaction and exchange may be facilitated.

References

Anderson, M. (2006) '*Adaptation*: The Self-Proclaiming Rhetoric of Charlie Kaufman and of the Apostle Paul', *Journal of Religion and Popular Culture*, XIII, Summer, accessed 19 July 2010, www.usask.ca/relst/jrpc/art13-adaptation.html.

Arthur, C. (1997) 'Maitreya, the Buddhist Messiah', in Bowie, F. and Deacy, C., *The Coming Deliverer: Millennial Themes in World Religions*. Cardiff: University of Wales Press, pp 43–59.

Augustine, St (1961) *Confessions*. Harmondsworth: Penguin.

Badham, P. and Badham, L. (1984) *Immortality Or Extinction?* London: Society for Promoting Christian Knowledge.

Bonhoeffer, D. (1963) *Letters and Papers from Prison*. London: Fontana.

Christianson, E. (2005) 'An Ethic You Can't Refuse? Assessing *The Godfather* Trilogy', in Telford, W., Christianson E. and Francis P. (eds) *Cinéma Divinité: Readings in Film and Theology*. London: SCM Press, pp 110–23.

Collins, A. Y. (1999) 'The Book of Revelation', in Collins, J. J. (ed.) *The Encyclopedia of Apocalypticism, Volume I: The Origins of Apocalypticism in Judaism and Christianity*. New York: Continuum, pp 384–414.

Cox, H. (1975) 'The Secular City – Ten Years Later', Religion-Online, accessed 19 July 2010, www.religion-online.org/showarticle.asp?title=1861.

Deacy, C. (2001) *Screen Christologies: Redemption and the Medium of Film*. Cardiff: University of Wales Press.

Deacy, C. (2005) *Faith in Film: Religious Themes in Contemporary Cinema*. Aldershot: Ashgate.

Deacy, C. (2008) 'A Time to Kill? Theological Perspectives on Violence and Film', in Deacy, C. and Ortiz, G. (eds) *Theology and Film: Challenging the Sacred/Secular Divide*. Oxford: Blackwell, pp 123–42.

Delumeau, J. (2000) *History of Paradise: The Garden of Eden in Myth & Tradition*. Urbana and Chicago, IL: University of Illinois Press.

Ferm, V. (ed.) (1976) *An Encyclopedia of Religion*. Westport, CT: Greenwood Press.

Fiddes, P. S. (1989) *Past Event and Present Salvation: The Christian Idea of Atonement*. London: Darton Longman & Todd.

Ford, D. (1999) *Theology: A Very Short Introduction*. Oxford: Oxford University Press.

Garrett, G. (2007) *The Gospel According to Hollywood*. London and Louisville, KY: Westminster John Knox.

Gibson, E. C. S. (1902) *The Thirty-Nine Articles of the Church of England*. London: Methuen.

Giles, P. (1992) *American Catholic Arts and Fictions: Culture, Ideology, Aesthetics*. Cambridge: Cambridge University Press.

Hick, J. (1973) 'Towards a Christian Theology of Death', in Penelhum, T. (ed.) *Immortality*. Belmont, CA: Wadsworth, pp 141–57.

Hick, J. (1976) *Death and Eternal Life*. London: Collins.

Jewett, R. (1999) *Saint Paul Returns to the Movies: Triumph over Shame*. Cambridge: Eerdsmans.

Jewett, R. and Lawrence, J. (2009) 'Heroes and Superheroes', in Lyden, J. (ed.) *The Routledge Companion to Religion and Film*. Abingdon: Routledge, pp 384–402.

Kelly, J. N. D. (1980) *Early Christian Doctrines*. London: Adam & Charles Black.

Lyden, J. C. (2007) 'Theology and Film: Interreligious Dialogue and Theology', in Johnston, R. K. (ed.) *Re-Viewing Theology and Film: Moving the Discipline Forward*. Grand Rapids: Baker Academic, pp 205–18.

Lyden, J. C. (2008) 'Teaching *Film as Religion*', in Watkins, G. (ed.) *Teaching Religion and Film*. Oxford: Oxford University Press, pp 209–18.

Lynch, G. (2005) *Understanding Theology and Popular Culture*. Oxford: Blackwell.

Marsh, C. (1998) 'Religion, Theology and Film in a Postmodern Age: A Response to John Lyden', *Journal of Religion and Film*, 2(1), April, accessed 19 July 2010, http://avalon.unomaha.edu/jrf/marshrel.htm.

Marsh, C. (2004) *Cinema and Sentiment: Film's Challenge to Theology*. Carlisle: Paternoster Press.

Marsh, C. (2007) *Theology Goes to the Movies: An Introduction to Critical Christian Thinking*. Oxford: Routledge.

Mitchell, J. (2007) *Media Violence and Christian Ethics*. Cambridge: Cambridge University Press.

Nellis, M. (2009) 'The aesthetics of redemption: Released prisoners in American film and literature', *Theoretical Criminology*, 13(1), February: 129–46.

Norris, R. A. (1980) *The Christological Controversy*. Philadelphia, PA: Fortress Press.

Ostwalt, C. (2003) *Secular Steeples: Popular Culture and the Religious Imagination*. Harrisburg, PA: Trinity International.

Reed, E. (2004) 'Redemption', in Jones, G. (ed.) *The Blackwell Companion to Modern Theology*. Oxford: Blackwell, pp 227–42.

Reinhartz, A. (2003) *Scripture on the Silver Screen*. Louisville, KY: Westminster John Knox.

Richardson, A. (1986) *Creeds in the Making*. London: SCM Press.

Russell, J. B. (1997) *A History of Heaven: The Singing Silence*. Princeton, NJ: Princeton University Press.

Stanford, P. (2002) *Heaven: A Traveller's Guide to the Undiscovered Country*. London: HarperCollins.

Stone, B. (1999) 'Religion and Violence in Popular Film', *Journal of Religion and Film*, 3(1), April, accessed 19 July 2010, www.unomaha.edu/jrf/Violence.htm.

Taylor, S. J. (2003) 'It all happens here: Locating Salvation in Abel Ferrara's *Bad Lieutenant*', *Journal of Religion and Film*, 7(1), April, accessed 19 July 2010, www.unomaha.edu/jrf/Vol7No1/ferrarabadlt.htm.

Vaux, S. A. (1999) *Finding Meaning at the Movies*. Nashville, TN: Abingdon Press.

Walsh, R. and Aichele, G. (2002) 'Introduction: Scripture as Precursor', in Aichele, G. and Walsh, R. (eds) *Screening Scripture: Intertextual Connections Between Scripture and Film*. Harrisburg, PA: Trinity Press International, pp vii–xvi.

Chapter 2

Steps towards desistance among male young adult recidivists

*Anthony Bottoms and Joanna Shapland**

In recent years there has been a marked increase in scholarly interest in the topic of desistance from crime. Desistance and persistence have been researched for several age-groups (e.g. Farrall 2002; Laub and Sampson 2003; Ezell and Cohen 2005), but there has also been a significant renewal of interest in a phenomenon that has been observed 'for centuries', that is, 'the dramatic decrease in criminal behavior during young adulthood' (Siennick and Osgood 2008: 161). In this chapter, we provide an overview of some of the principal results from a fresh longitudinal research study that focuses on the early stages of desistance among young adult recidivists. But first, we will briefly sketch some key aspects of the existing research literature, because this has provided a set of invaluable way-markers for our study.

The age-crime curve and its explanation

Desistance among young adult recidivists is a topic that is closely linked to the so-called 'age-crime curve'. Although this is a standard criminological term, it is not always recognised that there are several different methods of constructing such curves, and that these differences have potential explanatory consequences. Perhaps the most usual method is that adopted in Figure 2.1, which shows, for England and Wales in 2000, age-crime curves for males and females, constructed using a *cross-sectional offender-based methodology*. Here, the unit of measurement is the offender, and each offender counts as one whether s/he has committed one or a hundred offences; also, the diagram is cross-sectional, taking a 'snapshot' of all recorded offenders in the year. There are two main possible alternatives to this basis of measurement. The first is to adopt a *cross-sectional offence-based methodology* (counting the total number of offences committed by offenders at each age point); and as van Mastrigt and Farrington (2009: 563–65) have recently shown, when this method is used the peak age is higher than in Figure 2.1.[1] The second and more radical alternative is the *longitudinal* curve, which measures, for a specified population of offenders, the frequency of their offending over their lifetime (or a portion of it). In principle, there is no reason

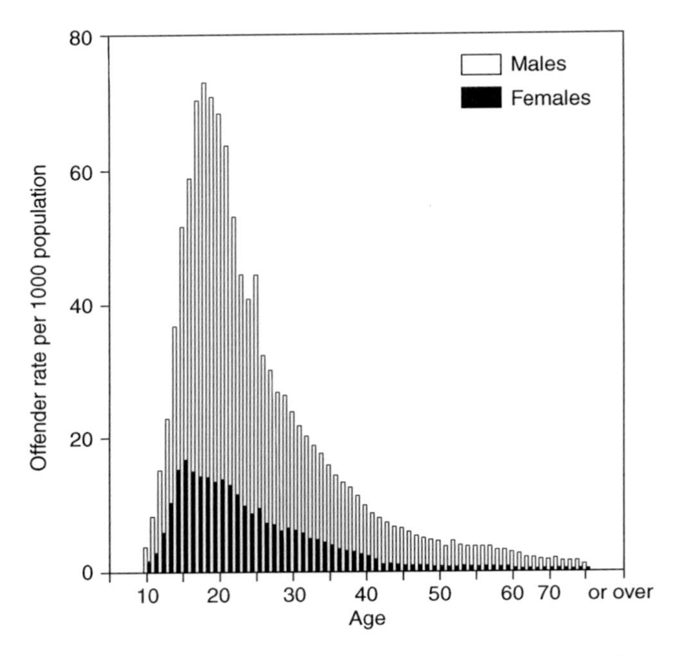

Figure 2.1 A cross-sectional offender-based age-crime curve: recorded offender rates per 1,000 relevant population by age-year and sex, England and Wales, 2000.

why the shape of a cross-sectional offender-based curve must be similar to a longitudinal curve, because cross-sectional curves include many one-off and short-career offenders, whereas longitudinal curves, if they are to contain more than a couple of data points for each individual, must necessarily be constructed on recidivist offenders. In practice, however, the shapes of longitudinal curves are often not very different from cross-sectional curves, as Figure 2.2 illustrates, using data on 'chronic offenders' from the well-known Cambridge Study in Delinquent Development[2] (see also Laub and Sampson : 86; Ezell and Cohen 2005). This is an important and intriguing result, suggesting that the criminality of even recidivist offenders declines sharply in the age range 20–30.

Perhaps four main theories are available in the criminological literature to explain the shape of (one or more varieties of) the age-crime curve. In the first explanation, offered by Gottfredson and Hirschi (1990), offenders' actual experiences in young adulthood are not considered to be of great importance. Rather, these authors contend that there is an 'invariance of the age [reduction] effect' across different offender populations, widely scattered historically and geographically. Moreover, they argue, in young adulthood there is no 'drastic reshuffling of the criminal and noncriminal populations based on unpredictable,

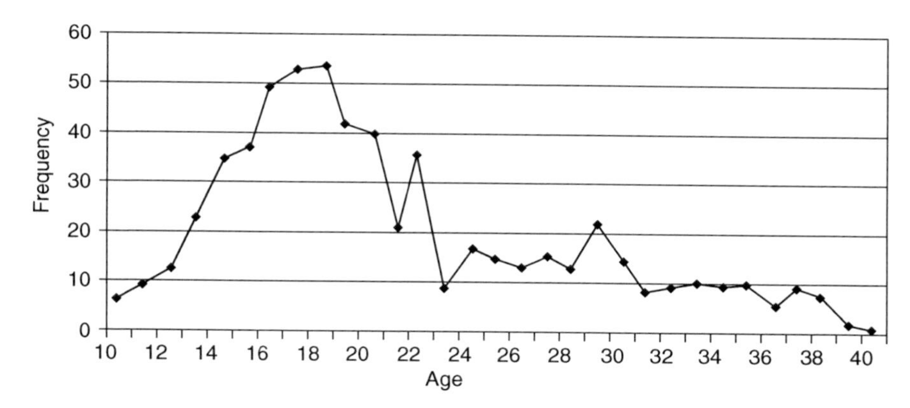

Figure 2.2 A longitudinal age-crime curve: frequency of convictions from age 10 to age 40 among 'chronic offenders' in the Cambridge Study in Delinquent Development.

Note: Reproduced with permission from: A. Piquero, D. P. Farrington and A. Blumstein (2007), *Key Issues in Criminal Career Research: New Analyses of the Cambridge Study in Delinquent Development*. Cambridge: Cambridge University Press, Figure 9.3, p 136.

situational events'. Instead, 'individual differences in the likelihood of crime' – based in these authors' view on high or low degrees of self-control, established early in life – 'tend to persist across the age-course' (Gottfredson and Hirschi 1990: 141). However, since crime does decline with age – among both persistent and occasional offenders – 'we are left with the conclusion that it is due to the inexorable aging of the organism' (Gottfredson and Hirschi 1990: 141).

Empirical studies have raised difficulties with this approach. The suggestion that individual differences in crime propensity tend to persist over the life course has been challenged by studies showing that it is not easy to predict adult offending from variables available for the adolescent period (Laub and Sampson 2003: Chapter 5; Kazemian *et al* 2009). Moreover, research from the Pittsburgh longitudinal study (Stouthamer-Loeber *et al* 2004) suggests that the factors predicting desistance or otherwise in the twenties are not simply the reverse of adolescent criminogenic factors, but seem to involve the operation of a different set of processes – a hypothesis that has been called 'asymmetric causation' (Uggen and Piliavin 1998).

Gottfredson and Hirschi's (1990) theoretical approach is, however, not restricted to their self-control hypothesis. They also argue that even persons with low self-control will not commit offences if what might be described as the 'surrounding opportunity structure' does not favour a criminal response. This point is highly congruent with the later demonstration by Horney *et al* (1995) that recidivism, or its absence, is often linked to immediate social circumstances, and alerts desistance researchers to the need to consider such (sometimes transient) factors, as well as personality factors with their roots in childhood (see further, van der Laan *et al* 2009). There is obviously some potential tension between the empirical outworking of this insight and Gottfredson and Hirschi's self-control thesis, but in the final analysis the latter is, for these authors, the dominant concept.

A second theoretical approach, proposed by Terrie Moffitt (1993, 2006), argues that we may need different explanations of crime, and of age-crime patterns, for different kinds of offenders. Moffitt's 'dual taxonomy' hypothesis distinguishes sharply between 'life-course persistent' and 'adolescence-limited' offenders: the former, it is suggested, start their criminality earlier and have more deep-seated neurological and personality deficits; the latter's offending starts later, and is more of a situational response to the turbulence of adolescence. Accordingly, Moffitt (1993: 691) posits that in young adulthood the two groups will 'go different ways': the former will tend to persist with their offending, while most of the latter will desist as they confront the choices of adulthood, and recognise that continued offending will be maladaptive to an acceptable adult identity. However, the 'recovery' process for the adolescence-limited might be delayed if they have fallen into 'snares', such as 'incarceration, addiction, or truncated education without credentials' (Moffitt 2006: 691).

In her original article, Moffitt (1993: Figure 3) proposed that the dual taxonomy thesis can explain the shape of the classic cross-sectional offender-based age-crime curve; she argued that the upper section of the bell-curve contains adolescence-limited offenders, while the life-course persistent group, starting early and finishing late, contribute especially to the lower 'flanges'. Doubt was however cast on this suggestion by Laub and Sampson's (2003) later publication of long-term follow-up data (to age 60+) from the Gluecks' (1950) offender sample, a population that has many of the characteristics of a 'life-course persistent' group.[3] The resultant longitudinal age-crime curve (Laub and Sampson 2003: 86) was a classic bell-shape, rather than the relatively flat trajectory that Moffitt had suggested for such a group.[4]

Unlike the first two theories, the third approach, offered by Sampson and Laub (1993) after their first reanalysis of the Gluecks' data, postulates that what actually happens to a recidivist offender in early adulthood may be crucial in explaining subsequent patterns of offending or desistance. For Sampson and Laub, while prior experiences are certainly important, they do not determine a persistent offender's future. This is because the young adult must – as Moffitt had also suggested – adapt to adult roles and responsibilities, and the consequent social bonds formed in (for example) marriage and employment can be very effective in providing both incentives to comply and informal social controls, *independently of* prior childhood experiences. Thus, and contrary to Gottfredson and Hirschi's view (see above), Sampson and Laub by implication suggest that in adulthood 'drastic reshuffling' does often take place between persons who had differing offending levels in adolescence. An interesting variation on the 'social bonds' thesis was later proposed by Warr (2002), who suggested that the apparent influence of marriage (or partnership) in promoting desistance may be caused largely by reduced time spent with delinquent peers. Also, Blokland and Niewbeerta's (2005) Dutch study, while it supports the social bonds approach in finding that 'changes in life circumstances considerably affect the development of offending at the individual level', nevertheless also suggests that such transitions account for only a modest amount of the population-level (aggregate) age trend in offending in young adulthood (Blokland and Niewbeerta 2005: 1229).

The previous paragraph deliberately cites only the earlier work of Sampson and Laub. In later work, Laub and Sampson (2003) traced and interviewed 52 of the Gluecks' original offender sample when the men were in their sixties; the authors also modified their previous theoretical approach, in particular by adding 'human agency' or choice as an element in the desistance process. At about the same time, a similar theoretical approach was put forward by Giordano *et al* (2002). In their empirical study, and contrary to the results of Sampson and Laub (1993), Giordano *et al* found little evidence of the influence of adult social bonds on desistance. Instead, they postulated the existence of four closely-related 'cognitive transformations' that, they argued, together help to produce the reduction of offending in young adulthood; and of these, the first two are of special interest for the early stages of desistance (the main subject of this chapter). They are, first, 'a shift in the actor's basic openness to change'; and, second, the actor's 'exposure to a particular hook or set of hooks' for change (e.g. marriage or employment) *in interaction with* his/her 'attitude toward [that hook]', especially the extent to which s/he regards it as 'incompatible with continued deviation' (Giordano *et al* 2002: 1000–01). Subsequent desistance-related 'cognitive transformations', for these authors, focus especially on changes in perceptions of the self, and its relation to offending (on which see also Maruna 2001).

Thus, theorists of the fourth persuasion emphasise that individuals think actively for themselves as they enter potential desistance-related transitions in young adulthood. It is surprising, but true, that this is innovative in developmental criminology; as Britta Kyvsgaard (2003: 241) has pointed out, until recently the criminal career literature 'has paid little attention to the subjective aspects of maturation in terms of personal philosophy or one's perception of one's place in the world and the potential connection that such changes might have to changes in offending'. Such a perspective also potentially alters the interpretation of role transition effects, such as marriage, since 'any effect of a role transition ..... [may be] subsequent to the emergence of a cognitive openness to change that spurs interest in both marriage and reform' (Siennick and Osgood 2008: 169–70). Empirically disentangling the temporal order and relative importance of role transition effects and cognitive change then tends to resemble the classic 'chicken-and-egg' conundrum, though a recent study suggests the priority of cognitive change (Le Bel *et al* 2008).

These various theoretical approaches together create a rich range of suggestive leads for the contemporary desistance researcher. These include possible major differences between early starters and others; the effects of various fresh social circumstances including marriage, employment and declining peer involvement; the presence or absence of 'drastic reshuffling'; and the study of 'subjective effects' and 'cognitive transformations'. Some of these themes have already been effectively utilised as a basis for empirical studies – for example, in Californian research based on official records, Ezell and Cohen (2005) tested the first (Gottfredson/Hirschi), second (Moffitt) and third (Sampson/Laub) theoretical approaches, and concluded that the third fitted the data best. The present study offers a fresh opportunity to revisit these important issues, concentrating particularly on the early stages of desistance. As will become clear, our theoretical approach places agency in a central position, but sees it as interacting with longer-term familial, personality and social-structural dimensions, and with more immediate social situations, in a complex process of gradual change.

The Sheffield desistance study

The Sheffield Desistance Study has four principal characteristics.[5] First and most innovatively, the study recruited the sample at approximately the apex of the age-crime curve, in order to focus special attention on the personal and social processes operating at the start of the apparent 'dramatic decrease' (Siennick and Osgood 2008: 161) in offending in the early twenties. Second, the research adopted a prospective longitudinal design, because only such designs can adequately address issues of temporal order. Third, the research sample was restricted to 'non-occasional offenders', because such persons have by definition repeated their criminal behaviour, and thus have more than a single event from which to desist. Fourth, given our interest in a variety of potential influences on desistance, including human agency (on which see Bottoms 2006), the study deliberately adopted a mixed qualitative and quantitative research approach, aiming to collect data on, for example, several formal scales or checklists, as well as information on subjects' world views, their perceptions of developing situations and relationships, and so on.

The mixed quantitative and qualitative nature of our research requires emphasis, although we are certainly not alone among desistance researchers in adopting it (see for example Giordano *et al* 2002; Farrall 2002; Laub and Sampson 2003). A reviewer of one of our research reports suggested that we should separate out the quantitative and qualitative aspects of the study, and present them in separate papers. Although the advice was intended constructively, we reject it because, in a nutshell, it appears to prioritise methodological assumptions over what we regard as the main task of social science, which is to gain an overall *understanding* of selected social phenomena (see further Runciman 1983 and our discussion below; also Bottoms 2008). Adequate understanding of desistance processes certainly requires quantitative analysis (for example, concerning the extent to which later offending levels are predicted by earlier crime patterns), but it also requires, we believe, 'softer', more subjective data (for example, as to how agents themselves perceive various relevant changes). We see no reason of principle why, in the quest for understanding, the two kinds of data may not be used in conjunction with each other, and we therefore have no hesitation in sometimes interpreting our quantitative results by reference to findings from the qualitative study, and vice-versa.

In the Sheffield research, the main research method used was a series of four lengthy (on average about 90 minutes) one-to-one interviews, administered at intervals of 9–12 months, which is a shorter interval than in most previous longitudinal studies.[6] Additional data were obtained from the police on subjects' official criminal records, enabling the study to examine measures of both official and self-reported offending.

The first round of interviews began in 2003. The police kindly agreed to conduct searches on the Police National Computer (PNC) in order to identify potential research sample members. For this purpose, two principal criteria were used, both deriving from the overall research design:

- born in 1982, 1983 or 1984 (i.e. aged 19–22 at the commencement of the study);
- having been convicted on at least two separate occasions for one or more 'standard list offences' (a Home Office category which includes offences such as theft, burglary and violence, but not most motoring offences).

In addition, for reasons of practicality, it was necessary for potential respondents to have had recent contact with the criminal justice system; to have an address in Sheffield; and, if in prison, to be due for release before the end of the research.

These procedures yielded a population of 679 males and 94 females, but the requirements of the Data Protection Act 1998 meant that the police were unable to allow the research team to approach these people directly. Rather, it was necessary for the probation service, acting on behalf of the police as data holders, to approach identified persons to ask whether they would be willing to become research participants; and any who were not currently in prison or under probation supervision could not be approached. This procedure worked well, but it had two consequences. First, for practical reasons, the probation service made approaches by letter to offenders in custody, and orally whenever practicable to offenders being supervised in the community. The former method produced a more positive response, hence 82 per cent of first research interviews took place in custody. As a direct result of this, the achieved sample had on average a significantly more criminally active profile than the minimum criterion of two standard list conviction occasions. Second, the inability of the research team to make direct approaches to potential respondents meant that the final research sample was smaller than had originally been hoped, and it also prevented the recruitment of a meaningful female sample. Nevertheless, the final sample comprised 113 males, which is very similar to the number of offenders with two or more convictions in the leading British longitudinal study of criminal careers to date, the Cambridge Study in Delinquent Development (118 males with two or more convictions by age 50: Farrington *et al* 2006:24).

Because of these complexities in recruitment, it cannot be claimed that the sample is representative of the population of 679 males from which it was drawn. However, whereas for community research samples it is usually found that more disadvantaged people are more likely to be non-respondents,[7] in this case statistical analyses of basic data from the PNC summary records showed that the research sample is significantly more recidivistic than the rest of the male population.

Second interviews were successfully completed with 98 (87 per cent) of the 113 men, third interviews with 88 (78 per cent), and fourth interviews with a slightly different group of 88 (78 per cent). (In all, 97 men (86 per cent) were interviewed at *either* the third *or* the fourth interview.) These re-contact rates can be regarded as satisfactory for a recidivistic sample of this sort. Reassuringly, also, on four key variables – measuring age, self-described ethnic status, lifetime official criminality, and early social disadvantage – there were no statistically significant differences between those who completed, and those who did not complete, the fourth interview.[8]

Characteristics of the sample

At first interview, the mean age of the sample was 20 years 9 months. As regards self-described ethnicity, 89 (79 per cent) were white British; 14 (12 per cent) black or Mixed black/white; 8 (7 per cent) Asian or Mixed Asian/white; and there were two who classified themselves in other categories.

At the time of the first interview, sample members had, on average, been convicted on eight *separate* occasions ('conviction occasions') for 'standard list' offences, with an average of two offences per occasion. A comparison with the Cambridge Study in Delinquent Development is instructive; in that study, by age 40, 164 men had been convicted of a standard list offence, with the total number of standard list conviction occasions being 686 (Farrington *et al* 2006: 17). By contrast, at first contact (on average, just under age 21), the 113 men in the Sheffield sample had 909 standard list conviction occasions, and by the end of the data gathering period (August 2007) they had acquired a further 263. By any standards, therefore, this is a highly recidivistic sample. The offences were mostly what are often described by the police as 'volume offences'; that is, property offences (such as burglary, theft and taking cars); drugs offences; and a fair amount of violence, including robbery. There were however virtually no sexual offences.

The Home Office has developed a well-validated prediction instrument, the Offender Group Reconviction Score (OGRS2), which predicts the percentage probability of reconviction for a standard list offence within two years (Copas and Marshall 1998). The variables used as predictors in OGRS2 are chronological age and a bundle of key 'lifetime criminality' variables such as the total number of conviction occasions, age at first conviction, and the number of custodial sentences before age 21. For this sample, OGRS2 predictions were high: the mean predicted reconviction rate was 77 per cent, and the median 83 per cent. Thus, we might expect about four-fifths of this sample to be reconvicted of at least one standard list offence within two years.

A potentially key variable in relation to the retrospective identification of Moffitt's 'life-course persistent' group is age at first known criminality ('AFC': operationalised in this study as age at first conviction or caution). The mean AFC for this sample was 13 years 6 months. The distribution was perhaps surprisingly even, with roughly one-third of the sample being first convicted or cautioned before their thirteenth birthday (29 per cent), one-third at 13 or 14 (38 per cent), and one-third at 15+ (32 per cent). AFC was significantly related to total (lifetime) official criminality, measured at the time of first interview, and also to self-reported offending in the year before that interview, but not to official criminality in this recent period.

As in many other criminological studies, self-reported offending levels were much higher than official records suggested, and at first interview 33 per cent of the men admitted 150 or more offences in the previous year (data adjusted for time at liberty if they were in custody for part of that time).[9] The most frequently admitted offences in the year before the first interview were (in descending order): shoplifting; driving without insurance; burglary (residential and non-residential combined); handling stolen goods; theft from vehicles; and drug dealing.

It is often assumed that persistent criminality is necessarily associated with drugs. According to the men's self-reports, that was not always the case in this sample. At first interview, 47 per cent were classified as 'drug problem' offenders, the great majority of whom admitted to drug dependency.[10] Thus, when first encountered, the sample was equally divided between drug problem offenders and others.

Turning to the social lives of the sample, at the time of first interview (or, if first interviewed in prison, just before their imprisonment) just over half were, perhaps surprisingly given their age and criminality levels, living with one or more parents. (We return later to the possible influence of parents on desistance processes.) A fifth were living with a girlfriend or partner, and a further half either were currently or had recently been in a steady relationship with a girlfriend. Since the great majority of both parents and girlfriends disapproved of offending, these social ties produced a pull towards desistance. Set against these influences, however, most respondents said their friends ('mates') were very important to them, and they often trusted them deeply – but two-thirds of the sample said that at least three-quarters of their friends had criminal records. Thus, at the apex of the age-crime curve, there are often actively competing normative influences in the lives of persistent offenders, as between parents, girlfriends and mates.

Finally, the sample displayed many of the familiar social handicaps of persistent offender populations in the UK. For example, about half the men had been excluded from school for at least a month during their school career; 86 per cent had left school with no qualifications (though some had acquired some since, mostly in young offender institutions); and nearly 60 per cent had had no job of any kind (including casual jobs) during the year before the first interview. Such matters would clearly put sample members at a disadvantage in the employment market.

Since early social disadvantage has frequently been shown to be associated with adolescent criminality, we constructed an 'early disadvantage score', based on subjects' responses in the first interview to a range of retrospective questions relating to their childhood and adolescence. Topics included were parental criminality; placement in local authority care; parental attachment, supervision and communication scales; number of addresses during childhood; truancy; school exclusion; no school qualifications; and a negative attitude to school. Scores on this scale were, at the first interview, strongly related to lifetime criminality and to AFC, but not to recent official or self-reported offending – perhaps an indication that, in early adulthood, previous causal connections are beginning to change.

Offending subsequent to initial interview: Did respondents desist?

Official offending

Ninety of the 113 men in the sample (79.6 per cent) were reconvicted of at least one standard list offence in the period from their first interview to 31 August 2007, an average period of over three years. This was in line with the approximately 80 per cent reconviction prediction of OGRS2, although that prediction is for a two-year period. Thus, four-fifths of the men did not fully desist – and we also know from our self-report analyses that some of the official 'desisters' did in fact commit further offences.

However, if we consider the *frequency* of official offending over time, a different picture emerges. Thus, the mean number of standard list offences per year at risk[11] was 8.2 in the year before first interview (Period A), but only 2.6 in the time from Interview 3 to August 2007 (Period D*),[12] some two to three years later, a difference that is statistically significant (Wilcoxon signed ranks test, $z = -7.193$, $n = 99$, $p < 0.001$). The high figure before Interview 1 might be partly artefactual, given that most men's first interview was conducted while serving a prison sentence, and a large number of recent offences is more likely to lead a court to impose a sentence of imprisonment. Nevertheless, the difference in the figures is sufficiently striking to suggest that there is a real reduction in frequency. Overall, therefore, these data suggest *steps towards* desistance, but not (for most) the cessation of offending.

The previous paragraph is based on aggregate data. However, when we compare individuals' offending levels over time, the data do not fully support

Gottfredson and Hirschi's (1990) view (see introduction) that such levels persist over time, relative to other offenders. If we classify offenders as having, relatively speaking, high, medium or low official offending levels vis-à-vis their peers within each time period, then we find that, not surprisingly, there is some continuity: for example, among those who were among the most prolific offenders (i.e. the upper quartile) at Period A, 50 per cent were still in the upper quartile at Period D* (although given the overall declining frequency of offending in the population, their absolute level of convictions decreased) (Table 2.1A).[13] But there was also significant discontinuity: of those in the upper quartile at Period A, 29 per cent had moved into the least prolific category at Period D*, while among those in the least prolific category at Period A, 14 per cent had moved into the upper quartile at Period D*. Movement across categories is therefore clearly not rare.

Self-reported offending

The same self-reported offending questions were used in all four research interviews. Methodologically, the study used the 'card-sort' method adopted by (among others) the Cambridge Study researchers (Farrington 1989), and this was generally well received by respondents. Figure 2.3 shows the overall results, comparing self-reported offending levels for the same individuals at Interviews 1

Table 2.1 Comparisons of offending levels for individuals at the beginning and end of the study period

Table 2.1A Official offending†: relative ranking of individuals for frequency of standard list offences, period A compared to period D*

Offending category during period A	*Offending category during period D**			*Total*
	Low	*Medium*	*High*	
Low	29 59.2%	13 26.5%	7 14.3%	49 100.0%
Medium	13 50.0%	7 26.9%	6 23.1%	26 100.0%
High	7 29.2%	5 20.8%	12 50.0%	24 100.0%
Total	49	25	25	99

Figures include only those who had more than 31 days at risk in the community during both of the two time periods. Percentages are percentages within the offending categories at period A.

† Definition of categories: *Period A*: Low = 0–4.8 official offences per year at risk; Medium = 4.9–10.9 offences; High = 11+ offences. *Period D**: Low = zero offences; Medium = 0.1–2.5 official offences per year at risk; High = 2.51+ offences.

Table 2.1B Self-reported offending†† during period A as compared to period D

Offending category during period A	*Offending category during period D*			*Total*
	Low	*Medium*	*High*	
Low	12 92.3%	1 7.7%	0 0.0%	13 100.0%
Medium	18 47.4%	6 15.8%	14 36.8%	38 100.0%
High	4 20.0%	8 40.0%	8 40.0%	20 100.0%
Total	34	15	22	71

Figures include only those who had more than 31 days at risk in the community during both of the two time periods, and who completed the fourth interview. Percentages are percentages within the offending categories at period A.

†† Low = 0<25 offences per year at risk; Medium = 26<150 offences per year at risk; High = 150+ offences per year at risk.

and 4.[14] By Interview 4, a minority of men had completely stopped offending, but a reduction in frequency was more common. There is however an interesting polarisation between the two periods, seen in the U-shaped distribution of the second diagram. That is, there was still a significant minority who had very high offending levels, but the majority had reduced, leaving a more bipolar distribution than at the time of the first interview. Considering within-individual change, as with official offending there were movements in both directions, and overall 43 men (61 per cent) reduced their actual self-reported offending from Period A to Period D, while 28 (39 per cent) increased it (for a more detailed analysis by categories, see Table 2.1B).[15] However, since those who increased their offending tended to do so rather markedly, if we count *offences* rather than *offenders*, there is no significant change in the self-reported offence totals in the whole sample from Period A to Period D.[16] This important but uncomfortable paradox (most offenders reduce their offending, but there is no reduction in crime) echoes the results of van Mastrigt and Farrington (2009) on the age-crime curve (see introduction), though these authors were working with official data, and for the Sheffield sample this result was not replicated with official data. Among those who reported an increase in self-reported offending, the offence types that showed the greatest increase were: drug dealing; robbery of a business; handling stolen goods; carrying a knife; going equipped for stealing; and various motoring offences (drunk driving; driving while disqualified; driving without insurance). This suggests something of a shift towards a more purposeful pattern of offending.

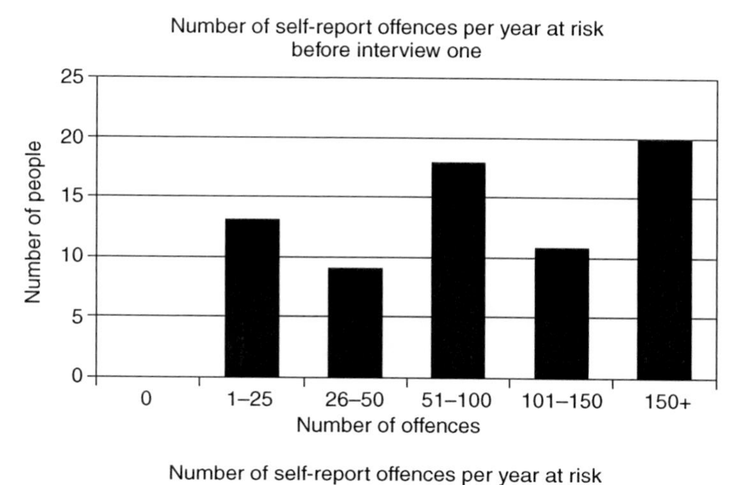

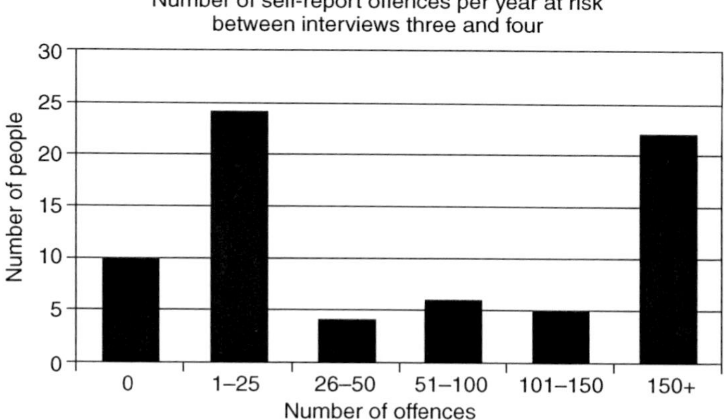

Figure 2.3 Comparison of distribution of self-reported offending at Period A and Period D.

Note: Comparison restricted to respondents interviewed at Interview 4, and with 31 days or more 'at risk' between Interviews 3 and 4 (N = 71). Data adjusted for time at risk.

In this and the previous section, we have provided basic data on the characteristics of the sample, and on the outcomes as measured by offending in the three years after the first interview. We now move on to consider some initial analytic results from the Sheffield research. In later papers, we will present fuller quantitative analyses (based on hierarchical linear modelling) and qualitative analyses (based on in-depth analysis of the tapes of the interviews with respondents who completed at least three taped interviews).[17] In what follows, we provide some initial quantitative analyses based on regression models, and some highlights of the qualitative analysis. Together, these give a good overview of some of the main findings of the research. It should be emphasised that the quantitative analyses presented here are primarily exploratory, rather than aimed at testing specific hypotheses, although at the end of the chapter we will consider how the analyses relate to the prior research considered in our introduction.

Views about future offending

In discussing her proposed 'adolescence-limited' group of offenders, Terrie Moffitt (2006: 279) suggests that 'most [such] delinquents are able to desist from crime when they age into real adult roles, returning gradually to a more conventional lifestyle', although this return might be delayed by 'snares' (see earlier discussion). This is, we think, an interesting part of Moffitt's argument, and for us it has three important features. First, she speaks of a 'return' to a more conventional lifestyle, implying that the offender has emerged from a fundamentally conformist background, and can return to it (see also Matza's (1964) classic text on similar themes). Second, the suggestion is that facing the realities of the transition to adulthood triggers this return (or attempted return), since there is an awareness that continued offending into adulthood will be dysfunctional at many levels. Third, however, any attempted return could be more complicated if the offender has – as the great majority in the Sheffield sample had – fallen into some 'snares' (see introduction). All three of these suggestions resonate strongly with our data, and we believe they are applicable – at least in terms of offenders' intentions – not only to the 'adolescence-limited' group, but also to many persistent offenders.[18]

At the first interview we asked respondents which of the following three formal statements was closest to their present view about the possibilities of their desistance:

- 'I have made a definite decision to try to stop'.
- 'I would like to stop but I'm not sure if I can'.
- 'I am unlikely to stop'.

In later interviews, a fourth possible response was added, namely 'I have stopped offending'.

At the first interview, 56 per cent said they had made a definite decision to stop; thereafter, the proportion saying they definitely intended to stop, or had stopped, increased from the first to the last interview (see Table 2.2). Very few men chose the 'I am unlikely to stop' response; rather, the great majority of those making a less positive statement said 'I would like to stop but I'm not sure if I can'. (In other words, given their practical circumstances, stopping offending did not seem a very realistic probability, although ideally they would like to do so.) On this evidence, therefore, even many persistent offenders, once they are in their twenties, do not wish to continue with a life of crime. For example, although 28 offenders self-reported an increase in their offending from Interview 1 to

Table 2.2 Respondents' views about future offending: Interviews 1–4 (%)

	Interview 1	*Interview 2*	*Interview 3*	*Interview 4*
'I have stopped offending'	–	36	32	36
'Definite decision to try to stop'	56	25	30	34
'Would like to stop but not sure if I can'	37	34	28	21
Unlikely to stop/other	7	5	10	9
Total	100	100	100	100
(N)	(112)	(97)	(88)	(88)

Interview 4, with an apparently more purposeful pattern of offending (see above), at the fourth interview only nine offenders said that they were 'unlikely to stop' their offending (Table 2.2).

The more qualitative evidence of our interviews suggested that most expressions of 'wishing to desist' were genuine. One rather striking finding of the study, which we shall be reporting in more detail elsewhere, was the conventionality of the aspirations of interviewees: the ambition of most was to live in a small house or flat in a decent working-class area of Sheffield, with a wife or partner, and a steady job which provided enough income to live on. A significant reason for such aspirations appears to be the onset of adulthood; there was much comment in the research interviews about 'growing up now', 'becoming more responsible', and so on, often linked to a triggering event such as the importance of a relationship or the birth of a child.

We carried out regression analyses on the 'views about future offending' variable as expressed at each of the four interviews, using variables from the interview in which the views were expressed, as well as appropriate variables from previous interviews. The results, and the procedures used, are set out in Table 2.3 and the Appendix to this chapter.[19] As will be noted, the final models were developed using, in part, a standard ('stepwise') model-building procedure. As Archdeacon (1994) has wisely cautioned, it is important not to over-interpret final models developed in this way, since automatic model-building procedures may on occasion generate a result 'chosen, on narrow technical grounds, over another that would have yielded an equally reasonable or even superior interpretation of the data'. Hence, those using standard model-building procedures should be 'willing ... to look critically at the intermediate as well as the final results and to think of the output not as a solution but as a source of insight' (Archdeacon 1994: 245). Such an interpretative framework is of course highly congruent with the exploratory analytic approach that we have chosen to adopt in this paper.

However, even bearing in mind this salutary advice, the results shown in Table 2.3 seem to point to an important conclusion. It will be noted that the OGRS2 score, although bivariately related to respondents' 'views about future

Table 2.3 Regression analyses on 'views about future offending' at each interview as the dependent variable†

Interview 1

	B	*S.E.*	*Sig.*	*95.0% C.I. for EXP(B)*		
				Lower	*Exp(B)*	*Upper*
Self-efficacy	0.801	0.195	0.000	1.520	2.227	3.263
Employment	1.609	0.487	0.001	1.926	4.998	12.969
Constant	–4.974	1.209	0.000		0.007	

N = 111. $R^2 = 0.37$ (Nagelkerke). Model $\chi^2 = 35.31$, $p < 0.001$.
Excluded variables together with their beta values and significance levels at step 1 are provided below:

Hopelessness B = –0.097, p = 0.251; impulsivity B = –0.102, p = 0.599; obstacles total B = 0.074, p = 0.539; percentage of mates in trouble B = –0.013, p = 0.223; used drugs in last 12 months B = 1.362, p = 0.241; general property factor (self-report offending) B = –0.269, p = 0.419; robbery/drugs factor (self-report offending) B = –0.332, p = 0.226; OGRS2 score B = 0.002, p = 0.930; total offences in lifetime official offending B = –0.017, p = 0.408.

Collinearity diagnostics indicated no cause for concern.

Interview 2

	Co-efficient estimate	*S.E*	*Wald*	*Sig.*	*95% confidence interval*	
					Lower bound	*Upper bound*
Self-efficacy (2)	–0.632	0.204	9.560	0.002	–1.033	–0.231
Empathy (2)	0.286	0.135	4.494	0.034	0.022	0.551
Obstacles total (2)	0.245	0.090	7.369	0.007	0.068	0.421
Drug Problem (2)	1.543	0.618	6.232	0.013	0.332	2.754

N = 93. Pseudo $R^2 = 0.46$ (Nagelkerke). Model $\chi^2 = 48.44$, $p < 0.001$.

Excluded variables together with their Wald values and significance levels at step 1 in the two starting models are provided below:

Starting Model 1: Obstacles total (1) Wald = 1.619, p = 0.203; parental attachment Giordano (1) Wald = 0.504, p = 0.478; parental attachment Hay (1) Wald = 0.293, p = 0.589; parental communication (1) Wald = 3.306, p = 0.069; partner attachment (1) Wald = 0.570, p = 0.450; hopelessness (1) Wald = 0.009, p = 0.924; self-efficacy (1) Wald = 0.043, p = 0.836; OGRS 2 score Wald = 0.398, p = 0.528; drugs problem (1) Wald = 0.233, p = 0.629.

Starting Model 2: Fairness of criminal justice system (2) Wald = 0.568, p = 0.451; partner attachment (2) Wald = 0.028, p = 0.867; hopelessness (2) Wald = 4.211, p = 0.040; impulsivity (2) Wald = 0.037, p = 0.847.

Collinearity diagnostics indicated no cause for concern.

Tests of parallel lines showed the assumption to be justified.

Interview 3

	Co-efficient estimate	*S.E*	*Wald*	*Sig.*	*95% confidence interval*	
					Upper bound	*Lower bound*
Impulsivity (1)	0.409	0.193	4.477	0.034	0.030	0.787
Parental attachment now (Giordano) (3)	–0.898	0.267	11.345	0.001	–1.421	–0.375
Obstacles total (3)	0.180	0.083	4.682	0.030	0.017	0.343
Employment (1)	–1.755	0.546	10.340	0.001	–2.824	–0.685

N = 76. Pseudo $R^2 = 0.52$ (Nagelkerke). Model $\chi^2 = 47.27$, $p < 0.001$.

Excluded variables together with their Wald values and significance levels at step 1 in the three starting models are provided below:

Starting Model 1: Parental attachment Giordano (1) Wald = 1.658, p = 0.198; parental attachment Hay (1) Wald = 0.046, p = 0.831; parental communication (1) Wald = 1.277, p = 0.258; hopelessness (1) Wald = 0.645, p = 0.422; self-efficacy (1) Wald = 0.132, p = 0.716; OGRS 2 score Wald = 2.934, p = 0.087; early disadvantage score Wald = 2.398, p = 0.121.

Starting Model 2: Fairness of CJS (2) Wald = 2.742, p = 0.098; hopelessness (2) Wald = 2.385, p = 0.122; self-efficacy (2) Wald = 0.866, p = 0.352; Obstacles total (2) Wald = 1.329, p = 0.249; drugs problem (2) Wald = 1.200, p = 0.273.

Starting Model 3: Parental attachment now (Hay) (3) Wald = 0.119, p = 0.730; parental communication now (3) Wald = 0.090, p = 0.764; parental supervision now (3) Wald = 3.462, p = 0.063; employment status (3) Wald = 1.301, p = 0.254; sleeping rough (3) Wald = 0.517, p = 0.472; drugs problem (3) Wald = 1.199, p = 0.273.

Collinearity diagnostics indicated no cause for concern.

Tests of parallel lines showed the assumption to be justified.

Interview 4

	Co-efficient estimate	*S.E*	*Wald*	*Sig.*	*95% confidence interval*	
					Lower bound	*Upper bound*
Obstacles total (4)	0.333	0.084	15.720	0.000	0.168	0.498
Empathy (4)	0.606	0.159	14.465	0.000	0.294	0.919

N = 88. Pseudo $R^2 = 0.39$ (Nagelkerke). Model $\chi^2 = 37.86$, $p < 0.001$.

Excluded variables together with their Wald values and significance levels at step 1 in the four starting models are provided below:

Starting Model 1: Hopelessness (1) Wald = 2.014, p = 0.156; impulsivity (1) Wald = 0.178, p = 0.673; obstacles total (1) Wald = 0.690, p = 0.406; OGRS 2 score Wald = 0.015, p = 0.902; general property factor (official offending) Wald = 1.986, p = 0.159.

Starting Model 2: Obstacles total (2) Wald = 5.938, p = 0.015.

Starting Model 3: Obstacles total (3) Wald = 1.761, p = 0.184; parental attachment now Giordano (3) Wald = 0.281, p = 0.596; partner attachment (3) Wald = 0.742, p = 0.389.

Starting Model 4: Fairness of CJS (4) Wald = 0.721, p = 0.396; ego resilience (4) Wald = 2.294, p = 0.130; resilience (4) Wald = 2.006, p = 0.157; self efficacy (4) Wald = 2.402, p = 0.121; drugs problem (4) Wald = 2.048, p = 0.152.

Collinearity diagnostics indicated no cause for concern.

Tests of parallel lines showed the assumption to be justified.

† See Appendix for procedures. The independent variables used in the final models for Interviews 2, 3 and 4 were those from that interview plus previous interviews. Numbers in parentheses after variables indicate the interview at which data on that variable was collected.

offending' at all four interviews, did not significantly contribute to any of the multivariate 'starting models' (see the Appendix for details of procedures), and therefore of course does not appear in any of the final models. By way of contrast, the variables that did appear in the final models – although varying in detail at particular interviews – can be readily grouped into two principal categories: first, those measuring psychological characteristics (using formal psychological scales); and, second, those measuring various *current* aspects of the men's lives (e.g. employment, drug-taking). The consistency of such patterns across four separate interviews strongly suggests that what we have called 'views about future offending' – such as a willingness to say 'I have made a definite decision to try to stop' – usually arises at least partially independently of prior criminality levels (as measured by OGRS2).

Let us then consider in more detail the variables in the final models that measure psychological characteristics and current circumstances. Two psychological measures were especially prominent in the final models, namely 'self-efficacy' and 'empathy'. The self-efficacy scale was included only within Interviews 1 and 2, and it was strongly related to views about future offending at both of those interviews. Bandura (1997: 37), a leading authority on self-efficacy, explains that it 'is not a measure of the skills one has, but a belief about what one can do under different sets of conditions with whatever skills one possesses'; thus, it is integrally linked to conceptions of human agency (Bandura 1997: 3–7). Bandura (1997: 39) further refers to substantial research evidence that 'efficacy beliefs affect thought processes, the level and persistency of motivation, and affective states, all of which are important contributors to the types of performances that are [subsequently] realised'. In the light of this, it is worth noting that in this study, although individuals' desistance intentions did sometimes fluctuate from interview to interview, an expressed 'definite intention to stop' at Interview 1 significantly predicted lower self-reported offending in Period D, two to three years later (Mann-Whitney U test, $z = -2.40$, $p < 0.02$); although interestingly it did not predict official offending levels at Period D*.

By contrast to self-efficacy, the short empathy scale[20] was most strongly associated with 'views about future offending' at Interview 4 (by which time only one-third of the sample were saying 'I would like to stop but I'm not sure if I can' or 'I am unlikely to stop'; see Table 2.2). Perhaps those who were least empathetic and most egotistic were by this point self-declaring as unlikely desisters.

Turning now to the 'current circumstances' variables in the final models shown in Table 2.3, these vary from interview to interview but, consistently with the earlier literature, include both 'employment' and 'drug problems'. Most recurrently, there are strong associational links between views about future offending and scores on an 'obstacles scale' that we developed from the recidivism/desistance study of Ros Burnett (1992: 82).[21] Thirteen 'obstacles to going/staying straight' (such as 'lack of money' or 'drugs' – see Table 2.4 for the full list) were offered to respondents at each interview. We then converted these responses into

Table 2.4 Perceived obstacles to going straight or staying straight: Interviews 1–4

	Interview 1		*Interview 2*		*Interview 3*		*Interview 4*	
	%	*Rank*	N	*Rank*	%	*Rank*	%	*Rank*
Lack of money	77	1	66	1	67	1	61	1
Opportunity for easy money	69	2	52	3	66	2	48	3
Need for excitement or to relieve boredom	61	3	48	4	50	3	47	4
Lack of work	60	4	47	5	49	4	51	2
Having a record	54	5	57	2	36	8	39	5
Taking drugs	46	6	40	6	43	5 =	34	6
Anger/stress/depression	44	7	35	8 =	43	5 =	25	9
Police harassment	42	8	36	7	27	11	24	10
Where I live	41	9	35	8 =	37	7	30	7
Alcohol	35	10	30	10	33	9	28	8
Pressure from mates	33	11	21	11 =	25	12	18	11
Family problems	28	12	21	11 =	29	10	17	12 =
Pressure from partner	18	13	16	13	18	13	17	12 =
(N)	112	–	95	–	88	–	88	–

a simple score for each respondent by summing the total number of identified 'obstacles'. As Table 2.3 shows, this score was strongly negatively associated with views about future offending at Interviews 2, 3 and 4.[22] Table 2.4 gives details of the specific obstacles mentioned by respondents at each interview, and shows also that there was strong consistency in the rank order of obstacles across interviews. Among the most frequently cited obstacles were those relating to money (lack of it; opportunities for easy 'takes') and to the excitements of offending.[23] The financial aspects of desistance have been rather neglected in the developmental criminology literature,[24] but in this study there were many narrative comments along the lines that, in trying to desist, the offender was in effect taking a self-imposed pay cut, entailing a significant change in lifestyle (although of course also reducing the risk of imprisonment). As to the excitements of offending, respondents' honest awareness of the continued emotional pull of offending (on which see for example Katz 1988) also seems to us to be very important, and it was backed up by fairly frequent descriptions about how respondents deliberately tried to avoid places and situations where, they thought, they might easily succumb to that excitement, despite their genuine wish to desist (Bottoms 2009).

A final comment on Table 2.3 concerns attachments to partners and parents. Like the OGRS2 scores, the 'partner attachment' scale was (at some interviews) significantly bivariately related to views about future offending, but it did not appear in any of the final regression models. The qualitative study, however, suggested that – in line with previous research such as that of Sampson and Laub

(1993) and Giordano *et al* (2002) – attachment to a partner was frequently a 'hook' factor that helped men to take seriously the possibility of attempting to desist. The issue of parental attachment as an aid to desistance is much less prominent than partner attachment in the prior criminological literature, and was less frequently commented on in the narrative sections of our interviews. However, scores on formal parental attachment and communication scales were significantly associated with views about future offending in all interviews except the first, and they were especially prominent in Interview 3, when the questions were specifically focused on *current* links with parents.[25] For this age-group, the issue of attachment to and communication with parents as an aid to desistance therefore seems to merit more attention than it has previously received (see further below).

Predicting later offending

In this section, we consider factors that predict self-reported and official offending levels at the end of the study period (Periods D and D* respectively). As with the 'views about future offending' analysis, we have used an exploratory regression approach. However, whereas in the earlier analysis we adopted a *correlational* strategy (examining all variables up to and including those collected in the same interview in which the views about future offending were expressed), on this occasion we have used a more strictly *predictive* strategy (only considering independent variables that were collected *at or before* Interview 3, while the dependent variable is either self-reported offending during Period D, or official offending during Period D*, i.e. periods *beginning at* Interview 3). This predictive strategy was adopted in order to gain a more robust understanding of the temporal sequencing of factors related to offending, or its absence, at the end of the study period.

Before we report the results, one important technical point needs to be emphasised. Neither for official criminality nor for self-reported offending is it possible to have much confidence in the validity of the precise figures for subsequent offending levels, as opposed to the general message that is conveyed by the data. That is especially the case given that an adjustment has to be made for any periods in custody.[26] An analytic strategy that uses broad categories of offending levels as the dependent variable largely eliminates these difficulties, so that is the approach we have adopted; and that choice has again led us to adopt ordinal regression as the appropriate analytic tool.[27]

Details of the final regression model for *self-reported offending* are shown in Table 2.5 and the Appendix.[28] As before, it is important not to over-interpret the model, but one feature stands out – namely, that the principal predictors comprise variables measuring *both* lifetime criminality (the OGRS2 score) *and* two variables that relate firmly to the offender's current situation at Interview 3 (employment and the obstacles score). Relating this result to the theoretical frameworks with which we began, the data seem to be simultaneously supporting different strands

Table 2.5 Final ordinal regression model in relation to the prediction of self-reported offending between Interviews 3 and 4†

	Co-efficient estimate	*S.E*	*Wald*	*Sig*	*95% confidence interval*	
					Lower bound	*Upper bound*
OGRS 2 score	0.053	0.019	7.760	0.005	0.016	0.090
Most recent obstacles total (3)	0.251	0.101	6.252	0.012	0.054	0.448
Most recent employment status (3)	−1.192	0.564	4.467	0.035	−2.297	−.087

N = 63. Pseudo R^2 = 0.42 (Nagelkerke). Model $\chi^2 = 28.89$, $p < 0.001$.

Analysis includes only those with more than 31 days at risk in the community between Interviews 3 and 4.

Excluded variables together with their Wald values and significance levels at step 1 in the three starting models are provided below:

Starting Model 1: Fairness of CJS (1) Wald = 1.383, p = 0.240; hopelessness (1) Wald = 1.015, p = 0.314; self-efficacy (1) Wald = 0.422, p = 0.516; general property factor (self-report offending) Wald = 0.037, p = 0.847; obstacles total (1) Wald = 1.689, p = 0.194; age at first criminality Wald = 0.780, p = 0.377, total offences in lifetime official offending Wald = 0.684, p = 0.408; early disadvantage score Wald = 0.184, p = 0.668; general property factor (official offending) Wald = 0.662, p = 0.416; drugs problem (1) Wald = 0.945, 0.331; employment status (1) Wald = 1.325, p = 0.250.

Starting Model 2: Obstacles total (2) Wald = 4.149, p = 0.042.

Starting Model 3: Parental attachment now (Hay) (3) Wald = 0.479, p = 0.489; parental communication (3) Wald = 0.376, p = 0.540; parental supervision now (3) Wald = 1.598, p = 0.206, social identity commitment/esteem (3) Wald = 0.481, p = 0.488.

Collinearity diagnostics indicated no cause for concern.

Tests of parallel lines showed the assumption to be justified.

† See Appendix for procedures. Numbers in parentheses after variables indicate the interview at which data on that variable was collected.

of the prior theorisation. In more detail, the strength of the OGRS2 variable as a predictor draws attention to the difficulty of breaking a pattern of criminality that has become well established – a point alluded to in different ways in the work of both Gottfredson and Hirschi and Terrie Moffitt (both in her 'life-course criminality' and in her 'snares' discussions). In this connection it is also, we think, important that prior criminality (as measured by OGRS2) featured much more strongly as a predictor of self-reported offending than it did as a correlate of 'views about future offending'(Table 2.3).[29] The implication of this contrast would seem to be that, for potential desisters, changing a pattern of behaviour is more difficult than forming the wish to change behaviour.

But, returning to Table 2.5, the presence of the 'employment' and 'obstacles' variables in the final model also directs our attention to a different strand in the prior literature, namely that which focuses on the importance of current situations in relation to further offending, especially the role-transitional factors emphasised by Sampson and Laub (1993). In this connection the bivariate strength of several measures of current parental links at Interview 3 is additionally noteworthy. Also relevant in this interpretive context is that, as previously reported, a definite 'intention to desist' at Interview 1 significantly predicts self-reported offending at Period D. Although this variable was not strongly enough related to self-reported offending to appear in any final model, the bivariate relationship provides a useful link to the theorisation of Giordano *et al* (2002).[30]

Turning now to the prediction of *officially recorded offending*, details of the final regression model are shown in Table 2.6 and the Appendix.[31] In broad terms, the predictors in the final model are similar to those in Table 2.5, in that they comprise variables measuring both prior offending and current circumstances. As regards prior offending, on this occasion it is not OGRS2 that constitutes the main predictor, but rather a direct count of 'total lifetime offences' before Interview 1, together with a principal components variable labelled the 'robbery factor' (i.e. showing particularly those who had been convicted of robbery).[32] But it is again the case that the best prediction of offending (this time, official offending) at the end of the study period comes not from prior offending alone, but from a combination of *both* prior criminal record *and* variables measuring current circumstances. With respect to these later circumstances, once again the 'obstacles score' is a significant predictor. The other principal 'current circumstances' predictor in the final model concerns, in effect, delinquent friends: it is a score, obtained at Interview 3, on a self-categorisation scale derived from social identity theory (Capozza and Brown 2000),[33] and it measures the extent to which the respondent regards his self-identity as being strongly linked to his peer-group (e.g. 'My group of friends is an important reflection of who I am').

This 'self-categorisation (friends)' variable resonates strongly with data from our qualitative analysis. We know from that analysis that by Interview 3 many offenders, having taken tentative first steps towards desistance, were re-evaluating their commitment to delinquent friends. It therefore makes sense that those with a continuing group commitment to such friends, linked to self-categorisation, should have higher levels of offending at the end of the study period. But why should this variable predict official criminality but not self-reported offending?[34] The answer to this question is not entirely clear at this stage, and merits further exploration.

In looking back over the analyses in Tables 2.5 and 2.6, it is notable that neither the AFC variable nor the early disadvantage score has featured prominently among the variables predicting either self-reported or official offending at the end of the research period (in other words, persistence in offending.) Yet these are the variables in our study that are most closely related to Moffitt's proposed 'life-course persistent' categorisation. Of course, AFC is one of the variables included within the OGRS2 score, and AFC is also significantly correlated with lifetime

Table 2.6 Final ordinal regression model in relation to the prediction of standard list offences between Interview 3 and 31 August 2007†

	Co-efficient estimate	*S.E*	*Wald*	*Sig.*	*95% confidence interval*	
					Lower bound	*Upper bound*
Total lifetime offences from official offending	0.064	0.022	8.603	0.003	0.021	0.107
Most recent obstacles total (3)	0.206	0.085	5.912	0.015	0.040	0.371
Social identity: self-categorisation (friends) (3)	–0.572	0.199	8.225	0.004	–0.963	–0.181
Robbery factor from official offending	–1.872	0.531	12.446	0.000	–2.912	–0.832

N = 80. Pseudo R^2 = 0.44 (Nagelkerke). Model 2 = 39.01, $p < 0.001$.

Analysis includes only those with more than 31 days at risk in the community between Interview 3 and 31 August 2007, and who completed an interview later than Interview 2.

Excluded variables together with their Wald values and significance levels at step 1 in the three starting models are provided below:

Starting Model 1: Motoring factor (self-report offending) Wald = 3.210, p = 0.073; violence factor (self-report offending) Wald = 2.221, p = 0.136; age at first criminality Wald = 1.442, p = 0.230; OGRS 2 score Wald = 0.356, p = 0.551; general property factor (official offending) Wald = 0.488, p = 0.485; drugs problem (1) Wald = 1.089, p = 0.297.

Starting Model 2: Obstacles total (2) Wald = 2.232, p = 0.135; drugs problem (2) Wald = 4.007, p = 0.045.

Starting Model 3: Status actual/ideal difference (3) Wald = 2.518, p = 0.113; social identity commitment/esteem (3) Wald = 0.179, p = 0.672; most recent employment status (3) Wald = 3.073; p = 0.080; drugs problem (3) Wald = 0.042, p = 0.837.

Collinearity diagnostics indicated no cause for concern.

Tests of parallel lines showed the assumption to be justified.

† See Appendix for procedures. Numbers in parentheses after variables indicate the interview at which data on that variable was collected.

total criminality; but it seems to be these variables – based on the totality of official convictions – rather than AFC itself, which best predict later criminality. As for early disadvantage, this has been clearly less prominent in the regression analyses than current difficulties.

With regard to current difficulties, one of the surprises of our analysis has been the prominence of the 'obstacles score' – as perceived by respondents – among the associational and predictive variables in Tables 2.3, 2.5 and 2.6. This suggests that such a score could, after appropriate replication, perhaps be considered as a useful working tool for probation officers and others working with young adult recidivist offenders – not least because it appears to be *both* a useful predictor *and* an instrument that can provide specific information about the nature of offenders' self-perceived current difficulties.[35]

The overall results from the analyses presented above may perhaps be summarised as follows:

- Even in this highly criminal sample, the great majority wish to desist, though not all regard desistance as practicable. Over time, however, a growing proportion do regard it as practicable; and their ambitions for the future are both modest and conventional. These findings seem to be closely connected to a realisation that, in the early twenties, it is desirable to re-adapt one's lifestyle to face the demands of adult life.
- Despite the high incidence of wishing to desist, there is a good deal of reoffending. But many offenders reduce their frequency of offending, so 'steps towards desistance' are frequently (but not universally) taken.
- Desistance, where it occurs, is usually a gradual, not a sudden, process.
- A minority have high offending levels even at the end of the follow-up period, and this means that, in self-report analyses, there is no aggregate reduction in offending in the sample as a whole. There is, however, greater polarisation between high-rate and low-rate offenders at the end of the study.
- There are significant obstacles to be faced by those wishing to desist, and among the more important, in their perception, are financial issues and the continued emotional pull of offending.
- Some psychological variables are related to views about future offending, notably self-efficacy (beliefs about what one can achieve) and empathy (extent to which one cares about other people's views).
- Current circumstances of various kinds are also strongly related both to views about future offending and to actual desistance or persistence.
- The importance of current beliefs and perceptions, and of current circumstances (previous two bullet points) appears to be related to the fact that, on a within-individual basis, changes in offending levels over time do occur in young adulthood, in both directions. There is therefore evidence of change in the relative offending of sample members during the period of the study.
- There is apparently no sharp differentiation in this sample between 'life-course persistent' and 'adolescence-limited' offenders, though this might perhaps be due to the undoubted and near-universal importance of 'snares' (for example, weak employment prospects).
- A result of particular interest is that past offending is not strongly related to offenders' assessments of their 'views about future offending', yet it is strongly related both to future self-reported offending and to future official criminality. This suggests (as do the interviews in the qualitative study) that it is easier to form sincere intentions to change than it is actually to alter patterns of behaviour. Achieving desistance is not, for most recidivist offenders, a straightforward process.

A case study

The Cambridge sociologist W. G. Runciman (1983) has cogently argued that social scientists, when doing empirical work, need to be able to answer three questions: *What* happened ('reportage')?; *Why* did it happen ('explanation')?; and *What was it like* for various participants (appreciative 'description')? Appreciative description, Runciman (1983: 18) suggests, might or might not constitute a *necessary* dimension of explanation in any given context; but even where it does not, a social scientist who is unable to answer the 'What is it like?' question – the experiential question – in relation to a particular empirical topic 'may fairly be told that he writes of things which he knows little or nothing about' (Runciman 1983: 34). It is this kind of methodological advice that has led us, like a number of other desistance researchers (including Maruna 2000; Giordano *et al* 2002; Farrall 2002; Laub and Sampson 2003) to include narratives and case histories as well as quantitative analysis within our research approach; for we are convinced that a healthy developmental criminology cannot ignore Kyvsgaard's (2003) call for it to take seriously the need for data on subjects' 'perception of their place in the world' (see introduction). In previous sections, we have attempted to utilise such a perspective in our interpretation of various aspects of the data from our study. The value of Runciman's 'appreciative description' dimension is however most fully understood through case histories, as we hope to show more fully in later publications.

Space here allows only one case history, which well illustrates both the gradual nature of desistance in this sample (see above) and some of the transitions involved. At the time of the first interview, 'John' was aged 20, and in prison. He had a total of nine conviction occasions for standard list offences, and had received his first caution at age 11. His OGRS2 score was above 90 per cent. He had recently split up with a girlfriend; he had been living rough, which he had found physically and emotionally difficult; he was long-term unemployed; he had been, before his prison sentence, addicted to heroin and crack; and his mother, who he loved, had severed relations with him because of his persistent offending. Perhaps not surprisingly, when asked in the first interview 'What are the good things about your life just now?', he answered: 'Nothing'. However, in response to a further question asking what kind of person he would like to be in five years' time, he answered: 'Confident. Hardworking. Trustworthy. A good person to get on with'. We see here, therefore, a stark contrast between the very unpromising current context, and a dream of something much better.[36] Otherwise stated, there are significant normative links to mainstream society which – in appropriate circumstances – could pull John back towards the conformity that his recent actions had denied. As for intended desistance, John rated himself at first interview as someone who would like to stop offending, but he was not sure that this was possible.

After release from prison, John was helped to obtain suitable accommodation. He initially returned to heroin and crack, but probation helped him to switch instead to a drug-substitute. At about this time, he met a girl with whom he began a steady relationship, which meant a lot to him; she moved in with him, and the relationship lasted to the end of the research period. By that time, the couple had had a much-loved son, with another child expected. John began to reduce his offending. He was in court for one offence between the first and second interviews, for which he received a community penalty, but there was no further official criminality. Self-reported offending continued, but at steadily reducing levels, and tended to occur particularly on occasions when the family finances were rocky. John also went back to drugs, but this time to cannabis. His relationship with his mother significantly improved as his offending reduced, assisted also by the birth of his son. To avoid being tempted, he deliberately stayed away from an area of the city where he might encounter former criminal friends. In his final interview, he at last allowed himself to tick the statement: 'I have made a definite decision to try to stop'.

This all-too-brief sketch allows us to see in action a reasonably typical set of desistance processes, and their uncertain character ('two steps forward, one step back'). John's case also well illustrates the first two stages of Giordano *et al*'s (2002) proposed desistance-related 'cognitive transformations', namely 'a shift in the actor's basic openness to change', and his 'exposure to a set of hooks for change', coupled with his attitude towards those hooks. Thus, from this case history we can glean at least some sense of 'what it is like' to take initial steps towards desistance.

An interactive model of the early stages of desistance

Desistance can look different from differing vantage points. One valuable approach to the study of desistance has been to take samples already identified from records as 'desisters' and 'persisters', and ask the offenders to trace retrospectively how they reached these respective destinations (Maruna 2001; Laub and Sampson 2003). In the case of desisters, such analyses can also involve studying the development and maintenance of a crime-free identity (Maruna 2001; Giordano *et al* 2002).

The sample for the Sheffield study consists of recently-active recidivist offenders, initially recruited at the apex of the age-crime curve. The research has therefore captured a different dimension of desistance – its beginnings. As John's case illustrates, these beginnings are often very uncertain.

Given this focus on early-stage desistance, how do the results of the Sheffield study relate to the previous research traditions summarised at the beginning of this chapter? We have seen that, in this sample, some of the detailed propositions in the work of Moffitt (1993) and of Gottfredson and Hirschi (1990) are not well supported empirically. On the other hand, indices of total previous official criminality are good predictors of later offending (both official and self-reported), so in a more general sense these theories are pointing to the important truth that, in part, past behaviour predicts future behaviour. This is really not surprising: after all, offending for most of this sample has been a persistent activity for several years, and, like any ingrained habit, it will generate dispositions that may be hard to break (see Mouzelis 2008: Chapter 8, modifying Bourdieu's theory of practice). Moreover, we know that there are, in the perceptions of these men, both practical (cash-related) and emotional (excitement-related) reasons for continuing rather than stopping (Table 2.4).

Yet, given the onset of adulthood, the great majority do want to stop. The Sheffield data support the contention of Sampson and Laub (1993) and Warr (2002) that factors such as current unemployment and continued identification with delinquent friends predict later recidivism, *over and above* variables relating to previous offending. The qualitative data also, however, strongly support the 'agency'/'cognitive transformation' approach of, for example, Giordano *et al* (2002), and suggest that how an individual approaches the 'hooks for change' and 'obstacles' that he encounters can be of vital significance for the outcome. The importance of agency and self-perception is even seen quantitatively in some contexts, for example in the way that self-efficacy is associated with early intentions to desist; and in the astonishing strength as a predictor (for several outcomes) of the 'self-perceived obstacles score'.

We have tried to represent some of these themes in a heuristic model of the early stages of desistance (Figure 2.4), though we need to emphasise that much of the detail in this proposed model is derived from qualitative analyses not fully discussed in this chapter.[37] In the centre of the diagram are two circles, respectively representing: (a) the individual's dispositions (the result of his personal, social and criminal history), and (b) the social capital (both 'bonding' and 'bridging': see Halpern 2005: 19–22) that is available to the individual. Both of these of course can, and do, change over time, so they are not static but potentially interactive elements within the model. Across the top of the diagram is represented a gradual decrease in offending levels – as we have seen, a frequently observed phenomenon in this sample. Around the perimeter, an individual's tentative steps towards desistance are shown, influenced at each step by his dispositions, and also by the available social capital (bonding or bridging), which might form what Giordano *et al* (2002) describe as a valuable 'hook' in the steps towards desistance. Almost inevitably, however, difficulties will be encountered – perhaps in the form of tempting offers of lucrative criminal activity from former friends, or the provocation of a fight in a bar, or the difficulty of finding legitimate employment. These difficulties undoubtedly often present real challenges, and – as Figure 2.4 tries to show – the repercussions can develop in either a positive or a negative direction. If relapse occurs, however, it does not necessarily push the would-be desister right back to his starting-point; and this is how gradual desistance is possible.

So, the Sheffield study points to a more fully interactive model of the early stages of desistance than does most previous theorisation. It presents a complex picture of the continuing importance of criminal history and habits, and the desistance-inducing potential of fresh employments and personal ties, but all held

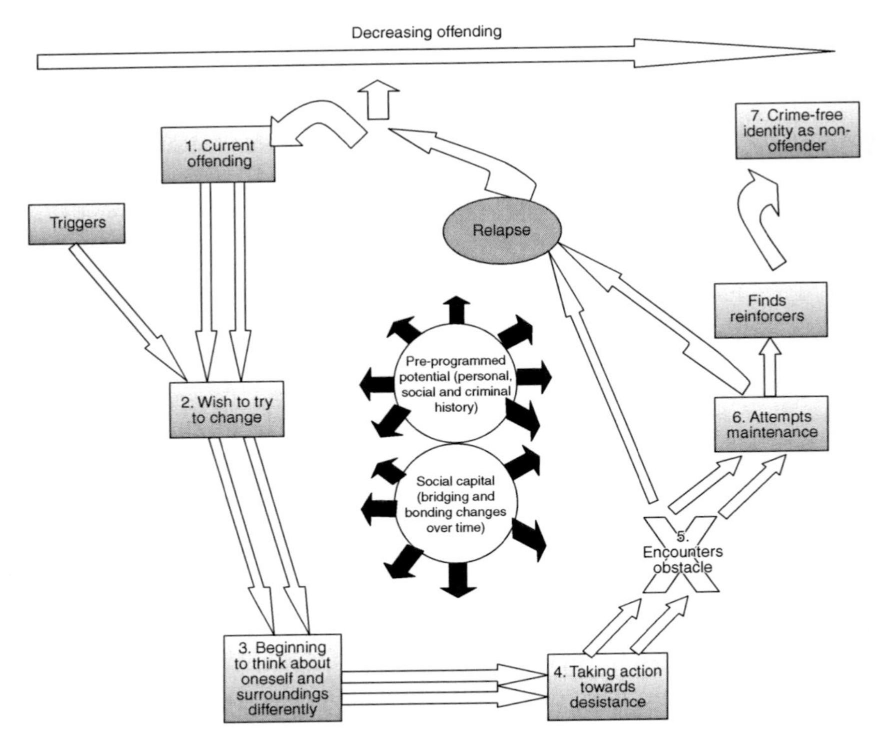

Figure 2.4 A heuristic and interactive model of the early stages of desistance.
Note: Drawn using Creately software (https://creately.com).

together by the individual agent, who must attempt to negotiate a new way of living, breaking with the habits of the past with the support of whoever is willing and able to act as a 'significant other' (including, interestingly, parents), all within a shifting surrounding social context.

Where does the criminal justice system fit into this picture? We shall be publishing separately on this topic, but a few remarks can usefully be made here (see also, and congruently, Farrall 2002; McNeill 2006; Farrall *et al* 2010). There is some qualitative evidence in our study that custodial sentences may have an impact by strengthening offenders' desires to change their way of life, but it is clear also that the lived experience of desistance is primarily a process of learning new ways of living in the community. For a persistent offender who has been committing crimes which bring in income (burglary, theft, drug dealing, etc.), money is central to this process: desisting requires acquiring new or increased sources of legal income, and/or learning to do without so much income. Either of these strategies may be linked to changes in surroundings, changes in leisure patterns, changes in peer relationships, or the acquisition of new routines and habits. How then might the criminal justice system aid or hinder these lifestyle transformations?

In terms of aiding, there is a clear potential role for community correctional personnel, such as the Probation Service in England and Wales (as well as others in the public sector who may be able to help with issues such as housing or employment). Surmounting the 'difficulties' at stage 5 of Figure 2.4 (the 'snares' described by Moffitt 2006), is hard for those with little human or social capital. Yet helping those who are trying to desist to overcome such practical obstacles has not always been seen as a valued activity in recent supervision practice in England; instead, practice has tended to focus especially on enforcement (given the political climate of a 'culture of control': Garland 2001) and on attitudinal change (following some of the recommended approaches of the so-called 'What works?' movement: see generally Raynor and Robinson 2009). It is also true that offenders are sometimes seen to be less deserving of the time of potential sources of help in the public sector because they have offended. However, on a harm reduction approach – that is, one which weighs against current expenditures both the harms and losses to potential future victims and the cost to the public purse of dealing with future crimes – offenders genuinely trying to desist might be seen as reasonable recipients of aid from the public sector.

It also seems important that criminal justice system personnel do not label would-be desisters simply as 'high risk' individuals. If desisters are indeed continuing to offend (even if at a lower rate), clearly that offending must be pursued. However, if they have ceased offending, being 'turned over' as the 'usual suspects' is not necessarily very helpful, either in encouraging offenders to move towards a non-offending self-identity or in maintaining pro-social ties or employment. The key predictors of further offending in our study were *both* prior official offending *and* various aspects of current circumstances. Heavy policy emphasis on the first of these may make it more difficult for offenders to overcome the obstacles that they presciently perceive on the path to desistance. One of the faults of our ways of dealing with offending may be that we have many mechanisms (including PNC files and 'risk scores') for making sure that prior offending is not forgotten, but not so many for helping would-be offenders to overcome the obstacles they face, or for welcoming back into conventional society those who are succeeding or have succeeded in the process of desistance. Perhaps we need to re-learn the lesson that criminal justice personnel are there not only to stamp on crime, but also to celebrate conformity.

Notes

* The research reported in this chapter was conducted at the Centre for Criminological Research, University of Sheffield, as part of an Economic and Social Research Council (ESRC)-funded Research Network on Social Contexts of Pathways in Crime (SCoPiC), co-ordinated by Professor P-O. Wikström of the Institute of Criminology, University of Cambridge. We acknowledge with deep gratitude some fundamental debts to funders, colleagues, and those who helped us with research fieldwork: (a) *Funders*:

to the ESRC for the main grant, and to the Leverhulme Foundation for the later grant of an Emeritus Fellowship to AEB; (b) *Colleagues*: to Grant Muir, Deirdre Healy, Deborah Holmes, Helen Atkinson, Angela Sorsby and Andrew Costello, for indispensable contributions to our joint endeavours – we are particularly grateful to Angela Sorsby for undertaking many of the analyses reported in this chapter; (c) *Fieldwork*: to South Yorkshire Police, the National Probation Service (South Yorkshire), and to the staff of many prisons for their generous co-operation; and last but certainly not least, to the young men who agreed to participate as research subjects, and to many of their families and friends, for their patience and often considerable interest in the research.

1 An important reason for this is that offences committed by adolescents are much more likely to involve co-offending, hence the offender:offence ratio is higher in adolescence.
2 In this analysis, 'chronic offenders' were defined by the authors as those with five or more convictions by the age of 40 (Piquero *et al* 2007: 132f). For this purpose, a 'conviction' is, as in most Cambridge Study analyses, a criminal act leading to a conviction, with the proviso that if two or more offences were committed on the same day, only the most serious one is counted (Farrington *et al* 2006: 17).
3 The Gluecks' offender sample was selected from the populations of two correctional schools in Massachusetts. At the commencement of the research, the average age of the sample was 14 years 8 months. At that time, their average number of conviction occasions was 3.5, and their average age at first conviction was 12.5 (Glueck and Glueck 1950: 37, 293, 295).
4 See Moffitt (2006: 298–301) for her response to Laub and Sampson (2003). She makes no specific comment on the longitudinal age-crime curve, but does emphasise that her original publication predicted only that life-course persisters would 'continue offending well beyond the age when most young men in their cohort population desisted' (Moffitt: 299–300).
5 See Bottoms *et al* (2004) and Shapland and Bottoms (2007) for earlier discussions of the theoretical frameworks of the Sheffield Study.
6 We invited each respondent to his next interview nine months after the previous interview; but respondents were frequently elusive, and the average period between interviews was 11–12 months.
7 This is true, for example, of surveys of the general population (such as the British Crime Survey) which attempt to contact respondents at their home address. For data on non-response in the British Crime Survey, see Aye Maung (1995: 212–14).
8 In these comparisons, lifetime criminality was measured by the OGRS2 score, and disadvantage by the 'early disadvantage score'; these measures are both described later.
9 For those (the majority) who were first interviewed in prison, these data refer to the year before their current period in custody.
10 A 'drug problem offender' was identified as someone who *either* admitted to being dependent on drugs (of any kind), *or* to taking hard drugs and regarding this as a problem. At first interview, 41 per cent admitted to recent drug dependency.
11 That is, excluding periods of custody during any measured period. In this and all subsequent statements relating to offending over a specific period, the data given omit those who were at liberty for less than 31 days during the period in question.
12 Period A is a period before Interview 1 – either one year before the interview, or, if interviewed in prison, one year before the start of the current prison sentence. Period B is the period between the first and second interviews, and Period C the period between the second and third interviews. Period D is the period between the third and fourth interviews, and Period D* is the period from Interview 3 to the last collection of official offending data from the Police National Computer (31 August 2007).

13 Because of the sharp decline in official offending levels during the study period, it is necessary in Table 2.1A to use different cut-off points for the categories in Period A and Period D*. For Period D*, we have used the same categories as in the regression analysis on official criminality (see Table 2.6). For Period A, we have – as for Period D* – used the upper quartile as the highest category, plus a similar proportionate division between the other two categories.

14 Obviously, only persons completing Interview 4 can be included in this analysis. Some others also had to be excluded because they did not have a sufficient period (minimum 31 days: see fn 11) at liberty in Period D; hence, although 88 men completed Interview 4, the N for this analysis is 71. We compared these 71 men with the 42 others in the full sample on the four variables of age, self-declared ethnic status, OGRS2 score, and early disadvantage score; the only statistically significant difference was that the 71 cases had a disproportionate number of those self-declaring as 'White British'.

15 Unlike the similar analysis for official offending (see Table 2.1A and fn 13), these comparisons are based on actual, not relative, offending levels.

16 Of course, if frequency amongst those decreasing continues to decline, the offences total will eventually show a reduction.

17 Not all interviews were taped, especially because of the reluctance of some prisons to allow tape-recording, and some tape malfunctions.

18 Moffitt (1993: 684) in fact originally used the term 'snares' in relation to her 'life-course persistent' group, pointing out that, for them, snares can 'diminish the probabilities of later success by eliminating opportunities for breaking the chain of cumulative continuity'.

19 The dependent variable was the 'views about future offending' variable (see Table 2.2), but because of the small numbers stating that they were 'unlikely to stop', that category was combined with the group saying that they 'would like to stop but not sure if I can'. There were therefore three values for the dependent variable at Interviews 2, 3 and 4, and two values for Interview 1 (see Table 2.2). For Interviews 2, 3 and 4, as these values are in a clear rank order, ordinal regression was chosen as the appropriate method of analysis. Moreover, as required by the assumptions of ordinal regression, the difference between responses A and B, and B and C, are impossible to quantify accurately, and the difference between responses A and B may be greater or less than the difference between responses B and C. For Interview 1, where the dependent variable had only two values, logistic regression was used as the appropriate method of analysis.

20 There were two items in the empathy scale, namely: 'If things I do upset people it's their problem not mine', and 'I do not care much about whether other people think what I do is wrong'.

21 In a slightly different way, the research on probationers by Stephen Farrall (2002: 73ff, 209–10) also highlighted obstacles and their resolution as central to the motivations of and outcomes for would-be desisters.

22 We ran initial analyses for each obstacle separately, and also for groups of obstacles (e.g. 'economic obstacles'), but the obstacles total was consistently the most powerful indicator.

23 There are several other interesting features of the data in Table 2.4, for example the generally declining percentages as one moves from Interview 1 to Interview 4. Four items decline faster than most, namely 'police harassment', 'pressure from mates', 'anger/stress/depression' and 'family problems'.

24 Though not in all criminology: see for example Wright and Decker's (1994) important ethnographic study of active burglars in St Louis, Missouri, where 'in the overwhelming majority of cases, the decision to commit a residential burglary arises in the face of what offenders perceive to be a pressing need for cash' (Wright and Decker 1994: 36).

25 Various parental scales were included in Interviews 1 and 3. At Interview 1, they were prefaced by the phrase 'When I was growing up ...', and all statements were in the past tense (e.g. 'My parents trusted me'). At Interview 3, the focus was on *current* relationships with parents (excluding cases where the respondent had no current contact with his parents). Essentially the same scales were used, but the present tense was used throughout, and where necessary the wording was changed (e.g. 'My parents still want to know how my life is going' instead of 'My parents would ask about what I was doing at school').

26 There are three relevant issues here: (a) the number of official offences recorded for a given period will be partly dependent on success in detection and on charging practices; (b) self-reported offence totals given by still-active offenders are often simply estimates; and (c) adjustments for periods in custody, although necessary, inevitably produce their own distortions: for example, an offender with only three months at liberty in a 12-month follow-up period would very likely not have sustained the same rate of offending had he remained at liberty throughout, yet the statistical adjustment necessarily assumes that he would have done so.

27 For both the self-report and official offending analyses, the essential requirements for the use of an ordinal regression approach (set out in fn 19) were fully met. The categories that were used for the dependent variables are set out in the Appendix.

28 The N for Table 2.5 is 63. There were 71 subjects who completed Interview 4 and had at least 31 days at risk between Interviews 3 and 4 (see fn 14), but eight of these had to be excluded from the regression analysis in Table 2.5 because of missing data on one or more relevant independent variables.

29 Additionally, it is methodologically interesting that the OGRS2 score, based primarily on official criminality variables, is a good predictor of *self-reported* offending two to three years later.

30 The 'views about future offending' variable was not included as one of the independent variables in the regression models reported in Tables 2.5 and 2.6. The statement in the text is based on a special analysis in which this variable was added to the other Interview 1 variables listed in the regression procedure for Table 2.5.

31 The N for Table 2.6 is 80. There were 101 offenders who had at least 31 days at risk in Period D*, but because the analysis includes (as a crucial component) variables from Interview 3, it was necessary for subjects to have completed that interview (N = 88), or, in a few cases, a fourth interview after a third interview had been missed. The remaining exclusions resulted from missing data on one or more relevant independent variables.

32 Pre-Interview 1 patterns of both official criminality (on a 'lifetime' basis) and self-reported offending (for Period A) were subjected to principal components analyses. The official offending analysis produced four components: (a) a general property offending component linking to theft and handling, burglary, unlawful taking of a motor vehicle and criminal damage (accounting for 23 per cent of the variance); (b) a violence and criminal damage component (16 per cent); (c) a drugs and motoring offences component (11 per cent); and (d) a robbery and motoring component (9 per cent). Overall, the analysis accounted for 59 per cent of the variance. The self-reported offending analysis also produced four components: (a) a general property offence component (accounting for 29 per cent of the variance); (b) a motoring offence component (11 per cent); (c) a violence and criminal damage component (13 per cent); and (d) a robbery, drug dealing and theft component (10 per cent). Overall, this analysis accounted for 67 per cent of the variance. Scores on components from both of these analyses were included in the various regression analyses reported in this chapter.

33 This particular scale was adapted from the work of Ellemers *et al* (1999).

34 It is noteworthy that in the analyses for Table 2.5, this variable is not significantly related to self-reported offending between Interviews 3 and 4 even on a bivariate basis.

35 In this connection it is also worth noting that the study by Farrall (2002: 75–6) found only partial agreement as between probationers and probation officers as regards the assessment of obstacles to desistance.

36 In their interesting chapter on 'existential aspects of desistance', Farrall and Calverley (2006) present a case study of a successful desister ('Sandra'), at the conclusion of which they emphasise that 'Sandra did not become a completely different person', but rather 'found a new way of "being Sandra"' (Farrall and Calverley 2006: 93). This is a very important observation which fits closely with the self-perceptions of respondents in the Sheffield study. As the quotation in the text makes clear, even among the chaos of his life at Interview 1 'John' saw himself as fundamentally 'trustworthy' and 'a good person to get on with'. He was struggling to find ways to make that side of himself more prominent, and the bad things currently surrounding him less prominent. On similar themes, see further Giordano *et al* (2002) and Maruna (2000). We shall be developing these issues in later publications.

37 We are particularly grateful to Deirdre Healy for her contribution to the qualitative study, and to earlier versions of this model.

References

Archdeacon, T. J. (1994) *Correlation and Regression Analysis: A Historian's Guide*. Madison, WI: University of Wisconsin Press.

Aye Maung, N. (1995) 'Survey design and the interpretation of the British Crime Survey', in M. A. Walker (ed.) *Interpreting Crime Statistics*. Oxford: Clarendon Press, pp 206–27.

Bandura, A. (1997) *Self-Efficacy: The Exercise of Control*. New York, NY: W. H. Freeman and Co.

Blokland, A. A. J. and Nieuwbeerta, P. (2005) 'The effects of life circumstances on longitudinal trajectories of offending', *Criminology*, 43: 1203–33.

Bottoms, A. E. (2006) 'Desistance, social bonds and human agency: a theoretical exploration', in Wikström, P. -O. H., Sampson, R. J. (eds) *The Explanation of Crime*. Cambridge: Cambridge University Press, pp 243–90.

Bottoms, A. E. (2008) 'The relationship between theory and empirical observations in criminology', in King, R. D. and Wincup, E. (eds) *Doing Research in Crime and Justice*, 2nd edn. Oxford: Oxford University Press, pp 75–116.

Bottoms, A. E. (2009) 'Desistance and diachronic self-control'. Paper presented at a conference to celebrate the 50th anniversary of the founding of the Institute of Criminology, University of Cambridge.

Bottoms, A. E., Shapland, J., Costello, A., Holmes, D. and Muir, G. (2004) 'Towards desistance: theoretical underpinnings for an empirical study', *The Howard Journal of Criminal Justice*, 43: 368–89.

Burnett, R. (1992) *The Dynamics of Recidivism*. Oxford: Centre for Criminological Research.

Capozza, D. and Brown, R. (2000) *Social Identity Processes*. London: Sage.

Copas, J. B. and Marshall, P. (1998) 'The Offending Group Reconviction Scale: a statistical reconviction score for use by probation officers', *Applied Statistics*, 47: 159–71.

Ellemers, N., Kortekaas, P. and Ouwerkerk, J. W. (1999) 'Self-categorization, categorization, commitment to the group and group self-esteem as related but distinct aspects of social identity', *European Journal of Social Psychology*, 29: 371–89.

Ezell, M. E. and Cohen, L. E. (2005) *Desisting from Crime*. Oxford: Oxford University Press.

Farrall, S. (2002) *Rethinking What Works with Offenders*. Cullompton: Willan Publishing.

Farrall, S. and Calverley, A. (2006) *Understanding Desistance from Crime: Emerging Theoretical Directions in Resettlement and Rehabilitation*. Maidenhead: Open University Press.

Farrall, S., Bottoms, A. E. and Shapland, J. (2010) 'Social structures and desistance from crime', *European Journal of Criminology*, 7(6): 546–70.

Farrington, D. P. (1989) 'Self-reported and official offending from adolescence to adulthood', in Klein, M. W. (ed) *Cross-National Research in Self-Reported Crime and Delinquency*. Dordrecht: Kluwer, pp 399–423.

Farrington, D. P., Coid, J. W., Harnett, L., Jolliffe, D., Soteriou, N., Turner, R. and West, D. J. (2006) *Criminal Careers up to Age 50 and Life Success up to Age 48*, Home Office Research Study No 299. London: Home Office.

Garland, D. (2001) *The Culture of Control*. Oxford: Clarendon Press.

Giordano, P. C., Cernovich, S. A. and Rudolph, J. L. (2002) 'Gender, crime and desistance: toward a theory of cognitive transformation', *American Journal of Sociology*, 107: 990–1064.

Glueck, S. and Glueck, E. (1950) *Unraveling Juvenile Delinquency*. Cambridge, MA: Harvard University Press.

Gottfredson, M. R. and Hirschi, T. (1990) *A General Theory of Crime*. Stanford, CA: Stanford University Press.

Halpern, D. (2005) *Social Capital*. Cambridge: Polity Press.

Horney, J., Osgood, D. W. and Marshall, I. H. (1995) 'Criminal careers in the short term: intra-individual variability in crime and its relation to local life circumstances', *American Sociological Review*, 60: 655–73.

Katz, J. (1988) *Seductions of Crime: Moral and Sensual Attractions in Doing Evil*. New York, NY: Basic Books.

Kazemian, L. Farrington, D. P. and LeBlanc, M. (2009) 'Can we make accurate long-term predictions about patterns of de-escalation in offending behavior?', *Journal of Youth and Adolescence*, 38: 384–400.

Kyvsgaard, B. (2003) *The Criminal Career: The Danish Longitudinal Study*. Cambridge: Cambridge University Press.

van der Laan, A. M., Blom, M. and Kleemans, E. R. (2009) 'Exploring long-term and short-term risk factors for serious delinquency', *European Journal of Criminology*, 6: 419–38.

Laub, J. H. and Sampson, R. J. (2003) *Shared Beginnings, Divergent Lives*. Cambridge, MA: Harvard University Press.

Le Bel, T. P., Burnett, R., Maruna, S. and Bushway, S. (2008) 'The "chicken and egg" of subjective and social factors in desistance from crime', *European Journal of Criminology*, 5: 131–59.

McNeill, F. (2006) 'A desistance paradigm for offender management', *Criminology and Criminal Justice*, 6: 39–62.

Maruna, S. (2001) *Making Good*. Washington, DC: American Psychological Association.

van Mastrigt, S. B. and Farrington, D. P. (2009) 'Co-offending, age, gender and crime type: implications for criminal justice policy', *British Journal of Criminology*, 49: 552–73.

Matza, D. (1964) *Delinquency and Drift*. New York, NY: John Wiley and Sons.

Moffitt, T. E. (1993) 'Adolescence-limited and life-course-persistent antisocial behavior: a developmental taxonomy', *Psychological Review*, 100: 674–701.

Moffitt, T. E. (2006) 'A review of research on the taxonomy of life-course persistent versus adolescence-limited antisocial behavior', in Cullen, F. T., Wright J. P. and Blevins K. R. (eds) *Taking Stock: The Status of Criminological Theory*. New Brunswick, NJ: Transaction Publishers, pp 277–311.

Mouzelis, N. (2008) *Modern and Postmodern Social Theorizing*. Cambridge: Cambridge University Press.

Piquero, A., Farrington, D. P. and Blumstein, A. (2007) *Key Issues in Criminal Career Research: New Analyses of the Cambridge Study in Delinquent Development*. Cambridge: Cambridge University Press.

Raynor, P. and Robinson, G. (2009) *Rehabilitation, Crime and Justice*, 2nd edn. Basingstoke: Palgrave Macmillan.

Runciman, W. G. (1983) *A Treatise on Social Theory, vol. 1, The Methodology of Social Theory*. Cambridge: Cambridge University Press.

Sampson, R. J. and Laub, J. H. (1993) *Crime in the Making*. Cambridge, MA: Harvard University Press.

Shapland, J. and Bottoms, A. E. (2007) 'Between Conformity and Criminality: Theoretical Reflections on Desistance', in Müller-Dietz, H., Müller, E., Kunz, K-L., Radtke, H., Britz, G., Momsen C. and Koriath H. (eds) *Festschrift für Heike Jung*. Baden-Baden: Nomos, pp 905–20.

Siennick, S. E. and Osgood, D. W. (2008) 'A review of research on the impact on crime of transitions to adult roles', in Lieberman, A. M. (ed.) *The Long View of Crime*. New York, NY: Springer, pp 161–87.

Stouthamer-Loeber, M., Wei, E., Loeber, R. and Master, A. S. (2004) 'Desistance from persistent serious delinquency in the transition to adulthood', *Development and Psychopathology*, 16: 897–918.

Uggen, C. and Piliavin, I. (1998) 'Asymmetrical causation and criminal desistance', *Journal of Criminal Law and Criminology*, 88: 1399–422.

Warr, M. (2002) *Companions in Crime*. Cambridge: Cambridge University Press.

Wright, R. and Decker, S. (1994) *Burglars on the Job*. Boston, MA: Northeastern University Press.

Appendix

Procedures in relation to regression equations

Views about future offending (Table 2.3)

Interview 1

Dependent variable: 1 = 'Definite intention to stop'; 2 = other responses.

Procedures: All the variables measured at Interview 1 that had a significant relationship to 'views about future offending' at Interview 1 in bivariate Spearman's correlations were entered into a stepwise binary logistic regression in SPSS using the backward Wald method.

Interview 2

Dependent variable: 1 = 'Have stopped offending'; 2 = 'Definite intention to stop'; 3 = other responses.

Procedures: All the variables measured at Interview 1 that had a significant relationship to 'views about future offending' at Interview 2 in bivariate Spearman's correlations were entered into an ordinal logistic regression (PLUM) in SPSS. Variables were excluded stepwise based on the probability of the Wald statistic until only variables with a significant Wald statistic were left in the model. This procedure was repeated for Interview 2 variables that had a significant relationship to 'views about future offending' at Interview 2 in bivariate Spearman's correlations. Finally the procedure was repeated using together the Interview 1 and 2 variables that went into the two final models for Interviews 1 and 2 run separately.

Interview 3

Dependent variable: 1 = 'Have stopped offending'; 2 = 'Definite intention to stop'; 3 = other responses.

Procedures: All the variables measured at Interview 1 that had a significant relationship to 'views about future offending' at Interview 3 in bivariate Spearman's correlations were entered into an ordinal logistic regression (PLUM) in SPSS. Variables were excluded stepwise based on the probability of the Wald statistic until only variables with a significant Wald statistic were left in the model. This procedure was repeated for Interview 2 variables and then again for Interview 3 variables that had a significant relationship to 'views about future offending' at Interview 3 in bivariate Spearman's correlations. Finally the procedure was repeated using together the Interview 1, 2 and 3 variables that went into the three final models for Interviews 1, 2 and 3 run separately.

Interview 4

Dependent variable: 1 = 'Have stopped offending'; 2 = 'Definite intention to stop'; 3 = other responses.

Procedures: All the variables measured at Interview 1 that had a significant relationship to 'views about future offending' at Interview 4 in bivariate Spearman's correlations were entered into an ordinal logistic regression (PLUM) in SPSS. Variables were excluded stepwise based on the probability of the Wald statistic until only variables with a significant Wald statistic were left in the model. This procedure was repeated for Interview 2 variables, then again for Interview 3 variables and then again for Interview 4 variables that had a significant relationship to 'views about future offending' at Interview 4 in bivariate Spearman's correlations. Finally the procedure was repeated using together the Interview 1, 2, 3 and 4 variables that went into the four final models for Interviews 1, 2, 3 and 4 run separately.

Self-reported offending (Table 2.5)

Dependent variable: 1 = 0<25 offences per year at risk in the period between Interviews 3 and 4; 2 = 26<150 offences per year at risk; 3 = 150+ offences per year at risk.

Procedures: All the variables measured at Interview 1 that had a significant relationship to self-reported offending between Interviews 3 and 4 in bivariate Spearman's correlations were entered into an ordinal logistic regression (PLUM) in SPSS. Variables were excluded stepwise based on the probability of the Wald statistic until only variables with a significant Wald statistic were left in the model. This procedure was repeated for Interview 2 variables and then again for Interview 3 variables that had a significant relationship to self-reported offending between Interviews 3 and 4 in bivariate Spearman's correlations. Finally the procedure was repeated using together the Interview 1, 2 and 3 variables that went into the three final models for Interviews 1, 2 and 3 run separately.

Official offending (Table 2.6)

Dependent variable: 1 = No recorded offences in the period from Interview 3 to 31 August 2007; 2 = Some offences, but not in upper quartile for the sample; 3 = those in the upper quartile.

Procedures: All the variables measured at Interview 1 that had a significant relationship to the number of standard list offences between Interview 3 and 31 August 2007 in bivariate Spearman's correlations were entered into an ordinal logistic regression (PLUM) in SPSS. Variables were excluded stepwise based on the probability of the Wald statistic until only variables with a significant Wald statistic were left in the model. This procedure was repeated for Interview 2 variables and then again for Interview 3 variables that had a significant relationship to the number of standard list offences between Interview 3 and 31 August 2007 in bivariate Spearman's correlations. Finally the procedure was repeated using together the Interview 1, 2 and 3 variables that went into the three final models for Interviews 1, 2 and 3 run separately.

Chapter 3

Youth justice?

The impact of system contact on patterns of desistance

Lesley McAra and Susan McVie

Introduction[1]

Over the past decade, youth justice discourse in many Western jurisdictions has become dominated by the mantra of 'evidence-based' policy (see Gatti and Verde 2002; Walgrave 2002; McAra 2004a; Muncie and Goldson 2006). Informed by the results of research on risk and protective factors and (more especially) the precepts underpinning the 'What works?' agenda, huge resources have been devoted to early intervention initiatives, for 'at risk' children and their families, as well as to specialist programmes aimed at reducing re-offending amongst older, more persistent offenders. This has been accompanied (particularly in the UK) by a massive increase in government sponsored research, focused on evaluating programme effectiveness and establishing value for money (see Pitts 2003; Hope 2004).

Evidence-based policy, as currently conceived, has a particularly seductive quality for politicians, not least because its scientific imprimatur suggests political neutrality and because it has the capacity to enhance central (government) control over youth justice agencies, through national standards, performance indicators and evaluation research – all considered integral to the delivery of 'programme integrity' (see Farrall 2002; Muncie 2002; McAra 2004a). It also has a seductive quality for certain sectors of academia (providing a major source of research income and sustaining a new generation of contract researchers) and some practitioners (as for example within Scotland, where the 'What works?' agenda has functioned to re-professionalise and re-legitimise the social work contribution to criminal justice, see McAra 2005a). Consequently a range of more or less powerful groups now have a strong vested interest in maintaining the evidence-based approach.

As a counterweight to this, however, there is a growing body of research which is beginning to question the actual evidence-base of the preventative and offending reduction elements of contemporary youth justice policy frameworks. This attack comes from two main directions. First, from a range of commentators who claim that the scientific foundations of the 'What works?' principles are inherently flawed and/or that programmes based on such principles have been imported into youth justice systems in inappropriate ways; and, second, from a number of studies which have explored the longer-term (mostly damaging) impact of system (rather than individual programme) contact on young people.

Flaws in scientific foundations of policy

The 'What works?' agenda stems from a range of meta-analytic reviews conducted during the 1980s and 1990s (see Garrett 1985; Andrews *et al* 1990; Lipsey 1992). These reviews reanalysed data from a range of individual studies on offender treatment programmes, to record changes from pre-test to post-test expressed as standard deviation units. They concluded that programmes based on six core principles could be effective in reducing reoffending, in particular programmes which calibrated intensity of intervention to level of risk; tackled criminogenic need; were community-based and multi-modal in orientation; and appropriately resourced with well trained and highly motivated staff (McGuire 1995).

The results of meta-analysis are, of course, only as good as the quality of the individual studies from which they derive their data. Concerns have been expressed that some of the most influential meta-analytic studies have drawn on relatively poor quality research; that there is a publication bias towards evaluation studies showing large effect sizes, which may overstate the effectiveness of 'What works?' measures; and that there is reliance on police reports or reconviction data as outcome measures which are insensitive measures of re-offending (see in particular Gaes 1998; Smith 2005).

Other criticisms of 'What works?' relate less to meta-analysis as a method, and more to the use to which the science has been put. Much of the enthusiasm with which 'What works?' principles have been taken up by policy-makers has been based on over-optimistic assumptions about what specialist programmes will be able to deliver in terms of crime reduction. Even the best and most rigorously conducted meta-analytic studies only ever claimed that re-offending could be reduced by a small amount. For example, Lösel (cited in Smith 2005) in a review of 13 meta-analyses (drawing on the results of over 500 evaluations) found that the average effect size was about 0.1 of a standard deviation, which was equivalent to a reduction in the re-offending rate of about 5 per cent in comparison with control groups (see Smith 2005: 187). This has not prevented policy-makers from setting (what may be) unrealistic targets for youth justice agencies (as for example in Scotland, where the youth justice system was charged with effecting a 10 per cent reduction in the number of persistent offenders by 2006, from a baseline of 1,201 identified offenders in 2004; a target which it failed to meet).

Arguably, the efficacy of specialist offender programmes on offer within a particular youth justice system is a poor measure of the effectiveness of the system as a whole. Only a small minority of the offenders processed by any system will ever access such programmes, and then only after a long-term sequence of interactions with a range of different agencies (e.g. the police, social work/probation, court or tribunal). A core limitation of meta-analytic review is that such studies often fail to take account of potential selection effects caused by the gate-keeping practices of agencies at earlier stages of the youth justice process, and the broader (and possibly cumulative) impact of systemic contact on individual offenders as they move from stage to stage. More particularly, there has been (some would argue) a rather naïve assumption amongst policy makers that measures that appear to work in one jurisdiction can be successfully transplanted into others, without any need to consider differences in the cultural and social contexts within which such measures are to be implemented (see especially Muncie 2002; Muncie and Goldson 2006).

System contact and deviancy amplification

In contrast to the precepts of the 'What works?' agenda, there is a growing body of research across a range of jurisdictions, including England/Wales, Germany and the US (but not Scotland), which indicates that contact with the youth justice system and experience of more severe forms of sanctioning, in particular, are as likely to result in enhanced as diminished offending risk (see Sherman *et al* 1998; Klein 1986). Taken to its extremes this research would suggest (in a manner akin to labelling theory) that contact with the youth justice system is inherently criminogenic.

Much of this body of work is longitudinal in design. As such it is able to redress some of the methodological limitations of programme evaluation mentioned above. In particular, longitudinal research enables the tracking of individual offenders through the youth and adult criminal justice systems and is able to test for the impacts of particular criminal justice pathways on subsequent behaviour. Moreover, longitudinal research is able to undertake a longer term follow-up of cases than is possible in most government-sponsored evaluation research.

Examples from this literature include the Cambridge Study (Farrington 1977),[2] which found that self-reported delinquency was significantly higher amongst cohort members who were first convicted between the ages of 14 and 18 than amongst a matched group of unconvicted boys. Similar results were found for those with first convictions between the ages of 18 and 21 again compared with a matched group of the unconvicted (Farrington *et al* 1978). Furthermore, Tracy and Kempf-Leonard (1996) in their follow-up study of the 1958 Philadelphia birth cohort, found that boys who were committed to a correctional facility at any stage were more likely to continue offending into adulthood than those who were not, after controlling for other influences. However, they also found that criminal careers tended to be shorter where there was early intervention in the form of probation, than in cases where first intervention came much later.

Perhaps the most powerful evidence of the negative consequences of youth justice interventions, comes from a comparative study undertaken by Huizinga *et al* (2003). Drawing on data from two longitudinal projects (one sited in

Bremen, Germany and the other in Denver, US), the authors found that arrests and sanctions had only a limited impact on offending, resulting, for the most part, in the maintenance or increases in the previous level of offending (with increases being more likely in the case of the individuals given the most severe sanctions). The similarity in outcomes is particularly striking given the very different ethos of the youth justice system in Germany (more lenient, focused on diversion) from that of Denver (more punitive, propels offenders quickly into court, limited diversion). The authors conclude that it may not be the severity or otherwise of the sanctions on offer which is significant in terms of tackling offending, but rather the 'simple certainty of response' (Huizinga *et al* 2003: 5).

Aim of the chapter

The aim of this chapter is to explore the impact of the Scottish model of youth justice on future offending in the light of the above debates on the effectiveness of 'evidence-based' policy. It does so principally by drawing on findings from the Edinburgh Study of Youth Transitions and Crime, a prospective longitudinal study of youth offending.[3] Taken together, our findings provide some support for the broader international longitudinal research just mentioned. As we aim to demonstrate: selection effects at each stage of the youth justice process mean that certain categories of young people – 'the usual suspects' – become propelled into a repeat cycle of referral into the system whilst other equally serious offenders escape the tutelage of agencies altogether. Importantly, the deeper the usual suspects penetrate the youth justice system the more this is associated with *inhibited* desistance from offending.

Our principal message, therefore, is that the key to tackling serious and persistent offending lies in minimal intervention and maximum diversion. While the Scottish system[4] is better placed than most other Western juvenile justice systems to deliver such an agenda, as currently implemented, it appears to be failing many young people.

Structure of the chapter

The chapter begins with a short overview of the Scottish system of youth justice to contextualise the research findings. We then provide a brief description of the aims and design of the Edinburgh Study. A series of key findings which indicate systemic selection effects and the impact of contact on desistence from offending are presented. The chapter concludes with a discussion of the findings and their implications in relation to the broader literature on effectiveness.

Scottish youth justice in comparative context

Over the past 35 years, the youth justice system in Scotland has differed from a number of its US and European counterparts, due to its continued commitment to welfare values (McAra 2004a). Predicated on the Kilbrandon philosophy (see below) and located in a social and political culture committed to social welfare and mutual support, the system was initially able to resist the increasingly punitive turn taken in other western jurisdictions between the 1970s and early 1990s (see Paterson 1994; Garland 2001; Crawford 2002; McAra 2004a, 2005a). A further key difference has been the central role accorded to a lay tribunal in the Scottish youth justice process in contrast to the court-based structures which inhere in many other jurisdictions (as for example Italy, Germany and a range of US states, see Winterdyk 2002).

History and philosophy

The current system in Scotland was set in train by the Social Work (Scotland) Act 1968. This Act abolished the existing juvenile courts and introduced a new institutional framework for youth justice: the children's hearing system.[5]

The hearing system is underpinned by the Kilbrandon philosophy (named after the chairman of the committee set up to review youth justice in the early 1960s). According to this philosophy, the problems faced by child offenders and those in need of care and protection stem from the same source: namely deeper social or psychological malaise and/or failures in the normal upbringing process (Kilbrandon Committee 1964). As a consequence the overall aim of the hearing system is to deal with the needs of the child, with 'best interests' to be paramount in decision-making. The system is predicated on early and minimal intervention and, in the case of offenders, is intended to avoid the criminalisation and hence stigmatisation of young people (see McAra, 2002, 2004a, 2006).

Key institutions and procedures

Referrals to the children's hearing system are made to the Reporter. While anyone can make a referral, the overwhelming majority of referrals on both offence and non-offence grounds are made by the police (SCRA 2005; McAra and McVie 2005).[6]

At the time of writing, the police in Edinburgh are expected to follow a set of guidelines when making referral decisions in respect of children who offend. Up to two written warnings can be given in cases of non-serious offences where the child admits guilt. Cases in which a formal charge has been issued, those involving serious offences and all those in which the child does not admit guilt should be referred by the police juvenile liaison officer (JLO) to the Reporter (see McAra and McVie 2005). Importantly, there is always some delay between the time at which the child is apprehended by police 'beat' officers and when the case is formally recorded as a warning or charge. Police 'beat' officers issue charges to children (usually at a police station in front of their parents) and then pass the papers on to a JLO. In practice, a high proportion of charges are quietly dropped by the JLO (McAra and McVie 2005).

Once a child has been referred to the hearing system, the principal role of the Reporter is to investigate the case to determine whether at least one of the statutory grounds for referral to a hearing has been met *and* that the child is in need of compulsory measures of care. A high proportion of cases result in no further action. In 2003–04, for example, only 11 per cent of children referred to the Reporter were brought to a hearing (SCRA 2005).

The principal decision makers at a hearing are the lay panel of three trained members of the public (who live within the local government area). The overall task of the hearing is to decide whether compulsory measures of care are indeed necessary, in which case a supervision requirement will be made ensuring statutory social work involvement. In practice, the majority of hearings result in a supervision requirement (in 2003–04, only a fifth of cases were discharged by panels, SCRA 2005).

Recent changes

Although welfarist principles continue to underpin the hearing system, a number of changes have been made over the past decade. The first signs of change were introduced by the Children (Scotland) Act 1995 which enabled Reporters and panel members to place the principle of risk above that of best interests in cases where the child was considered to be a risk to him/herself or others. Policy transformation, however, has gained momentum in the wake of devolution (1999),[7] as Ministers in the newly formed Scottish Executive have gradually embraced the 'New Labour' crime agenda (McAra 2006).

Key changes since devolution include: the piloting of youth courts for 16–17 (and some 15) year old offenders; new national objectives and standards for youth justice; a new administrative framework which includes multi-agency youth justice teams with responsibility for the direction and implementation of policy; the expansion of restorative justice initiatives; the importation of 'What works?' principles into a range of specialist programmes; a gradual elision between the new social inclusion, community safety and youth justice policy agendas, with increased emphasis on early targeted intervention to support at risk children and their families (see McAra 2006); and a new policy focus on anti-social behaviour, with the extension of anti-social behaviour orders to the under 16s, the introduction of parenting orders and facilities for the electronic monitoring of children. Importantly, these changes have introduced a range of competing and somewhat contradictory rationales into the youth justice system (it is variously punitive, actuarial and restorative in orientation). Moreover, its holistic and child-centred ethos has been gradually eroded as the new apparatus of youth justice is increasingly being utilised by the Scottish Executive as a mechanism through which its broader public reassurance and community regeneration strategies can be effected (see McAra 2006; Armstrong and McAra 2006).[8]

Taken as a whole these changes are indicative of a degree of policy convergence with the system south of the border in England/Wales, with the new pilot youth courts bringing Scotland more into line with other US and European jurisdictions (see McAra 2004a).

The Edinburgh study of youth transitions and crime

The Edinburgh Study is a longitudinal programme of research on pathways into and out of offending for a cohort of around 4,300 young people who started secondary school in the City of Edinburgh in 1998, when they were aged around 12. One of the key objectives of the study is to explore the extent, nature and impact of the cohort's contact with formal agencies of social control, including the police and the other institutions comprising the youth justice system (social work, the children's hearing system and the courts).

Children from all school sectors are included (mainstream, special, and independent). A census method was employed resulting in 89 per cent coverage of the eligible school population within Edinburgh (excluding non-participating schools and children opted out by parents). Response rates amongst the achievable population have been uniformly high (as indicated in Table 3.1).[9]

Information has been collected over six annual sweeps from a range of sources including: questionnaires completed by cohort members; school records; and files held by police juvenile liaison officers, the Reporter, and the social work department. At each sweep of the study, the period covered is the previous 12 months (with the exception of sweep 1 in which the reference period was 'ever'), so that the study provides a continuous account of events in the lives of the cohort, and not just an account of selected time segments. Key themes included in the questionnaire are: self-reported offending, drug and alcohol use; experience of victimisation; friendship patterns, gang membership and friends' offending; leisure activities including hanging around; family structure and parenting; school experience; contacts with the police and youth justice agencies; neighbourhood dynamics; and a number of personality variables such as self-esteem and impulsivity.

Table 3.1 Edinburgh study response rates

Study year	*Number achieved*	*Per cent response*
Sweep 1 (age 11½–12½)	4300	96.2
Sweep 2 (age 12½–13½)	4299	95.6
Sweep 3 (age 13½–14½)	4296	95.2
Sweep 4 (age 14½–15½)	4144	92.6
Sweep 5 (age 15½–16½)	3861	89.1
Sweep 6 (age 16½–17½)	3531	80.5

Note: Response rates exclude children attending non-participating schools but include those opted out by their parents.

Form of analysis

Two phases of analysis were carried out. Phase 1 explored selection effects at three different stages of the youth justice process: police beat officer decisions to charge; JLO decisions to refer the charged cases to the Reporter on offence grounds; and Reporter decisions to bring offence grounds cases to a hearing. Sweep 4 was chosen for this phase as it spans the peak age of referral to the Reporter (around the age of 15 – both in terms of national statistics and Edinburgh Study findings) and thus maximises the number of cases which can be used. Phase 2 of the analysis examined the impact of these three different stages of agency contact on future offending, drawing on data from both sweeps 4 and 5. Detailed descriptions of all the variables used can be obtained from the authors of this chapter.

Phase 1: selection effects

Police beat officer decisions to charge

While experience of adversarial police contact is fairly common amongst the youngsters in the cohort, most contact is minor in nature (for example being told off or told to move on, see McAra and McVie 2005). At sweep 4, for example, only 464 (11 per cent) cohort members had been charged by the police in the past year.

Descriptive analysis was carried out to explore differences in characteristics between those who reported being charged by beat officers and those who did not. This analysis revealed a range of variables that differentiated between these two groups: (a) gender; (b) social deprivation as measured by family socio-economic status, neighbourhood deprivation, and free school meal entitlement; (c) family structure (a binary measure differentiating between children who had *always* lived with two birth parents and children who had lived, at any time, in another form of family); (d) offending behaviour including prevalence of drug and alcohol use and involvement in serious offending (our measure of serious offending comprises seven self-reported items: theft from a motor vehicle, riding in a stolen motor vehicle, carrying an offensive weapon, housebreaking and attempted housebreaking, fire raising, robbery, and involvement in six or more incidents of violence); (e) factors pertaining to visibility and 'availability' for policing, in particular hanging around, truanting from school[10] and level of parental supervision; and (f) previous and current police contact, as measured by volume of adversarial police contacts over the past 12 months, experience of being charged by the police or referred by the police to the Reporter in earlier years, and whether the child's friends had been in trouble with the police in earlier sweeps of the study.

Multivariate analysis was then undertaken to determine which factors best predicted being charged when controlling for each of the other variables. The method used was binary logistic regression. The dependent variable used was 'police charge' in the last year (which had values of 1 for 'charged' and 0 for 'not charged'). The independent, or explanatory, variables were entered into the models using a forward stepwise procedure, thereby allowing the statistical package to exclude those variables that did not meet the significance criteria. A maximum likelihood paradigm with a p-value for entry into the model of 0.05 (i.e. there is less than 5 in 100 chance that the variables entered might not be predictive of the dependent variable) and for exclusion from the model of 0.1 was used.

The results of the analysis are presented in Table 3.2. The left-hand column sets out all of the variables included in the modelling (namely those variables found to be significant at the descriptive analysis stage). The other columns show the variables that emerged as significant within the final model, including the odds ratio and p values for each of the categorical and continuous variables. The odds ratio (OR) is the standardised coefficient which indicates the strength

Table 3.2 Police charges multivariate analysis

First model	*Final model N = 3325 Charged = 315 Not charged = 3010*	*Odds ratio*	*p value*	*Lower CI*	*Upper CI*
Male	Male	1.5	0.013	1.1	2.1
Low socio-economic status household	–	–	–	–	–
Mean neighbourhood deprivation	High mean neighbourhood deprivation	1.3	0.001	1.1	1.5
Free school meal entitlement	Free school meal entitlement	1.5	0.034	1.0	2.1
Non two-parent family	–	–	–	–	–
Volume parental supervision	–	–	–	–	–
Taken illegal drugs in past year	Taken illegal drugs in past year	1.6	0.005	1.2	2.3
Drink weekly	–	–	–	–	–
Serious offender	Serious offender	1.9	0.000	1.4	2.7
>5 times truancy	>5 times truancy	1.8	0.002	1.2	2.5
Hang out most evenings	Hang out most evenings	1.7	0.005	1.2	2.3
Self-report charged by police at earlier sweeps	Self-report charged by police at earlier sweeps	7.4	0.000	5.4	10.3
Volume of police contact at current sweep	High volume of police contact at current sweep	1.9	0.000	1.7	2.2
Friends in trouble with police	–	–	–	–	–

of effect of each independent variable in the model on the dependent variable. Odds ratios for the categorical variables can be directly compared, and indicate the ratio of the odds of being charged by the police amongst one group (e.g. males) relative to the odds of another group (e.g. females). Odds ratios for each of the continuous variables can also be compared directly, since they were standardised before insertion into the models. The odds ratio for a continuous variable shows how the odds of being referred by the police are increased by a difference of one standard deviation on the scale of the variable.

As might be expected, involvement in serious offending continued to be an important predictor of being charged even when controlling for a range of other factors. Those who reported involvement in at least one form of serious offending were just under twice as likely to be charged as those reporting no such involvement. Illegal drug use was also a moderate predictor of being charged (OR 1.6) but not weekly alcohol use. Again as one would expect, the greater the number of times a youngster comes to the attention of the police over a 12-month period, the more likely they are to be charged. Moreover measures indicating availability for policing also continue to be important predictors of being charged, including persistent truancy (OR 1.8) and hanging around the streets most evenings (OR 1.7).

Those factors aside, the findings also suggest that police beat officers discriminate against certain categories of youngsters: in particular boys and disadvantaged children (as measured by free school meal entitlement and neighbourhood deprivation, although household socio-economic status dropped out of the final model). To rule out any potential effect of bias in police decision-making according to area of residence, individuals were clustered into neighbourhoods using multi-level modelling. As clustering did not have any impact on which factors were significant within the final model, the findings suggest that the police are more likely to refer children from poor areas in general rather than from specific areas which are more heavily policed or which have become notorious or disreputable in the view of the police.

Importantly, however, even when controlling for the other factors much the strongest predictor of being charged is having previous police charges. Children who reported that they had been charged in previous years were *over seven times* more likely to be charged at age 15 than children with no such history – a factor which is completely independent of their current involvement in serious offending, and their more recent history of police adversarial contact. Interestingly, the peer effect of having friends as perceived troublemakers, disappears in the context of multivariate analysis, suggesting that the raw difference between the charged and non-charged groups found in the descriptive analysis is fully accounted for by the other variables in the regression model.

Police juvenile liaison officer decisions to refer cases to the reporter

Although current protocols state that all youngsters who are charged by the police should be referred to the Reporter, our findings would suggest that police juvenile liaison officers exercise a high level of discretion in this regard. At sweep 4 over two-fifths (43 per cent) of children who reported that they had been charged by the police were *not* subsequently referred to the Reporter.

Descriptive analysis was again undertaken to identify factors that differentiated between those in the charged group who were subsequently referred to the Reporter (n = 265) from those who were not (n = 199). The same basic variables were included at this stage of analysis as above but with two additions: a binary variable relating to whether the child had been referred by the JLO to the Reporter at an earlier sweep of the study or not; and a volume of serious offending measure (to determine whether *persistent* serious offending was associated with referral).

As before, those variables that proved to be significantly related to referrals to the Reporter during descriptive analysis were entered into a binary logistic regression model to determine the best explanatory factors when controlling for each of the others. The dependent variable was 'referral to the Reporter' (which had values of '0' for not referred and '1' for referred). Importantly the descriptive analysis showed that neither gender nor volume of serious offending discriminated between the groups and thus these variables were not included in the regression modelling. The results of the multivariate analysis are presented in Table 3.3.

Although all our measures of social deprivation were highly related to Reporter referral in descriptive analysis, none of these measures remained significant within the regression models once other factors were controlled for. By contrast, family structure did appear to be a key driving force behind the referral process. Children who were not currently living in a two-parent family were almost twice as likely to be referred to the Reporter as those living with both

Table 3.3 JLO referral to reporter multivariate analysis

First model	*Final model* *N = 462* *Referred = 263* *Not referred = 199*	*Odds ratio*	*p value*	*Lower CI*	*Upper CI*
Low socio-economic status household	–	–	–	–	–
Mean neighbourhood deprivation	–	–	–	–	–
Free school meal entitlement	–	–	–	–	–
Non two-parent family	Non-two birth parent family	1.9	0.002	1.3	2.8
Self-report charged by police at earlier sweeps	–	–	–	–	–
Referred by JLO in previous years	Referred by JLO in previous years	4.2	0.000	2.8	6.3

birth parents. However, as with police decisions to charge, much the strongest predictor of referral relates to previous system contact. Youths who had a history of referral to the Reporter by the JLO at earlier sweeps of the Study, were just over four times as likely to be re-referred as youngsters with no such history. Just as an early history of being charged propels youngsters into a repeat cycle of charges, so too does an early history of referral into the hearing system lead to a repeat cycle of referral by the police in later years.

Reporter decisions to refer a case to a hearing

As noted earlier, the Reporter to the children's hearing system investigates all referrals to determine whether at least one of the statutory grounds has been met and whether the child is in need of compulsory measures of care. Of the 265 children in our cohort, who were referred to the Reporter on offence grounds at sweep 4, only 80 (30 per cent) were referred by the Reporter to a hearing. What factors then discriminated between the children referred by the Reporter to a hearing from those who were not?

The explanatory variables used in this stage of the analysis differed in certain key respects from those used to explain police referral practices, since the information available to Reporters is normally based only on reports (e.g. from the police, education or social work) rather than on face-to-face contact with the child or family at point of referral. Thus in addition to basic demographic variables (gender, socio-economic status, family structure and social deprivation), a range of variables were derived from information in Reporter files: grounds for referral (whether single offence grounds, or joint offence and care and protection grounds); volume of police charges (as a measure of officially recorded offending); vulnerability in terms of the volume of identified needs (relating to the personal, family and/or school circumstances of the child see McAra 2005b); and current and previous hearings contact in terms of the total volume of referrals received by the Reporter within the past year, and whether the child was known to the Reporter by the first sweep of fieldwork (by the age of 12 approximately).

Again, analysis started with descriptive statistics to identify factors which differentiated between offenders referred to a hearing from those against whom no formal action was taken. All of the variables which were significantly associated with referral to a hearing at the descriptive stage were then included in logistic regression analysis. The dependent variable was 'hearing held' (which had values of 0 for 'no hearing' and 1 for 'hearing held'). The results are presented in Table 3.4.

Table 3.4 confirms that vulnerability is a strong driving force behind Reporter decisions to refer children to a hearing. At sweep 4, being brought to a hearing was strongly predicted by a greater volume of needs. Family structure also remained an important predictor of a hearing being held, when other factors were held constant, with those living in non two-parent families being almost four and a half times more likely to be referred to a hearing than those living with

Table 3.4 Reporter referral to hearing multivariate analysis

Variables entered in first model	*Final model N = 253 No hearing = 178 Hearing = 75*	*Odds ratio*	*p value*	*Lower CI*	*Upper CI*
Hearings record by sweep 1	Hearings record by sweep 1	2.9	0.012	1.3	6.7
Free school meal entitlement	–	–	–	–	–
Non two-parent family	Non two-parent family	4.4	0.008	1.5	13.3
Volume of needs	High volume of needs	4.8	0.000	3.0	7.7
Volume referrals in past year	–	–	–	–	–
Volume of charges	High volume of charges	2.9	0.003	1.4	5.9
Grounds (joint or offence only)	–	–	–	–	–

both parents. Similarly the greater the volume of police charges over the past 12 months the more likely the child was to be referred to a hearing. Importantly, however, having a hearings record by the age of 12 was a strong predictor of further system involvement in later years. Children with an early record were almost three times as likely to be referred to a hearing at sweep 4 as their counterparts with no such history. Thus, even after controlling for risky behaviour and vulnerability, early system involvement appears to result in a repeat cycle of referral.

It is important to note that all but one of those brought to a hearing received a supervision requirement. The child who did not was already on supervision, which was terminated at this point. This highlights the crucial role played by the Reporter in terms of access to services and supervision for children. Since the panel very rarely discharge cases, it is effectively the Reporter who determines which children end up on supervision.

In summary, phase 1 of the analysis has shown that decision-making at each stage of the youth justice referral process is strongly influenced by previous police and system contact. Even when controlling for involvement in serious offending, social deprivation, family structure and factors which render children more available for policing, children who have been identified by the police as troublemakers in previous years are significantly more likely to be charged and subsequently referred to the Reporter than serious offenders with no such history. Similarly, even when controlling for level of need and officially recorded offending, youngsters who have an early hearings record are more likely to be referred to a hearing by the Reporter than other equally 'needy' offenders who are coming to the attention of the Reporter for the first time.

Phase 2: The impact of agency contact on subsequent behaviour

The second phase of analysis was designed to explore the impact of police and Reporter contact on subsequent behaviour in terms of involvement in serious offending. The focus is on system contact experienced at sweep 4, as described above, with a view to exploring change in serious offending at sweep 5. In line with phase 1, three progressively more intensive levels of system contact were evaluated:

- being charged by the police but resulting in *no further action* (i.e. the police do *not* refer the case to the Reporter, the charge amounting, therefore, to a form of moral scolding);
- being referred by the police to the Reporter on offence grounds *but not being brought to a hearing* (i.e. the case is diverted away from the formal system by the Reporter);
- offence ground referrals being brought to a children's hearing and the child placed on supervision.

To take account of any differences in the characteristics of those who progressed through the system from those who did not, and to legislate against the effect of potential bias caused by the systemic selection effects identified at phase 1, a process of synthetic case control analysis was carried out using a technique known as propensity score matching (PSM). This quasi-experimental technique involves pairing individuals or 'cases' who receive a form of intervention with a closely matched comparison group of 'control' subjects who do not (see Rosenbaum and Rubin 1983). The analysis was carried out using a series of binary logistic regression models which were bootstrapped with 200 replications to minimise variance and produce robust standard errors (see Cummings and McKnight 2004; Becker and Ichino 2002).[11]

Three sets of propensity scores were calculated, each one representing the probability that an individual would have received intervention at one of the three stages examined. The probabilities were conditional upon a set of observed characteristics that were available for both those who received intervention and the potential comparators. Ten control variables that emerged as significant in predicting selection through the various stages of the system were taken from the phase 1 analysis to match the groups. These were: gender, non two-parent family, free school meal entitlement, drug use in past year, hanging out most days, truancy, neighbourhood deprivation, early police contact, number of times in trouble with the police and volume of serious offending. Only three variables could not be used from phase 1 (volume of needs, number of charges and hearings record at sweep 1), as they were derived from the Reporter's files, hence this information was not available for the non-referred groups.

Only those variables that were significant in the final regression models were retained for matching, to prevent constructing over-parameterised models which may have reduced matching power and increased model variance (Caliendo and

Table 3.5 Summary of the matched groups from propensity score matching

	Intervention group	*Comparison group*
Stage 1: Police charge	Charged by police at sweep 4 but no further action taken and never referred to the Reporter (n = 99)	Had adversarial police contact but not charged at sweep 4 and never referred to the Reporter (n = 238)
Stage 2: Referral to reporter	Referred by police to the Reporter at sweep 4 on offence grounds but no further action taken and never attended hearings (n = 130)	Had adversarial police contact (including charges) but never referred to the Reporter (n = 322)
Stage 3: Brought to a hearing	Referred by police to the Reporter at sweep 3 or 4 on offence grounds and brought to a hearing at sweep 4 (n = 59)	Had adversarial police contact (including charges) but never referred to the Reporter (n = 117)

Note: Comparison group numbers are larger than for the intervention group due to over-sampling; weighting was used during analysis to balance the samples.

Kopeinig 2005). The exception to this rule was the serious offending variable which was always retained to ensure that the groups were matched as closely as possible on the outcome measure. The PSM procedure was set to allow for multiple matches (4:1) for each person who had intervention since the pool of potential matches at each stage was larger than the intervention group. This over-sampling approach both maximises the use of available data and minimises the potential impact of large standard errors on the outcome measures (Bryson *et al* 2002).

Table 3.5 presents a summary of the characteristics of the intervention group and the matched comparison group for each stage of the analysis. The groups were constructed so as to ensure that the impact of system contact at each stage would not be confounded by the effects of other system contact, especially earlier contact with the children's Reporter. Therefore, the pool of potential matches at all three stages was restricted to those individuals who had never experienced a referral to or contact with the children's hearing system (either before or subsequently).

Results of analysis

The three intervention groups were compared with their matched comparison groups on the basis of both prevalence and frequency of self-reported serious offending at sweep 4 (the point of intervention) and sweep 5 (one year later). The results of these analyses (summarised in Table 3.6) confirm that the matching

Table 3.6 Inter-group comparison of serious offending at sweeps 4 and 5

	Sweep 4		*Sweep 5*	
	Prevalence (%)	*Frequency (mean)*	*Prevalence (%)*	*Frequency (mean)*
Stage 1: police charge				
Charged group (n = 99)	74.7	8.17	49.0	4.07
Comparison group (n = 237)	71.0	7.89	49.5	4.53
Difference (p-value)	0.552	0.458	0.942	0.774
Stage 2: referral to reporter				
Referred group (n = 130)	69.2	8.03	50.0	4.91
Comparison group (n = 322)	63.6	7.75	47.0	4.51
Difference (p-value)	0.338	0.452	0.625	0.848
Stage 3: brought to a hearing				
Hearing group (n = 59)	67.8	9.63	71.7	6.64
Comparison group (n = 117)	67.8	8.88	52.5	4.51
Difference (p-value)	1.000	0.691	0.037	0.076

Note: Difference in mean volume between groups was calculated using the Wilcoxon Mann-Whitney test of mean ranks.

Analysis was based on imputed offending data and weighted to take account of oversampling within the matched groups.

process was successful in ensuring that there was no significant difference in either prevalence or frequency of serious offending at sweep 4 between any of the intervention and comparison group pairings.

Overall, the figures show a marked reduction in self-reported serious offending between sweeps 4 and 5 amongst all of the groups, regardless of the stage at which they had reached in the system. Nevertheless, comparison between the groups at sweep 5 shows some interesting differences. At the police charge and Reporter referral stages, there was no significant difference in prevalence or frequency of serious offending between the intervention and comparison groups at sweep 5. However, those who were brought to children's hearings at sweep 4 were significantly more likely to report involvement in serious offending one year later than their comparable counterparts. The overall mean frequency of serious offending was also greater amongst the hearings group than the comparison group, although the difference was just outside the bounds of the 95 per cent confidence level.

In order to explore intra-group change in self-reported serious offending between the two time periods, the overall percentage change in offending was calculated and Wilcoxon non-parametric testing was carried out. The results of these analyses are summarised in Table 3.7. The first point to note is that all of the groups had reduced their involvement in serious offending by a sizeable amount, which corresponds with a general pattern of desistance amongst the cohort as a whole (see Smith 2005). Interestingly, the biggest reduction in serious

Table 3.7 Intra-group change in self-reported serious offending between sweeps 4 and 5

	% change in mean frequency of serious offending	*Difference (p-value)*
Stage 1: police charge		
Charged group (n = 99)	–50.2	0.000
Comparison group (n = 237)	–42.6	0.001
Stage 2: referral to reporter		
Referred group (n = 130)	–38.9	0.001
Comparison group (n = 322)	–41.9	0.000
Stage 3: brought to a hearing		
Hearing group (n = 59)	–31.0	0.222
Comparison group (n = 117)	–49.2	0.001

Notes: Change in mean volume within groups was tested using Wilcoxon signed rank test.
Analysis was based on imputed offending data and weighted to take account of over-sampling within the matched groups.

offending amongst the intervention groups is observed at the level of the police charge (50 per cent); while the biggest reduction amongst the comparison groups was at the hearings level (49 per cent).

Most importantly, Table 3.7 reveals that at the police charging and Reporter referral stages, the reduction in serious offending amongst those who received either of these forms of intervention and amongst those who did not is statistically significant. However, amongst those who were brought to a children's hearing on offence grounds and made subject to compulsory measures of care, there was no significant reduction in their self-reported frequency of serious offending. This compares with a much larger and statistically significant drop in serious offending amongst the comparison group. In other words, significant desistance from offending is apparent amongst young people who have either no or minimal system contact. Whereas those who are drawn farthest into the system with the aim of receiving intervention intended to address their behavioural problems are inhibited in this regard.

Although random assignment to groups was not possible within this study, the quasi-experimental nature of the analytical approach and the integrity of the matching process has ruled out the possibility that the poorer outcomes for the intervention group are due to system selection of the most incorrigible or intractable cases. Indeed, phase 1 of the analysis has shown that the most persistent serious offenders are not always referred by the JLO to the Reporter. An alternative explanation for these findings is that children who attend hearings are more likely to disclose their offending than the comparison group, possibly as a direct result of system contact (i.e. that they have nothing to lose by doing so). However, there are several arguments that might be levelled against such a claim.

There is a considerable body of literature that has explored the issue of reliability in relation to self-reports of delinquency by young people, and these have indicated a consistently high level of truthfulness amongst respondents (see Gold 1970; Hindelang *et al* 1981; Huizinga and Elliot 1986; Junger-Tas 1994). Following a comprehensive review, Thornberry and Krohn (2000) conclude that 'self-reported measures of delinquency are as reliable as, if not more reliable than, most social science measures'. Sutterer and Karger (1994) found that willingness to give written consent for examination of official (police and court) files was a positive indicator of the validity of individual self-report data. Coincidentally, at sweep 4 of the Edinburgh Study respondents were asked to sign a permission slip for access to their police records. Comparison of the results reveals no significant difference in consent rates between those who were placed on supervision and their matched comparison group. This further refutes the suggestion that there was any difference in the validity of these individual's self-reported delinquency at this stage. Testing of the Edinburgh Study data on a number of other dimensions supports these findings (McAra and McVie 2010, forthcoming).

Nature of social work contact and services offered

While the children's hearing system is the administrative body that decides whether children should be made subject to compulsory measures of care, it is social workers who are responsible for implementing supervision requirements and securing access to relevant interventions. It is not possible within the remit or scope of this chapter to conduct an in-depth evaluation of the nature and extent of the intervention put in place for each child who attended a hearing. However, data collected from social work files do reveal some interesting details, in particular the relative paucity of regular one-to-one contact with child offenders and that social workers, despite political pressures to the contrary, continue to adhere to a social educational model of intervention when selecting suitable services for young offenders.

Table 3.8 shows that the most common form of disposal for the group who were brought to hearings was a home supervision requirement, which was the case for half of these individuals. Only one in ten was detained in secure care as a result of their referral. Social work contact mainly comprised regular work carried out with the family as a whole (see Table 3.9); by contrast only a quarter of these children received regular individual work. In a further quarter of cases, social work contact was either sporadic or on an emergency basis only.

Most of those brought to hearings were referred to specialist services in addition to receiving general social work. In the majority of cases, some kind of educational service was contacted, such as a referral to an educational welfare officer or psychologist (56 per cent) or the Youth Strategy Group (49 per cent) (a service predominantly aimed at tackling truancy and school exclusion, see McAra 2005b). Importantly, Table 3.9 also reveals that only one in three of these children were in receipt of any offence-focused work.

Table 3.8 Children's hearing disposals for the intervention group (n = 59)

Most serious disposal given in current year	%
Home supervision requirement	51
Placement with family/foster care	15
YPC/CSU	5
Residential school	5
Secure care	10
Voluntary social work measures	14

Table 3.9 Nature of social work contact and services offered for intervention group (n = 59)

Nature of social work contact	%	*Nature of services offered*	%
Child and family work	63	Educational welfare/psychologist or special education	56
Regular individual	25	Youth strategy group	49
Irregular contact	20	Work on offending	36
Monitoring/duty only	7	Psychiatry/mental health services	10
		Befriending	9
		Medical/GP	7
		Other (voluntary sector)	9

Note: Numbers total over 100 as some children had more than one form of social work contact and more than one type of service

Discussion and implications

The overall aim of this chapter was to conduct an exploration of the impact of the Scottish model of youth justice on future offending within the context of ongoing debates about the effectiveness of evidence-based policy. Taken together, our findings indicate that the key to reducing offending may lie in minimal intervention and maximum diversion: that doing less rather than more in individual cases may mitigate against the potential for damage which system contact brings.

Filtering and labelling

The findings have shown a complex filtering process is at work in terms of gate-keeping practices, which means that certain groups of youngsters – who might readily be termed the usual suspects – become the principal focus of agency attention. These youngsters are recycled into the hearing system again and again no matter whether their offending has diminished in seriousness or frequency, or whether their formally assessed levels of need have been addressed.

Such working practices on the part of gate-keepers, place serious limitations on the capacity of the Scottish youth justice system to deliver the current offending reduction programme and achieve set performance indicators. Our findings suggest that targeted early intervention strategies, far from diminishing the number of offence referrals, are likely to widen the net of potential recipients even further. Greater numbers of children will be identified as at risk and any early hearing involvement will result in constant recycling into the system, thereby swelling rather than diminishing the number of youngsters retained in the system until their sixteenth or even eighteenth birthdays.

The dominance of previous police and Reporter contact within gate-keeping practices also means that even if the 'usual suspects' manage to access programmes or services which address offending behaviour, this in itself will not diminish their chances of re-referral into the system. Police and Reporter decision-making thus may be setting up the youth justice system as a whole, as well as the children who come within its purview, to a high risk of 'failure'. As such the findings show how the working cultures of agencies within youth justice can serve to de-rail 'evidence-based' policy (albeit unintentionally), indicating the need for a more careful understanding of the vagaries of the cultural and social environment before transplanting policies from jurisdiction to jurisdiction.

Damaging consequences of agency contact

More significantly, our findings provide some support for the international longitudinal research discussed earlier. In particular, they confirm that repeated and *more intensive* forms of contact with agencies of youth justice may be damaging to young people in the longer term, even within the confines of a predominantly welfare-based system. As we have shown, forms of diversion that serve to caution without recourse to formal intervention, such as police decisions to warn rather than refer to the JLO and Reporter decisions not to hold a hearing, are associated with desistance from serious offending. By contrast, crossing the threshold into the realm of actual intervention through being brought to a hearing and placed on social work supervision, is not linked with a significant decline in serious offending. Such findings are supportive of a maximum diversion approach.

Why intervention may be failing

As noted above, the Bremen/Denver research concluded that certainty of response to offending may be of greater import in tackling offending than the severity or otherwise of sanctioning (Huizinga *et al* 2003). The labelling processes which we have identified as endemic within the Scottish youth justice system, mean that official action taken against youngsters is spurred on by factors for the most part *in addition* to their offending (at the police beat officer and Reporter stages) and sometimes to *the exclusion* of their offending (at the JLO stage).

Importantly, youngsters are powerless to alter the majority of the factors which propel them further and further into the system at the age of 15 (including family structure, social deprivation, gender, and being known to the police and Reporter in earlier years). The only real certainty for such children is that the *master-status* of troubled/troublesome youngster results in amplified levels of intervention. The fact that children cannot readily shrug off ascribed labels may in turn create the self-fulfilling prophecy identified by labelling theorists such as Becker (1963) and Lemert (1964) (a topic which is explored in McAra and McVie 2010, forthcoming).

A second factor, which may be linked to system failure, is the nature and extent of social work supervision on offer. The information available for our intervention group indicates that supervision is often intermittent in nature and geared overwhelmingly towards educational provision, with few youngsters receiving offender-focused work. In addition, social work tends to be directed at the level of the family rather than the individual child, with only a quarter of children meeting their social worker regularly on a one-to-one basis. Of course, even if social work intervention at the individual level was to be improved in terms of resource allocation and targeted provision, the extent to which such services would impact on reducing aggregate rates of offending is questionable. As we have shown, the number of offenders who progress through to the hearing stage of the system is relatively small, and the selection effects inherent in the system determine that it is not always the most persistent or serious offenders who progress to this point.

As was noted, the emphasis on education and family within supervision, indicates that social workers (in spite of political pressures to the contrary) are continuing to work within a predominantly welfarist paradigm (which was the core ethos of youth justice in Scotland until at least the mid-1990s). We would argue that it is not the welfarist paradigm per se that is damaging to young people (nor indeed the nature of social work services on offer), but rather the cumulative effect of systemic contact over many years which, our findings suggest, has the potential to stigmatise and criminalise.

Is doing nothing better than doing something?

Reducing offending is of course only one of a complex set of aims which many western youth justice systems are now required to deliver (with youth justice agencies also contributing to the delivery of community safety and public reassurance strategies). A key challenge for youth justice professionals and politicians is to balance the needs of the offender against the rights of the community and the broader public interest. Arguably, however, policy in many jurisdictions, including Scotland, is increasingly favouring the community and public interest over that of children (McAra 2006; Muncie and Goldson, 2006). Concern for the community and the wider public has manifested itself in 'tough' talk about youth crime. Under these circumstances an evidence-base which suggests that less intervention is rather more effective in reducing offending becomes 'politically' untenable.

The original Kilbrandon vision, underpinning the Scottish system, was one of *active* communities involved in the process of youth justice through the lay panel and *common ownership* of the problems posed by troubled/troublesome children. This vision we would argue should be the starting point for any minimal-interventionist approach. It is a vision which is under threat within Scotland, as political debates about youth crime are increasingly conducted within a lexicon of punishment and exclusion.

Conclusion

Current policy convergence across many Western jurisdictions – and the UK in particular – is characterised by an uneasy mixture of penal rationales. Thus punitive and emotive political discourse about youth crime is overlaid by the neutral and scientific language of new public management, and the apparently rich promise of restoration, reparation and social inclusion.

The findings from the Edinburgh Study add further weight to the international research evidence that youth justice systems may be congenitally unable to deliver the reductions in offending that both current performance indicators demand and so-called evidence based policy suggests are possible. This of course raises broader questions about what the aim of youth justice ought to be.

We have argued that the key to reducing youth offending lies in maximum diversion and minimum intervention. As noted earlier, the Scottish system should be better placed than a number of its counterparts across Western Europe and the US, to deliver such an agenda, principally because its founding principles were explicitly aimed at decriminalisation and destigmatisation. However, these principles have been subverted by the working cultures of agencies within the system (including the police and the Reporter), the fragmented and sometimes chaotic nature of social work services and supervision, and recent political interference. Somewhat ironically the early welfarist underpinnings of the system may have exacerbated this process, given the capacity which welfare-based systems in general have, for lengthy periods of intervention (which in Scotland can be extended from birth to the age of 18, depending on grounds) and the characteristically high levels of discretion which are often afforded to the experts which colonise them.

Accepting that, in some cases, doing less is better than doing more requires both courage and vision on the part of policy makers. A realisation of this vision in turn requires acceptance that youth justice agencies *by themselves* cannot make the wider public feel safer nor can they mend broken families and remake shattered communities. To the extent that systems appear to damage young people and inhibit their capacity to change, then they do not, and never will, deliver justice.

Notes

1 Grateful thanks are due to Rod Morgan and David J. Smith for comments made on an earlier draft of this paper presented at the Nuffield Foundation (May 2006).
2 The Cambridge Study followed 411 boys who grew up in a working class district of London (Farrington 1977).
3 The Edinburgh Study has been funded by grants from the Economic and Social Research Council (R000237157; R000239150), The Scottish Executive and the Nuffield Foundation.
4 In this chapter, we use the term 'youth justice system' to refer to all institutions and procedures for dealing with child offenders under the age of 18. This includes, but is not restricted to, the Scottish children's hearing system, see below.
5 At that time Scotland remained under the tutelage of the UK national Parliament at Westminster; however, it had its own separate education and legal system. Moreover policy was administered through the then Scottish Office which had its headquarters in Edinburgh. These arrangements facilitated a degree of policy divergence between Scotland and England/Wales in matters relating to youth and adult criminal justice (see McAra 2004a, 2005a).
6 Children can be referred from birth until the age of 15 on care and protection grounds and from the age of eight (age of criminal responsibility) until the age of 15 on offence grounds. They can be retained in the system until their eighteenth birthdays through the extension of supervision requirements (see below). Offenders aged 16–17 are generally dealt within the adult criminal courts but can be remitted to the hearing system for advice and disposal (only small numbers are ever remitted, see McAra 1998). It should be noted that the Crown reserves the right to prosecute children aged from eight to 15 in the criminal courts in cases of extreme seriousness, e.g. homicide or rape, and in certain specified motor vehicle offences (see McAra 2004a).
7 Scotland now has its own Parliament and justice and education have become separate departments in the newly formed Scottish Executive. These departments are jointly involved in policy relating to the youth justice system.
8 Indeed, at the launch of the pilot youth courts, Cathy Jamieson (Minister for Justice, at the time of writing) stated that 'punishment is a key part of the youth justice process' (McAra 2006).
9 A range of strategies has been used to achieve a very high response rate amongst the cohort. Children who have difficulty with reading or writing are given an appropriate level of help in completing the questionnaire, or are interviewed where necessary. Children not present at school after several visits are seen elsewhere (normally at home). Missing data were dealt with using a mixture of weighting and multiple imputation. (Further information on the aims and methods of the study can be found in Smith and McVie 2003).
10 Truanting is associated with availability for policing as the findings show that a high proportion of truants spend their time away from school hanging around the streets and other public places (see McAra 2004b).
11 For a detailed explanation of the PSM technique used, please contact the authors of this chapter.

References

Andrews, D. A., Zinger, I., Hoge, R. D., Bonta, J., Gendreau, P. and Cullen, F. T. (1990) 'Does correctional treatment work? A clinically relevant and psychologically informed meta-analysis', *Criminology*, 28: 369–404.

Armstrong, S. and McAra, L. (2006) 'Audience, borders, architecture: the contours of control', in Armstrong, S. and McAra, L. (eds) *Perspectives on punishment: The contours of control*. Oxford: Oxford University Press.

Becker, H. (1963) *Outsiders*. New York, NY: Free Press.

Becker, S. O. and Ichino, A. (2002) 'Estimation of average treatment effects based on propensity scores', *The Stata Journal*, 2(4): 358–77.

Bryson, A., Dorsett, R. and Purdon, S. (2002) 'The use of propensity score matching in the evaluation of labour market policies', Department for Work and Pensions, Working Paper No 4. London: HMSO.

Caliendo, M. and Kopeinig, S. (2005) 'Some practical guidance for the implementation of propensity score matching' (Institute for the Study of Labor, Germany, Discussion Paper No 1588), *Journal of Economic Surveys*, 2008, 22(1): 31–72.

Crawford, A. (2002) 'La Réforme de la Justice des Mineurs en Angleterre et au Pays de Galles', *Deviance et Societe*, 26(3): 387–402.

Cummings, P. and McKnight, B. (2004) 'Analysis of matched cohort data', *The Stata Journal*, 4(3): 274–81.

Dehejia, R. H. and Wahba, S. (1998) 'Propensity score matching methods for non-experimental causal studies', National Bureau of Economic Research, Working paper 6829. Cambridge, MA: National Bureau of Economic Research.

Farrall, S. (2002) *Rethinking what works with offenders: probation, social context and desistance from crime*. Cullompton: Willan Publishing.

Farrington, D. P. (1977) 'The effects of public labelling', *British Journal of Criminology*, 17(2): 112–25.

Farrington, D. P., Osborn, S. G. and West, D. J. (1978) 'The persistence of labelling effects', *British Journal of Criminology*, 18(3): 277–84.

Gaes, G. (1998) 'Correctional Treatment', in Tonry, M. (ed.) *The Handbook of Crime and Punishment*. Oxford: Oxford University Press.

Garland, D. (2001) *The Culture of Control*. Oxford: Oxford University Press.

Garrett, C. J. (1985) 'Effects of residential treatment on adjudicated delinquents: ameta-analysis', *Journal of Research in Crime and Delinquency*, 22: 287–308.

Gatti, U. and Verde, A. (2002) 'Comparative youth justice: an overview of Italy', in Winterdyk, J. (ed.) *Juvenile Justice Systems: International Perspectives*, 2nd edn, Toronto: Canadian Scholars Press.

Gold, M. (1970) *Delinquent behaviour in an American city*. Belmont, CA: Wadsworth.

Hill, M., Walker, M., Moodie, K., Wallace, B., Bannister, J., Khan, F., McIvor, G. and Kendrick, A. (2005) *Fast Track Children's Hearings Pilot: Final Report of the Evaluation of the Pilot*, accessed 23 July 2010, www.scotland.gov.uk/Publications/2005/06/14103237/32402. Edinburgh: Scottish Executive.

Hindelang, M. J., Hirschi, T. and Weis, J. G. (1981) *Measuring delinquency*. Beverley Hills, CA: Sage.

Hope, T. (2004) 'Pretend it works: Evidence and governance in the evaluation of the Reducing Burglary Initiative', *Criminal Justice*, 4: 287–308.

Huizinga, D. and Elliott, D. S. (1986) 'Reassessing the reliability and validity of self-report delinquency measures', *Journal of Quantitative Criminology*, 2(4): 293–327.

Huizinga, D., Schumann, K., Ehret, B. and Elliot, A. (2003) *The effects of juvenile justice processing on subsequent delinquent and criminal behaviour: a cross-national study*, final report to the National Institute of Justice. Washington: National Institute of Justice.

Junger-Tas, J. (1994) 'The International Self-Report Delinquency Study: Some methodological and theoretical issues', in Junger-Tas, J., Terlouw, G. J. and Klein, M. W. (eds) *Delinquent Behaviour among young people in Western World*. Amsterdam: Kugler publications.

Kilbrandon Committee (1964) *Report on children and young persons, Scotland*. Edinburgh: HMSO.

Klein, M. (1986) 'Labelling theory and delinquency policy – an empirical test', *Criminal Justice and Behaviour*, 13: 47–79.

Lemert. E. (1964) 'Social structure, social control and deviation', in Clinard, M. (ed.) *Anomie and deviant behaviour*. New York, NY: Free Press.

Lipsey, M. W. (1992) 'The effect of treatment on juvenile delinquents: results from meta-analysis', in Lösel, F., Bliesener, T. and Bender, D. (eds) *Psychology and Law: International Perspectives*. Berlin: De Gruyter.

McAra, L. (1998) *Social work and criminal justice volume 2: Early arrangements*. Edinburgh: The Stationery Office.

McAra, L, (2002) 'The Scottish juvenile justice system: Policy and practice', in Winterdyk, J. (ed.) *Juvenile Justice Systems: International Perspectives*, 2nd edn, Toronto: Canadian Scholars Press.

McAra, L. (2004a) 'The cultural and institutional dynamics of transformation: Youth justice in Scotland and England and Wales', *Cambrian Law Review*, 35: 23–54.

McAra, L. (2004b) *Truancy, school exclusion and substance misuse*, Edinburgh Study of Youth Transitions and Crime, Research Digest No 4. Edinburgh: Centre for Law and Society, University of Edinburgh.

McAra, L. (2005a) 'Modelling penal transformation', *Punishment and Society*, 7(3): 277–302.

McAra, L. (2005b) *Patterns of referral to the children's hearing system for drug or alcohol misuse*, Edinburgh Study of Youth Transitions and Crime, Research Digest No 6. Edinburgh: Centre for Law and Society, University of Edinburgh.

McAra, L. (2006) 'Welfare in crisis? Youth justice in Scotland', in Muncie, J. and Goldson, B. (eds) *Comparative Youth Justice*. London: Sage.

McAra, L. and McVie, S. (2005) 'The usual suspects? Street-life, young offenders and the police', *Criminal Justice*, 5(1): 5–35.

McAra, L. and McVie, S. (2010, forthcoming) 'The impact of youth justice on patterns of desistance: a dual trajectory approach'.

McGuire, J. (1995) 'Reviewing what works past present and future', in McGuire, J. (ed.) *What works: reducing offending guidelines from research and practice*. Chichester: Wiley.

Muncie, J. (2002) 'Policy transfers and what works: Some reflections on comparative youth justice', *Youth Justice*, 1(3): 27–35.

Muncie, J. and Goldson, B. (2006) *Comparative youth justice*. London: Sage.

Paterson L. (1994) *The autonomy of modern Scotland*. Edinburgh: Edinburgh University Press.

Pitts, J. (2003) 'Changing youth justice', Youth Justice, 3(1): 3–18.

Rosenbaum, P. and Rubin, D. (1983) 'The central role of the propensity score in observational studies for causal effects', *Biometrika*, 70: 41–50.

SCRA, Scottish Children's Reporter Administration (2005) *Annual statistics*. Stirling: Scottish Children's Reporter Administration.

Sherman, L. W., Gottfreson, D. C., Mackenzie, D., Ecj, J., Reuter, P. and Bushway, S. D. (1998) 'Preventing crime: what works, what doesn't, what's promising', Research

Brief, National Institute of Justice. Washington DC: US Department of Justice, Office of Justice Programmes.
Sianesi, B. (2004) 'An evaluation of the active labour market programmes in Sweden', *Review of Economics and Statistics*, 86(1): 133–55.
Smith, D. J. (2005) 'The effectiveness of the juvenile justice system', *Criminal Justice*, 5(2): 181–95.
Smith, D. and McVie, S. (2003) 'Theory and method in the Edinburgh study of youth transitions and crime', *British Journal of Criminology*, 43: 169–95.
Sutterer, P. and Karger, T. (1994) 'Methodological annotations on retrospection in criminological research', in Weitekamp, E. G. M. and Kerner, H. J. (eds) *Cross-national longitudinal research on human development and criminal behavior*, NATO Science Series D: Behavioural and Social Sciences, Vol. 76. Springer.
Thornberry, T. P. and Krohn, M. D. (2000) 'The self-report method for measuring delinquency and crime', *Criminal Justice*, 4: 33–82.
Tracey, P. E. and Kempf-Leonard, K. (1996) *Continuity and discontinuity in criminal careers*. New York, NY: Plenum.
Walgrave, L. (2002) 'Juvenile justice in Belgium', in Winterdyk, J. (ed.) *Juvenile justice systems: International perspectives*, 2nd edn. Toronto: Canadian Scholars Press.
Winterdyk, J. (2002) 'Introduction', in Winterdyk, J. (ed.) *Juvenile justice systems: International perspectives*, 2nd edn. Toronto: Canadian Scholars Press.

Chapter 4

Feminist research, state power and executed women

The case of Louie Calvert

Anette Ballinger

Introduction: condemned women, pardons and life after punishment

Analysis of statistics relating to women who were sentenced to death during the first half of the twentieth century reveals that 91 per cent were reprieved (Royal Commission 1953). Hence, most condemned women eventually experienced some form of life after punishment as free individuals. The vast majority of women who received the death penalty during this period had killed a close family member – most frequently their child or partner.[1] For example, of the 130 women sentenced to death for murder in England and Wales between 1900 and 1950, '102 had killed a child, nearly always their own' (Ballinger 2000: 1). Such crimes are exemplified by the cases of Florence Boxhall (1910), Hannah Wilson (1916), Ada Cook (1918) and Edith Roberts (1921), all of whom were sentenced to death for killing their infant or toddler and subsequently had their sentence commuted to life imprisonment. These women could expect to serve a sentence of between one and seven years, with the vast majority serving approximately three years in prison (National Archives HO144/1749/419784).

For many such women life after punishment meant being released into the custody of a semi-penal institution such as the Friendless and Fallen London Female Preventative & Reformatory Institution (National Archives PCOM8/29) or Women's Training Colony in Newbury (National Archives HO144/4526). Semi-penal institutions were frequently organised as private charities and overseen by wealthy (often female) philanthropists whose aim was to further reform the characters of the ex-prisoners to ensure they would be capable of leading a 'good and useful life' following their eventual release (National Archives HO144/4526; Barton 2005).

A similar form of life after punishment regularly awaited the second largest group of female murderers – those who had killed their partner. Many such cases indicated a relationship between the amount of provocation and/or violence the women had suffered prior to the killing and the prison sentence they were required to serve. Thus, women who had experienced extreme violence and abuse could expect to serve less than 30 months (see for example the cases of Laura

Lynn, Elizabeth Rhodes and Rene Duffy, National Archives HO144/19805; HO144/21405; HO144/21406; ASSI52/662; Ballinger 2007a), after which they could also be released into the care of reformatories (see for example the case of Emma Byron, National Archives HO144/687; Ballinger 2005).

As well as sharing a similar fate after being released from prison, the majority of reprieved women had also experienced similar types of hardship before committing the crime for which they were punished. In the case of mothers killing their children, the most common form of hardship included extreme poverty and abandonment by the father of the child which meant little or no prospect of supporting the child, let alone themselves as single mothers. The personal circumstances of battered women were equally desperate. Living in an era where few women enjoyed economic independence, and the term 'domestic violence' had not yet entered discourse, they faced a reality without formal support systems if they attempted to leave a violent partner. In short, prior to committing their crimes, the majority of reprieved women were united by their lack of alternatives and by insurmountable structural circumstances over which they had no control. Thus, during an era where women lacked formal equality, case-studies relating to reprieved women indicate that such desperate personal circumstances were recognised at an *informal* level by criminal justice staff who, in recommending a reprieve, ensured that these women would indeed be given the opportunity to experience life after punishment (Ballinger 2011).

It was a very different story, however, for the minority of women who were never to experience life after punishment – those who were executed. Many of these women had killed another adult – a crime usually associated with men. Statistically, women who had killed an adult were *less* likely to be reprieved than men (Ballinger 2000: 2), particularly women like Louie Calvert who offered no mitigating circumstances, but instead appeared to possess considerable independence and agency. Before turning to an in-depth analysis of her case and its relevance for thinking about life/death after punishment, it is important to situate it within a broader analytical context. The following section therefore explores this wider context at both an epistemological and theoretical level.

Feminist epistemology and the production of knowledge

> Subjugated knowledges are … blocks of historical knowledge that were present in the functional and systematic ensembles, but which were masked, and the critique was able to reveal their existence by using, obviously enough, the tools of scholarship … [In] both this scholarly knowledge and the disqualified knowledge people have contained the memory of combats, the very memory that had until then been confined to the margins.
>
> (Foucault 2004: 8)

> 'Breaking our silences, telling our tales, is not enough' ... In order to be politically mobilised, this truth must be shared, collectively analysed and strategically deployed in feminist political struggle.
>
> (Rich cited in Sawicki 1991: 106)

The impact that second wave feminism has had on criminology as a discipline and the challenge it has presented to the theory and practice of the legal system has been profound. In particular, this dual impact can be observed where the subject of knowledge production is concerned. Feminists have offered critiques of traditional, biologically determined, 'scientific' explanations of female behaviour in general, and their criminality in particular, by emphasising the socially constructed nature of femininity (Smart 1976; Heidensohn 1986; Allen 1987; Ballinger 2005). More specifically, discourses relating to femininity such as those of motherhood, domesticity, respectability, and sexuality have been exposed as playing a crucial role in defining the 'good' woman – 'someone who by *nature* is maternal, caring, gentle, modest, unselfish and passive' (Ballinger 2007a: 67). Furthermore, this work has demonstrated how traditional phallocentric knowledge about women can have specific, and immensely detrimental consequences for female criminals because they are judged according to double standards, that is, not only according to their crimes, but also according to their feminine conduct and behaviour, particularly in relation to these four discourses. Within this context feminists have identified those women who fail to fulfil gender role expectations and who also break the law as 'doubly deviant' (Smart and Smart 1978: 3; Morris 1987; Naffine 1990; Kennedy 1993; Ballinger 2000):

> ... the same ideological ingredients that slotted women into sexist stereotypes were essentially present in the contemporary studies of female criminality that also fraudulently claimed to be objective and scientific.
>
> (Smart cited in Carrington 2002: 115)

This was a crucial theoretical development because it rejected essentialist-tainted, simplistic comparisons regarding the treatment of male and female criminals by the legal system, and instead shifted the focus of analysis onto the terrain of 'the differential impact of law on distinct categories of women', a strategy which allowed a recognition of other factors such as the specific *type* of woman being judged (Ballinger 2007a: 460). Indeed, as Carlen stated, 'the majority of women ... are sentenced not according to the seriousness of their crime but primarily according to the court's assessment of them as wives, mothers and daughters' (Carlen 1983: 10), with those who are deemed to have failed to live up to acceptable feminine conduct likely to experience 'judicial misogyny' (Carlen 1985: 10).

In turn, these theoretical developments had a profound impact on law's claim to be objective, value-free and politically neutral. Feminists demonstrated that law was based on 'the Enlightenment principles of science, rationality and reason' – themselves constructed around, and reflecting male interests and values, and hence phallocentric in nature (Smart 1989; Ballinger 2007b: 66). Within this phallocentric perspective, the socially situated nature of knowledge claims is ignored 'and the failure of dominant groups … to critically and systematically' interrogate their privileged position, as well as the effect that such a position has on their personal beliefs, ensure that the knowledge generated will always be partial, subjective and open to challenge (Harding cited in Letherby 2003: 45).

These Enlightenment principles and values have also been responsible for creating a hierarchy of knowledge dominated by those 'experts' – 'judges of normality' – who can lay claim to 'truth' as a consequence of having produced 'scientific' and 'objective' knowledge (Foucault 1977: 304). The criminal justice system presents itself and communicates through the very discourses on which legitimacy for the law is founded – neutrality, objectivity, reason and rationality (Lacey *et al* 1990: 152), that holds the promise of a guarantee to a correct interpretation of events, 'or even a direct access to the truth which avoids the problem of human interpretation' (Smart 1989: 11). Moreover, while law is not a science, it is nonetheless able to present itself as if it is, setting 'itself apart from and above other discourses in the same way that science does' (Smart 1995: 73). In short, within Enlightenment discourses, a claim to 'scientificity' is a claim to speak the truth, drawing on this claim therefore further reinforces the credibility of the legal process. However, one of feminism's key achievements has been to expose such claims as social constructions, hence, far from stemming from scientific methods, 'the authority to identify "empirical truths" and to interpret observable, testable "facts" is dependent on existing power relations within given social contexts"' (Faith cited in Ballinger 2003: 219). Furthermore, within the legal system in particular, these claims to 'scientificity' and 'truth' disguise and mystify the subjugation and transformation of the defendant's own account:

> The legal process translates everyday experiences into legal relevances, it excludes a great deal that might be relevant to the parties, and it makes its judgements on the scripted or tailored account … parties are not always silenced, but … how they are allowed to speak, and how their experience is turned into something the law can digest and process, is a demonstration of the power of law to disqualify alternative accounts.
>
> (Smart 1989: 11)

In short, knowledge generated outside scientific discourses such as lived experiences, autobiographies and memories can be silenced, 'subjugated or disqualified' (Smart 1995: 73). In the case of convicted prisoners, such processes are further exacerbated by their construction as 'untruthful and unbelievable' (Pratt and Gilligan 2004: 3). Thus, prisoners' version of 'the truth' is located at the bottom of the hierarchy of knowledge – subjugated, disqualified, or 'muted' altogether (Worrall 1990: 21).

This is not to argue that the knowledge of the powerless and the vulnerable – particularly condemned prisoners – should automatically or necessarily occupy a privileged position, or that they should always be regarded as producers of 'true' and accurate versions of events. Drawing on personal experiences and recollections, they will, by their very nature, offer a subjective account, and motivations for writing or proclaiming specific versions of events must be considered. For example, from the viewpoint of a condemned prisoner, proclaiming one's innocence would appear to be a rational strategy. Nonetheless, with these qualifications in mind, Brown and Clare maintain that such documents and accounts can provide valuable insight as well as a challenge to official discourse (Brown and Clare 2005: 53). Tracing the relationship between criminology and history through prisoners' biographies to the mid-nineteenth century, Brown and Clare discovered a consistency and persistence which they argue, form a counter-discourse to official truth that makes 'an alternative reading of the identity of the prisoner' possible (Brown and Clare 2005: 63, 68). Similarly, Inglis argues that although 'they tend to dramatise or romanticise the past', biographies and autobiographies nonetheless 'have a crucial function in telling different stories, creating different perspectives and rewriting history':

> ... biographies can help link a macro perspective which emphasise the economic, political, social and cultural structure within which individuals live, and personal accounts which reveal the logic of the thinking and practices of people's everyday lives.
>
> (Inglis 2003: 5)

Moreover, it is worth noting, that there are several examples in existence of prisoners' autobiographies being *more* accurate than official state-driven accounts. Recent cases involving miscarriages of justice have demonstrated that a substantial number of convicted prisoners who persistently proclaimed their innocence, were being truthful, they were indeed innocent (see for example Cannings 2006; Batt 2004; Rose *et al* 1997; Conlon 1990).

Thus, given the potential of the legal system to have a serious impact upon defendants – a matter of life and death during an era where the death penalty was implemented – Gilligan argues that for those committed to social justice, it is imperative to deconstruct how truth is 'discovered, socially constructed and disseminated within a context of official discourse' (Gilligan 2004: 21). This point holds special significance for feminists who, as indicated earlier, argue that it is precisely the modernist approach to truth production which creates subjugated knowledge. Thus, while there are 'many competing, complementary or contradictory truths about the same set of social facts as various actors evaluate these facts from perspectives that are premised on their own inherent assumptions or presumptions' (Gilligan 2004: 21), not everyone has equal access to the means of truth production, or indeed *any* access, as the case-study of Louie Calvert below demonstrates. Conversely, Foucault maintains that 'far from preventing knowledge, power produces it' (Foucault 1980: 59); 'consequently institutions and experts who claim to speak the truth should be treated with wariness and critical reflection' (Inglis 2003: 3).

Within this context feminist epistemology – particularly standpoint feminism – has emphasised the importance of retrieving and excavating subjugated knowledge – that is to say – generating knowledge from 'below', the aim being to reconstruct new configurations of 'truth' which allows hitherto silenced groups to speak for themselves, and ultimately, 'leading to the creation of new spaces for subjugated knowledge to flourish' (Ballinger 2010, forthcoming). As Cain notes, the aim here is to 'evade dominant knowledges' and 'generate new knowledge from repressed common senses' (Cain 1990b: 134–35). Thus, the aim is *not* to generate another 'true' story or 'objective' body of knowledge, but to create opposition to, and critique of, *fake* stories through *alternative* knowledge (Letherby 2003: 57; Harding 1996: 298). Referring specifically to the feminist standpoint method of generating knowledge, Cain maintains that:

> There are as many knowledges as there are people. And it is to deal with precisely this point that the standpoint epistemologies have been developed.
> (Cain cited in Comack 1999: 290)

Yet, as already noted, not everyone has equal access to the tools of knowledge production. On the contrary, 'the state symbolically dominates society through maintaining a monopoly over the means of producing the truth' (Inglis 2003: 3). With this in mind standpoint feminist academics can use their relatively privileged position to engage in the political act of making the knowledge of the powerless visible, to 'put the women's words on paper':

> Giving women a voice, therefore, means quite literally sharing authority with them on the written page. This includes making it clear when they are speaking and giving their words space alongside [the author]. In the process, their accounts or stories – and the differences between them – become visible.
> (Comack 1999: 299)

While engagement with this overtly politically committed research strategy offers the promise of giving a voice to one of the most powerless groups within society – condemned prisoners – standpoint feminists emphasise that the final outcome of a given project will always and inevitably be an *interpretation* of the available data, which in turn, will always be open to challenge as further knowledge is excavated. Faith has summed up this key aspect of feminist epistemology:

> We cannot … presume now or into the future to have arrived at a definitive set of knowledges or understandings … But as new materials are produced, ideas can be reconstructed in new configurations of 'truth' which allow for

previously silenced groups to name themselves and to describe their own experiences.

(Faith 1993: 9)

This point has special significance for the data below which has culminated in the Louie Calvert case-study, because it provides both a theoretical and practical example of the process of knowledge production described by Faith. That is to say, during the 1990s when I first researched this case, all available documents *at that time*, were examined in what was then the Public Record Office. Thus, in 1996 I wrote of the Louie Calvert case, that of the 15 women who were executed during the twentieth century in England and Wales, hers was one of the most 'invisible' cases – 'her "muted" condition almost complete' (Ballinger 2000: 131). Less than a decade later, however, hitherto unlisted and unavailable documents were released to the National Archives for public inspection,[2] and it now became apparent that she was in fact the only woman (so far!) out of the 15 executed women, who had left behind her own hand-written autobiography. Hence, from a researcher's viewpoint, she had now moved from being 'muted' and 'invisible' to one of the most vociferous and 'visible' condemned prisoners in the entire study.

This experience thus provides an example of the *process* of knowledge production advocated by feminist epistemologists such as Cain, who has emphasised that this process can never be regarded as complete. Instead, standpoint feminist epistemology recognises that all knowledge produced will be influenced by the 'relational and historical site in the social world' which the researcher occupies – therefore, it will always be a socially constructed product (Cain 1990a: 133). Within this context returning to, and reflecting upon a past research project in the light of new knowledge having been excavated, is not only defensible, it is highly desirable – indeed it may be regarded as a key strength of standpoint feminism which encourages continuous engagement with theoretical reflexivity for the purpose of improving the quality of existing knowledge, or in the words of Faith above, reconstructing 'new configurations of 'truth' (Faith 1993: 9).

In sum, and in sharp contrast to the legal system's claims to truth which is constructed as scientific, 'unconditional and unalterable' with 'facts speak[ing] for themselves' (Inglis 2003: 172), when standpoint feminists draw conclusions from available knowledge, they do not claim to have arrived at an immutable 'truth', nor do they regard such conclusions as closure of the issue since the potential for excavating new knowledge always exists, necessitating further theoretical reflexivity. Instead, such conclusions are 'only the end of one act in a timeless play, with no known finish to it, as the next episode in the interplay of discourse unfolds' (Pratt and Gilligan 2004: 9).

Altogether, the impact of second-wave feminism on both criminology and the theory and practice of law has culminated in a profound challenge to established modernist forms of knowledge production, particularly in relation to the status and legitimacy of the rule of law and scientific or 'expert' knowledge, and thus, also to the status and legitimacy of official discourse itself. In presenting this challenge, feminist epistemology seeks to confront the power inequality between powerful state institutions such as the criminal justice system which is able to disqualify 'minor' knowledge 'in order to promote the centralisation, normalisation and disciplinarisation of dominant knowledges' (Foucault 2004: 288), and those consigned to the outer margins of knowledge production such as condemned prisoners, whose knowledge has been subjugated. The in-depth analysis of Louie Calvert's autobiography which follows is thus motivated by a desire to retrieve subjugated knowledge in order to increase historical knowledge of resistance and struggle (Sawicki 1991: 57). To help achieve this I shall employ Cain's three-stage epistemological strategy which she considers essential for feminist knowledge production. The first stage involves the *de*-construction of state-defined official discourse. This is followed by the *re*-construction of a new, alternative 'truth' from the specific site of standpoint feminism. The final stage involves engaging in 'theoretical reflexivity', a necessary third step before conclusive theorising about the difference between official discourse and the newly generated subjugated knowledge can take place (Cain 1990a: 6). The aim of this three-stage process is to contribute to the development of a new site on which the voices of the powerless – in this case the voice of a condemned prisoner – can be heard. In other words, this analytical process 'allows feminist epistemology to challenge the social construction of state-defined "truth"', and thus confront the power inequality between those in privileged positions who construct official discourse and the powerless at the receiving end of the consequences of such discourse (Ballinger 2003: 220). The remainder of this chapter will demonstrate how these aims can be achieved by applying Cain's three-stage strategy to this case.

The construction of official discourse: the state's story

Louie Calvert was in 1926 found guilty and sentenced to death for the murder of Lily Waterhouse – a woman in whose house she had been living for the previous three weeks.[3] Official discourse produced by different state servants and agencies of the criminal justice system about Louie displayed little ambiguity about the *type* of woman she was. For example, Home Office personnel described her and the circumstances of her crime in these terms:

> The prisoner … has been known as a prostitute of a low type in Leeds for some years. She has also a bad record of theft and housebreaking since she was 15 … She has had two illegitimate children aged 9 & 6.
>
> (National Archives HO144/6012)

> The prisoner was a bad character and, although the woman she murdered was also a prostitute, she seems to have befriended the prisoner, with the result

> that the prisoner robbed her while she was alive and then deliberately murdered her for the sake of obtaining the rest of her small possessions. The murder and removal of the goods were carried out with great deliberation.
>
> (National Archives HO144/6012)

The Chief Constable of Leeds Police Department echoed Home Office personnel:

> She is a known prostitute of a low class. Although she had worked as a weaver, she had been dismissed from both of her most recent jobs owing to her being a very unsatisfactory worker and time keeper … Calvert was not driven to crime through parental neglect. The prisoner is of idle and very dirty habits.
>
> (National Archives HO144/6012)

Furthermore, it was suggested that Louie had killed before:

> The prisoner has quite recently made a statement to a wardress who was sitting with her that about two years ago she caused the death of a man with whom she was living as housekeeper by pushing him down some cellar steps.
>
> (National Archives HO144/6012)

Those in a position to construct the official 'truth' about Louie Calvert therefore firmly identified her as a woman who had failed to conduct herself according to appropriate discourses around femininity, and hence, as falling within the 'doubly deviant' category outlined above. Other institutions with access to knowledge production, such as the media, were equally condemning. The *News of the World*, for example, described her thus:

> When standing her trial …, her shifting black eyes were a psychological study. She seemed callous and indifferent, and her hard, sharp-featured face was the face of a wicked woman
>
> (Anon 1926c)

Indeed, her career as a petty thief and occasional prostitute was confirmed by her 'previous convictions' sheet which indicated that she had accumulated 13 convictions between 1911 and 1925 (National Archives HO144/6012).
Ten days prior to her execution Louie was given an exercise book by prison staff:

> … to amuse herself with, and she was told she could write what she liked, and that it could not be sent out of the prison. On or about 15.6.26 the prisoner told the matron that she had started writing the history of her life.
>
> (National Archives HO144/6012)

She completed her life story on 18 June, and the matron took possession of it before passing it to the prison governor who, after reading it, sent it to the Prison Commissioners with a note which outlined his own interpretation of her account:

> I beg to enclose this history written by the prisoner in question. On p.26 will be seen what is practically a confession of the crime for which she was sentenced. On p.17 is the confession of another murder which has already been reported to the commissioners.
>
> (National Archives HO144/6012)

On receipt of the book the Prison Commissioners agreed with the governor's interpretation of Louie's account:

> The woman has written 'The Story of her life' in prison. In it she confesses to the murder.
>
> (National Archives HO144/6012)

This simplistic portrayal of Louie Calvert as a 'callous', 'wicked woman' and a double murderer quickly acquired the status of official 'truth' and has remained the dominant – possibly the only account – of her personality and crimes for nearly a century. However, through excavating subjugated knowledge in the form of Louie's *Life Story*, written after her conviction, her own account of events regarding her life and her involvement in these two deaths can now be heard and contrasted with the state's version of the 'truth' surrounding the case. The following section therefore employs Cain's first step for generating an 'alternative truth' – the de-construction of official 'truth' – within the context of newly excavated knowledge from 'below'.

The retrieval of subjugated knowledge: Louie's story

One central theme in Louie's *Life Story* which reinforces its authentic nature is her frankness about her past behaviour. There is no idealisation or sanitisation of her past in her autobiography, nor indeed did she proclaim her innocence. She did, however, provide a far more complex account of events which makes the case against her considerably more nuanced and ambiguous than that outlined by Home Office personnel. The credibility of her account is further reinforced by the level of self-reflection which she applied to key aspects of her life. Thus, for example, she appeared to agree with the Home Office opinion stated above, that she 'was not driven to crime through parental neglect' or indeed any other mitigating factors when she wrote:

> I had a very good school mistress and she taught me many things that was beneficial for me and at home I was taught … to say my prayers at

> my Mothers knee... Ours was a good Christian home and father always used to read prayers ... We were sent to Sunday school and had to go to church both morning and night. I was quite happy and contented with my surroundings and Mother never knew a moments worry from any of us.
>
> (Calvert 1926 in National Archives HO144/6012)[4]

She provided a frank account of her criminal past, including her participation in a prison riot:

> ... I went to work in the laundry and ... I hated washing so I was often in trouble and one day I was that fed up with Officer saying do this and do that – I burnt some very delicate work with a red hot iron and of course I was reported well that night me and three of the girls ... had a real smash up and we were all taken down to the punishment cells in the Kneebricks and I was put in the straight jacket for striking an officer ... given three days bread and water and seven days close confinement and lost some of my remission and not allowed to write home for two months ... and while on punishment ... was taken to hospital with pneumonia and of course that learnt me a lesson I never went into punishment again.
>
> (Calvert 1926 in National Archives HO144/6012)

Upon release Louie went into domestic service and for about three weeks 'all went well':

> then the daring spirit was in me and I robbed my employer of £50 and ran away to Blackpool where I had a good time and enjoyed myself for a month on the proceeds when I came back I was sent back to the Borstall to finish my time.
>
> (Calvert 1926 in National Archives HO144/6012)

Although gaining lawful employment upon release, when her prison record was discovered she was dismissed and consequently found it impossible to obtain employment elsewhere as a result of her criminal past. She then 'got into bad company', further criminal activity and imprisonment. One spell in prison turned out to be 'a hard sentence ... because I was confined whilst in doing my sentence of my little girl'. Louie reflected upon her situation:

> You would have thought that this would have made me different – but no – I had got past that, and prison did not bother me ... the love of daring and adventure was in me.
>
> (Calvert 1926 in National Archives HO144/6012)

Upon release Louie left her baby in the care of her mother and displayed a disarming honesty regarding her attitude towards motherhood:

> I used to send Mother £1 every week and clothes but never bothered to go home and see her … once or twice I would write and ask how my baby was going on but that was all I never bothered about her …
>
> (Calvert 1926 in National Archives HO144/6012)

Yet, after an encounter with the Salvation Army she made up her mind 'to be different' and became housekeeper to John Frobisher – the man whose murder she supposedly had confessed to – according to official accounts. Frobisher was a widower who initially was 'very good' to her and her second child, Kenneth, but after 12 months:

> He came home quite drunk and behaving in a disgusting manner and using foul language in front of the baby and when I told him to stop it he struck me when I started fighting back and struck him a foul blow which caused him to fall down the cellar steps and break his neck it was brought in as accidental death …
>
> (Calvert 1926 in National Archives HO144/6012)

While recognising the term 'domestic violence' had not yet entered official or popular discourse in 1926, this is nonetheless a powerful example of an issue which the *defendant* considered relevant to the case compared to the criminal justice workers, every one of whom failed to make a single reference to the wider context within which Frobisher died, but merely interpreted her words as a 'confession'. It is therefore an illustration of Smart's observation above, of the restricted ways in which parties are allowed to speak, and how their experience is turned into something the law can digest and process, thus demonstrating 'the power of law to disqualify alternative accounts'. What is left *unsaid* may be as important as what is *said* – both components play a part in creating subjugated knowledge. In this example, only those parts of Louie's account which were *consistent* with the dominant truth about her as a 'bad person' were selected for comment, thus strengthening the case against her.

Louie's account of the circumstances around the death of Lily Waterhouse was also considerably more complex than a simple confession. Journalistic accounts have consistently described Louie's husband, Arthur, as meek and naïve for putting up with her lies and criminal activities (Huggett and Berry 1956). Her account of life with Arthur illustrates a very different side to his personality. For example, he beat her son Kenneth so badly that he was hospitalised. Hospital staff reported Arthur to the 'cruelty officer'[5] and he was subsequently sentenced to '3 months hard labour'. When he was released he became a nightwatchman for four months – the only time he was in paid employment. Consequently the family lived in extreme poverty:

> I had to go out and get the money by fair means if I could and if not by foul at last I got that fed up with the way we were living and him constantly fighting and drinking that I left home … I got into the company of the young woman with whose death I am charged … we used to go out at night and visit the public houses with the intention of get old [*sic*] of any man who had money and get them drunk then rob them of whatever money they had left and leave them and the last Sunday I was there this woman brought a man home supposed to be a soldier from Becketts Park hospital for wounded soldiers and after he had been there a few days we began to quarrel about him she wanted him and he wanted me but I wanted neither I wanted to leave them and go home again as it was beginning to get a little bit to [*sic*] hot the detectives were on our tracks and we could not go out with them pulling up and getting us fined well on the Wednesday night the day I was going to leave her we went out and had a few drinks with this man and he fetched half a dozen pint bottles of beer and stout home and when we had been home about half an hour we all started to quarrel and it got to fighting oh the drink it is the ruination of everything for we do lots of things in drink and temper that we are most sorry for after well he said something nasty to her and she landed out with her fist at him and they both rolled on the floor when she got up and struck out again I picked up the poker which happened to be the nearest thing to me and my intention was to strike the man and make him leave of hitting her but instead it struck her on the head through him dodgeing [*sic*] out of the road and she fell dead at our feet he went mad then and got hold of her belt strangled her and carried her upstairs I got out and got home God knows how I did it I don't.
>
> (Calvert 1926 in National Archives HO144/6012)

Louie's account of events is noteworthy for its specificity about the man alleged to be present, its frankness regarding the women's criminal intentions and her admittance to accidentally injuring Lily – a very different crime from the premeditated, 'deliberate' and 'cruel' murder described in Home Office communications. Thus, it is hardly a statement which can be described as a 'confession to murder', but as with Louie's account of Frobisher's death, the Home Office interpretation of her account of Lily's death emphasised those parts of her story which were consistent with official discourse and marginalised those parts which provided a wider context for events and which stood as a direct challenge to her conviction and punishment. This point is further reinforced by a third example – the misrepresentation of Louie's words within her petition for a reprieve. She wrote:

> I know that I deserve to die yet why should I have to bear the brunt of the whole crime on my shoulders and the man who is responsible for this and who did the worst be allowed to go free I have not waited five weeks under

> conviction without realising the position I am now in I have prayed earnestly about it and I am truly sorry for the wrong that I have done.
>
> (Calvert 1926 in National Archives HO144/6012)

Expressing guilt or regret at Lily's death is *not* the same as making a confession and her words are entirely consistent with her account of having hit Lily accidentally during the fight described in her *Life Story*. Yet, the Home Office Minutes noted: 'She admits her guilt'[6] (National Archives HO144/6012).

Finally, Carlen's concept of 'judicial misogyny' was activated by presenting a negative interpretation of events in Louie's life not directly relevant to the case, but which nevertheless served to strengthen the image of her as 'a very bad character'. For example, while Home Office personnel claimed Louie had been dismissed from her jobs 'owing to her being a very unsatisfactory worker and time-keeper', Louie wrote that 'I fell out of work through the mill closing down and slack trade' (National Archives HO144/6012). While the exact details surrounding Louie's unemployment is likely to remain a matter for speculation, it is noteworthy that the case took place in the year of the General Strike, a period of severe unemployment and depression. Her explanation is therefore not beyond the bounds of possibility and is not disputed within Home Office documents.

With regard to the Home Office's claim that Louie was the mother of 'two illegitimate children', once again Louie's own account is more complex, stating that at the time of the children's birth she *believed* herself to be married: 'My husband was in the regulars and we lived in the married quarters … till my husband went out to France'.[7] After being home on leave:

> My husband went back this time to India where he met with a fatal accident and died the Friday has [*sic*] my son was born on the Friday following now when my boy was three months old I was sent to prison again for six months and whilst there I found out that I was not married as Jim had already a wife living at the time he had married me it was so hard because he had been so good to me and I could not realise it to be true.
>
> (Calvert 1926 in National Archives HO144/6012)

Home Office personnel did not dispute this part of Louie's story either; however, reducing it to the simplistic statement that she had 'two illegitimate children' during an era where illegitimacy carried severe moral judgement, served to further reinforce the image of Louie being of 'very bad character'. Having thus contributed to the assassination of her character, state servants were able to present personal opinions as if they were facts, for example, by claiming that 'the murder and the removal of goods were carried out with great deliberation'. While it is beyond dispute that Louie stole Lily's belongings after her death, being a thief does not prove she was also a murderer, and in a case relying solely on circumstantial evidence, no such evidence can prove whether the murder was deliberate or accidental, or whether the theft was an act of opportunistic burglary or carried out 'with great deliberation'.

In the following section I explore the plausibility and credibility of Louie's 'alternative truth' about events compared to that of state-defined 'truth'. This will involve employing the second stage of Cain's epistemological strategy for knowledge production by accompanying the de-construction of official discourse with a *re*-construction of the newly excavated knowledge outlined above, generated from the specific site of standpoint feminism.

Re-constructing subjugated knowledge – the creation of an 'alternative truth'

As noted above, despite having been told that whatever 'she wrote could not leave the prison', the matron passed Louie's *Life Story* on to the Governor who passed it on to the Prison Commissioners, who forwarded it to the Home Office where advisers to the Secretary of State now had only five days before the scheduled execution in which to consider its implications. After receiving Louie's *Life Story* the response of Home Office personnel was that 'the prisoner could have told this story in Court but did not give evidence' (National Archives HO144/6012). This statement serves as a powerful example of the false equality imposed upon defendants within the court-room, who statistically – then as now – were more likely to belong to a lower social class than members of the legal profession, yet were (and are) nonetheless credited with possessing equal knowledge of court-room protocol and procedure.[8] Carlen has described 'the judicial rhetoric of an adversary justice where … both prosecution and defence stand as equals before the law' as 'absurd':

> … the ideal of adversary justice is subjugated to an organisational efficiency in whose service body-movement and body-representation are carefully circumscribed and regulated, bewilderment and embarrassment openly fostered and aggravated, uncertainty coolly observed and manipulated.
>
> (Carlen 1976: 20)

Louie's lack of expertise in court-room protocol was exemplified by a much cited incident involving her sudden exchange of 'her hat for a more fashionable and expensive-looking one' whilst sitting in the dock (Ballinger 2000: 138–39; Anon 1926a; Anon 1926b). It may have been due to precisely such behaviour – stemming from the context of her status as an uneducated, petty criminal and penniless prostitute from the lowest social class, that she was advised *against* giving evidence by her counsel. Yet, as with other capital cases during the first half of the twentieth century, the non-appearance of defendants in the witness-box could reflect negatively on them and invariably carried implications of guilt (Ballinger 2000: 266).[9] Meanwhile, Home Office communications contain no critique of the role Louie's counsel would have played in the decision as to whether she should give evidence on her own behalf, or why he did not argue her case more convincingly. Within this context, Inglis has argued that:

> Being able to survive and operate successfully in the legal field depends on a number of factors not least of which are experience, social class background, and access to good advice and legal counsel.
>
> (Inglis 2003: 188)

Yet, as with the interpretation of her *Life Story*, Louie was once again judged outside a wider context, with the comments made regarding her failure to give evidence revealing a taken for granted assumption that she would understand the best way to present herself and her evidence in court, despite her status as a destitute prostitute with little or no knowledge of legal codes. Thus, the vast social and educational gulf, generated by deep-rooted class and gender divisions which existed between judges, barristers, Home Office personnel – and in 1926, also juries – and the defendant, was simply ignored. As noted by Inglis, 'ignorance of the law is no excuse for citizens of the state. But … those who have no familiarity with the law … can be easily manipulated if not made fools of' (Inglis 2003: 188). This is because:

> The law operates within the 'juridical' field with its own language, discourse and practices … The juridical field has its own distinctive habitus – that is, its own preordained, unquestioned ways of thinking and acting which become second nature to regular participants … Success comes from … being able to talk and give evidence using appropriate language and adopting proper postures and attitudes.
>
> (Inglis 2003: 177)

In Louie's case, this wider social and educational context, and the inevitable power relationships involved were rendered 'invisible' – within Home Office communications. Instead, her ignorance became interpreted as a *deliberate* attempt to deceive, once again reinforcing her status as a disreputable person.

With specific reference to Louie's account of a man's presence in Lily's house and his involvement in her murder, another Home Office worker stated that 'this is the first time the prisoner has told this story'. The inaccuracy of this statement is supported by the Home Office documents themselves. For example, one memo stated that the prosecutor, Mr Lowenthal:

> had F. Crabtree ready in C[our]t with all evi[dence] as to his alibi but there was no justification for calling him as there was a mere suggestion that someone other than & stronger than the pr[isoner] might have killed the woman in the kitchen and carried her upstairs. Mr Lowenthal was quite satisfied that the verdict was right.
>
> (National Archives HO144/6012)

It is unsurprising that Mr Lowenthal was satisfied with the verdict as he was the *prosecutor* in the case. More surprising however, is the fact that Mr Lowenthal had this man waiting to be called as a witness in the court, which begs the question why Home Office personnel claimed never to have heard Louie's story before. In fact, the same memo demonstrates knowledge of Fred Crabtree's existence from the very beginning of the investigation:

> The police, when they visited Calvert ... *the day after the murder*, had found in a handbag a paper with the [Canadian] address of a man called Crabtree... and ... careful inquiry was made as regards the movements of a miner named Frederick Crabtree ... This man was in fact an out-patient at Becketts Park Hospital.
>
> (National Archives HO144/6012; emphasis added)

Furthermore, Lily's next-door neighbour, Emily Clayton, testified at Louie's trial that 'the previous Sunday' a man had come to her 'house and asked for Mrs Waterhouse':

> Mr Chapple: Could you describe the man?
> He was tall ... He looked to be well built, and he said he was in Becketts Park Hospital, and he was going back to Canada the same week.
>
> (National Archives HO144/6012, Trial Transcript, p 18)

It would appear that the trial judge, Mr Justice Wright was aware of the potential significance of Emily's testimony for he referred to it in his 'Judge's Notes':

> On the Sunday about 9 a man came to my house and asked for Mrs Waterhouse. He ... said he came from Beketts Park Hospital and was going to Canada the next month.
>
> (National Archives HO144/6012)

The 'Judge's Notes' also referred to Detective Officer Chester's testimony that he had found 'papers with [the Canadian] address of a man called Crabtree' in Louie's handbag when she was first interviewed. Finally, providing indisputable proof that Louie had discussed Fred Crabtree the very first time she was interviewed by police, the judge noted Detective Superintendent Pass's statement, taken the day after Lily's body was found, where he testified:

> She said that Lily was expecting a man named Fred Crabtree to come and stay with her that night. I asked who Crabtree was. She said he was an ex-soldier from Beckett Park Hospital who is going to Canada on Saturday, and that Crabtree had been there last Sunday and stayed all night.
>
> (National Archives HO144/6012)

Indeed, the state's concern about any potential connection between Fred Crabtree and Lily's murder resulted in him being traced and interviewed:

> He appears to have been able, however, to satisfy the Police that he could not be the man who left his address at Mrs Waterhouse's house and who is the man to whom the prisoner now refers in her 'Life Story' … According to the witnesses whose statements were taken he had a complete alibi … The only suspicious circumstance was that on the 1st April he had a slight cut just below his eye, but this was accounted for by … a bat [which] had hit him in the face [at work].
>
> (National Archives HO144/6012)

Nonetheless, despite the considerable amount of evidence indicating a connection between Louie, Lily and Fred Crabtree, the Home Office Permanent Under-Secretary concluded:

> I have today discussed this fully with the Directors + they both agree that prisoner's story of the presence of a man etc now told for the first time is incredible on the evidence + may safely be disregarded.

He further concluded that the details of the Fred Crabtree found in Louie's bag:

> … was *another* patient at the Becketts Park Hospital, and that it seems *probable* he either borrowed Frederick Crabtree's name or that he was of the same name. Fred Crabtree the miner, has a sister in Canada … I do not *believe* the prisoner's story, that a man was present when she struck the deceased woman with the poker, and that he subsequently strangled her and carried her body upstairs.
>
> (National Archives HO144/6012; emphasis added)

Apart from questioning the likelihood of there being two men called Fred Crabtree living within close proximity to each other, who both attended the same hospital, were both ex- or current service-men and both had Canadian connections, it would also seem appropriate to question the Under-Secretary's use of the words 'believe' and 'probable'. In a capital case, it would seem to be of crucial importance to move *beyond* probabilities and beliefs. In this case, it would have meant carrying out a thorough investigation to establish the identity of this man who had been observed by an independent witness going into Lily's house – and whose details were found in Louie's bag upon arrest. However, as Gilligan and Pratt have noted:

> official discourse is … very wide ranging in its scope: it can be designed to bring closure to controversial incidents … and it can seem little more than

> simple documentation of the work … of a particular criminal justice bureaucracy, written by its chief executive. What such discourse does however, is to provide an official, objective truth about crime, criminal justice and punishment which puts a particular stamp on the available beliefs that individuals and social groups have of such matters …
>
> (Gilligan and Pratt 2004: 2)

This process of 'truth-production' engaged in by state servants was facilitated by Louie's failure to conform to discourses of acceptable femininity. As 'a prostitute of a low class', 'bad character' and 'very dirty habits' with 13 previous convictions and two illegitimate children – one of them in care – she had broken every one of the conventions associated with domesticity, motherhood, respectability and sexuality, and as such, became the target of judicial misogyny. As a doubly deviant woman she was precisely the *type* of woman who could easily be discredited as a witness. Thus, her attempt to produce 'truth' – based on lived experience and memories in the form of her *Life Story* – could be relegated to the very bottom of the hierarchy of knowledge. Svensson has noted:

> The usual way of piling up a criminal's life in the court records, as well as in the newspapers, is to refer to his [*sic*] life as if it simply consisted of his [*sic*] crimes. … The person is described as the symbol of evil … criminals are regarded as ruthlessly calculating individuals deliberately committing their crimes. There is no regard for the fact that most crimes are committed by people under the influence of drugs or alcohol, often frightened and under stress, or that these acts are often badly planned or unpremeditated …[by the] socially vulnerable. Since their voice has been taken away from them they cannot really be heard.
>
> (Svensson 1997: 89)

In Louie's case, this dominant portrayal of the defendant was exacerbated by her failure to comply with any of the discourses which contribute towards acceptable femininity. Meanwhile, 'establishment forces' were located at the top of the hierarchy of knowledge – largely as a result of their ability to forge official truth into something which 'simply fit[ted] the authorities' preconceived ideas of what really happened' (Gilligan and Pratt 2004: 5). This is further supported by examples of Home Office communications such as: 'The excuse of the murder I do not believe and the law must take its course', and: 'The prisoner did not give evidence and the circumstantial evidence of her guilt is overwhelming'. Hinting at the doubly deviant nature of Louie's crime, a third state servant responded: 'I agree. It is the sort of crime that men frequently commit but women very rarely' (National Archives HO144/6012).

This completes the *de*-construction of official truth and the *re*-construction of an alternative truth which includes recently excavated subjugated knowledge – that is – Louie's version of the truth. In the final section I employ the third step in the process of excavating subjugated knowledge advocated by Cain – the application of theoretical reflexivity to the first two steps of the excavation process.

Theoretical implications

This chapter has not sought to claim Louie Calvert's innocence. Indeed, as I have indicated, Louie herself did not make such a claim. Nor has it sought to suggest that Fred Crabtree – the miner interviewed in connection with the case – was implicated in Lily Waterhouse's murder. However, within the context of state servants themselves raising the possibility of the existence of another man of the same name – or alternatively – someone who had stolen Crabtree's identity, and, keeping in mind this was a capital case with a life at stake – this chapter has sought to suggest that the failure to carry out a full investigation into the exact identity and involvement of this man, constitutes a severe lack of adherence to the founding principles of the British criminal justice system, principles such as 'due process, the rule of law and presumption of innocence [which] play a crucial role in maintaining the legitimacy of the state and its ability to deliver justice' (Ballinger 2003: 219). Directly linked to this, it has thus also aimed to challenge law's claim to truth, impartiality and objectivity by uncovering the processes involved in creating subjugated knowledge – processes which usually remain invisible, as indeed do the processes involved in the construction of 'truth' through official discourse. These processes nonetheless confirm Foucault's observation cited above that 'far from preventing knowledge, power produces it'. It also confirms Inglis' point that 'institutions ... which claim to speak the truth should be treated with wariness and critical reflection' (Inglis 2003: 3). Only when such processes are challenged – for example by autobiographies, critical scholars or radical organisations – do they become *visible* – only *then* does the possibility arise for the precipitation of a crisis of legitimacy which may lead to the creation of a new terrain on which subjugated knowledge can flourish, and ultimately, to the formation of an 'alternative truth'.

However, the 'battle for the truth' (Foucault 1980: 132) is not fought between equals and the power difference between a condemned prisoner and the entire criminal justice apparatus is emphasised in this case by the state's ability to restore equilibrium after what turned out to be a very temporary crisis of legitimacy – by strengthening its own case through official discourse while simultaneously undermining already subjugated knowledge – to the point where Louie could be annihilated altogether. It was able to do so because 'official discourse is ... the systemisation of modes of argument that proclaim the state's legal and administrative rationality' (Burton and Carlen 1979: 48). Furthermore, Burton and Carlen's observation in relation to state inquiries can be applied to the inquiries carried out by the Home Office after learning about the existence of Louie's *Life Story*:

> The task of inquiries into particular crises is to represent failure as temporary, or no failure at all, and to re-establish the image of administrative and legal

> coherence and rationality. One of the political desiderata of official discourse is therefore to retain the intellectual confidence of parties, elites and functionaries within the state apparatuses. To create a discourse of unity and cohesion between parties ... [thus] demonstrating the state's sovereign reason.
>
> (Burton and Carlen 1979: 48)

The state's success in achieving this goal can be measured by the fact that 'the production of "truth" in official discourse ... [is] something that had come to be largely taken for granted', as indicated by its ability 'to deny or nullify alternative truth accounts' (Pratt and Gilligan 2004: 9). Within the context of this 'unequalled ability to marshal the available judicial resources ... and to use them effectively to win their case' (Inglis 2003: 178), an attempt to launch a battle 'on behalf of the truth' is unlikely to be successful; instead the purpose of excavating subjugated knowledge can be understood 'as a battle about the status of truth and the economic and political role it plays' (Foucault 1980: 132). Foucault argues that the intellectual can challenge 'the ensemble of rules according to which the true and the false are separated [as well as the] specific effects of power attached to the true':

> The essential political problem for the intellectual is not to criticise the ideological contents supposedly linked to science, or to ensure that his own scientific practice is accompanied by a correct ideology, but that of ascertaining the possibility of constituting a new politics of truth. The problem is not changing people's consciousnesses – or what's in their heads – but the political, economic, institutional regime of the production of truth.
>
> (in Gordon 1980: 132, 133)

Foucault's position is relevant to the central epistemological point outlined above, which argued against generating another 'true' story or 'objective' body of knowledge, (since this will inevitably create a new body of subjugated knowledge), but argued *for* a challenge to 'fake' stories. That is to say, feminist epistemology as applied in this chapter, has not attempted to prove that Louie's *Life Story* was more 'true' than the Home Office's version of the 'truth'. Instead, this chapter has provided a systematic challenge to the key 'fake' story that 'truth corresponds with reality and exists independently of people – facts speak for themselves' (Inglis 2003: 172), and that law has access to scientific methods guaranteeing they will be discovered. Far from possessing the scientific means which guarantees the production of an 'objective truth', the chapter has demonstrated the state's involvement in its own brand of knowledge production and truth manipulation – emphasising those aspects of the case which strengthened legitimacy of Louie's execution whilst simultaneously dismissing those aspects which had the potential to render the execution unsafe.

Within a hierarchy of credibility where official discourse crowns the pyramid and prisoners 'have the credibility of elves' (Chevigny cited in Davis 2001: 430), another hierarchy was also evident – that of gender. This gender hierarchy consisted of a 'male judiciary with male definitions and understandings of human behaviour … claimed as universal'; which furthermore, allowed knowledge claims to be made 'without any reliance on supporting evidence, empirical or evidentiary' (O'Donovan 1993: 428). This gender hierarchy was reinforced by Louie's failure to conform to acceptable standards of femininity, for as Smart has noted, 'law is not a free-floating entity, it is grounded in patriarchy, as well as in class and ethnic divisions' (Smart 1989: 86, 88). As such, it has a vested interest in reproducing 'the most secure foundations of patriarchal relations … the family and gender divisions' (Smart 1995: 129). As a prostitute with 13 previous convictions and 'very dirty habits', the mother of illegitimate children, one of them in care, and leaving her husband to spend time drinking with other men, Louie had made very little effort towards contributing to the foundations of hetero-patriarchal family life. Thus, her lack of conformity to appropriate feminine standards stood as direct challenge to the hetero-patriarchal social order as can be observed from the numerous derogatory comments made about her personality, life-style and demeanour, quoted earlier. In that sense, the process whereby state representatives ignored 'the personal … meaning and logic of what happened and instead construct[ed] a logic and understanding of events which [were] supplanted by the force of law' (Inglis 2003: 16), were in essence also the process of constructing masculinist official discourse which ultimately led to the creation of subjugated knowledge with Louie's words being disqualified and eventually silenced altogether.

Conclusion

Brown and Clare observed that 'given the susceptibility of the recording of memory to selectivity and interpretation, relying on prisoner accounts will always be vulnerable to criticism and accusation of bias' (Brown and Clare 2005: 68). In this chapter I have sought to demonstrate that the exact same observation can be made with regard to relying on official discourse. However, as a result of its position at the top of the hierarchy of knowledge, scrutinising its selectivity, interpretation and bias is fraught with difficulties, for 'once state representatives have determined what is "true", limits and controls are set on the production of other alternative, resistant truths' (Inglis 2003: 6). It is within this context that the value of feminist epistemology can be observed, for after having developed the tools for retrieving knowledge from 'below' it has been able to expose official discourse and the legal system – indeed the very foundations of the rule of law – as well as their claim to 'truth' as 'ideological mystifications' and socially constructed products (Box 1983: 13). The fact that the 'symbolic domination of juridical professionals' enables them 'to declare their opinions and theories as if they were facts' (Inglis 2003: 178), and the legal process has named its tools for knowledge production 'due process' and 'rule of law' does not guarantee that conclusions drawn are 'neutral and universally true' (Inglis: 2003: 178).

Instead, they demonstrate that 'truth is linked in a circular relation with systems of power which produce and sustain it, and to effects of power which induces and which extend it'. Hence:

> It is not a matter of emancipating truth from every system of power (which would be a chimera, for truth is already power) but of detaching the power of truth from the forms of hegemony, social, economic and cultural, within which it operates at the present time.
>
> (Foucault in Gordon 1980: 133)

Finally, this chapter began by discussing life after punishment for women who were reprieved from the death penalty. Clearly, executed women like Louie Calvert were not to experience life after their punishment. However, the phrase 'life after punishment' can be interpreted in more symbolic and metaphorical terms. Within the context of Carlen's insistence that 'feminists have a responsibility to use their knowledges to alter, whenever possible, the ... power relations which entrap some women in both victimisation and criminalisation processes (Carlen in Faith 1993: 69), knowledge produced by the methods of standpoint feminism can ensure that hitherto silenced voices are heard again:

> By giving name to lies about women who have been historically denied a forum for speaking in their own voices, we open the doors to the cacophony of dissent and reaction.
>
> (Faith 1993: 9)

In that sense, excavating the traces of lived experience and memories that individuals like Louie Calvert have left behind, ensures that there is indeed some remainder of her life still in existence after her punishment. With this in mind, this chapter has also argued for putting 'women's words on paper' and 'give their words space alongside the author'. It is therefore appropriate to conclude with Louie's words. Before starting to write her *Life Story* she wrote in her exercise book:

> There is so much good in the worst of us,
> There is so much bad in the best of us,
> That it ill becomes any of us,
> To find fault with the rest of us.
>
> (Calvert 1926)

It was not a sentiment she herself was to benefit from, however, by applying the tools of feminist epistemology to her autobiography, it has been possible to bring an end to her muted state and thus make her visible. In that sense, Louie's *Life Story* has played a crucial part, not only in extending 'a historical knowledge of resistance and struggle' (Sawicki 1991: 57), but also in 'the creation of new discourses and hence, new spaces on which state-defined truth and its claim to value-freedom can be challenged' (Ballinger 2003: 238). As such, both Louie and her story are entitled to be heard and furthermore, to be restored to their rightful place in history as testaments to the officially sanctioned violence that lurks behind the claim by state servants that their version of law and order is fair, reasonable and just.

Acknowledgements

Many thanks to Stephen Farrall, Inge Poulsen, David Scott and Joe Sim for their encouragement, support and helpful comments.

Notes

1 A pattern which still holds true today (see for example Brook 2005).
2 The document referred to in this chapter was released under the 75-year rule in 2002. Other authors such as Huggett and Berry who attempted to research this case also experienced difficulties and wrote: 'The case of Louie Calvert presented peculiar difficulties, which at first seemed insurmountable ... we were fortunate to find people who took part in the case and who remembered this ... woman. Without their help it would have been impossible to have obtained so much information about an obscure ... murder (Huggett and Berry 1956: 10).
3 For a detailed account of the Louie Calvert case see Ballinger 2000.
4 All quotes are direct reproductions of words, style, grammar and spelling as they appear in National Archives HO144/6012.
5 An early twentieth-century term roughly equivalent to the modern title of 'child protection officer'.
6 There are many other examples of condemned female prisoners expressing guilt or regret over the murder victim whose words were misrepresented as a confession by the Home Office. See for example the case of Louise Masset in Ballinger (2000).
7 Louie's husband was a soldier and was posted to France during the First World War.
8 It can also be seen as an example of an unintended consequence of the Criminal Evidence Act 1898 which in theory should be welcomed, yet, in practice created a new set of value-judgements with regard to prisoners who did not give evidence on their own behalf, who were now frequently regarded with suspicion and more likely to be guilty (see for example Ballinger 2000: 266).
9 In his summing-up the judge observed: 'Of course it has not escaped your attention that the prisoner has not thought fit to give evidence. Well of course she is entitled to take that course. She need not give evidence if she does not want to do it, the learned counsel has said there were reasons of health or nerves which induced her or her advisers to come to the decision that she should not give evidence; ... but when you have a difficult incident like that to explain, it certainly would have been – if there is an explanation – a very desirable thing that in a case of this sort, a case of this importance, especially to a prisoner, that she should place herself in a position in order to give her explanation. You will bear the fact in mind that you are left with this incident ... and from the point of view of the prisoner, you have no explanation' (National Archives HO144/6012, Trial Transcript, p 83). This statement suggests that a less favourable view was taken of prisoners who declined to give evidence on their own behalf.

References

Allen, H. (1987) *Justice Unbalanced*. Milton Keynes: Open University Press.

Anon (1926a) 'Woman Changes Hat in the Dock', *Evening News*, 14 April 1926.

Anon (1926b) 'Boots of the Dead', *News of the World*, 18 April 1926.

Anon (1926c) 'Murdress's Goodbye', *News of the World*, 27 June 1926.

Ballinger, A. (2000) *Dead Woman Walking: Executed Women in England & Wales 1900–1955*. Dartmouth: Ashgate.

Ballinger, A. (2003) 'Researching and Redefining State Crime: Feminism and the Capital Punishment of Women', in Tombs, S. and Whyte, D. (eds) *Unmasking the Crimes of the Powerful*. New York, NY: Peter Lang.

Ballinger, A. (2005) 'Reasonable Women Who Kill: Re-interpreting and Re-defining Women's Response to Domestic Violence in England and Wales 1900–1965', *Outlines: Critical Social Studies*, 7(2): 65–82.

Ballinger, A. (2007a) 'Masculinity in the Dock: Legal Responses to Male Violence and Female Retaliation in England and Wales 1900–1965', *Social & Legal Studies*, 16(4): 459–81.

Ballinger, A. (2007b) 'The 'worse' of two evils? Double murder trials and gender in England and Wales 1900–53', in Barton, A., Corteen, K., Scott, D. and Whyte, D. (eds) *Expanding the Criminological Imagination: Critical readings in criminology*. Cullompton: Willan Publishing.

Ballinger, A. (2011) *Capitalising on Punishment: Gender, Truth and State Power*. Aldershot: Ashgate.

Barton, A. (2005) *Fragile Moralities and Dangerous Sexualities: Two Centuries of Semi-Penal Institutionalisation for Women*. Aldershot: Ashgate.

Batt, J. (2004) *Stolen Innocence: The Story of Sally Clark*. London: Ebury Press.

Box, S. (1983) *Power, Crime and Mystification*. London: Tavistock.

Brook, F. (2005) *Understanding Homicide*. London: Sage.

Brown, A. and Clare, E. (2005) 'A History of Experience: Exploring Prisoners' Accounts of Incarceration', in Emsley, C. (ed.) *The Persistent Prison: Problems, Images and Alternatives*. London: Frances Boutle.

Burton, F. and Carlen, P. (1979) *Official Discourse: On discourse, analysis, government publications, ideology and the state*. London: Routledge & Kegan Paul.

Cain, M. (1990a) 'Towards Transgression: New Directions in Feminist Criminology', *International Journal of the Sociology of Law*, 18: 1–18.

Cain, M. (1990b) 'Realist Philosophy and Standpoint Epistemologies or Feminisit Criminology as a Succesor Science', in Gelsthorpe, L. and Morris, A. (eds) *Feminist Perspectives in Criminology*. Milton Keynes: Open University Press.

Calvert, L. (1926) *My Life Story*, in National Archives Document HO144/6012.

Cannings, A. (2006) *Against All Odds: A Mother's Fight to Prove her Innocence*. London: Time Warner Books.

Carlen, P. (1976) *Magistrates' Justice*. London: Martin Robertson.

Carlen, P. (1983) *Women's Imprisonment*. London: Routledge & Kegan Paul.

Carlen, P. (ed.) (1985) *Criminal Women*. Cambridge: Polity Press.

Carrington, K. (2002) 'Feminism and critical criminology: confronting genealogies', in Carrington, K. and Hogg, R. (eds) *Critical Criminology*. Cullompton: Willan Publishing.

Conlon, G. (1990) *Proved Innocent*. London: Hamish Hamilton.
Comack, E. (1999) 'Producing feminist knowledge: Lessons from women in trouble', *Theoretical Criminology*, 3(3) August: 287–306.
Davis, A. (2001) 'Writing on the Wall: Prisoners on Punishment', Punishment and Society, 3(3) July: 427–31.
Faith, K. (1993) *Unruly Women*. Vancouver: Press Gang Publishers.
Foucault, M. (1977) *Discipline and Punish*. London: Penguin Books.
Foucault, M. (1980) 'Truth and Power', in Gordon, C. (ed.) *Power/Knowledge Selected Interviews and Other Writings 1972–1977*. London: Harvester Wheatsheaf.
Foucault, M. (2004) 'Society Must Be Defended', in Bertani, B. and Fontana, A. (eds) *Michel Foucault*. London: Penguin Books.
Gilligan, G. (2004) 'Official inquiry, truth and criminal justice', in Gilligan, G. and Pratt, J. (eds) *Crime, Truth and Justice: Official Inquiry, Discourse, Knowledge*. Cullompton: Willan Publishing.
Gilligan, G. and Pratt, J. (eds) (2004) *Crime, Truth and Justice: Official Inquiry, Discourse, Knowledge*. Cullompton: Willan Publishing.
Gordon, C. (ed.) (1980) *Power/Knowledge Selected Interviews and Other Writings 1972–1977*. London: Harvester Wheatsheaf.
Harding, S. (1996) 'Feminism, Science and the Anti-Enlightenment Critiques', in Garry, A. and Pearsall, M. (eds) *Women, Knowledge and Reality*. London: Routledge.
Heidensohn, F. (1986) *Women & Crime*. Basingstoke: MacMillan.
Huggett, R. and Berry, P. (1956) *Daughters of Cain*. London: Allen & Unwin Ltd.
Inglis, T. (2003) *Truth, Power and Lies*. Dublin: University College Dublin Press.
Kennedy, H. (1993) *Eve Was Framed: Women and British Justice*. London: Vintage.
Lacey, N., Wells, C. and Meure, D. (1990) *Reconstructing Criminal Law*. London: Weidenfeld Paperbacks.
Letherby, G. (2003) *Feminist Research in Theory and Practice*. Open University Press: Buckingham.
Morris, A. (1987) *Women, Crime and Criminal Justice*. Oxford: Basil Blackwell.
Naffine, N. (1990) *Law & the Sexes*. London: Allen & Unwin.
National Archives DocumentsNational Archives Documents, HO144/6012; HO144/1749/419784; HO144/4526; HO144/19805; HO144/21405; HO144/21406; HO144/687; ASSI152/662; PCOM8/29.
O'Donovan, K. (1993) 'Law's Knowledge: The Judge, The Expert, The Battered Woman and Her Syndrome', *Journal of Law and Society*, 20(4), Winter: 427–37.
Pratt, J. and Gilligan, G. (2004) 'Introduction: crime, truth and justice – official inquiry and the production of knowledge', in Gilligan, G. and Pratt, J. (eds) *Crime, Truth and Justice: Official Inquiry, Discourse, Knowledge*. Cullompton: Willan Publishing.
Rose, J., Panter, S. and Wilkinson, T. (1997) *Innocents*. London: Fourth Estate.
Royal Commission (1953) *Royal Commission on Capital Punishment 1949–1953 Report*. London: HMSO.
Sawicki, J. (1991) *Disciplining Foucault*. London: Routledge.
Smart, C. (1976) *Women, Crime and Criminology*. London: Routledge & Kegan Paul.
Smart, C. (1989) *Feminism and the Power of Law*. London: Routledge.
Smart, C. (1995) *Law, Crime and Sexuality*. London: Sage.

Smart, C. and Smart, B. (eds) (1978) *Women, Sexuality and Social Control*. London: Routledge & Kegan Paul.

Svensson, B. (1997) 'The Power of Biography: Criminal Policy, Prison Life, and the Formation of Criminal Identities in the Swedish Welfare State', in Reed-Danahay, D. (ed) *Auto/Ethnography*. Oxford: Berg.

Worrall, A. (1990) *Offending Women*. London: Routledge.

Chapter 5

Paths of exclusion, inclusion and desistance

Understanding marginalised young people's criminal careers

Robert MacDonald, Colin Webster, Tracy Shildrick and Mark Simpson

Introduction

In this chapter we draw upon a range of qualitative studies of youth transitions in contexts of social exclusion and multiple deprivation in order, first, to see what they tell us about criminal careers amongst young men in these contexts and, second, to reflect critically upon and add to contemporary criminological theory about criminal careers, particularly in respect of desistance.

The chapter is organised as follows. Four research projects ('the Teesside studies') are described in terms of their aims, design and methods and their main, thematic findings, beyond issues of criminal career, are noted. Following this, our main findings about the formation of more serious criminal careers are sketched out. Attention then turns to processes of desistance as reported by these studies. Moving away from empirical description, and before concluding, the chapter then reflects on findings of the Teesside studies vis-à-vis key questions that we see as pertinent in contemporary theory in this field, namely questions of history, biographical context, contingency and generations.

The Teesside studies of youth transitions and social exclusion

We refer here to four, related studies (see Table 5.1).

The first two of these, *Snakes and Ladders* (Johnston *et al* 2000) and *Disconnected Youth?* (MacDonald and Marsh 2005), both explored how working-class young people (aged 15–25 years) made transitions to adulthood in contexts of multiple deprivation, with critical investigation of theories of the underclass and concepts of social exclusion as prime foci.[1] These projects were undertaken in the poorest wards of one of the poorest towns of England: perfect territory in which to grapple empirically and theoretically with popular concepts and theories of youth exclusion and marginalisation. At the time of fieldwork in the late 1990s and early 2000s, the seven wards that comprised our research sites all featured in the top 5 per cent most deprived nationally (DETR 2000) and two of them ('Orchard Bank' and 'Primrose Vale') were in the worst

Table 5.1 The Teesside studies of youth transitions and social exclusion: research design

Study 1 (Snakes & Ladders, Johnston et al 2000)
- Funded by Joseph Rowntree Foundation.
- Fieldwork in 1998–99, in one very deprived ward in Teesside.
- Twenty interviews with professional 'stakeholders'.
- Some limited observational work in the research site.
- Ninety-eight one-off, qualitative interviews with young adults, aged 15–25 years.

Study 2 (Disconnected Youth?, MacDonald and Marsh 2005)
- Funded by Economic and Social Research Council.
- Fieldwork in 1999–2001, in five, neighbouring, very deprived wards in Teesside.
- Thirty interviews with professional 'stakeholders'.
- Participation/observation with young people in three sites over a year.
- Eighty-eight qualitative interviews (some repeated) with young adults, aged 15–25.

Study 3 (Poor Transitions, Webster et al 2004)
- Funded by Joseph Rowntree Foundation.
- Fieldwork in 2003.
- Thirty-four qualitative interviews with young adults, aged 23–29, drawn from the samples of studies 1 and 2, exploring three sub-themes:
  - young parenthood (n = 11);
  - persistent 'poor work' (n = 11);
  - long-term criminal and drug using careers (n = 12).

Study 4 (Evaluation of Hartlepool Dordrecht Initiative, Simpson et al 2006)
- Funded by Hartlepool Dordrecht Initiative – a multi-agency, broad-based crime reduction partnership.
- Fieldwork 2002–05.
- Thirty qualitative interviews with 'clients' of the initiative, aged 18–30 years.
- Fifteen interviews with professional staff involved with the initiative.
- Key focus on evaluating the project and determining if/how/why 'it works' in terms of desistance from crime.

five – of 8,414 – in England. As is common in qualitative research, we use pseudonyms for research participants and particular neighbourhoods.

Both studies used 'participation/observation' (e.g. regular, repeated visits to particular sites to be in the company of groups of young people) and, in total, interviews with approximately 50 professionals who worked with young people (such as drugs advisors, youth workers, employment advisors). At their core, though, these studies relied on lengthy, tape-recorded, biographical interviews (Chamberlayne *et al* 2002) with 186 young people (82 females and 104 males) from the predominantly white, (ex)manual working-class population resident in 'one of the most de-industrialised locales in the UK' (Byrne 1999: 93).[2]

For the first two studies, sample recruitment was a mixture of purposive, theoretical and convenience sampling. The starting point was to recruit individuals of the right age (15–25 years) from these places. It was imperative to focus on aspects of young people's experiences that would help test the claims of underclass theory and understand better the (at that time) novel concept of social exclusion as well as being relatively open in terms of sample recruitment. Thus, we sought out individuals who were single parents, who had plentiful experience of unemployment and who had significant histories of offending (the core domains of underclass theory) but we also sought out people who were not parents, who were employed (or training/studying) and who were not known to us as offenders. Agencies and organisations were helpful in introducing us to potential interviewees (e.g. training schemes, further education colleges, New Deal for Young People programmes, drugs advice services, the Probation Service, local Young Offenders Institutes, community groups). From early interviewees we would seek suggestions for others (in a 'snowballing' method). These two strategies generated the bulk of interviewees.

Because of our recruitment methods we cannot claim that this combined sample of 186 people from the *Snakes and Ladders* and *Disconnected Youth?* studies is statistically representative of young adults in these neighbourhoods. We therefore do not seek to *quantify* aspects of youth experience (e.g. *how many* local young people were involved in offending). Because of our efforts to sample different experiences of youth transition, our varied points of contact and the relatively large size of the sample (for qualitative research), we do believe, however, that we achieved a sample that was representative of the range of transitions typical of young adults in these neighbourhoods.

The third study was *Poor Transitions* (Webster *et al* 2004). It was designed as a follow-up to the two, earlier ones. The key research question was where earlier youth transitions *led* individuals in their mid to late twenties. Fieldwork was undertaken in 2003, between two and four years after our first interviews. We re-interviewed 34 people (18 females and 16 males), now aged 23–29 years, from the two original samples. We sampled theoretically so as to understand key experiences in longer-term transitions, including the subsequent transitions of those with extensive criminal/drug-using careers as revealed in our first studies (see Table 5.1).

Again, no claim can be made that these 34 individuals are strictly representative of the larger samples of the first studies. Our knowledge of the research site and of *potential* re-interviewees makes us think that those we did speak to were broadly representative of the initial, larger samples (see Webster *et al* 2004).

Longitudinal qualitative youth research, as comprised in these first three Teesside studies, is relatively rare in British social science (see Henderson *et al* 2007, for a very good example) and very valuable for unravelling questions of criminal career.[3] The sort of (working-class) 'socially excluded' young adults we talked to are often described as 'hard to reach' in (middle-class) research and policy circles (Merton 1998). In fact, there was nothing *particularly* difficult about finding suitable participants and undertaking interviews with them (see MacDonald 2010). Our interviewees were very generous in the time they gave and the candour they expressed, providing the core of the empirical material of the studies.

Analysing youth transitions

Theoretically, we were interested in understanding youth transitions as the outcome of individual agency (e.g. choices made by people), local subcultural values and practices (e.g. how the perception of these choices was influenced by gender and class traditions) and social structural constraints (e.g. the range and nature of the structure of opportunities for working-class young adults, against which choices could be made). Our research focused on what Coles (1995) identifies as the key three strands of youth transitions, i.e. 'school to work careers' (e.g. the movement of young people through education, jobs, training, unemployment), 'family careers' (e.g. forming partnerships, becoming a parent) and 'housing careers' (e.g. leaving home, independent living). In addition, the research incorporated investigation of 'leisure careers' (e.g. changing patterns of peer associations and leisure activity), 'drug-using career' (e.g. engagement or non-engagement with different forms of drug use) and, the main subject of this chapter, 'criminal careers'.

We researched and analysed these six aspects of youth transition in the lives of the 186 young people in our first two studies. Standard, cross-sectional, comparative analysis of all cases (e.g. by common qualitative themes) was supplemented by longitudinal analysis of the biographies of these individuals.

Key, general findings

Given the mass of research data gathered and the sheer range of the topics of the research, space precludes anything but the briefest discussion of one or two *general* findings about the nature of youth transitions as revealed by these projects (i.e. beyond what they might say about criminal careers, to which we turn soon). In short, we come out strongly against the assertions of underclass theory – and many versions of theories of social exclusion. Despite the heavy burden of social and economic pressures bearing down on these lives, virtually all clung tight to traditional working-class values, practices and goals (in respect of employment and family and community life). Unemployment was a common, recurrent experience but so was employment. 'Economic marginality', rather than exclusion, characterised their churning, non-progressive movement around low-level jobs, training places and time on 'the dole'. Strong similarities in 'school to work careers', therefore, denied the possibility of more subtle typologies: economic marginality was the preserve of virtually all, with only a handful finding more secure, rewarding labour market transitions. Explanations of the relative success of the latter largely rested on contingency – such as finding themselves by chance in a job with a 'good employer' – rather than individual characteristics, such as agency.

Whilst economic marginality was the dominant, overall, shaping determinant of the lives of these samples, at the individual level, contingency, flux, indeterminacy and the power of unpredictable 'critical moments' reigned (see Thomson *et al* 2002). In general terms, the social characteristics – and 'risk factors' – that individuals carried (e.g. whether they were male or female, from step-parent or 'intact' family backgrounds, possessed some low level educational qualifications or had none, had completed government training programmes or had not) were of little use in predicting next biographical steps and the particularities of personal experiences at the level of individual lives (MacDonald 2006; Webster *et al* 2006). Overall, we conclude, therefore, that for these individuals in these locales at this time, broad sweep socio-economic processes of de-industrialisation, the economic dispossession of the traditional working-class, the dismantling of previously effective routes to working-class adulthood, the new vagaries of 'getting by' in the lack of these and the concentration of the hardships of poverty onto these lives did more to explain their biographical twists, turns and outcomes than did individual level factors, such as the particular choices of the people we interviewed.

To conclude this section, we make reference to a fourth study, which stands outside the thrust of the Teesside studies as usually described. This was an evaluation study, commissioned by the Hartlepool Dordrecht Crime Reduction Initiative (hereafter referred to as the Dordrecht Project). The approach was pioneered in the Dutch city of Dordrecht and Hartlepool was the second town in the UK to replicate it. In essence, its partnership (police and probation services led) drew in a wide range of support to aid offenders to desist from crime (health and mental health services, drug treatment, help with accommodation, training and employment, access to leisure options, etc). 'Persistent burglars' then other persistent criminals were offered these 'carrots' (participation was 'voluntary' for those otherwise facing a custodial sentence) which were backed up with the 'sticks' of intensive supervision and the threat of 'return' to prison/young offender institutes for breaches of conditions. Various statistical measures and qualitative approaches were used to assess the success or otherwise of the Dordrecht project. Our findings in relation to how and why the project seemed to 'work' for some, but not others, are relevant to the discussion of desistance that we come to later in the chapter.

The onset and establishment of criminal careers: Teesside findings in brief

Whilst it is important to re-iterate that these were not statistically representative samples, analysis of the biographical accounts of interviewees can help us sketch out the *nature* and *shape* of typical criminal careers. The numbers we cite are for qualitative not quantitative argument. One hundred and sixty-eight of the 186 interviewees across the *Snakes and Ladders* and *Disconnected Youth?* studies gave accounts of crime that were deemed detailed enough to use. One hundred of these reported no offending whatsoever and 21 described 'one-off' or very short-lived offending. Forty-seven reported recurrent offending, all of whom had convictions and 33 of who had been imprisoned. Twenty-six of these 47 were or had been opiate users. Only three of these 47 cases were young women. Compared with young men, the young women in the studies told a different story of their criminal and drug-using involvement; of abusive relationships with male partners and family members, of sexual exploitation and street prostitution entwined with 'heavy end' heroin use (see MacDonald and Marsh 2005). It is the 44 young men that are the focus of the chapter. Although each case differed there were enough of them and enough shared between them to allow valid, theoretical descriptions of criminal careers amongst young men like this, in this place, at this time.

As noted, 21 interviewees had a very short-lived 'criminal career', with typically one or two offences of shop-lifting or criminal damage in their early to mid-teenage years. For many, their transgressions ceased there. Two key movements can be identified in the consolidation of the most serious, longer-term criminal careers of 44 young men.

Street corner society and leisure time crime

The first of these was the hardening up of disappointing or disaffecting school experiences (common experience of the samples overall) into full-blown educational disengagement (see MacLeod 2004). This was usually displayed in frequent, persistent truancy. A process of simultaneous disengagement from school and engagement with 'street corner society' (MacDonald and Shildrick 2007) further established oppositional identities, reinforced sub-cultural commitment to friends and was the cornerstone for the evolution of most careers of crime that extended beyond early to mid-teenage: 'just me and this other lad used to nick off all the time… //… Just go and hang about the town… that was me starting days of crime and that, yeah. Shoplifting and pinching bikes, that's what it was' (Danny, 21, YOI inmate). Dull truant time spent 'doing nothing' (Corrigan 1976) was enlivened by the camaraderie of shoplifting jaunts, other petty thieving and speeding around the estates in stolen vehicles: crime as leisure for bored, out-of-school teenagers (see Stephen and Squires 2003).

The thieving of saleable items from garden sheds, garages and cars was the next most common offence of those listed by the sample and also appeared to be the offence to which (some) shop-lifters graduated in their criminal careers. Still of school age and still filling truant time, these were as much leisure-time crimes as anything else. Although Richy (age 17) said that he had often 'mooched [stolen from garden] sheds', he did not consider himself 'a bad lad, a real thief'. At this stage, crime provided exciting, thrill-driven moments in otherwise dull days: 'when you pinch summat, like a barbecue set you can sell on for £10, you can buy yourselves a few bottles of cider, can't you? You can cure your boredom then' (Richy). Reference to 'the buzz' was very frequent in attempts to explain earlier criminality and drug use and given as the sole motivation behind the instances of vehicle theft reported to us. Asked about this, Gazz (20, YOI inmate) commented:

> No, not bad crimes, not bad stuff. Just jumping in cars which were nicked. Not nicking them. Just jumping in with the lads for a spin round. Looking back, I can't see why I did it. Daft stuff. Just the buzz. Like these two bottles of pop I nicked – and a can of after-shave – that's my two shoplifting ones. I didn't really need them. I just did it. For the buzz I suppose.

For *some*, this period marked the early phases of criminal apprenticeships. They began to learn the routines of more acquisitively-oriented offending (e.g. how and what to thieve from cars) and were drawn into local criminal markets (e.g. the best shops and pubs for fencing stolen property, the market rate for 'knock-off gear', etc). For *many*, though, these sorts of infringements – coupled with underage drinking and recreational use of drugs such as cannabis, amphetamines and ecstasy – marked the extent, and end-point, of criminal careers. Because offending of this sort at this stage was not (perceived as) 'serious', 'bad' or 'real' crime (but as expressive leisure activity that passed time in structure-less days of truancy) – and because, therefore, it did not bring down serious criminal justice intervention – it was not determining of self-identities and next steps. Indeed, a few drifted back into attending school more frequently, describing the greater boredom of truant days in comparison. And after 16 there was nothing to truant from. For most, therefore, 'street corner society' and the occasional wrong-doing associated with it gave way to the post-16 education and labour market destinations that were normal for our samples: some re-engagement in training schemes and college courses, low level employment and episodic unemployment. In terms of leisure, for the majority the street was replaced by the pubs and clubs typical of working-class adult leisure. Thus, the relatively large numbers involved in (petty) offending in early teenage lessened as the years passed.

The entwining of criminal careers with dependent drug careers

The second, most significant moment – that helped to drag out a smaller number of individual's criminal career into later years and to transmute them into something more destructive – is when heroin enters the scene. Parker and colleagues (1998) map the 'second wave of heroin outbreaks' in Britain during the mid-1990s. Teesside provides a classic case. Local police and drugs workers reported how very cheap, smokable heroin flooded into its working-class housing estates in the mid-1990s, prior to which the area had had a negligible heroin using population:

> Heroin came in in about '95, didn't it? I didn't even *know* it was heroin. It was just brown powder on a bit of foil. Like tack [cannabis].

> No one was bang on to it then. Didn't know it was heroin or what the risks were.
>
> (Richard, 20)[4]

MacDonald and Marsh (2002) describe how some of Teesside's young people seemed unprepared to resist the temptations of this 'poverty drug' (that eased feelings of guilt, shame and exclusion) and made speedy transitions from occasional, recreational use of drugs such as cannabis and amphetamines to often daily, dependent use of heroin (and later in the 1990s, crack cocaine).[5] Richard (20) described how he and his friends made the shift from cannabis to heroin use:

> We'd all been smoking tack for ages. Ever since we were 14 or 15. We'd smoke it all day and it'd get to the point where it had no effect. It wasn't getting us stoned... [so]... me and my friends thought we'd have a daft go at it [heroin] and before we knew it a few of us were [cold] turkeying and then we all were. Hooked. It's dead hard to come off... they say 'once a smackhead, always a smackhead'. Maybe they're right.

For this minority (n = 23), dependent use of heroin was the driving force behind exclusionary transitions which distanced them from their families, their previous life-styles, from the labour market, entangling them in chaotic, damaging careers of drug-driven crime (see Simpson 2003). Persistent engagement in heroin use and crime both strengthened, and was strengthened by, the camaraderie, sub-cultural allegiance and particular form of social capital shared with friends on the same track. As years passed, the social networks of these young men became *increasingly* narrow, uniform, and local. People associated with others like them; partly by choice and partly because their drug and crime lifestyles carried much stigma locally. Inclusion in these peer groups was met with exclusion by others. Thus, allegiances and associations reinforced transition pathways, narrative possibilities and social identities, progressively closing down limited legitimate social and economic opportunities and non-criminal identities.[6]

Heroin use became central to an understanding of their unfolding biographies:

> That's the way it goes. Start off smoking a bit of ganga, breaking into cars and pinching car radios and then you end up on heroin and that and it fucks you up.
>
> (Jason, 21)

> Prior to 16 I'd had a few cautions. It just got worse as I was getting older. I went from E to heroin. Doing it daily to feed my habit so I was robbing everything in sight. Whatever I could sell, I'd rob. It did for me, heroin. Shoplifting, thefts, then burglary and robbery.
>
> (Barney, 20)

For individuals like Richard, increasingly desperate acquisitive criminality was fuelled by the need for daily drug money. He estimated that he had committed around 150 separate thefts from shops in different towns around the north-east during this period of his criminal career (having been 'barred out' of his local town centre by private security guards that were aware of his criminal record). At one point he was making around £300 per day from the selling on of stolen goods and 'most of it was going on heroin'. By the age of 20, this close combination of drug and crime careers had progressively closed down options for a more 'mainstream' lifestyle. He had failed to complete several government training programmes, had been employed only once (and briefly), had been unemployed recurrently, had become estranged from his family, had been homeless and slept rough, had a lengthy and worsening record of offending, had been imprisoned twice and, at the age of 20, was living in a bail hostel, struggling to maintain his commitment to a methadone programme and scratching around trying to find ways, beyond heroin, to fill tedious, direction-less days. We interviewed him again, three years later. The intervening period had been typified by a familiar pattern of heroin use, offending, prison, attempts to 'go straight' and relapse to heroin use. He said:

> It's like a vicious circle. It's like one, big, magnetic circle… when you get out of jail it start again, you're slowly getting drawn back in all the time… slowly you end up back on the circle again, moving round and round and back in the same direction all the time.

'Vicious circle' was a commonly used metaphor by young men in this group. We feel that it is does not capture the *deepening* problems they faced, as their lives circulated around drug use and crime over years. We prefer the metaphor of 'cork-screw heroin careers' to signal the downward trajectory typical of these young men; in Richard's case a story replete with instances of family estrangement, homelessness, recurrent joblessness, ill-health, bereavement, failed desistance, relapse to heroin, successive imprisonment, loss, regret, shame. Questions can be asked about the descriptive purchase provided by the concept – given the strong sense of *social inclusion* in neighbourhood-based social networks of friends and family common amongst our interviewees (MacDonald *et al* 2005) – but if anyone is 'socially excluded', Richard is. Cases like his represent perhaps the most intractable forms of social exclusion that were uncovered in the research.

Understanding desistance

Yet our follow up *Poor Transitions* study (Webster *et al* 2004), supplemented by our evaluation of the Hartlepool Dordrecht Project (Simpson *et al* 2006), uncovered a happier story. To recap, in the former, one of the 'types' of transition that we were particularly interested in tracking into the interviewees' mid and late twenties was that where careers of persistent offending and dependent drug use were combined.

Despite the depths of their troubles at earlier interviews, the majority of the 12 interviewees in this group in *Poor Transitions* were in a state of 'fragile desistance'. By this we mean that *we* agreed that they were making a sustained, new and – at that point – apparently successful attempt to take the long, precarious journey from the depths of a 'cork-screw heroin career' back to 'a normal life', as Richard, at the age of 23, described it. We are not positing a simplistic 'rock bottom' theory here; that there is a readily identifiable, uniform or fixed 'bottom' of the corkscrew that, once reached, returns people back upwards. As we discuss shortly in respect of 'critical moments', turning points were unpredictable in occurrence and outcome and quite varied in nature. Thus, we stress the fragility of the desistance *process* (rather than a single, simple event) because, of course, the biographies of this sub-sample were replete with failed attempts and because success was contingent on several factors beyond individual motivation.

Parenthood, partnerships and employment

Here we review briefly the factors that were significant in the movement to desistance for our interviewees. Unsurprisingly, many of those reported in the relevant criminological literature – specifically, the getting of more regular *employment*, the forming of new, stable *partnerships* (with 'straight', non-drug involved women) and the (usually unplanned) coming of *fatherhood* – were also found here to be significant in the process of desistance (Maruna 2001; Laub and Sampson 2003; Stephen and Squires 2003; Farrall and Calverley 2006). For this reason we do not provide qualitative illustration and detail of these factors; but we would wish to note that these three 'aids to desistance' also signal the key processes and symbolic markers said to signify the movement from youth to adulthood (Coles 1995). In thinking about the processes of 'growing out of crime' (Rutherford 1992), then, we can reflect on the relative normalcy of the factors that 'helped', seeing desistance as a normal process of maturation and the transition to adulthood. Yet we know that for the majority of young people in the UK transitions have become extended, fragmented and less clear (Furlong and Cartmel 2007). For working-class young people in deprived neighbourhoods beset by economic marginality, pathways to adulthood have become particularly blurred, unstable and circuitous. For working-class young people in these neighbourhoods who *also* carry the weight of personal histories of drugs and crime, achieving these 'normal' steps – of effective (re)engagement with employment, of parenthood, of 'growing out of crime' – was extraordinarily difficult (Farrall 2004). Perhaps surprisingly then, and in contradiction to some other reports of the values and practices of criminally involved young men in poor locales (Hall *et al* 2008), only a few appeared to have become wholly detached from conventional working-class attitudes to employment. Jason and Stu had long-records of offending, were imprisoned at the time of interview and were plotting more lucrative crime (as drug dealers) on release (see MacDonald and Marsh 2001). They said they knew:

> lads who 'were on the out' who were earning £450 per week working at the chemical plant. We should earn that! Taxis, night-clubs, trainers, a good haircut – it all adds up. How much does it cost the government to keep us in here [prison] for a week? They should just give us that money and I'd stop doing crime.

Jason and Stu (both 20) were unusual for our studies. Most seemed to be prepared to surrender the more lucrative proceeds of crime for the wages of local 'poor work' and most made attempts to access training and educational courses, in and out of prison, to improve their qualifications and labour market chances. For instance, in a letter from prison Danny (21) described how on release from his previous sentence he had failed to attend an interview for a welding training course at a local college:

> it was the Careers Service [in the last YOI] that arranged it for me. I got out but the interview was another two months away and I never really thought about it after a few weeks. Daft really cos I would've done sound as well. I never cared much then though. I've thought a lot now so I'll give it 100% next time around! I'm still interested in getting on a course. I'm not as keen as before about welding, like, but I'm gonna try my luck with a place on landscape gardening. If not then I'll go with welding. Either one's still a bonus.

Successful completion of training courses at best then placed them at the back of long queues for jobs and in competition with similarly qualified individuals who benefitted from the absence of a criminal history. Lying about or hiding as best as they could their criminal pasts was frequent amongst these ex-offenders as they sought to slough off their reputations and records and access limited opportunities. Low paid, low skilled, insecure 'poor work' that rarely required detailed CVs or formal qualifications was the sort typically available to young adults in our studies, *regardless of offending history*. That ex-offenders were not completely detached from employment and *did* sporadically manage to access this sort of work suggests that criminal records were of lesser importance to employers in this sort of depleted, casualised labour market.

For some, though, continued failure to (re)enter employment and continued 'hanging around' provided the context for relapse and the end, for the time being, of fragile efforts to 'go straight'. Spending many years in and out of prison, on heroin and out of work also limited the opportunities for this group to establish stable, loving partnerships. 'Settling down' was inhibited by their commitment to male friends, to drugs and to crime. Whilst others in the sample were making efforts to progress, the school-to-work, family and housing careers of this group were held on pause as they struggled to disentangle themselves from crime and drugs. Thus, a corollary of cumulative, sustained, heroin-driven crime is often largely 'empty' 'school-to-work careers' and faltering 'family careers' punctuated by repeated spells of imprisonment which together acted as a moratorium on the achievement of normal youth transitions to adulthood, limiting the potential of biographical resolutions to criminal careers. Young men like these are unlikely to appear attractive as potential employees, partners and fathers.

Separation from peer groups

Probably the most commonly cited factor as significant in the process of desistance was separation from peer groups. Earlier we described the weighty role of adolescent peer networks (as 'street corner society') in directing and encouraging the transitions of these young men, particularly towards offending and drug use. Many of our interviewees described how they also acted as the main obstacle to desistance. Even when people had come to a point where they felt a desire or a need to 'go straight' they perceived no easy way forward because of their long-standing, primary allegiance to friends who continued to be involved in drugs and crime. Echoing homelessness research, the life-worlds and 'street culture' of drug users and offenders can be a serious barrier to desistance (Blackman 1997).

This was true of all those with extended criminal careers but particularly exemplified by those interviewees for whom these had become entangled with drug careers.[7] Dependent heroin users were virtually unanimous on this point; their lives since mid-teenage had been lived within social networks that reinforced drug behaviour. Escaping these networks was crucial to going straight. Matthew, 19, was a recurrent heroin user and had served several custodial sentences for drug-related offences. He reflected on his frustrating attempts to get away from his past:[8]

> ... first day I was out [of YOI] this time I was thieving, do you know what I mean, Miss? I'm just sick of it, doing the same thing over and over again, getting locked up and that... //... if I had the money, Miss, I wouldn't even do it... even a £100 a week would do me. Yeah, I could get £200 a week at the turkey factory but I could get that in one day off one [stolen] car... //... but I'm sick of all these places. I've seen too much of it. //... I grow out if then I get back into it... //... I'm sick of pinching, I'm sick of doing all the crime and that. I wanna chill out for a good bit, do you know what I mean?... //... [but] the lads my age and a bit older, they're all into crime. I'm close to them. I dunno, but I think it's hard making new friends and that again....

For many, imprisonment provided a welcome opportunity to do their 'rattle' (albeit often under a harsh, non-therapeutic regime).[9] A few had even purposefully sought a prison sentence (rather than probation supervision) as a way of escaping the recurrent drug temptations 'of the street'. Release from prison was normally viewed with trepidation because it signalled a return to the generative environment of their initial drug dependency: 'you're just going back to the same place, the same group of people and it's easy to get back into it' (Stu, 20). Separation from drug-using and criminally inclined peers often called forth an allied process of (re)engagement with and acceptance by non-criminal and non-drug dependent others. In this respect, the formation of new partnerships with non-drug using women, as significant others who could be trusted and who gave trust, emerged as a key aspect of desistance for some of the young men interviewed. Re-contacted three years after we first spoke to him, Richard's plans for desistance hinged around re-integrating with non-drug using friends that he knew from earlier days:

> I'm planning to go out drinking with some of the lads from Primrose Vale. I've already written to a few of 'em. I used to talk to them when I was on it [heroin], like when I used to pass them. [But] I didn't used to, like, stand and knock about with 'em. I'd always be on my way somewhere, going for a score [to purchase heroin] or summat.

Pushed on the reasons for his previous relapses into heroin use and offending, Richard said:

> It's 'cos I don't occupy myself. No job to keep me busy. It does me head in just wandering around. Nothing to do. I end up knocking around with me old [drug-using] mates. I just get back into it. I don't have enough to do. I just hang around here. Play pool. *I need more purpose*. I want to go to college. I wish it would come around quicker. (Richard's emphasis)

Purposeful activity

This stress on 'purpose' captures, we think, why factors such as parenthood and employment are significant aids to desistance. We use the phrase 'purposeful activity' (MacDonald and Marsh 2005) to include activities such as these but also other, broader activities and roles that might be available given the difficulty of achieving these normal resolutions for the subjects of this chapter. 'Purposeful activities' can share the five latent functions that the social psychologist Marie Jahoda (1982) argues are typically found in work and that she deems as crucial for sustaining individual, positive, social psychological health: the structuring of time; the enforcement of personal activity; the provision of personal goals; the development of social contacts; and the ascription of a social identity (see Farrall 2002, for further discussion). For the subjects of this chapter, these latent functions have predominately, over their recent years, been fulfilled by their engagement in drug-related, peer associated offending. Work's *manifest* function, to generate income, has also been met in this way.

For places and populations where work, as employment, is limited in quantity and quality and unable to meet the economic, social and psychological needs of all, drug-related crime can provide work-like, purposeful activity. Therefore, just as the perceived purposelessness of school had provided the context for the earlier drift into delinquency and the 'leisure time crime' that spiced up the spaces of truancy (Matza 1964, 1969) – and post-school worklessness became both effect and cause of continued, peer-based offending – the availability of purposeful activity, in which individuals could invest their time, energy and identity helped these young men terminate drug and criminal careers, as they reached their early twenties.

Employment, partnerships and parenting provided purposeful activity. So did some local agencies. Participation in their organised leisure activities and vocationally-oriented, basic short courses helped to re-orient lives away from the more anti-social aspects of street corner society, fill time in and divert energies into more positive activities. These voluntary-sector, estate based, youth projects stood out from the generally negative assessment received from informants about the majority of the agencies and organisations they encountered (i.e. schools, training schemes, employability courses, criminal justice services). The wholly voluntary nature of young men's participation, the fact that attendance by pre-existing friendship groups was encouraged, that employability outcomes were not explicit targets, that they were run by workers sympathetic to their situations (in some cases because of similar biographical experience), and that they provided purposeful activities to replace the busyness of criminal careers, are all factors that help explain their positive appeal.

The significance of 'critical moments'

Yet why did some interviewees persist in crime when most in our samples did not? Why did some *not* seek out purposeful activities? Why did interventions like the Dordrecht project 'work' well for the majority of offenders but not for all? Even with longitudinal, detailed, narrative accounts it is sometimes difficult to untangle processes of cause and effect (e.g. might gaining employment be an *outcome* of desistance rather than a precursor to it?). Similarly, the relative importance of personal agentic disposition, 'natural' processes of maturation away from crime and the role of policy and practice interventions in aiding rehabilitation remains fuzzy (Farrall and Sparks 2006; Maruna *et al* 2004). For us, these remain questions and the following discussion, that shifts attention from sociological to social-psychological levels of analysis, is necessarily speculative.

In answering our question about the only partial success of the Dordrecht Project, a unanimous response from staff and offenders alike was that individuals 'had *to want* to change'. This begs the obvious question why (or how) did some want to change where others in objectively similar situations did not?

Across all our studies, informants talked about the significance of what we call 'critical moments' (see Thomson *et al* 2002); instances of biographical insight and reflection from which new directions in life are pursued. Williamson (2004), in reviewing the life-courses of the 'Milltown Boys' 40 years on, uses the term 'wake-up calls' in a similar way. 'Turning points' (Hodkinson and Sparkes 1997) and 'fateful moments' (Giddens 1991) are synonyms, more or less. For us, critical moments are events or experiences that, in the mind of the informant in reflecting on their lives, were remembered as highly consequential. They could be superficially trivial in nature (e.g. a negative, throw-away comment by a teacher about a pupil's poor prospects) or more readily identifiable 'serious life events' (such as parental separation, housing moves or bereavement).

That the critical moment happened in the individual's life – and at the time it did – was unpredictable, as were the consequences that followed. We uncovered many instances of traumatic, single episodes apparently leading people to re-orient their lives away from drug and criminal careers. Lisa (23) used to be 'in with a crowd getting into trouble and doing drugs' until she was raped by one of them. Zack (24) said that 'the turning point' in his life was when 'my best mate hung himself'. He had now 'calmed down' and given up 'all sorts of mad stuff'. Critical moments could turn people *away* from and *toward* crime and drug careers – even within a single biography. Micky (25) reported that the death of his sister, in his teens, catalysed his heroin use. The death of his mother, in his twenties, was a critical moment that spurred his desistance from crime and drug use. In short, we think that the spread and effects of 'critical moments' in our samples – and how and where they sit biographically in relation to other key pressures toward persistence or processes of desistance – might go some further way to understanding how and why some do or do not 'want to change'.

To sum up this discussion of our current conclusions about desistance from crime, we would argue that a social structure of legitimate opportunities providing purposeful activity (e.g. provided by the labour market) coupled with suitable policy/practice interventions that might also provide purposeful activity and other valued support (such as the Dordrecht Project and the sort of youth work projects valued by our informants) can *help* desistance from crime but cannot wholly explain it; personal psychological re-orientation towards these opportunities is also essential and, from our research, 'critical moments' of one sort or another can spur this re-orientation. These conclusions chime directly with promising research in criminology about desistance from drug use and the rehabilitation of offenders (e.g. Farrall and Sparks 2006; Farrall 2004; Maruna *et al* 2004), some of which we discuss next in thinking more broadly about what our research says.

The Teesside studies and contemporary criminology: some theoretical reflections

Historical and biographical context

Our studies have emphasised consistently how conditions of economic marginality placed severe restrictions on the capacity of individuals to make informed choices about and steps towards meaningful educational, training and employment opportunities. The discussion in this chapter so far has kept ethnographic faith with the stories related to us by individuals; the focus has been on the biographical telling of the story of criminal and drug careers, in summary form. But, as C. Wright Mills (1959: 12) informed us, 'no social study that does not come back to the problems of biography, of history and of their intersections within a society has completed its intellectual journey'. We now need to consider more fully how the 'private troubles' of biography and individual milieu found in the lives of Richard, Danny, Stu, Jason, Barney and the others cited here relate to 'public issues' of history and social structure.[10]

Despite the far-reaching social and economic transformations of late modernity and the immense changes they have made to the patterns of life of particular places, the criminological study of social, spatial and historical context in individual criminal careers has mostly proved elusive; more aspiration than reality (Laub and Sampson 2003; Godfrey *et al* 2007; Wikstrom and Butterworth 2006; McVie and Norris 2006a, 2006b; Smith 2007).[11] Here, we affirm the importance of such an approach.

The places we studied are but extreme examples of a general disruption, then collapse, of traditional working-class transitions in the UK since the 1970s. Our Teesside cohort was born between 1974 and 1983; on the cusp or in the depths of severe and rapid deindustrialisation. This was a place that, until the 1970s, had been a successful industrial conurbation, famous worldwide for its industrial prowess in chemicals and steel. This economic base underwrote Teesside's traditional forms of highly gendered and predominantly working-class community. Global economic change had profound repercussions locally (Beynon *et al* 1994). Restructuring of its industrial mainstays brought massive redundancies that severely curtailed local labour market prospects for young people growing up here and rapidly destabilised gender and class pathways and destinies. As social networks of support and stable marriages in traditional working-class communities declined and social cohesion came under increasing threat, changes in the occupational structure disadvantaged the relatively unskilled and unqualified working-class, especially men, compared to women's growing participation in the labour market (Ferri *et al* 2003). This sharp decline in previously established working-class routes to adulthood, in this place at this time, we believe, offers the best clue as to why criminality and dependent drug use became more likely for some, and why *purposeless* activity emerged from collapsed opportunity, aspiration and direction for many.

There are some strong resonances between our findings and Shadd Maruna's (2001) examination of desisting ex-offenders and active offenders in Liverpool in the 1980s. The processes involved in the formation and maintenance of criminal careers – particularly in terms of the hardening and deepening effects of entwined careers of drug dependency (associated, in his case, with the arrival of a 'first wave heroin outbreak' in Liverpool in the 1980s and in our case with the UK's 'second wave heroin outbreak' in Teesside in the 1990s) and, in both places and times, the dearth of decent employment opportunities – are striking and affirm our argument here about the significance of the historical contingencies of the places in which lives are lived out. As with our research 20 years later, for those seeking to desist in Maruna's study the obstacles and temptations placed in their way were considerable and repeat offenders faced a 'brick wall', returning again and again to crime, and mostly prison. Indeed, in the contemporary period the social consequences of conviction have become much harsher and resettlement of prisoners much harder, especially in the context of mass imprisonment (Farrall and Sparks 2006).

This is not to say that the individuals we (or Maruna) interviewed lacked resilience or agency towards the conditions they met in their lives. 'Desisters' possessed hope, were imagining the future and taking steps towards it, despite the bleakness of their lives. Despite this sense of agency (or perhaps because of it) a final similarity worthy of attention is the relative lack of *sociological* understanding of their lives, displayed across Maruna's interviewees and ours.[12] To us, as researchers, the conditions of history, place and class are critical in understanding the biographies of our informants and the stories they told us. This 'sociological imagination', this placing of biographies in social and historical context, was however strikingly absent from our interviews. Time and time again interviewees refused to seek explanations of their criminal careers that went beyond their own personal failings and mistakes. Whilst in retrospect, in making sense of their lives, they might point to critical moments, contingencies and pressures that presaged criminality or drug use, overall a discourse of individual responsibility ruled. Compare this with Laub and Sampson's (2003: 185) study of a sample of male offenders, born during the Great Depression and growing up in the middle decades of the twentieth century in Boston, US. Laub and Sampson report a strong sense of class-based injustice and defiance against authority amongst interviewees who were highly aware of the historical and class situations they were born into.

Explaining this difference between findings from Teesside (and from Liverpool) in latter twentieth century and Laub and Sampson's would involve quite lengthy speculation.[13] Here, though, we would point only to a general process of apparently increasing individualisation in youth transitions to adulthood in the UK under late modernity. This has engendered what Furlong and Cartmel (2007) call the epistemological fallacy. Young people – removed from the traditional class cultural apprenticeships associated with modernity (Cohen 1997), endowed with *apparently* more choice and room for personal agency by an array of post-16 options in an educational and training market place, and subject to powerful government-backed rhetoric of aspiration, achievement and possibility – fail to see the continuing force of social origin in shaping biographical outcomes.

Career, contingency and generation

We have argued elsewhere that it was difficult to predict who amongst our samples would pursue criminal and drug-using careers (Webster *et al* 2006). We have also described in this chapter how the transitions of these young men were replete with contingent events and critical moments that had unpredictable consequences. Yet we now present a paradox. Compared with the transitions of non-offenders in our studies, those with the most serious criminal and drug-using careers were at the same time the most chaotic and socially excluded *and* had the clearest shape and most predictable direction.

Because we are amply aware of, and have criticised (Webster *et al* 2006; MacDonald 2006), the flawed, deterministic approaches of previous criminal career research, which has emphasised the strong, predictive, individual aspects of careers, we want to explain what we mean by the unpredictable nature of 'contingency' and context. We do *not* use 'contingency' in the sense of merely random occurrences to oppose determinism. Rather, we use the term in Abrams' (1982: 272) sense of occurrences that are incident upon distinctive patterns of behaviour:

> They [contingencies] are significant conjunctures of uncertain outcome, decisive moments at which the career is framed and structured one way or another. Emphasising the importance of contingencies in the deviant career is not therefore to reduce the process of becoming to a record of chance happenings. Rather, what is being stressed is the way in which the process is organised in terms of sequences of characteristic but not pre-determined interactions, probable but not prescribed episodes of action and response in which the individual moves or is moved from one status to another.

So we do not mean what happened to individuals was pure chance – although sometimes this came into it – we mean that among the people to whom we spoke, and given their commonality of class background, poverty and place, some 'risks' and contingencies (accidents, ill health, bereavement, unexpected and irresolvable financial costs and pressures, drug-use opportunities, particular sorts of street encounters) were more 'typical'. Thus, not all *individuals* will experience all or any such contingencies, but as a *group* they have a greater chance of doing so. So whilst, for example, the incidence of bereavement and poor personal and family health seemed very high – and Fate seemed to dealt some informants a shockingly bad hand – what we know of the socio-spatial concentration of health inequalities reminds us of the *likelihood* of finding these and other 'risky' experiences among this group, living in these places.

In a sense we are arguing that the collapse of classed certainties and subsequent poverty are the main driver of greater contingency, 'risk' and the inability to plan or anticipate what might come next in individual lives, made precarious by social change and the limits of resources to cope with the multifarious contingencies, exigencies and pressures of poverty. At least among those young men following criminal and/or drug dependent careers, their trajectories were increasingly laid out for them through, firstly, the addictive demands of drug dependency and, secondly, the formal and staged interventions of criminal justice and drug treatment agencies. As Everett Hughes (1945) argued long ago, when a 'master status trait' such as criminality and/or dependent drug use is assigned by others it increasingly over-shadows all other aspects of life for the individual concerned. Or, as Richard put it, 'once a smack-head, always a smack-head'. Again, paradoxically, criminalisation in contrast to mere impoverishment, raises profound issues of self-definition and affiliation, focuses self-consciousness, raises sharply the question of 'guilt', and how to conduct oneself in the future.

This finally brings us to the 'problem of sociological generations'.[14] Different to a mere succession of biological generations, 'sociological' generations embody a cycle growing up within the same terms of reference, unable to change those terms of reference, in 'the mutual phasing of two different calendars: the calendar of the life cycle of the individual and the calendar of historical experience' (Abrams 1982: 240). The Teesside cohort faced very particular conjunctions and predicaments of economic marginalisation and disrupted transitions to work and family formation, such that it is difficult to separate individual life and contemporary crises in historical development because the two help to define each other. For most, traditional (non-criminal) working-class values and aspirations have retained their hold. For some, criminality and drug dependency took over completely. All grew up within the same terms of reference. The difference between non-criminal and criminal trajectories for us is explained largely in terms of typical contingencies – the range of possibilities given within the same highly circumscribed and disrupted terms and conditions faced by this generation of working-class young people.

Conclusion

To summarise, the chapter has provided a sketch of the more serious criminal and drug-using careers of young men in Teesside, north-east England as revealed to us through a series of qualitative studies. We have charted two key processes in their formation: firstly, of sustained educational disengagement in early teenage years, of allegiance to 'street corner society' and the appeal of 'leisure time crime' amidst the purposelessness of truancy; secondly, of the hardening up and prolongation of some criminal careers with the onset of persistent, dependent drug use, which then typically propelled young men along 'cork-screw heroin careers' of deepening social exclusion. A third key process relates to desistance from criminal and drug-using careers, as uncovered in our later studies. These described well-known factors correlated with desistance and 'growing out of crime', such as the getting of employment, the formation of partnerships and the coming of parenthood. Opportunities for purposeful activity, as found in these roles but as also provided by local youth work projects for example, seemed crucial to our interviewees' attempts to 'go straight'. This was also true of physical and sub-cultural separation from teenage peer groups; identified here as a particularly important facet of desistance. The question of how and why some desisted where others did not drew our attention, more speculatively, to the influence of critical moments in re-orienting interviewees' views of themselves, their lives and their futures.

In retrospect, participants told us *their* stories, but they did not tell us the *whole* story. In bemoaning the often marked absence of social context – of biography, contingency, place, generation, social structural and historical change – in criminal career research, we give credit where credit is due. Inexplicably, Godfrey *et al*'s (2007) *Criminal Lives* has been sorely neglected. This is a study of criminal careers and the influence of family and occupational change in Crewe from 1880 to 1940. The authors emphasise the importance of historical change and continuity, arguing that:

> These changes help us to make sense of crime and offending as part of a social process as well as simply the outcome of a series of individual choices. Societies change, and 'change' at that level is often about change in structural factors foremost and individual-level change which follows it. As societies change they reveal continuities and discontinuities which can help us to make sense of the processes at play when individuals desist from criminality.
>
> (Godfrey *et al* 2007: 170–71)

Theoretically, we are also inspired by the work of the late Phillip Abrams (1982). For Abrams, just as for others working in the tradition of the sociology of crime and deviance, moral careers – whether criminal or not – are lived in particular conjunctions of life history and social history. Whilst lived by individuals, they are socially organised and are the typical experiences and destinies of particular sociological categories of people – as well as the actual biographies of particular individuals. For our working-class informants, growing up during the 1980s and 1990s amongst the economic wreckage of one of the most de-industrialised places in Britain, the conditions of their lives allowed criminal 'solutions' for some and alternative, newly economically marginal ones for many. For us, group conditions as well as individual life circumstances must form the basis of criminal career research, so that studies can grasp how the *collective* conditions and 'public issues of social structure' set the frame of possibilities for individual biographies and their attendant 'private troubles'; showing how possibilities for desistance from, or persistence in, crime are socially, economically and historically structured as well as individually made.

Notes

1 We are grateful to Paul Mason, Jane Marsh and Donald Simpson who worked as researchers on our Teesside studies. Other colleagues – Andrea Abbas, Mark Cieslik, Les Johnston and Louise Ridley – also helped with the projects. We are grateful to them, and to the ESRC and JRF for funding.

2 The majority of informants in the Disconnected Youth? study were interviewed twice over a one year fieldwork period. Snakes and Ladders held one-off interviews.

3 A further study is underway in this series (Shildrick et al 2011, forthcoming). Although not centrally concerned with issues of criminal career, it has included 30 people (now aged 30–40 years) interviewed in earlier studies. A proportion of these have possessed the sort of criminal and drug-using careers described in this chapter and further analytical attention will be given to processes of desistance and persistence amongst them.
4 Maruna (2001: 68) makes this remarkably similar comment, in reflecting on the consequences of the '*first* wave' heroin outbreak in the 1980s in Liverpool: 'only after becoming addicted to the new drug (which was largely smoked or 'chased' rather than injected) did they even realize they had been using heroin, some said'.
5 These findings are not presented in support of 'gateway theories' of drug careers. Most cannabis users on Teesside do not become heroin users and, of course, the dynamics and complexities of drug careers cannot be discussed in any detail here (see Simpson 2003; MacDonald and Marsh 2002). To be clear, however, looking back retrospectively, the majority of those with more serious criminal careers *had* made this sort of speedy transition from use of drugs such as ecstasy and cannabis to heroin and identified this as a highly significant moment in their criminal careers.
6 The role of social support, social networks and social capital was important in understanding the transitions and inclusion/exclusion of all young adults in these studies. What we describe here might be an example of the 'destructive' social capital identified by Perri 6 (1997). More typically positive 'bonding social capital' – the informal social support of networks of family and friends – helped made life liveable for young people growing up in hard circumstances and, in all cases, shaped early adult destinations.
7 Easy access to therapeutic, non-punitive drug treatment services was also reported as a significant aid to the process of desistance, as was housing moves away from the home neighbourhood; space disallows further discussion here but we would not wish to understate their importance (see MacDonald and Marsh 2005).
8 Mathew insisted on calling Jane Marsh, a researcher on one of our studies, 'Miss' throughout his interview.
9 'Rattle' refers to the physical effects of the process of heroin detoxification.
10 'The problems of social science, when adequately formulated, must include both troubles and issues, both biography and history, and the range of their intricate relations. Within that range the life of the individual and the making of societies occur; and within that range the sociological imagination has its chance to make a difference in the quality of human life in our time' (Mills 1959: 226).
11 One notable, recent exception is Savoleinen's (2009) testing of some key claims of Sampson and Laub's influential, US-based theory of desistance, using Finnish data. Quite rightly, Savolainen emphasises – and demonstrates – the *impact of cultural context* on the *role* and *efficacy* of particular adult bonds (e.g. marriage, employment, partnerships, parenthood) in explaining desistance.
12 Admittedly, Maruna comments that his interviewees were keenly aware of 'their unique misfortune of growing up in the wrong place at the wrong time' (Maruna 2001: 68) but this largely refers to their recognition of the impact of a new heroin outbreak on their lives, rather than a widespread, broader understanding of issues of class inequality and injustice.
13 On a slightly different tangent, Jay MacLeod (2004) provides a close, ethnographically based theorisation of the development of disadvantaged young people's *differential* senses of social justice, opportunity and class situation.
14 'Sociologically, a generation is that span of time within which identity is assembled on the basis of an unchanged system of meanings and possibilities' (Abrams 1982: 256).

References

Abrams, P. (1982) *Historical Sociology*. Shepton Mallet: Open Books.

Blackman, S. (1997) 'Destructing a Giro', in MacDonald, R. (ed.) *Youth, the 'Underclass' and Social Exclusion*. London: Routledge.

Beynon, H., Hudson, R. and Sadler, D. (1994) *A Place Called Teesside*. Edinburgh: Edinburgh University Press.

Byrne, D. (1999) *Social Exclusion*. Milton Keynes: Open University Press.

Chamberlayne, P., Rustin, M. and Wengraf, T. (eds) (2002) *Biography and Social Exclusion in Europe*. Bristol: Policy Press.

Cohen, P. (1997) *Rethinking the Youth Question*. London: Palgrave.

Coles, B. (1995) *Youth and Social Policy*. London: UCL Press.

Corrigan, P. (1976) 'Doing Nothing', in Hall, S. and Jefferson, T. (eds) *Resistance through Rituals*. London: Hutchinson.

DETR (Department of the Environment, Transport and the Regions) (2000) *Index of Multiple Deprivation*. London: DETR.

Farrall, S. (2002) *Re-thinking what works with offenders*. Cullompton: Willan Publishing.

Farrall, S. (2004) 'Social capital and offender re-integration: making probation desistance focused', in Maruna, S. and Immarigeon, R. (eds) *After Crime and Punishment*. Cullompton: Willan Publishing.

Farrall, S. and Calverley, A. (2006) *Understanding desistance from crime: Theoretical directions in resettlement and rehabilitation*. Maidenhead: Open University Press.

Farrall, S. and Sparks, R. (2006) 'Introduction', *Criminology and Criminal Justice*, 6(1): 7–17.

Ferri, E., Bynner, J. and Wadsworth, M. (eds) (2003) *Changing Britain, Changing Lives: Three Generations at the Turn of the Century*. London: Institute of Education.

Furlong, A. and Cartmel, F. (2007) *Young People and Social Change*, 2nd edn. Maidenhead: Open University Press.

Giddens, A. (1991) *Modernity and Self-identity*. Cambridge: Polity Press

Godfrey, B. S., Cox, D. J. and Farrall, S. D. (2007) *Criminal Lives: Family Life, Employment, and Offending*. Oxford: Oxford University Press.

Hall, S., Winlow, S. and Ancrum, C. (2008) *Criminal Identities and Consumer Culture*. Cullompton: Willan Publishing.

Henderson, S., Holland, J., McGrellis, S., Sharpe, S. and Thomson, R. (2007) *Inventing Adulthoods*. London: Sage.

Hodkinson, P. and Sparkes, A. (1997) 'Careership: a sociological theory of career decision making', *British Journal of Sociology of Education*, 18(1): 29–44.

Hughes, E. C. (1945) 'Dilemmas and Contradictions of Status', *American Journal of Sociology*, 50: 353–59.

Jahoda, M. (1982) *Employment and Unemployment: A Social Psychological Analysis*. Cambridge: Cambridge University Press.

Johnston, L., MacDonald, R., Mason, P., Ridley, L. and Webster, C. (2000) *Snakes & Ladders: Young People, Transitions & Social Exclusion*. Bristol: Policy Press.

Laub, J. H. and Sampson, R. J. (2003) *Shared Beginnings, Divergent Lives: Delinquent Boys to Age 70*. London: Harvard University Press.

MacDonald, R. (2006) 'Social exclusion, youth transitions and criminal careers: five critical reflections on risk', *Australian and New Zealand Journal of Criminology*, 39(3): 371–83.

MacDonald, R. (2010) 'Idle, Thieving Bastards? Researching the Youth Underclass', in Meadows, P. and Francis, P. (eds) *Doing Criminological Research*, vol 2. London: Sage.

MacDonald, R. and Marsh, J. (2001) 'Disconnected Youth?', *Journal of Youth Studies*, 4(4): 373–91.

MacDonald, R. and Marsh, J. (2002) 'Crossing the Rubicon: Youth Transitions, Poverty Drugs and Social Exclusion', *International Journal of Drug Policy*, 13: 27–38.

MacDonald, R. and Marsh, J. (2005) *Disconnected Youth? Growing up in Britain's Poor Neighbourhoods*. Basingstoke: Palgrave.

MacDonald, R. and Shildrick, T. (2007) 'Street Corner Society', *Leisure Studies*, 26(3): 339–55.

MacDonald, R., Shildrick, T., Webster, C. and Simpson, D. (2005) 'Growing up in poor neighbourhoods', *Sociology*, 39(5): 873–92.

MacLeod, J. (2004) *Ain't no makin' it: aspirations and attainment in a local income neighbourhood*. Oxford: Westview Press.

Maruna, S. (2001) *Making Good: How ex-Convicts Reform and Rebuild Their Lives*. Washington, DC: American Psychological Association Books.

Maruna, S., Immarigeon, R. and LeBel, T. (2004) 'Ex-offender reintegration: theory and practice', in Maruna, S. and Immarigeon, R. (eds) *After Crime and Punishment*. Cullompton: Willan Publishing.

Matza, D. (1964) *Delinquency and Drift*. New York, NY: Wiley.

Matza, D. (1969) *Becoming Deviant*. Upper Saddle River, NJ: Prentice Hall.

McVie, S. and Norris, P. (2006a) *The Effect of Neighbourhoods on Adolescent Property Offending*, Edinburgh Study of Youth Transitions and Crime, Research Digest No 11. Edinburgh: Centre for Law and Society, University of Edinburgh.

McVie, S. and Norris, P. (2006b) *Neighbourhood Effects on Youth Delinquency and Drug Use*, Edinburgh Study of Youth Transitions and Crime, Research Digest No 10. Edinburgh: Centre for Law and Society, University of Edinburgh.

Merton, B. (1998) *Finding the Missing*. Leicester: Youth Work Press.

Mills, C. Wright (1959) *The Sociological Imagination*. New York, NY: Oxford University Press.

Parker, H., Bury, C. and Eggington, R. (1998) *New Heroin Outbreaks Amongst Young People in England and Wales*, Police Research Group, Paper 92. London: Home Office.

Perri 6 (1997) *Escaping Poverty: From Safety Nets to Networks of Opportunity*. London: Demos.

Rutherford, A. (1992) *Growing Out of Crime: the New Era*. London: Waterside Press.

Savolainen, J. (2009) 'Work, Family and Criminal Desistance: Adult Social Bonds in a Nordic Welfare State', *British Journal of Criminology*, 49: 285–304.

Shildrick, T., MacDonald, R., Webster, C. and Garthwaite, K. *et al* (2011, forthcoming) *Two steps forward, two steps back: understanding recurrent poverty*. Bristol: Policy Press.

Simpson, M. (2003) 'The relationship between drug use and crime', *International Journal of Drug Policy*, 14: 307–19.

Simpson, M., Shildrick, T., MacDonald, R., Harrison, J. and Abbas, A. (2006) *Evaluation of Hartlepool Dordrecht Project, Final Report*. Teesside: Youth Research Group.

Smith, D. J. (2006) *Social Inclusion and Early Desistance from Crime*, Edinburgh Study of Youth Transitions and Crime, Research Digest No 12. Edinburgh: Centre for Law and Society, University of Edinburgh.

Smith, D. J. (2007) 'Crime and the Life Course', in Maguire, M., Morgan, R. and Reiner, R. (eds) *The Oxford Handbook of Criminology*, 4th edn. Oxford: Oxford University Press.

Stephen D. and Squires, P. (2003) '"Adults Don't Realize How Sheltered They Are". A Contribution to the Debate on Youth Transitions from Some Voices on the Margin', *Journal of Youth Studies*, 6(2): 145–64.

Thomson, R., Bell, R., Holland, J., Henderson, S., McGrellis, S. and Sharpe, S. (2002) 'Critical moments: choice, chance and opportunity in young people's narratives of transition', *Sociology*, 36(2): 335–54.

Webster, C., Simpson, D., MacDonald, R., Abbas, A., Cieslik, M., Shildrick, T. and Simpson, M. (2004) *Poor Transitions*. Bristol: Policy Press.

Webster, C., MacDonald, R. and Simpson, M. (2006) 'Predicting Criminality? Risk Assessment, Neighbourhood Influence and Desistance', *Youth Justice*, 6(1): 7–22.

Wikstrom, P. H. and Butterworth, D. A. (2006) *Adolescent Crime: Individual differences and lifestyles*. Cullompton: Willan Publishing.

Williamson, H. (2004) *The Milltown Boys Revisited*. London: Berg.

Chapter 6

The reintegration of sexual offenders

From a 'risks-' to a 'strengths-based' model of offender resettlement

Anne-Marie McAlinden

Recent trends in penal policy in the UK as elsewhere have focused increasingly on risk management and surveillance of former prisoners as control is extended from prison into the community (Ericson and Haggerty 1997; Hudson 2001; Wargent 2002). This has been particularly evident in relation to sex offenders where 'risk' has been the touchstone of both academic and policy debates on sex offender management and reintegration (Simon 1998; Kemshall and Maguire 2001; Matravers 2003). Indeed, the reintegration of sexual offenders has captured both popular imagination and official attention over the last decade or more (McAlinden 2006). In line with broader governmental concerns about 'managerialism', a pantheon of 'risk-based' (Maruna and LeBel 2002) initiatives have been implemented to increase the surveillance of released sex offenders and to extend the didactics of control from prison to the community. Recent initiatives have included a spate of legislative measures, including sex offender notification and a range of orders under the Sexual Offences Act 2003 such as risk of sexual harm orders and sexual offences prevention orders. In tandem with the legislative and policy framework, formal inter-agency procedures have also been put in place to risk assess and manage sex offenders.

It is argued, however, that these largely situational approaches to offender rehabilitation may ultimately undermine effective risk management and reintegration. The failure of the risk-based model has been demonstrated, inter alia, by violence and vigilante action in the public arena which may isolate the offender from the rest of society. In effect, via the process of 'disintegrative shaming' (Braithwaite 1989), the offender may at best be singled out as different from the rest of the community, and at worst subjected to public harassment or attack by vigilante groups. The net result may ultimately be an increase or displacement of the risk of re-offending – the offender may return to their former offending pattern as a coping mechanism or relocate undetected elsewhere (McAlinden 2005, 2007). These failures have in turn led to calls for the development of an alternative strategy for sex offender resettlement.

There is a fundamental dichotomy which lies at the heart of the reintegrative process for this particular category of offender: for most sex offenders community re-entry at the end of their prison sentence is inevitable. On the other hand, many communities are unwilling to accept a sex offender in their midst either in terms of local housing or employment. Indeed, communities are particularly intolerant and unforgiving of those who have offended against children (McAlinden 2007: 10; Wilson *et al* 2007a: 1–2, 2007c: 328). In this respect, this chapter considers the alternative 'strengths-based' model of rehabilitation (Maruna and LeBel 2002), linked to the restorative justice tradition, which is characterised by the themes of repair, reconciliation and community partnership.[1]

Through the process of 'reintegrative shaming' (Braithwaite 1989), sex offenders are encouraged to develop innate motivations for personal change. There is a 'cognitive restructuring towards responsibility' (Toch 2000) as the offender is actively encouraged to develop community orientated concepts of self in order to secure their place within civil society (Bazemore 1999). It is argued that such approaches offer a more constructive, viable and proactive means of addressing the myriad of problems which relate to offender reintegration which relate not only to the offender but also to the community in which they are placed. Measures such as circles of support and accountability which operate with high risk sex offenders across a growing range of jurisdictions encapsulate the 'strengths-based' philosophy. They acknowledge in particular the critical contribution of the community to supporting offender rehabilitation as well as the concomitant effort required by the offender. By addressing both the individual and structural obstacles to reintegration, which are well established in the literature, they offer a more effective mechanism for securing offender reintegration and reducing the risk of re-offending (Wilson *et al* 2002, 2007a, 2007b, 2007c; Bates *et al* 2007).

In this respect, it is useful to begin this chapter with a broad overview of the key themes emerging from the general literature on ex-offender 'resettlement' or community 're-entry'[2] (Sampson and Laub 1993; Maruna 2001; Petersilia 2003) and the related literature on 'what works' in achieving desistance from crime (Farrall and Bowling 1999; Farrall 2002; Maruna and Farrall 2004; Maguire and Raynor 2006; McNeill 2006), and how this may be related to sex offenders as a particular offender group. The discussion will then move to critically examine the key features and merits of both 'risk-based' and 'strengths-based' models of offender resettlement.[3]

Resettlement and desistance from crime

There have been a number of recent developments in penal policy, both in the UK and the US, which have prompted renewed academic interest in life after crime and punishment (Maruna 2001; Travis and Petersilia 2001; Farrall 2002, 2003; Maruna and Immarigeon 2004). These trends have included the rise in rates of imprisonment, and extended supervision and restrictions placed on dangerous violent and sexual offenders after a period of custodial detention via, for example, the development of multi-agency panels on the assessment and management of risk and the use of rehabilitative strategies via community disposals and reintegrative shaming (Rose 2000: 321). As Farrall and Sparks have argued, as a result, 'the social consequences of a criminal conviction have become not just more prevalent but also weightier and "stickier" than in previous decades' (Farrall and Sparks 2006: 7). The social and personal consequences of conviction are arguably particularly onerous for sex offenders whose crimes attract such public abhorrence and are the subject of often emotive and hostile reactions from the local community.

Desistance is a process usually attributed to a range of factors including the efforts of offenders themselves, informal support from 'significant others' such as family and friends or the local community, and assistance by professional agencies (Maruna 2001; Maruna *et al* 2004; McEvoy 2008: 20). In this vein, a number of significant themes emerge from the general resettlement literature which relate to both the structural and individual obstacles to successful reintegration. In relation to the latter, these have been framed largely in terms of risk factors and serious social and economic disadvantages and include a history of abusive and criminal behaviour with physical or emotional abuse, persistent offending and the associated stigma, and long-term addictions; and an impoverished background resulting from lack of employment opportunities, poor education and housing provision and economic instability. The social context has had an adverse effect not only on the offender but also on the local community, thereby undermining effective informal social controls and promoting deviance (Rutter and Giller 1983; Sampson and Laub 1994; Hagan 1997; Hope 2001; Farrall, 2002: 145–92).[4] With sex offenders in particular, the research demonstrates that a combination of stable employment, accommodation, supportive relationships and treatment are part of a 'good lives' approach or positive reintegrative work with sex offenders (Ward and Marshall 2004; Marshall *et al* 2005; Ward *et al* 2007) and are firmly associated with reductions in subsequent sexual offending (Cumming and Buell 1997; Kruttschnitt *et al* 2000; Zevitz and Farkas 2000: 381–82).

In relation to the former, the key structural correlate perhaps which may both facilitate and impede effective sex offender management and reintegration is 'the community' to which almost all offenders are returned at the end of their sentences. As Farrall and Sparks argue, in a general sense but which, as this chapter will hope to demonstrate, has particular resonance with sex offenders, 'at some level a "reconnection with" the community is an important step in the process by which they put their "pasts behind them"' (Farrall and Sparks 2006: 8). The importance of community in sex offender reintegration is rather neglected by risk-based models but embraced by strengths-based approaches.

Apart from a few isolated early studies which directly addressed the axis between crime, persistent offending and the local community in both British (Mays 1952; Hobbs 1989) and American settings (MacLeod 1995), the preponderance of studies have retained a firm offender-based focus and as such have tended to neglect the social/structural dimension. The seminal text by Maruna (2001) establishes that individual or offender-centred factors also have a bearing on the extent to which offenders can 'make good' (Maruna 2001). These relate chiefly to the offender's subjective thought processes and degree of self-motivation for change (Zamble and Quinsey 1997; Farrall and Bowling 1999; Farrall 2002; Giordano *et al* 2002; Farrall and Calverley 2005: Chapter 8). Ultimately, via the construction of offending 'narratives' (Maruna 2001: Chapter 2) or 'redemption scripts' (Maruna 2001: Chapter 5) ex-offenders attempt to 'account for and understand their criminal past' (Maruna 2001: 7). In this way, even the most persistent offenders can manage to become non-offenders and useful members of the community by making sense of their lives (Maruna 2001).

A body of work by Sampson and Laub (Sampson and Laub 1993, 1994; Laub *et al* 1998; Laub and Sampson 2003), however, was instrumental in shifting the parameters of thinking about persistent offending by re-focusing attention away from individual factors towards reintegrative social processes that underlie 'trajectories of change' (Laub *et al* 1998). As will be discussed further below, the 'risk-based' model is more singularly focused on the management of offender-centred factors which might exacerbate the risk of recidivism, to the neglect of the social dimension. The 'strengths-based' model, however, provides a more holistic approach to sex offender resettlement by addressing both the individual obstacles to reintegration in terms of supporting offenders in altering their behaviour as well as the structural correlates and community-based relationships that underpin social inclusion and successful rehabilitation.

'The risk-based model'

The legislative and policy framework on sex offender reintegration has largely been focused on a 'risk-based' model of offender resettlement (Maruna and LeBel 2002). Sex offending has become more prominent in criminal justice agendas largely as a result of the emergence of 'risk' and related notions within social and political discourses. The concept of 'risk' has been reflected in contemporary criminal justice debates generally and, in particular, in the resulting legislative and policy framework on regulating the behaviour of sex offenders on release from custody.

'The new penology': risk, governance and precautionary logic

Recent debates within social and political theory have focused on the importance of risk management and social governance within civil society (Giddens 1984, 1990; Beck 1992). According to these discourses, social order is thought of as something which cannot merely be preserved and sustained but which must be actively constructed and controlled (Cohen 1985, Lyon 1994). In post-modern society, risk has become institutionalised. The late-twentieth century shift towards crime control and community risk management is evidenced by a range of offender-based risk-reduction strategies (Brown 1996; Hebenton and

Thomas 1996b). Indeed, accurate risk prediction and management relating to individual offenders has become the core business of almost all complex organisations, including probation (Robinson 2002; Hudson 2001), social services (Kemshall *et al* 1997) and the police (Ericson 1994; Johnston 2000).

These broader theoretical constructs concerning 'risk' have in turn been reflected in both official and popular penal policy discourses on how best to manage selected dangerous offenders (Ericson and Haggerty 1997). Indeed, the contemporary politics of crime control place a strong emphasis on public protection, risk management and preventative governance as part of, what has variously been termed, the 'new penology' (Feely and Simon 1992), 'risk society' (Beck 1992; Ericson and Haggerty 1997) or 'the new regulatory state' (Braithwaite 2000; Shearing 2000). Risk assessment and management and its association with 'actuarial justice' (Feely and Simon 1994) form the basis of preventative strategies such as selective incapacitation, risk of custody scales, preventative intervention with 'at risk' groups and community-based initiatives (Crawford 1999: 86).

This risk penality has been particularly evident in relation to concerns over the risk posed by released sex offenders living in the community where assessing, managing and reducing those risks has become the primary concern (Simon 1998; Kemshall and Maguire 2003; Matravers 2003). In this vein, it has been argued that the notions of risk management (Parton *et al* 1997: 232–40; Robinson 2002; Hudson 2001) and governance (Ashenden 2002, 2004; Wargent 2002) have become the touchstone of the regulation of child (sexual) abuse and managing the behaviour of sex offenders on release from custody, both in terms of policy and practice (McAlinden 2006: 200). More recently, criminal justice policy has notably shifted from 'From Dangerousness to Risk' (Castel 1991) towards a defining contemporary framework based on 'precautionary logic' (Ericson 2007). This pre-emptive approach to penal policy is characterised by the pursuit of security via the imposition of risk-averse policies which seek to control 'worst case scenarios' and address every possible manifestation of future risk (Zedner 2009). A good example of this in the field of sexual offending is the new legislative framework on vetting, contained in the Safeguarding Vulnerable Groups Act 2006, which expands significantly the range of individuals who will be subject to continous criminal records monitoring (McAlinden 2010).

The regulation of sexual offenders in the community post-release can also be usefully examined in terms of the proactive 'management' of knowledge about individual offenders and the production of measures designed to compensate against risk (Hebenton and Thomas 1996a, 1996b: 430–32, 439–40). 'Knowing' offenders' activities and their whereabouts allows for risk assessment and preventative action where offenders are made objects of knowledge in order to classify them into risk categories (Hebenton and Thomas 1996a: 108, 1996b: 440). Following Ericson and Haggerty's (1997) model of 'knowledge-risk-security', the primary purpose of recent legislative measures on sex offender management or reintegration is to increase public safety by having knowledge of the whereabouts of those convicted or cautioned of sexual offences.

The legislative and policy framework

Successive governments, mindful of the need to deliver 'populist punitiveness' (Bottoms 1995) and to counter mounting public hysteria concerning released sex offenders, have developed an increasingly punitive legislative framework which lays emphasis on the effective management of the dangerous. However, while the governance or control of the dangerous and those who pose a risk to society, particularly sex offenders, has been a mainstay of criminal justice debates in recent years, there is conflict and wide variation in the methods of social control employed (Garland 1996, 2001; O'Malley 1999, 2002; Rose 2000). There have been a range of developments, for example, which have provided for longer and indeterminate sentences for sex offenders in both the US and the UK. Recent legislative activity has, for the most part, however, been concentrated on the area of post-release control.

The 1996 government White Paper, *Protecting the Public* (Home Office 1996a: para 8.2), advocated strengthening the arrangements for supervising convicted sex offenders following their release from custody. These recommendations led to a consultation document on the sentencing and supervision of sex offenders (Home Office 1996b; Cobley, 1997a) where its five main proposals were eventually embodied in a range of legislation. One of the most notable and high profile of these recent legislative measures is sex offender notification, which has been the subject of considerable study and debate (Marshall 1997; Soothill *et al* 1997; Soothill and Francis 1998; Cobley 2003). Registration, as it is more colloquially known, requires certain categories of sex offenders to register their name and address and any changes to these details with the local police. Measures were first enacted under Sex Offenders Act 1997, Part I and then replaced by extended provisions in Sexual Offences Act 2003, Part 2.[5]

The Sexual Offences Act 2003 also introduced a range of other mechanisms to control the activities of sex offenders in the community. For example, the risk of sexual harm order[6] and sexual offences prevention order are new civil preventative orders which are designed to protect children from sexual harm (Shute 2004).[7] The latter can be used to prohibit the offender from frequenting places where there are children such as parks and school playgrounds. The former seeks to criminalise the preparatory acts involved in abuse, such as the 'grooming' of children, and can be used whether or not the individual has a prior record of offending. These measures, like notification, are also founded on the basic premise that the best way to protect the community and secure offender reintegration is through increased restriction, surveillance and monitoring of sex offenders (Kemshall 2001). The proliferation of legislative measures, in the UK in particular, is indicative of the high level of attention afforded in recent years to reintegrating sex offenders in the community within the context of a risk-based regulatory framework. The key criminal justice organisations that work to manage the risk posed by these offenders and to protect the public have therefore been given greater powers to carry out their work.

In the UK, there is a strongly embedded inter-agency culture of risk assessment and management which is firmly linked to working practices (Kemshall and Maguire 2001; Maguire *et al* 2001). Previously informal initiatives by various agencies (Sampson *et al* 1998) have been reinforced by the adoption of 'joined up' working (Cowan *et al* 2001: 439) and 'the end to end management of the offender'.[8] All work with sex offenders now takes place on a multi-agency basis via the work of Multi-Agency Public Protection Panels (MAPPPs) (Kemshall *et al* 1997; Bryan and Doyle 2003; Lieb 2003). Formal risk assessment and management is routinely undertaken by these inter-agency panels comprising members of the police, social services and probation, and additonally, voluntary sector agencies involved in the provision of accommodation and training and employment initiatives. The degree of agency intervention is based on whether sex offenders have been risk assessed and subsequently categorised as being of a low, medium or high risk of re-offending. These arrangements which require agencies to co-operate to identify, assess and manage the risk posed by sex offenders and other dangerous offenders in the community (Home Office 1997) have now been placed on a statutory footing.[9]

Popular discourses on sex offender reintegration

Media and public discourses on sex offender reintegration have prompted and sustained risk-based state responses through public protests about the presence of released sex offenders in the local community and the media-led cry for a more punitive criminal justice response. As a consequence, the reintegration of sex offenders post-release from custody is a difficult issue to address meaningfully in the public context. At times, the reaction of the public to the placement of sex offenders in their area has been an emotive, hostile and even violent one. In this respect, one of the most difficult issues for MAPPPs is that of public disclosure of information about the identity or whereabouts of sex offenders within the local community (Kemshall and Maguire 2003). The question of when the community should be notified about the presence of sex offenders living in their area in the UK is nowhere near as widespread as in the US and currently operates on a strict 'need to know' basis (Power 2003). Certainly, the difficulties related to community reaction to the resettlement of the sex offenders in the local community make it clear that this is an especially volatile issue.

The press and public response in this respect can be best epitomised by the adoption of 'name and shame' campaigns for the public outing of paedophiles. Following the abduction and murder of eight-year old Sarah Payne in Sussex in July 2000, the *News of the World* developed its 'Name and Shame' campaign which centred on printing the photographs, and names and addresses of known and suspected paedophiles, along with brief details of their offending history (Silverman and Wilson 2002: 146–66).

This campaign encouraged public outcry, wide spread hysteria and often vigilante justice (Ashenden 2002). Residents on the Paulsgrove estate in

Portsmouth protested nightly at the presence of paedophiles in their community and the failure of the authorities to notify them of their whereabouts (Williams and Thompson 2004a, 2004b). Protesters demonstrated outside the homes of suspected paedophiles, smeared slogans on their walls, issued threats and overturned and burned cars. As a result of this activity, one convicted paedophile disappeared and two alleged paedophiles committed suicide (Ashenden 2002: 208). One woman's house was attacked merely because she had the same surname as a known sexual offender. Famously, the offices of a local paediatrician were also targeted because the community had mistakenly made the association with the word 'paedophile'.

As will be discussed further below, risk-based approaches to sex offender reintegration in the form of a controlling legislative framework and a punitive reaction on the part of the media and the public undermine offender rehabilitation. They simply serve to label, stigmatise and isolate the offender from the rest of the community and impede their successful reintegration (Winick 1998: 539, 556; McAlinden 2005).

The risks of the 'risk-based' model

The risk-based model of sex offender reintegration which has dominated recent official and popular discourses is challenged signficantly by a number of factors. These relate chiefly to the undermining of risk and security, contrary to official intention, and the process of 'disintegrative shaming' (Braithwaite 1989).

Knowledge-risk-security

The opprobrious reaction of the media and the public to sex offender reintegration, which we have witnessed to date, are clearly at odds with the criminal justice system's calculated knowledge of risk and security. In the main, the only discernible level of engagement between authorities and the public in relation to the issue of sex offender reintegration is through possible community notification, which is usually in itself limited. As noted above, through community notification in particular, the intention of control is undermined potentially by a punitive media and public who are intent on removing offenders from their area rather than securing their reintegration. This then works to undermine knowledge of the offender's whereabouts and public security and ultimately to increase risk.

Somewhat paradoxically perhaps, 'risk management' within the context of measures such as sex offender registration is rooted in and itself constitutes 'insecurity' (Ewald 1986; Hebenton and Thomas 1996b: 440). Consistent with Ericson and Haggerty's (1997) model of knowledge-risk-security, outlined above, sex offender registration or notification appeared to be produced, in part, from an assumption that simply having knowledge about an offender's whereabouts would promote offender reintegration. The legislation failed, in particular, however, to develop a clear concept of how this information could be used effectively, beyond the transcarceration of the offender, to reduce the risk of future offending, promote reintegration, and protect the community (McAlinden 2007: 25). Failure to address a number of key practical issues during the formulation of the legislation, such as adequate policing resources (Marshall 1997; Cobley 2003: 60–61), has meant that the expansion of regulatory framework for controlling of sex offenders in the community post-release effectively ends up producing the opposite (Hebenton and Thomas 1996b: 441).

Disintegrative shaming

As noted above, the aftermath of the 'Name and Shame' campaign underlines the potential for disintegrative shaming (Braithwaite 1989) which may lead to harassment or even physical attack by vengeful members of the community on suspected sex offenders. This singling out of the offender via public shaming sanctions which underpin the risk-based model, however, may also have a number of other negative effects on sex offender reintegration, beyond the physical element.

First, it may impede their successful reintegration into the community, their ability to get a job or accommodation and therefore ultimately, their rehabilitation (Bedarf 1995: 885, 910–11; Cobley 1997a: 103; Soothill and Francis 1998: 291). Second, heightening the offender's sense of isolation may ultimately increase the chance of subsequent delinquent behaviour as a coping mechanism (Edwards and Hensley 2001). The application of a criminal label, which these measures inevitably entail, can confirm an offending identity which the sex offender may find easier to live out rather than to try to break from it (Winick 1998: 539, 556). Third, from the 'deviancy amplification spiral',[10] also of the labelling perspective (Wilkins 1964), the offender who is isolated from 'normal' law-abiding society may be forced to associate with similar offenders where they learn more sophisticated techniques. Fourth, if an offender becomes known or ostracised in the area where he lives he will not be deterred from future crime. The offender may simply go underground where he could be of even greater danger and displace risk elsewhere (Bedarf 1995: 90–10; Prentky 1996: 295–96; Soothill and Francis 1998: 288–89).

Therefore, consistent with Braithwaite's (1989) thesis of shaming, disintegrative shaming practices in the form of coercive criminal justice risk-based responses will not stop levels of sexual offending and may even lead to an increase in such crimes (Berliner 1996: 292; Earl-Hubbard 1996: 856; Prentky 1996: 296; Cobley 1997b; Edwards and Hensley 2001). Without structured support programmes in the community to assist in offender readjustment and to help them desist, risk-based models of reintegration may result in more incidents of sexual offences in the long term (Finstad 1990; Braithwaite and Daly 1994; Hudson 1998: 237). As will be discussed further below, shaming, however, can also be used to positive effect in the process of sex offender management and reintegration.

developing reintegrative social support systems, such as circle programmes, which are individually tailored to particular sex offenders (McEvoy 2008: 20–23, 43; McAlinden 2007: Chapter 7).

Circles of support and accountability

Circle programmes which originated in Canada, operate with selected high risk sexual offenders who are re-entering the community on release from prison (Cesaroni, 2001; Petrunik 2002: 503–05; Silverman and Wilson 2002: 167–84; Wilson *et al* 2002, 2007a). Canada is a society which has traditionally balanced discourses on 'risk' with a rights-based legal and policy framework, transforming the politics of crime control (Mantel 1994; Hudson 2003: 220). This has arguably stopped Canada from adopting some of the more punitive managerialist interventions witnessed in recent times in the UK. The scheme is based on the twin philosophies of safety and support – it addresses public concerns surrounding the reintegration of sex offenders and also the offender's rehabilitative needs. The circle is focused on the development of a network of social support built around the offender, the core member, involving the wider community together with state and voluntary agencies. The offender and other members of the circle sign a covenant which specifies each member's area of assistance. The scheme provides high levels of support, treatment, guidance and supervision for the offender, mediating between the police, media and the general community to minimise risk and assist in reintegration. This also includes practical assistance with finding stable accommodation and employment. The offender agrees to relate to the circle of support, pursue treatment and to act responsibly in the community. The offender has daily contact with someone from the circle each day in the high risk phase just after release which eventually diminishes (McAlinden 2005, 2007: 168–77). The circle remains in place as long as the risk to the offender and the community are above average.

Circles have also been extended to a number of jurisdictions, including the US, the Netherlands, Scotland (Armstrong *et al* 2008; Kirkwood and Richley 2008), the Republic of Ireland and Northern Ireland. In England and Wales in particular they have been used to support the work of MAPPPs, which were discussed above. Circles were initially developed in Thames Valley, the Hampton Trust and the Lucy Faithful Foundation to support statutory agencies in the effective management of high risk sex offenders released into the community. For example, circles have been used to report areas of concern back to the MAPPPs. This then enabled agencies to tighten control of the offender through targeted surveillance (Quaker Peace and Social Witness 2005: 14).

It is important to note, therefore, that there is a clear distinction between the dominant circle models adopted in Canada and England and Wales respectively. It has been said that while the Canadian model is organic, the English model is more systemic (Quaker Peace and Social Witness 2005: 6). To put it another way, and to return to the literature outlined above, the differences between the models can also usefully be explained by reference to Maruna and LeBel's (2002) dichotomy of 'strengths-based' and 'risk-based' approaches. That is, the former grew out of the need of a faith community to support individual offender reintegration on an ad hoc basis, while the latter is characterised instead by risk-based coercive agendas which are heavily focused on offender management. It is argued that the Canadian model in this sense offers an enhanced and potentially more effective means of meeting offender's resettlement needs in terms of effective community-based support. Circles address many of the core problems involved with sex offender reintegration – in terms of reducing sexual recidivism and securing the involvement of the local community in this process – as well as reflecting the ethos of the strengths-based approach.

Addressing the problems with reintegration

Empirical research shows that circles have been effective in reducing recidivism rates among high risk sex offenders (McAlinden 2007: 180–83). One early evaluation of circles in Ontario found that recidivism was reduced by more than 50 per cent where each incident of re-offending was less invasive and severe than the original offence for which the offender had been imprisoned (Wilson *et al* 2002). More recent evaluations have further demonstrated that circles have greatly assisted released high-risk sex offenders in desisting from re-offending by increasing offender responsibility and accountability as well as enhancing community safety (Wilson *et al* 2007b). In the most recent evaluations, for example, a sample of 60 high risk sex offenders who participated in the circles programme had significantly lower rates of re-offending than those that did not: a 70 per cent reduction in sexual recidivism, a 57 per cent reduction in all types of violent recidivism (including sexual), and a 35 per cent reduction in all types of recidivism (Wilson *et al* 2007c).

Early evaluations of these projects in England and Wales have also shown that circles have been effective in reducing expected rates of recidivism and assisting in offender reintegration through, for example, securing employment and housing (Quaker Peace and Social Witness 2005). A follow-up to the Thames Valley project investigated the outcome of circles with 16 core members. None of the core members had been reconvicted of a new sexual offence and of the 10 core members displaying recidivist behaviour, in six cases this was detected by the circles and the information passed to the relevant professional agencies (Bates *et al* 2007).

Moreover, circles have proven effectiveness in enhancing perceptions about community safety and in providing reassurance to the local community in a way that simple community notification or other aspects of risk-based approaches cannot. In the research by Wilson and colleagues, for example, circle members were given a 'hypothetical knowledge' that a high-risk sex offender had moved into their community. Initially, 33 per cent of respondents said they would feel unsafe in this knowledge. However, 68 per cent of respondents said they would feel more secure if they knew that the offender was part of a circle programme (Wilson *et al* 1997b: 3000). Equally in England and Wales, professional agencies have also been convinced of the effectiveness of circles (Wilson *et al* 2007b; Armstrong *et al* 2008). An evaluation of the MAPPPs arrangements recommended expanding the availability of longer-term intervention strategies such as circles of support (Wood and Kemshall 2007).

Circles and the 'strengths-based' approach

Circles of support are based on a 'partnership' approach to crime prevention where the local community works in tandem with statutory and voluntary agencies (Crawford 1999). In place of a model of professional 'expertise', therefore, is one that emphasises shared information and the importance of diverse knowledgeable agencies and an informed public (Crawford 1999: 59). As noted above, these programmes have given professional agencies a clear means of actively and positively engaging with the local community on contentious sex offender issues (Quaker Peace and Social Witness 2005: 18). Circles have successfully encouraged communities to play a constructive role in the reintegrative process (Quaker Peace and Social Witness 2005). Circles have opened up the work of statutory agencies by providing an opportunity for the general public to contribute to the resettlement of individual offenders. In short, rather than being part of the resettlement conundrum in terms of how professionals may placate the local community or find a safe and suitable place to relocate a released sex offender, the community itself can play a role in solving these often difficult issues. Moreover, a small group of community members may also offer a practical means of addressing the concerns of the wider community in relation to the placement of sex offenders in their area.

Indeed, circle programmes accord with the central tenets emerging from the review of the literature above. In essence, they recognise the wide range of social and personal problems which all offenders may face which may have a bearing on reintegration and, in particular, they address the three core themes which underline the 'strengths-based' approach which have been outlined above: (a) the importance of 'place'; (b) the role of hope; and (c) reintegrative shaming.

The importance of 'place'

This idea is one of the cornerstones of restorative justice initiatives with sex offenders such as circles of support. Circle programmes are focused on the development of supportive networks to assist with practical aspects of offender reintegration, such as obtaining housing and employment. Circles provide the offender with many of these 'benevolent' (Farrall and Sparks 2006: 12) factors and a suitable social space in which offenders can publicly affirm to themselves and others their commitment to a future non-offending identity. Circles of support have helped to shape the offender's relationships with the local community and have provided an effective forum in which the interchange between local community structures and the offender's rehabilitation has been successfully played out.

The role of hope

As outlined above, some of the most recent work on desistance from crime has focused on the role of 'hope' in fostering and sustaining offender desistance (Burnett and Maruna 2004; Farrall and Calverley 2005). Community forums like circles may be able to provide these crucial ingredients of emotional support, help with practical aspects of reintegration such as accommodation and employment, and psychological or cognitive support in terms of effective treatment or rehabilitative programmes. In short, they may provide both a symbolic and actual means of hope of offender desistance and reintegration by supporting the ex-perpetrator in their efforts to change. Indeed, this is consistent with the general research literature on offender resettlement which demonstrates that reintegrative approaches which combine cognitive-motivational programmes with practical services have produced encouraging early results (Maguire and Raynor 2006: 19).

Reintegrative shaming

Braithwaite's (1989) theory of reintegrative shaming is inextricably linked to that of restorative justice. Unlike risk-based punitive criminal justice responses, restorative justice is focused on 'changing the normative orientation of law from retribution to restoration' (Hudson 1998: 238). It views crime not as a violation of a general legal category which merits punishment but as harm to individual people and relationships and, as the term suggests, seeks to redress or restore that harm (Consedine 1995; Van Ness and Strong 1997/2002). The dynamics of initiatives such as circles of support, which have been outlined above, fully address these central facets of restorative, reintegrative shaming processes chiefly by empowering sex offenders to take responsibility for what they have done in a context of positive reinforcement. By shaming the offender rather than the offence (Braithwaite and Mugford 1994) and by helping the offender find their place again in civil society, measures such as circles of support encapsulate the strengths-based philosophy. As Burnett and Maruna put it, they recognise that 'individuals emerging from a shameful past need high levels of support in nurturing their pro-social inclinations, to restore their sense of belonging, mastery, independence…' (Burnett and Maruna 2006: 101).

Conclusion

In post-modern Western societies, arguably sex offenders remain one of the most difficult groups to rehabilitate and reintegrate. This is due in large part to societal reactions to released sex offenders, particularly those who have offended against children. Strengths-based approaches to offender reintegration are fundamentally different from punitive risk-based agendas by focusing instead on developing intrinsic motivations for personal change in a socially supportive environment. Such a model or process may ultimately offer a means of moving away from current risk-management discourses which may lead to public disclosure of offender status with all its attendant negative consequences towards the real and effective social reintegration of sex offenders in the absence of prejudice and stigma (Goffman 1963). As Maruna argues in the general context but which can apply equally to sex offenders, 'such rituals, if they were to be institutionalised as part of reintegration practice, might improve efforts to reintegrate ex-offenders into society' (Maruna 2001: 13).

At the theoretical level, at the time of writing, initiatives based on restorative or reintegrative theory are gaining ground in the criminal justice terrain for a growing number of serious offences (McAlinden 2007), despite the concerns of critics (Cossins 2008). Indeed, its general principles of repairing relationships, and promoting offender reintegration are now well recognised and accepted (Johnstone 2001; Sullivan and Tift 2001; McEvoy *et al* 2002). Indeed, at the practical level, as noted above, there is some professional support for expanding the availability of reintegration strategies such as circles of support with sex offenders (Wood and Kemshall 2007).

A difficulty, however, as even proponents recognise, is that the current popular and political concern with public protection and managing the dangerous which lies at the heart of risk-based managerialist retributive approaches has the potential to undermine strengths-based restorative policies (Burnett and Maruna 2006: 102). There are an increasing number of evaluations, however, which demonstrate the effectiveness of strengths-based restorative or reintegrative initiatives with sex offenders such as circles of support across a range of variables including reducing recidivism rates and increasing the level of positive and proactive community involvement. Such mounting evidence will become hard for the public and policy makers to ignore in the current 'what works' criminal justice climate.

Notes

1 For the sake of completeness, the other type of 'deficit' model outlined by Maruna and LeBel (2002) is 'needs-based' strategies which focus on helping ex-offenders to overcome addictions or learn basic skills in order to reduce the risk of re-offending.
2 There have been several theoretical attempts to define precisely what is meant by 'resettlement' (Maguire and Raynor 2006; McNeil 2006) and, indeed, it has also been questioned whether this is actually possible, particularly where an elderly inmate population is concerned (Crawley and Sparks 2006).
3 The central arguments in this chapter are based on previous work by the author. See in particular: McAlinden 2005 and 2007: Chapters 2, 3 and 7.
4 This thesis is also linked to strain theory which seeks to explain crime as a process whereby those with limited social and individual resources are more likely to resort to

deviant activities due to the tension between material aspirations and social advantages (Merton 1993).

5 Following a twin review of the law on sexual offences (Home Office 2000) and the Sex Offenders Act 1997 (Home Office 2001), a White Paper set out to address the issues raised by these reviews (Home Office 2002). This resulted in the Sexual Offences Act 2003 which also redefined and widened the scope of sexual offences.
6 Sexual Offences Act 2003, ss 104–113.
7 Sexual Offences Act 2003, ss 123–129.
8 See National Offender Management Service (NOMS), accessed 1 July 2009, www.noms.homeoffice.gov.uk.
9 Criminal Justice and Courts Services Act 2000, ss 67–68, which place a duty on the police and probation services as 'the responsible authority' to establish these arrangements, were further enhanced by the Criminal Justice Act 2003. This Act extended the responsible authority to include the prison service (s 325(1)) and established a reciproical 'duty to co-operate' between the responsible authority and a number of other agencies such as local education, housing, health and social services authorities (s 325(6)).
10 The amplification spiral begins when society becomes less tolerant of particular forms of behaviour. This leads to more acts being defined as deviant, since people are now more conscious of this behaviour. As a result there is more action against criminals who are more severely punished or segregated, and more alienation of deviant groups who now only mix with one another. In turn this generates more crime by deviant groups. The net result is even less tolerance of deviants by conforming society and the process begins again.

References

Armstrong, S., Chistyakova, Y., Mackenzie, S., Malloch, M. (2008) *Circles of Support and Accountability: Consideration of the Feasibility of Pilots in Scotland*. Glasgow: The Scottish Centre for Crime and Justice.

Ashenden, S. (2002) 'Policing Perversion: The Contemporary Governance of Paedophilia', *Cultural Values*, 6: 197–222.

Ashenden, S. (2004) *Governing Child Sexual Abuse: Negotiating the Boundaries of Public and Private, Law and Science*. London: Routledge.

Bates, A., Saunders, R., Wilson, C. (2007) 'Doing Something About It: A Follow-up Study of Sex Offenders Participating in Thames Valley Circles of Support and Accountability', *British Journal of Community Justice*, 5: 19–42.

Bazemore, G. (1999) 'After Shaming, Whither Reintegration: Restorative Justice and Relational Rehabilitation', in Bazemore, G. and Walgrave, L. (eds) *Restorative Juvenile Justice: Repairing the Harm of Youth Crime*. Monsey, NY: Criminal Justice Press.

Beck, U. (1992) *Risk Society: Towards a New Modernity*. London: Sage.

Bedarf, A. (1995) 'Examining Sex Offender Community Notification Laws', California Law Review, 83: 885–937.

Berliner, L. (1996) 'Community Notification of Sex Offenders: A New Tool or a False Promise?', *Journal of Interpersonal Violence*, 11: 294–300.

Bottoms, A. E. (1995) 'The Philosophy and Politics of Punishment and Sentencing', in Clarkson, C. and Morgan, R. (eds) *The Politics of Sentencing Reform*. Oxford: Oxford University Press.

Bottoms, A. E., Wiles, P. (1992) 'Explanations of Crime and Place', in Evans, D.J., Fyfe, N.R. and Herberts, D.T. (eds) *Crime, Policing and Place*. London: Routledge.

Braithwaite, J. (1989) *Crime, Shame and Reintegration*. Sydney: Cambridge University Press.

Braithwaite, J. (2000) 'The New Regulatory State and the Transformation of Criminology', *British Journal of Criminology*, 40: 222–38.

Braithwaite, J. and Daly, K. (1994) 'Masculinities, Violence and Communitarian Control', in Newburn, T. and Stanko, E. (eds) *Just Boys Doing Business? Men, Masculinity and Crime*. London: Routledge.

Braithwaite, J. and Mugford, S. (1994) 'Conditions of Successful Reintegration Ceremonies', *British Journal of Criminology*, 34: 139–71.

Brown, M. (1996) 'Serious Offending and the Management of Public Risk in New Zealand', *British Journal of Criminology*, 36: 18–36.

Bryan, T. and Doyle, P. (2003) 'Developing Multi-Agency Public Protection Arrangements', in Matravers, A. (ed.) *Sex Offenders in the Community: Managing and Reducing the Risks*. Cullompton: Willan Publishing.

Burnett, R. and Maruna, S. (2004) 'So "Prison Works", Does It? The Criminal Careers of 130 Men Released from Prison under Home secretary, Michael Howard', *The Howard Journal of Criminal Justice*, 43: 390–404.

Burnett, R. and Maruna, S. (2006) 'The Kindness of Prisoners: Strengths-based Resettlement in Theory and in Action', *Criminology & Criminal Justice*, 6: 83–106.

Castel, R. (1991) 'From Dangerousness to Risk', in Burchell, G., Gordon C. and Miller P. (eds) *The Foucault Effect: Studies in Governmentality*. Chicago, IL: University of Chicago Press.

Cesaroni, C. (2001) 'Releasing Sex Offenders into the Community Through "Circles of Support" – A Means of Reintegrating the "Worst of the Worst"', *Journal of Offender Rehabilitation*, 34: 85–98.

Cobley, C. (1997a) 'Sentencing and Supervision of Sex Offenders', *Journal of Social Welfare and Family Law*, 19: 98–104.

Cobley, C. (1997b) 'Keeping Track of Sex Offenders: Part 1 of the Sex Offenders Act 1997', *Modern Law Review*, 60: 690–99.

Cobley, C. (2003) 'The Legislative Framework', in Matravers, A. (ed.) *Sex Offenders in the Community: Managing and Reducing the Risks*. Cullompton: Willan Publishing.

Cohen, S. (1985) *Visions of Social Control*. Cambridge: Polity Press.

Consedine, J. (1995) *Restorative Justice: Healing the Effects of the Crime*. Lyttleton: Ploughshares Publications.

Cossins, A. (2008) 'Restorative Justice and Child Sex Offences: The Theory and the Practice', *British Journal of Criminology*, 48: 359–78.

Cowan, D., Pantazis, C., and Gilroy, R. (2001) 'Social Housing as Crime Control: An Examination of the Role of Housing Management in Policing Sex Offenders', *Social & Legal Studies*, 10: 435–57.

Crawford, A. (1999) *The Local Governance of Crime: Appeals to Community and Partnerships*. Oxford: Oxford University Press.

Crawley, E. and Sparks, R. (2006) 'Is There Life After Punishment? How Elderly Men Talk About Imprisonment and Release', *Criminology & Criminal Justice*, 6: 63–82.

Cumming, G. and Buell, M. (1997) *Supervision of the Sex Offender*. Brandon, VT: Safer Society.

Curtis, R.L. and Schulmann, S. (1984) 'Ex-offenders, Family Relations, and Economic Supports: "The Significant Women" Study of the TARP Project', *Crime and Delinquency*, 30: 507–28.

Earl-Hubbard, M. (1996) 'The Child Sex Offender Registration Laws: The Punishment, Liberty, Deprivation and Unintended Results Associated with the Scarlet Letter Laws of the 1990s', *North Western Law Review*, 90: 788–862.

Edwards, W. and Hensley, C. (2001) 'Contextualising Sex Offender Management Legislation and Policy: Evaluating the Problem of Latent Consequences in Community Notification Laws', *International Journal of Offender Therapy and Comparative Criminology*, 45: 83–101.

Ericson, R. V. (1994) 'The Division of Expert Knowledge in Policing and Security', *British Journal of Sociology*, 45: 149–76.

Ericson, R. V. (2007) *Crime in an Insecure World*. Cambridge: Polity Press.

Ericson, R. V. and Haggerty, K. D. (1997) *Policing the Risk Society*. Oxford: Clarendon Press.

Ewald, F. (1986) *L'Etat Providence*. Paris: Grasset.

Farkas, M. A. and Miller, G. (2007) 'Reentry and Reintegration: Challenges Faced by the Families of Convicted Sex Offenders', *Federal Sentencing Reporter*, 20: 88–92.

Farrall, S. (2002) *Rethinking What Works with Offenders: Probation, Social Context and Desistance from Crime*, Cullompton: Willan Publishing.

Farrall, S. (2003) '"J" accuse: Probation, Evaluation-Research Epistemologies (Part Two: This Time Its Personal and Social Factors)', *Criminal Justice*, 3: 249–68.

Farrall, S. and Bowling, B. (1999) 'Structuration, Human Development and Desistance from Crime', *British Journal of Criminology*, 39: 252–67.

Farrall, S. and Calverley, A. (2005) *Understanding Desistance From Crime*, London: Open University Press.

Farrall, S. and Maltby, S. (2003) 'The Victimisation of Probationers', *The Howard Journal of Criminal Justice*, 42: 32–54.

Farrall, S. and Sparks, S. (2006) 'Introduction' (Special Issue: What Lies Beyond? Problems, Prospects and Possibilities for Life After Punishment), *Criminology & Criminal Justice*, 6: 7–16.

Farrant, F. and Levenson, J. (2002) *Barred Citizens: Volunteering and Active Citizenship by Prisoners*. London: Prison Reform Trust.

Feely, M. and Simon, J. (1992) 'The New Penology: Notes on the Emerging Strategy of Corrections and Its Implications', *Criminology*, 30: 449–74.

Feely, M. and Simon, J. (1994) 'Actuarial Justice: the Emerging New Criminal Law', in Nelken, D. (ed.) *The Futures of Criminology*. London: Sage.

Finstad, L. (1990) 'Sexual Offenders Out of Prison: Principles for a Realistic Utopia', *International Journal of the Sociology of Law*, 18: 157–77.

Garland, D. (1996) 'The Limits of the Sovereign State: Strategies of Crime Control in Contemporary Society', *British Journal of Criminology*, 36: 445–71.

Garland, D. (2001) *The Culture of Control: Crime and Social Order in Contemporary Society*. Oxford: Oxford University Press.

Giddens, A. (1984) *The Constitution of Society*. Cambridge: Polity Press.

Giddens, A. (1990) *The Consequences of Modernity*. Cambridge: Polity Press.

Giordano, P., Cernkovich, S. and Rudolph, J. (2002) 'Gender, Crime and Desistance: Toward a Theory of Cognitive Transformation', *American Journal of Sociology*, 107: 990–1064.

Goffman, E. (1963) *Stigma*. Harmondsworth: Penguin Books.

Hagan, J. (1997) 'Crime and Capitalization: Toward a Developmental Theory of Street Crime in America', in Thornberry, T. (ed.) *Developmental Theories of Crime and Delinquency*. New Brunswick, NJ: Transaction Press.

Hagan, J. and McCarthy, B. (1997) *Mean Streets: Youth Crime and Homelessness*. Cambridge, MA: Harvard University Press.

Hebenton, B. and Thomas, T. (1996a) 'Tracking Sex Offenders', *The Howard Journal of Criminal Justice*, 35: 97–112.

Hebenton, B. and Thomas, T. (1996b) 'Sexual Offenders in the Community: Reflections on Problems of Law, Community and Risk Management in the USA and England and Wales', *International Journal of the Sociology of Law*, 24: 427–43.

Hobbs, D. (1989) *Doing the Business: Entrepreneurship, the Working Class, and Detectives in the East End of London*. Oxford: Clarendon Press.

Home Office (1996a) *Protecting the Public: The Government's Strategy on Crime in England and Wales*, Cm 3190. London: HMSO.

Home Office (1996b) *Sentencing and Supervision of Sex Offenders: A Consultation Document*, Cm 3304. London: HMSO.

Home Office (1997) *The Sex Offenders Act 1997*, Home Office Circular 39/97. London: Home Office.

Home Office (2000) *Setting the Boundaries: Reforming the Law on Sex Offences*. London: Home Office.

Home Office (2001) *Consultation Paper on the Review of Part I of the Sex Offenders Act 1997*. London: Home Office.

Home Office (2002) *Protecting the Public: Strengthening Protection Against Sex Offenders and Reforming the Law on Sexual Offences*, Cm 5668. London: HMSO.

Hope, T. (2001) 'Community Crime Prevention in Britain: A Strategic Overview', *Criminal Justice*, 1: 421–39.

Hudson, B. (1998) 'Restorative Justice: The Challenge of Sexual and Racial Violence', *Journal of Law and Society*, 25: 237–56.

Hudson, B. (2001) 'Human Rights, Public Safety and the Probation Service: Defending Justice in the Risk Society', *The Howard Journal of Criminal Justice*, 40: 103–13.

Hudson, B. (2003) *Justice in the Risk Society: Challenging and Re-affirming Justice in Late Modernity*. London: Sage.

Johnson, J. L. (2006) 'Sex Offenders on Federal Community Supervision: Factors that Influence Revocation', *Federal Probation*, 70: 18–32.

Johnston, L. (2000) *Policing Britain: Risk, Security and Governance*. Essex: Longman Publishing.

Johnstone, G. (2001) *Restorative Justice: Ideas, Values, Debates*. Cullompton: Willan Publishing.

Kemshall, H. (2001) *Risk Assessment and Management of Known Sexual and Violent Offenders: A Review of Current Issues*, Police Research Series Paper No 140. London: Home Office.

Kemshall, H. and Maguire, M. (2001) 'Public Protection, Partnership and Risk Penality: The Multi-agency Risk Management of Sexual and Violent Offenders', *Punishment and Society*, 3: 237–64.

Kemshall, H. and Maguire, M. (2003) 'Sex Offenders, Risk Penality and The Problem of Disclosure', in Matravers, A. (ed.) *Sex Offenders in the Community: Managing and Reducing*. Cullompton: Willan Publishing.

Kemshall, H., Parton, N., Walsh, M. and Waterson, J. (1997) 'Concepts of Risk in Relation to the Organisational Structure and Functioning within the Personal Social Services and Probation', *Social Policy and Administration*, 31: 213–32.

Kirkwood, S. and Richley, T. (2008) 'Circles of Support and Accountability: The Case for their Use in Scotland to Assist in the Community Reintegration and Risk Management of Sex Offenders', *SCOLAG*, 372: 236–39.

Kruttschnitt, C., Uggen, C. and Shelton, K. (2000) 'Predictors of Desistance among Sex Offenders: The Interactions of Formal and Informal Social Controls', *Justice Quarterly*, 17: 61–88.

Laub, J. and Sampson, R. J. (2001) 'Understanding Desistance from Crime', *Crime and Justice: A Review of Research*, 28: 1–69.

Laub, J. and Sampson, R. J. (2003) *Shared Beginnings, Divergent Lives*. Harvard, MA: Harvard University Press.

Laub, J. H., Nagin, D. and Sampson, R. J. (1998) 'Trajectories of Change in Criminal Offending: Good Marriages and the Desistance Process', *American Sociological Review*, 63: 225–38.

Lieb, R. (2003) 'Joined-up Worrying: the Multi-Agency Public Protection Panels', in Matravers, A. (ed.) *Sex Offenders in the Community: Managing and Reducing the Risks*. Cullompton: Willan Publishing.

Lyon, D. (1994) *The Electronic Eye: The Rise of Surveillance Society*. Cambridge: Polity Press.

Maguire, M. and Raynor, P. (2006) 'How the Resettlement of Prisoners Promotes Desistance from Crime: Or Does It?', *Criminology & Criminal Justice*, 6: 19–38.

Maguire, M., Kemshall, H., Noakes, L., Wincup, E. and Sharpe, K. (2001) *Risk Management of Sexual and Violent Offenders: The Work of Public Protection Panels*, Police Research Series Paper No 13. London: Home Office.

Mantel, M. (1994) *The Charter of Rights and the Legalization of Politics in Canada*. Toronto: Thompson Educational Publishing Inc.

Marshall. P. (1997) *The Prevalence of Convictions for Sexual Offending*, Home Office Research Bulletin No 55. London: Home Office.

Marshall, W. L., Ward, T., Mann, R. E., Moulden, H., Fernandez, Y. M., Serran, G. and Marshall, L. E. (2005) 'Working Positively with Sexual Offenders', *Journal of Interpersonal Violence*, 20: 1096–114.

Maruna, S. (2001) *Making Good: How Ex-Convicts Reform and Rebuild Their Lives*. Washington, DC: APA Books.

Maruna, S. and Farrall, S. (2004) 'Desistance From Crime: A Theoretical Reformulation', *Köeitschrift für Soziologie und sozialpsychologie*, 43: 171–94.

Maruna, S. and Immarigeon, R. (eds) (2004) *After Crime and Punishment: Pathways to Offender Reintegration*. Cullompton: Willan Publishing.

Maruna, S. and LeBel, T. P. (2002) 'Revisiting Ex-prisoner Re-entry: A Buzz-word in Search of a Narrative', in Rex, S. and Tonry, M. (eds) *Reform and Punishment*. Cullompton: Willan Publishing.

Maruna, S., Immarigeon, R. and T. LeBel (2004) 'Ex-offender Reintegration: Theory and Practice', in Maruna, S. and Immarigeon, R. (eds) *After Crime & Punishment*. Cullompton: Willan Publishing.

MacLeod, J. (1995) *Ain't No Makin' It*, 2nd edn. Oxford: Westview Press.

Matravers, A. (ed.) (2003) *Sex Offenders in the Community: Managing and Reducing the Risks*. Cullompton, Willan Publishing.

Mays, J. B. (1952) 'A Study of a Delinquent Community', *British Journal of Delinquency*, 3: 5–19.

McAlinden, A. (2005) 'The Use of "Shame" with Sexual Offenders', *British Journal of Criminology*, 45: 373–94.

McAlinden, A. (2006) 'Managing Risk: From Regulation to the Reintegration of Sexual Offenders', *Criminology & Criminal Justice*, 6: 197–218.

McAlinden, A. (2007) *The Shaming of Sexual Offenders: Risk, Retribution and Reintegration*. Oxford: Hart Publishing.

McAlinden, A. (2010) 'Vetting Sexual Offenders: State Over-extension, the "Punishment Deficit" and the Failure to Manage Risk', *Social & Legal Studies*, 19(1): 25–48.

McEvoy, K. (2008) *Enhancing Employability in Prison & Beyond: A Literature Review*. Belfast: NIACRO.

McEvoy, K., Mika, H. and Hudson, B. (2002) 'Introduction: Practice, Performance and Prospects for Restorative Justice' (Special Issue: Restorative Justice), *British Journal of Criminology*, 42: 469–76.

McNeil, F. (2003) 'Desistance-Focused Probation Practice', in Chui, W. -H. and Nellis, M. (eds) *Moving Probation Forward: Evidence, arguments and Practice*. Harlow: Pearson Longman.

McNeil, F. (2006) 'A Desistance Paradigm for Offender Management', *Criminology & Criminal Justice*, 6: 39–62.

Meisenhelder, T. (1977) 'An Exploratory Study of Exiting From Criminal Careers', *Criminology*, 15: 319–34.

Merton, R. K. (1993, first published 1938) 'Social Structure and Anomie', in Lemert, C. (ed.) *Social Theory: The Multicultural Readings*. Boulder, CO: Westview Press.

Niven, S. and Stewart, D. (2005) 'Resettlement Outcomes on Release from Prison in 2003', Home Office Research Findings No 248. London: Home Office.

O'Malley, P. (1999) 'Volatile Punishments: Contemporary Penality and the Neo-Liberal Government', *Theoretical Criminology*, 3: 175–96.

O'Malley, P. (2002) 'Globalizing Risk? Distinguishing Styles of "Neo-liberal" Criminal Justice in Australia and the USA', *Criminal Justice*, 2: 205–222.

Parton, N., Thorpe, D. and Wattam, C. (1997) *Child Protection: Risk and the Moral Order*. Hampshire: Macmillan.

Petersilia, J. (2003) *When Prisoners Come Home: Parole and Prisoner Re-entry*. Oxford: Oxford University Press.

Petrunik, M. G. (2002) 'Managing Unacceptable Risk: Sex Offenders, Community Response, and Social Policy in the United States and Canada', *International Journal of Offender Therapy and Comparative Criminology*, 46: 483–511.

Power, H. (2003) 'Disclosing Information on Sex Offenders: The Human Rights Implications', in Matravers, A. (ed.) *Sex Offenders in the Community: Managing and Reducing the Risks*. Cullompton: Willan Publishing.

Prentky, R. A. (1996) 'Community Notification and Constructive Risk Reduction', Journal of Interpersonal Violence, 11: 295–98.

Quaker Peace and Social Witness (2005) Circles of Support and Accountability in the Thames Valley: The First three Years – April 2002 to March 2005. London: Quaker Communications.

Robinson, G. (2002) 'Exploring Risk Management in Probation Practice: Contemporary Developments in England and Wales', *Punishment and Society*, 4: 5–25.

Rose, N. (2000) 'Government and Control', *British Journal of Criminology*, 40: 321–39.

Rutter, M. and Giller, H. (1983) *Juvenile Delinquency: Trends & Perspectives*. New York, NY: Guildford.

Sampson, A., Stubbs, P. Smith, D., Pearson, G. and Blagg, H. (1988) 'Crime, Localities and the Multi-Agency Approach', *British Journal of Criminology*, 28: 478–93.

Sampson, R. J. and Laub, J. H. (1993) *Crime in the Making: Pathways and Turning Points Through Life*. London: Harvard University Press.

Sampson, R. J. and Laub, J. H. (1994) 'Urban Poverty and the Family Context of Delinquency', *Child Development*, 65: 523–40.

Seleznow, E. (2002) 'Time to Work: Managing the Employment of Sex Offenders Under Community Supervision', accessed 1 March 2009, www.csom.org/pubs/timetowork.pdf, Center for Sex Offender Management. Washington, DC: US Department of Justice, Office of Justice Programmes.

Shearing, C. (2000) 'Punishment and the Changing Face of Governance', *Punishment and Society*, 3: 203–20.

Shute, S. (2004) 'The Sexual Offences Act 2003: (4) New Civil Preventative Orders – Sexual Offences Prevention Orders; Foreign Travel Orders; Risk of Sexual Harm Orders', *Criminal Law Review*, 417–40.

Silverman, J. and Wilson, D. (2002) *Innocence Betrayed: Paedophilia, the Media and Society*. Cambridge: Polity Press.

Simon, J. (1993) *Poor Discipline*. Chicago, IL: University of Chicago.

Simon, J. (1998) 'Managing the Monstrous: Sex Offenders and the New Penology', *Psychology, Public Policy and Law*, 4: 452–67.

Soothill, K. and Francis, B. (1998) 'Poisoned Chalice or Just Deserts? (The Sex Offenders Act 1997)', *Journal of Forensic Psychiatry*, 9: 281–93.

Soothill, K., Francis, B. and Sanderson, B. (1997) 'A Cautionary Tale: the Sex Offenders Act 1997, the Police and Cautions', *Criminal Law Review*, 482–90.

Sullivan, D. and Tifft, L. (2001) *Restorative Justice: Healing the Foundations of Our Everyday Lives*. Monsey, NY: Willowtree Press.

Toch, H. (2000) 'Altruistic Activity as Correctional Treatment', *International Journal of Offender Therapy & Comparative Criminology*, 44: 270–78.

Travis, J. and Petersilia, J. (2001) 'Re-entry Reconsidered: A New Look at an Old Question', *Crime and Delinquency*, 47: 291–313.

Van Ness, D. and Strong, K. H. (1997/2002) *Restoring Justice*. Cincinnati, OH: Anderson Publishing Co.

Ward, T. and Marshall, W. L. (2004) 'Good Lives, Aetiology and the Rehabilitation of Sex Offenders: A Bridging Theory', *Journal of Sexual Aggression*, 10: 153–69.

Ward, T., Mann, R. E. and Gannon, T. A. (2007) 'Good Lives Model of Offender Rehabilitation: Clinical Implications', Aggression and Violent Behaviour, 12: 87–107.

Wargent, M. (2002) 'The New Governance of Probation', *The Howard Journal of Criminal Justice*, 41: 182–200.

Wilkins, L. (1964) *Social Deviance: Social Policy, Action and Research*. London: Tavistock.

Williams, A. and Thompson, B. (2004a) 'Vigilance or Vigilantes: The Paulsgrove Riots and Policing Paedophiles in the Community: Part 1: The Long Slow Fuse', *Police Journal*, 77: 99–119.

Williams, A. and Thompson, B. (2004b) 'Vigilance or Vigilantes: The Paulsgrove Riots and Policing Paedophiles in the Community: Part 2: The Lessons of Paulsgrove', *Police Journal*, 77: 193–205.

Wilson, R. J., Huculak, B. and McWhinnie, A. (2002), 'Restorative Justice Innovations in Canada', *Behavioural Sciences and the Law*, 20(4): 363–80.

Wilson, R. J., McWhinnie, A., Picheca, J. E., Prinzo, M. and Cortoni, F. (2007a) 'Circles of Support and Accountability: Engaging Community Volunteers in the Management of High-Risk Sexual Offenders', *The Howard Journal of Criminal Justice*, 46(1): 1–15.

Wilson, R. J., Picheca, J. E. and Prinzo, M. (2007b) 'Evaluating the Effectiveness of Professionally-Facilitated Volunteerism in the Community-Based Management of High-Risk Sexual Offenders: Part One – Effects on Participants and Stakeholders', *The Howard Journal of Criminal Justice*, 46(3): 289–302.

Wilson, R. J., Picheca, J. E. and Prinzo, M. (2007c) 'Evaluating the Effectiveness of Professionally-Facilitated Volunteerism in the Community-Based Management of High-Risk Sexual Offenders: Part Two – A Comparison of Recidivism Rates', *The Howard Journal of Criminal Justice*, 46(4): 327–37.

Winick, B. (1998) 'Sex Offender Law in the 1990s: A Therapeutic Analysis', *Psychology, Public Policy and Law*, 4(1–2): 505–70.

Wood, J. and Kemshall, H. (2007), *The Operation and Experience of Multi-Agency Public Protection Arrangements (MAPPA)*, Home Office Findings 285. London: Home Office.

Zamble, E. and Quinsey, V. (1997) *The Criminal Recidivism Process*. Cambridge: Cambridge University Press.

Zedner, L. (2009) 'Fixing the Future? The Pre-emptive Turn in Criminal Justice', in McSherry, B., Norrie, A. and Bronitt, S. (eds) *Regulating Deviance: The Redirection of Criminalisation and the Futures of Criminal Law*. Oxford: Hart Publishing.

Zevitz, R. G. and Farkas, M. A. (2000) 'Sex Offender Community Notification: Managing High Risk Criminals or Exacting Further Vengeance?, *Behavioural Sciences and the Law*, 18: 375–91.

Chapter 7

All in the family

The importance of support, tolerance and forgiveness in the desistance of male Bangladeshi offenders

Adam Calverley

Introduction

In contrast to the widespread (and, rightly, controversial) public and academic focus on ethnicity in relation to engagement in offending, existing research has largely overlooked whether processes associated with desistance from crime vary by ethnicity. This is despite known ethnic differences in factors frequently identified as affecting disengagement from offending, such as employment, place of residence, religious affiliation and family structure, suggesting good reasons for believing differences may exist. This relative neglect of ethnicity as a potentially important factor in the desistance process has not gone unnoticed. Indeed, the leading researchers in this field, Laub and Sampson, have speculated:

> We expect that variations by race, ethnicity and structural context in promoting successful transitions to young adulthood will have effects on the desistance process. We know that rates of marriage and employment vary by race and social class. We also know neighbourhood contexts vary as well, and it is expected that these neighbourhood differences will interact with individual differences to increase the probability of crime and violence. But exactly how these interactions between person and context affect the desistance process is the key research question.
>
> (Laub and Sampson 2001: 55–56)

Therefore, if we are to adequately address this 'key research question' we need to look at how the 'variety of contexts – developmental, historical, and environmental – that bear on desistance' (Laub and Sampson 2001: 12) may vary according to different ethnic groups. This forces us to examine issues of community and their role in shaping these 'variety of contexts'. Moreover, if we are to understand the significance of these differences we must seek to explore the accounts of desisters from these different ethnic communities to better understand their experiences of desistance: whether these are shared with others' of the same ethnicity, and if so what factors are responsible.

In this chapter I will seek to address this oversight by considering the processes which are associated with desistance amongst a sample of male UK-based offenders who share the same ethnic origin: their families once originated from Bangladesh. In contrast to other minority ethnic groups, such as those of African and African-Caribbean ethnic origin, 'British Asian Bangladeshis' (to use the national census categorisation) have received relatively little criminological interest and, to date, no attention in relation to their experiences of stopping offending. Following an outline of the history, and social and economic position of Bangladeshis in the UK, I will focus on the important role that their families played in influencing their desistance and how the strong message of forgiveness and promise of future support they offered enabled the Bangladeshi desisters to envision and access a future away from crime. Finally, I will discuss the significant role of religion which many Bangladeshi respondents reported had helped to initiate and maintain their efforts to desist.

An overview of the UK Bangladeshi population

According to the last two censuses of 2001 and 1991, the UK's Bangladeshi population was the youngest, poorest and most mono-religious of all the ethnic populations it categorised. They comprised 0.5 per cent of the country's total population; primarily resided in England's urban areas, especially Greater London where more than half lived and 93 per cent described themselves as Muslim (ONS 2007). Compared with the white British population and other UK-based minority ethnic groups they are more economically deprived, geographically segregated and socially conservative, representing what Eade *et al* term an 'encapsulated community' (Eade *et al* 1996: 150).

South Asian family structures have been described as 'Pre-modern or Victorian', to use Peach's somewhat value-laden phrase (Peach 2006: 143), in that they tend to comprise a large number of children, under the auspices of a married couple with the father as the head of the household. Typically patrifocal, they tend to be organised around the father's wishes and instructions. They are usually 'nuclear', that is households are headed by two parents who are married. In addition to being shaped by this cultural expectation Bangladeshi households are also characterised by their large size and a youthful age structure. According to census data, British Bangladeshis have the largest households of any ethnic group in the UK, at 4.5 persons per household compared to 2.3 persons per household for white British and black British households. This is, in part, because Bangladeshi households have on average the largest number of dependent children which mean the population is characterised by a youthful age structure (ONS 2007). Research has identified Bangladeshis as less likely than other ethnic groups to co-habit (Berthoud and Beishon 1997: 28); have the lowest percentage of households of all ethnic groups to be headed by a lone parent (ONS 2007); have much lower rates of divorce (Berrington 1996: 144) and to be more likely to get married younger than the white British population (Berthoud and Beishon 1997: 25).

Religious and cultural practices have been posited to account for the high levels of marriage, low rates of cohabitation and the predominance of arranged marriages amongst Bangladeshis. Qualitative research has revealed that young Bangladeshis share with their parents an expectation that they will get married and that this will involve the latter, often in conjunction with other senior family members, helping to decide who their partner will be. Furthermore, the fact that those respondents who were already married Bangladeshis were more likely than respondents of other South Asian groups to report that their parents had 'chosen' their partners for them indicates a culture of acceptance greater to the wishes of their parents amongst Bangladeshis (Beishon, Modood and Virdee 1998: 50–51). Samad and Eade (2003: 27–28) found that the view that parents had a 'moral obligation to marry their children and intimate relationships should only develop within this context' was held across generations and gender.

Bangladeshis in UK society are poorly situated in terms of many socio-economic indicators. A Joseph Rowntree Foundation report found that Bangladeshis suffered from the highest rates of poverty of all ethnic groups with 65 per cent living in income poverty and child poverty rates exceeding 70% compared with 25% of white British children (Platt 2007: 40). Furthermore, according to Piggott (2004), poverty rates were far worse for Bangladeshis living in London. The unemployment rate for Bangladeshis living in London was 20 per cent compared with an average of 7 per cent for London as a whole. This represented the highest rate of unemployment for any ethnic group, whilst the economic activity rate for Bangladeshis was the lowest of all ethnic groups in the UK (ONS 2007). Male Bangladeshi pupils repeatedly perform below the national average when it comes to GCSE results: while the national average for achieving five passes at A* to C grade was 55 per cent, this was 43 per cent of Bangladeshi boys and 54 per cent of Bangladeshi girls, compared with the equivalent of 50 per cent for white British boys and 50 per cent for white British girls (DfES 2006).

In terms of housing, Bangladeshis in the UK are significantly more likely than other minority ethnic groups (such as African-Caribbeans, Indians and Pakistanis) to reside in more segregated neighbourhoods (Phillips 1998) and to rent and live in public sector social housing (Peach 1998). The latter owes much to the later timing of Bangladeshi migration, the majority of which took place after the Race Relations Act 1976, which prohibited direct and indirect discrimination on the basis of race. This meant that much of the worst discrimination practices involved in allocating council housing, which previous ethnic migrants were subject to, was now largely absent. However, with the best housing stock already secured, the public sector housing that they could access was poor in quality; a situation further compounded by the Housing Act 1980, which enabled tenants to purchase their own homes from councils and meant that housing that remained available to Bangladeshi tenants comprised poorer quality stock that no one else wanted.

Methodology

The findings reported in this chapter have been taken from interviews that I conducted with 11 Bangladeshi male probationers as part of my Doctoral research into processes of desistance amongst minority ethnic offenders (Calverley 2009). The research study relied on interviews with 33 male probationers who were desisting, or who had desisted from crime, and who were drawn from London probation area offices. They were one of the three principal minority ethnic groups who I sampled. Of the other two ethnic groups, eight were Indian and 14 were either black or dual heritage. To be included in the study probationers had to have three previous convictions (not exclusively for motoring offences); had grown up or spent a significant part of their life in the UK; and to have stopped offending, or at least shown evidence of having made significant progress toward desistance. By focusing on these three groupings, which occupy different positions in terms of their social and economic statuses, I was able to further explore the issue of wider social, economic and cultural formations on processes of desistance in general. The attendance to such factors (gleaned from census data and the wider literature on ethnic minority experiences in the UK) also meant that I was able to locate processes of desistance within the wider social and economic processes which have helped to shape my respondents' lives. The semi-structured qualitative interviews with the probationers were supplemented by interviews with 10 criminal justice practitioners who provided further insight into desistance amongst ethnic minorities. Data from interviewed scripts were coded and analysed using methods of grounded theory (Glaser and Straus 1980; Glaser 1998).

Re-connecting with families

Eight out of the 11 Bangladeshi respondents I interviewed had been sentenced to custody and were coming to the end of their licence at the time of interview, most had been given quite long sentences for robbery and violence of between four and five years. Prison was viewed as having given them a number of benefits, for example heroin addicts cited prison as the place where they were able to address their habit and stop using, while others cited opportunities that they took to improve their reading and writing skills or other educational courses. In keeping with studies of other groups of offenders and ex-offenders (Shover 1985), time spent in prison was seen as wasted time which had foreclosed potential opportunities. Others reflected on how they had lost the respect of those who mattered to them, namely families and friends: 'I've lost a lot of time, freedoms, respect from families and, you know, friends due to the fact that I was inside [and] a drug addict' (Kabir).

However, it is important to note that the positive meanings that the Bangladeshi respondents attributed to the effects of prison did not owe its significance to the punitiveness of their sentence or the harsh 'pains of imprisonment', but to the way it raised their *awareness* of their relationship with significant others in their lives: namely, their parents, wives, children and siblings. Despite the physical and geographical dislocation of prison, and the isolation from family that this entailed, for the Bangladeshis the *potential* opportunity of repairing these damaged relationships was still available to them. This process was reliant on two reciprocal conditions being met. First, there had to be a willingness on behalf of the (then) would-be desister that they *wanted* to re-build relationships with significant others; and second, there had to be a corresponding willingness on behalf of their significant others that *they too wanted* to help repair the relationship and will take the necessary steps in order for this to occur. Significantly, for the majority of the Bangladeshi interviewees who had spent time in prison, these two conditions were present.

The idea that 'acquiring something' new is a common feature of factors related to desistance (Farrall and Calverley 2006: 8) and the importance of recognition of characteristics of oneself in others has been identified by Maruna *et al* (2004) in terms of importance of 'the looking glass self', and at a subconscious level by Gadd (2006). For Bangladeshi respondents these processes came about through the realisation that the relationships they had with their family had value. On occasions this was revealed to them in contrasting their situation to that of white and black inmates:

> See that I'm not being racist or nothing, yeah, see like for white people, black people yeah, some people they like, see with me, with Asian people I've realised when you've got a family, yeah, they'll like support you. See I've got white mates and that they're like, they've been in and out, in and out so many times it's unbelievable. I mean they're even like, 'what are you doing? Why can't you fix your self up?' It's like the only thing – they're telling me now, yeah, why they can't fix themselves up – they ain't got support! They need support! I goes, 'what kind of support'. He goes, 'family support mate. I ain't got mum. I ain't got a Dad. I don't even know where they are'. 'Nah, don't tell me that'. But now when I'm looking at it in that way it is true. You do need a bit of support from someone. You can't do it on your own. You might, yeah, if you've got strong willpower you might do it on your own but you do need some kind of support and the best support I see is family.
>
> (Abdul)

Consequently, they recognised that they 'have' something which was denied to others (in the form of the support, love and affection of their family) and in making this realisation they actually 'acquired' something new: the realisation that the family support that they had was of real value and had implications for the rest of their lives, which, in turn, underlined the importance of making efforts to maintain it. The existence of this awareness that family support was available to them produced an openness to make use of that resource as a 'hook for change' (Giordano *et al* 2002). This, then, rather than acting as a deterrent, was the real significance of prison for Bangladeshi desisters.

However, the process through which the Bangladeshis re-engaged with their families and started to appreciate the value of the family support that they had was not an instantaneous epiphany of recognition. It was a slow process that was dependent on a series of small stages: from making contact with family in prison and discussing future plans to actually being accepted and supported by their family upon release. It is worth quoting the following extract by Abdul at length to illustrate the point as to how this process unfolds:

> Didn't need no prison sentence to open my eyes up, whatever. I just needed that space of time and that's what prison gave me basically. See like [pause] I've seen people go in and out in and out so many times even when I was in there yeah? For six months, one year, people don't realise, yeah? I'm not saying that I used to [be] like a hypocrite or something no, because I used to tell people: 'look this is what you're doing mate, look I've been in here for the last one year and you've gone out and come back. Why?' And he goes 'oh it's family man I ain't got no this that and that and that.' And I used to think, man it don't make sense though. But now thinking of that and looking back, you know thinking; yeah man, you do need family support. *That's what basically built up myself again; that relationship on the phone; speaking to them on the phone; and I knew that I was going to come back and stay with them again*. Things like that. Even my brothers and sisters: didn't speak to them. Never did. Can't remember the last time I spoke to them properly sitting down and laughing and enjoying ourselves having a meal together. Nah, can't remember that, but now in this three month [since release, I've] done that so many times it's like every time I do it I feel good. I feel happy. So to get off heroin and crack and whatever you need family support. That's my experienced way of saying it. You definitely need family support. If you ain't got that, well it's going to be hard man.
>
> (Abdul, emphasis added)

For Abdul, the support he received from his family *began* in prison. Through talking to them it enabled him to envisage an alternative future with them as a non-offender. This vision of a possible life away from offending, unlike the desisters at the start of Farrall and Calverley's (2006) emotional schema, was based not on hope but on the certainty that he 'knew' that he was 'going to come back and stay with them again'. This reassurance provided emotional comfort and security. However, perhaps the greatest message relayed to the inmate was that he and his past behaviour were not going to impact negatively on his future. This tolerance for past actions in the light of (assumed) future 'goodness' appeared to ensure that reform was achieved. Tolerance of those who had done wrong in the past and maintaining close contact with them whilst they were in prison appeared to be a great emotional support for the Bangladeshi members of my sample to draw upon. It communicated to them that their futures would not be defined by their pasts – or at worst, only the criminal aspects of their past.

Re-constructing a future together: re-building trust and shared emotions

Trust has been identified as a key component of social capital (Putnam 2000; Coleman 1990) and a necessary pre-condition for its successful creation is that members should 'expect that if they co-operate they will not be exploited or defrauded, but can at some time or other expect to benefit similarly in return' (Field 2003: 62). In the case of the Bangladeshi interviewees, who often had a long history of exploiting and defrauding their families, trust needed to be re-built. This was an incremental process whereby they proved that they were capable of being trusted through their actions.

One way of demonstrating that they were trustworthy was through closely negotiating their behaviour with their immediate family, such as parents and wives, particularly in areas where trust was integral, such as the management of money. Nasir described how for him building up trust was a collective process, which was negotiated and communicated openly but helped by his new role as a contributor to the family budget rather than a liability:

> Now yeah, the trust is coming in really like fast, my parents have started trusting me really fast because I'm giving in money every week, they're happy, you know, they're happy with the money I'm giving because they know that I can't, I won't be doing things. If I was doing things then I wouldn't be able to give that amount of money so they have a trust and all that. If I say, 'ah, I couldn't give money this week because for this reason I'm gonna buy this' 'Go ahead.' You know, anything that has happened in the house they'll confirm that with me as well. So it's like everything is coming back as it was before, before I was getting into drugs, you know, things are happening for me, like really fast.
>
> (Nasir)

For Mohammed negotiating the strict acceptability of his whereabouts was his own initiative. It not only built up trust but guarded against the risk of meeting other drug users when outside and reduced the risk of him going back to prison:

> … Because the first one, two, three, months I have to stay out. It doesn't matter what happens: stay out. So I mainly stay home. If I need to go to the shop; my mum sends me to the shop; I go to the shop. I tell her I go to the shop. I come back. If I need to go somewhere to an office or something and then I tell her and go, so she knows how long I'm going to be and in between that time I'll come back. So it's okay.
>
> (Mohammed)

The strict conditions that he imposes on his movements were, as he saw it, for his own benefit; and his mother's cooperation provided him with security.

Feelings of 'guilt' for past behaviour and indebtedness also explain why other Bangladeshi desisters accepted such strict controls placed upon their behaviour too. Thus, consensually agreeing a framework for being policed by family members was an important means for regaining trust.

A common feature of the processes through which Bangladeshi desisters rebuilt their relationships with their families was the way in which emotions were held not in isolation, but between both parties as they interacted with each other. Family members provided an important 'stage' upon which changes in the desisters behaviour could be recognised and their efforts and achievements could be certified. One way this was done was by acknowledging how these changes had been responsible for positive effects, as evident in positive emotions of significant others. This, in turn, bolstered Bangladeshi desisters' self-respect. Abdul, again:

> … See my brother, yeah, he's told me when he used to see my daughter and he used to see my son looking at other people's fathers and that and they're like depressed kind of thing but, where I've come back now my brother sees me like walking with them, walking my daughter and my son yeah, it's like; 'I can see the change in your daughter and your son, the expressions on their faces. They're happier and more cheerful and that'.
>
> (Abdul)

By sharing his observation on Abdul's children's new found happiness Abdul's brother engendered feelings of pride and a sense of achievement within Abdul. This experience and the emotions it generated was closely shared between both siblings, meaning they both felt good about these changes and the actions Abdul had taken to produce them.

Similarly, planning for the future is something that was done collectively. For Nasir, hope was a shared emotion held by him and his family for what his future might be:

> They're really supportive and they're really happy with me now. They've got a future, you know, they've got a future with me now. They know like I'm doing all right now. They're really happy for me and anything I ask them they're willing to give. They're like hoping to get me married and all that, so everything's going all right with my family.
>
> (Nasir)

As well as positive emotions, a number of negative emotions were also shared between the Bangladeshi desisters and their families. Most notable of these was the emotion of shame which their involvement in offending had brought on the family and the damage it had brought to the family's name and reputation. Kabir said that the pressures of gossip meant that his family was forced to adopt an isolationist strategy with regard to seeking help outside the 'family circle':

> I think I brought a lot of shame to the family. Erm, You know, in the end they would not associate with a lot of [people] outside the circle. They always kept everything around a circle, a family circle, you know? Reason why is because other people would need advice from the wrong people. You know, people talking; like 'my son's done this, my son's done this, what's your son done?' You know? So my father and mother were basically shamed of what I'd brought to the family. So it has affected them.
>
> (Kabir)

He goes on to admit that the shame had affected him individually, 'I'm ashamed of myself, I'm ashamed of me, and what I've brought to the family especially coming from an Asian culture'. Guilt was also present in the interviewees' accounts. There was awareness that they had caused fear and anxiety amongst their family, and consequently, were responsible for much worrying and suffering.

Marriage and desistance for Bangladeshis

The establishment of meaningful relationship with a partner or spouse has been identified throughout research literature as a principal factor associated with desistance (Shover 1983; Parker 1976; Sampson and Laub 1993, 2004). While this finding also applied to Bangladeshi men in my sample, how this process operated was affected by the specific cultural and structural context they inhabited. This included a shared cultural rule (held by themselves, their family and others in their social network) that marriage was desirable; the cultural practice of arranging marriages with spouses from Bangladesh; and the weak socio-economic position of their wives. These all influenced, at different times, the meanings they gave to marriage and, in turn, shaped their future expectations and motivations to desist.

At the time of interview more than half of the Bangladeshi respondents had got married (six out of 11). These married respondents shared many things in common. First, they had married whilst comparatively young (at around 19 and 20 years old compared to the average age of first marriages of 31 for men in England and Wales (ONS 2007). Second, all had had marriages arranged with spouses who originated from Bangladesh. Third, they all married either when they were experiencing either a lull in their offending or their criminal career had not begun yet. In the interim period between marrying their wives in Bangladesh and being re-united with them in the UK (typically 12 months due to immigration procedures) these Bangladeshi offenders relapsed or became involved in offending for the first time. Consequently, when their spouses arrived in the UK the majority of them faced the depressing, and until then hidden reality, that their new husband had a drug use problem or was in prison. Thus, the Bangladeshi members of the sample who had been married had not previously been committed to marriage.

Initially, therefore, marriage did not act effectively as a mechanism for impeding offending as their spouses knew few people, were not in employment, did not speak English so were isolated from access to wider support networks, and were therefore in a weak position to exert influence over their husbands' behaviour. However, what had previously been a weakness on the part of marriage as a mechanism for promoting desistance, that is that their spouses were isolated and could not easily withdraw from the relationship, became an advantage. There was a guarantee that someone would be waiting for them in the future. The fact that they were not going to go away meant that if they were willing to apply their motivation there were roles available for them to move into if they wished to be a good parent, son or husband. Abdul explained that his wife, whose family all lived in Bangladesh, had 'no one else in the country except me', thus giving some credence to his certainty that she would be there when he was released from prison. This implied two things; first, that he had an *obligation* and a *role* to deliver on, and second, that she would definitely not have moved away or be in a position to turn her back upon him. Her structural position as a non-English speaking housewife meant that she had nowhere else to go. Once out of prison his inclusion within the family, particularly when contrasted with his previous treatment, not only reinforced the strength of the family bonds and their importance to him, such as making him feel good about himself, but also confirmed the hopes that he had in prison and that were originally formed there through the discussion about his future life that he had with his family.

For the five Bangladeshis in my sample who had not married, the cultural tradition of locating and agreeing with parents a suitable marriage partner was a significant joint project for the future and a shared hope that they can both take part in. Families were also active in organising, and looking for future partners. For Mohammed, there was an expectation that he get married and that the process whereby he gets married should be a collective one: 'everyone is looking, relatives and all that stuff, see what they find and me as well to see if I can find anyone'. It was expected that he saved too, either to pay for the marriage or if he has to marry someone from Bangladesh for her to come over to the UK. For this group of Bangladeshi desisters the fact that they had not 'settled down', and married and many of their brothers and sisters had, was seen as an indication of their own failings in comparison to the success of their siblings who had done so. Consequently, they shared the expectation of their parents that they should marry in the future, and marry quickly.

Family support: practical assistance and structuring time

There was further evidence of other examples of family support which began during the Bangladeshis' time in prison. This came in the form of practical support such as sending money into prison, and taking care of family duties for those with a wife and children. Both the 'rallying around' and the social capital provided by families created a sense of respect and indebtedness within offenders towards their family, making them obliged to make good on any commitments not to not go back to crime. The knowledge that someone would 'be there' was integral to creating and sustaining the 'hope' of a drugs and crime free future and provided the necessary motivation to see the vision implemented. For others, the feeling of indebtedness that they felt they owed their family was further engendered, in addition to the financial and emotional support they received whilst in custody, by an awareness that they have made their family suffer:

> It is not like they wanted to disown me or anything but obviously they were very upset and I have heard from my brothers and sisters that they used to always pray and cry for me and, you know, they were always stressing over me while I was inside. Every week they would send me money, my family sent me money every week, they came and visited me every month, so I owe something back to them and I owe something back to myself.
>
> (Salman)

There was also evidence of families offering 'practical support' after their release from prison. This was also comforting for Bangladeshi desisters, producing further feelings of indebtedness as a result. Salman described how when he came out of prison, for his last sentence, his brothers and sisters were very keen to make him aware that he should come to them if he needed financial assistance. This was coupled with constant questioning of his whereabouts and behaviour. However, he says he did not resent this interference because he was happy that someone was looking out for him and had his best interests at heart.

Family support also provided opportunities to structure time more efficiently. One of the advantages for Bangladeshi desisters of being from large families was that even without paid employment they could structure their time running errands and be a useful productive member of the family:

> During the daytime I'm running around because of the family, picking up the kids, dropping them in the school in the morning, taking my sisters to the doctors or the hospital or … I have a lot of nieces and nephews that are ill and are in and out of hospital constantly with appointments and all that. So, by doing these kinds of responsibilities I'm filling my time in the daytime and the evening when I have a lot of free time.
>
> (Abhra)

The death of a father, or both parents also meant that interviewees were burdened with extra responsibilities and a duty to provide for other family members. For example, since Parvez's father died when he was still at school there was an obligation that he should provide financial assistance to his mother and siblings, as well as relatives from his father's first marriage in Bangladesh which placed pressure on him to earn money and provide financial support. This he initially did, but as he became more heavily involved in drinking, which his family were unaware of, he repeatedly failed to meet this responsibility. However, following the shame of his most recent conviction he pledged to re-invest himself in his previously neglected role of provider/supporter for the family. This enabled Parvez to publicly demonstrate his commitment to reform.

Islam and desistance: forgiving the past, supporting the future

Whilst several studies have identified religion as an important factor in promoting desistance (Giordano *et al* 2002, 2008; Maruna 1997; Chu 2007; Chu and Sung 2008), participants of these studies have identified themselves as Christian.[1] The issue of whether or not it is the religion adopted as opposed to religiosity *per se* which alters or modifies in some way the trajectory associated with desistance has not, as yet, been fully considered. The fact that Bangladeshi desisters in my sample were Muslim and many cited their religion as important to their efforts to stop offending gives us an insight into this question. My findings suggest that religiosity and religion were complementary factors in supporting this process. Islamic teachings place great importance on tolerance of those who have transgressed and a duty of believers to provide appropriate forgiveness. Significantly, these values were adopted by the parents and families of Bangladeshi desisters who as followers of Islam attached importance to living in accordance with their religious beliefs. This provides a plausible explanation as to why they were so willing to forgive their errant sons.

Over half the Bangladeshi respondents reported a renewed engagement with Islam as a significant event in their life responsible for helping them in their efforts to 'go straight'. It helped achieve this through supporting processes that have been identified elsewhere as supportive in enabling desistance. For example, similar to the processes of identity change among Maruna's sample (2001), embracing Islam provided Mohammed with the opportunity to adopt a new identity which was at the same time non-offending but contiguous with his past and in doing so enabled him to find his 'true self':

> ... I know I was like this before, I just messed up in between for a year or two, you know? I regret doing one, two years, but you know it was just that I wasn't actually well during them kind of times. That's how I'd put it. Because I wasn't well during them kind of times it affected me, you know? But now it's like I'm okay. It wasn't really me you know. It was me, but it's

> just mainly I was taking drugs and that was the thing that influenced me and slowly then I got into trouble. You know?
>
> (Mohammed)

Likewise, the narrative of Islam as found in the Koran provided interviewees such as Kabir with a reference on how to conduct his life. Here he tells how religion helped to provide him with strength and a resource which he could draw on to control his anger:

> I can manage my anger now. I know sometime, you know, if someone says something to me I don't have to talk back to them and I just remember and remind myself of the way of the Prophet of Islam. He was always patient. If someone insulted him he never said anything back to him or anything. These are the examples that I'm trying to follow …
>
> (Kabir)

Similarly for Mohammed Islam provided a future blueprint for the self to work towards; it provided a useful reference point for good behaviour inimical to future offending:

> I'm [pause] making the effort to become good and try to lose my bad habits that I have. … Get rid of all of my bad habits and replace them with good stuff like, you know, reading the Koran, reading books or going to a friend and then inviting them to come and go and sit down and have a chat, and all that stuff, good stuff, understand one another, you know, be friends. Mainly being good to people, being generous to people, loving one another yeah, and thinking always when you make an intention how your intention is, you know, if it's a bad intention try to remove that and replace that with a good intention.
>
> (Mohammed)

By associating with new religious friends Mohammed re-engagement with Islam provided him with a safe non-offending peer group to socialise with and respectable certifiers who could recognise and confirm his desistance, as well as space where this could take place. Thus, religion provided a structured environment where others can recognise the legitimacy of desisters' good intentions:

> I go to work at nine o'clock come back at six o'clock. Mostly I'm in the mosque from half-six to half-seven. I come back and then I have time for myself; I've got one hour. And then I've got religious friends. Though we go around and see brothers, meet brothers, socialise with brothers for an hour or so, you know? And that's it. It's nearly ten, half-ten, we don't have anything else to do. So. Eat in. Go to sleep. Wait for the next day.
>
> (Mohammed)

While the above examples may apply universally to the effects of all religions, it can be argued that what is significant about the religion of Islam in the case of my respondents was that those who comprised their 'community', by which I mean their family, friends and those living in their immediate neighbourhood were also Muslim. This meant when Bangladeshi desisters re-engaged with religion their actions were valued. In the case of their friends it also meant they gained a sense of communion with others with whom they had all but previously lost contact. A further advantage was that the adoption of the identity of a 'good' Muslim provided these Bangladeshis with a readily available, pre-packaged 'script' which if acted upon could provide them with a feasible and realistic pathway out of crime (Rumgay 2004).

Like other religions Islam has strict rules of observance (e.g. praying five times a day, abstinence from alcohol and drugs), and responsibilities and duties (caring for family, fasting, donating to charity). Originating from, and residing within, social networks characterised by their high levels of religiosity meant observance of these rules was more likely to be valued by those around them. This provided a greater incentive for Bangladeshi desisters to invest in living within these rules as their efforts would be recognised. Furthermore, the outcome of abiding by these Islamic rules resulted in more than just a re-orientation of Bangladeshi respondents' belief and value systems: it contained a performative function too. The self-discipline needed and the structuring of their time which were a result of adhering to these guidelines re-enforced the motivation of Bangladeshi desisters and protected them from spending time in places and among the company of people who were likely to pose a threat to their efforts to desist.

Embracing the Islamic religion had other effects that further embedded their desistance. For example, similar to other religions, Islam provided neural stimulation and occupied their time, preventing them from getting bored (Ellis and Thompson 1989). As a journey of self-education and learning it provided desisters with a continual project which will be forever under construction. The consequence of this is that it produces many other aspects of self-improvement:

> [Islam] helps you in so many ways, concentration, punctuality, I'm learning, I've began to learn so much, been learning a lot, every day I try to learn, I try to read. They say you can't never stop learning basically. So I try to learn, because they say, it's like saying Islam is like an ocean and the brain, the human brain is like a cup, so even if I try so hard to put that ocean into a cup. It's like knowledge is an ocean and the human brain is a mere cup, you can't fit that ocean into that cup. What you have to do is you have to gradually consume day by day, year by year, you have to take it in slowly, so that's the way I sort of play it. It gives me something to do, it keeps me busy, it keeps me focused. It's interesting because that's the way I'm looking at it. It's something to do, something I enjoy doing. I like learning, I learn something every day, it's a learning experience where at the same time I'm disciplining

> myself, I'm setting myself rules, regulations, because I'm following a religion, there's commandments that you have got to follow, God given commandments that you've got to follow and while doing that I'm filled with self-discipline and there's nothing more satisfying than self-restraint, meaning that you are able to control your actions, you're able to control your thoughts…that's the best thing about it really is it keeps you focused all around, not in just one place, all around, I'm really focused and that makes me think positive really.
>
> (Zahir)

The paradox for desisters such as Zahir is that while Islam literally means resignation and submission to the will of God, by choosing this route and strictly observing the religion's rules and instructions he finds himself far from passively burning out and fading away. Instead, and again similar to the experience of Maruna's desisters (2001), he finds himself fired up and zealous in his new mission. Similarly, Nasir describes his new life since becoming 'a better' Muslim:

> I think every day is a new day for me now, you know. When I wake up in the morning I don't yawn, I don't go 'I can't move.' I wake up, jump up and like get ready, you know, do whatever I want straight away, when before I couldn't open my eyes because I was too stoned or I was clucking or anything. Every day when I look at the sky, you know, it's a new day for me and try to do whatever I can. Boredom, I try to cover my boredom now, every time, I don't even really have boredom no more because I've covered it with so many things in my life, work, coming home, seeing my family, seeing my mates, new mates, you know?
>
> (Nasir)

Furthermore, Islam was also associated with re-orientation aspirations:

> The person I want to be is just a normal person basically now. I don't want wealth. If it is there I'll take it. If it's there and I can make money I will make it, but I'm not the person who is going to think that wealth is my life. Obviously we all need some kind of sustenance to sustain, but my mind is now I'll work for it. I just want a spiritual life, you know, be a humbler, you know what I mean? As I've said I've been a violent person all my life really, you know what I mean? [3-second pause] But I want to be … I've been told I'm a very caring person. All this kind of character came from my spiritual life.
>
> (Kabir)

For Kabir his spiritual life allowed him to re-order his goals and become more modest. Not only does this help redirect his life away from crime, as an ex-offender with poor skills, living in an area of high unemployment, it also, arguably, realistically reconciles him with his situation. One of the notable features of Bangladeshi desistance was that it took place despite the absence of engagement in the labour market.

Shared aspirations: 'buying back a future'

Modest aspirations were very important for Salman who said he just wanted to 'lead a normal life like everybody else'. Interestingly, the aspirations that he had for his own life were shared by his father, pointing to the fact that the future image of himself as successful and 'normal' is not a project of self-construction, but one of joint construction between himself and his family. He aspired to 'give something back' and re-pay some of the debt that he owes his family:

> I have put my family through a lot. I have taken money from the house before but they have never thrown me out of the house, the support has been always there, and is still there, and you know I count myself lucky and I want to give them something back for the support they have given me, that is the main thing. ... My father has made it clear that he doesn't want anything from me, what he has done he has done, he says 'we just want to see, we will be happy if we can see you stay off the drugs, have a job, have a car, get married, settle down and have kids and lead a normal life' and you know 'that is all I am asking [of] you. I am not asking you for money, all the money I gave you while you were in prison I don't want any of this back. All the money you wasted. All the money you took from the house, I don't want any of it back, I don't want anything, all I want you to do is show me that you can lead a normal life like everybody else in this family', that is all my father wants from me. He is not even telling me 25 times a day, do this, do that, he is just telling have a normal life and get a job so in that sense I feel I am very happy and I couldn't ask for anymore you know, so I am very happy with the support I am getting from my family and I would be lost without them. I wouldn't last without them; I don't think I would be able to cope without my family.
>
> (Salman)

Just as emotions are not singularly owned by desisters, but are affected by and interact with, the emotions of others, particularly close family relations (see above and Farrall and Calverley 2006: 128–29), the above extract underlines how Bangladeshi desisters' aspirations were held in conjunction with those of their family: they both wish to invest in the same future together. As Salman said, 'I want to give them something back for the support they've given me'. Like other desisters, the Bangladeshis I interviewed wished to achieve redemption by 'buying back their futures' (McNeill 2004: 432) However, their families' attitude of forgiveness to their past criminal actions meant not only was the opportunity to do so available, the fact that it was not burdened with pre-conditions that they first demonstrate sincerity, other than living a 'normal life', meant it came at a price which was reasonable, and so more likely to be achievable. This future was very much a joint project – one shared between offenders and their families – as illustrated by the following quote from Nasir:

> You know, my family is more close now, you know, *we're* getting somewhere in life, you know. Before when I was stuck, you know, in some nowhere, financial ways, family ways, *we* were all stuck and now everything is giving *us* a path to like move on, make something out of life.
>
> (Nasir, emphasis added)

As Maruna's (2001: 148–49) accounts of successful desisters highlighted the emphasis of 'I' in successful desisters' narratives, the importance of family in the lives of Bangladeshis and their desistance highlighted the return of 'we', or the 'us'.

Conclusion

The key factor that emerges from the above descriptions of Bangladeshis' experiences of desistance was that their families were central to their reform. In particular, the attitude of forgiveness that the Bangladeshi families held towards their convicted kin was critical to enabling their desistance. Despite the distressed and strained nature of their previous relationships, their families displayed a laudable willingness to intervene in their lives whilst they were in prison and made it clear that their assistance and support would be available in the future. Many of them reported that, despite what they had done, their families wished to accept them back after their release and they would be included within the family in the future. This created an awareness among the Bangladeshi respondents I interviewed that they had choices and opportunities for a future that did not have to involve crime. In doing so it created an awareness that they had some degree of control over their lives; that if they took the right steps (such as coming off drugs and staying away from criminal peers) they could ensure this future became a reality. In short, their families' approach created a sense of agency. This not only facilitated Bangladeshis' initial desire to desist, but also, having been forgiven at an early stage, generated a sense of personal indebtedness towards their family, which provided them with further incentive to maintain their efforts.

Re-building trust and relationships with their family provided Bangladeshi desisters with access to valuable resources of support that they could draw upon to maintain their desistance. These included emotional and psychological support such as offering encouragement and certifying their achievements; to practical support like help with finances and accommodation; to offering structured roles within the family of father, brother, carer, 'good Muslim', that they could move in to and which helped protect them from threats to their desistance. In addition, pro-social friends, often formed around religion, also offered support and protection. In all, this created a social context for Bangladeshis which was generally favourable to sustaining their desistance. This was despite them being economically and socially disadvantaged.

Of course, the finding that the quality of family relationships affects desistance is by no means new. Neither is it exclusive to Bangladeshi desisters. The findings of this chapter should be seen as lending support to McNeill's (2003) argument that criminal justice interventions that wish to be 'desistance-focused' should concentrate on building positive relationships between offenders and their families: 'like everyone else, offenders are most influenced to change (and not to change) by those closest to them and those whose advice they respect and whose support they value' (Weaver and McNeill 2007: 1). If so, then wider criminal justice policy has much to learn from how the strength of relationships between Bangladeshis and their families helps pull them towards processes associated with desistance. In addition, the tolerance that Bangladeshi families show towards their sons who have been sent to prison has much to teach wider society regarding its attitudes towards ex-offenders and their possibility of redemption. While the Bangladeshi community is more typically used to being publicly vilified by the media, particularly with respect to Islam (see Salgado-Pottier 2008), its forgiveness-oriented culture stands in stark contrast to the retributive approach found elsewhere in UK justice policy. In addition to what it can tell us that may assist Bangladeshi desisters, it offers a model for how to help those who have been sentenced to punishment which those who wish to help non-Bangladeshi desisters would also do well to examine.

Note

1 Deane *et al's* (2007) research amongst Canadian urban aboriginal gangs, which identified the significance of promoting pro-social values 'through traditional aboriginal teachings', provides an exception to this rule.

References

Beishon, S., Modood, T. and Virdee, S. (1998) *Ethnic Minority Families*. London: Policy Studies Institute.

Berrington, A. (1996) 'Marriage patterns and inter-ethnic unions', in Coleman D. and Salt, J., *Ethnicity in the 1991 Census: demographic characteristics of the ethnic minority populations*. London: HMSO, pp 178–212.

Berthoud, R. and Beishon, S. (1997) 'People, Families and Households', in Modood, T., Berthoud, R., Lakey, J., Nazroo, J., Smith, P., Virdee, S. and Beishon, S., *Ethnic Minorities in Britain: Diversity and Disadvantage*. London: Policy Studies Institute, pp 18–59.

Calverley, A. (2009) 'An exploratory investigation into the processes of desistance amongst minority ethnic offenders'. unpublished PhD thesis, Keele University, Keele.

Chu, D. C. (2007) 'Religiosity and Desistance From Drug Use', *Criminal Justice and Behavior*, 34(5): 661–79.

Chu, D. and Sung, H. (2008) 'Racial Differences in Desistance From Substance Abuse: The Impact of Religious Involvement on Recovery', *International Journal of Offender Therapy and Comparative Criminology* (online) 22 July, accessed 1 October 2008, http://ijo.sagepub.com/cgi/rapidpdf/0306624X08320207v1.

Coleman, J. S. (1990) *Equality and Achievement in Education*. Boulder, CO: Westview Press.

Deane, L., Bracken, D. and Morrisette, L. (2007) 'Desistance within an urban Aboriginal gang', *Probation Journal*, 54(2): 125–41.

DfES (Department for Education and Skills) (2006) *Ethnicity and Education: The Evidence on Minority Ethnic Pupils aged 5–16. Research Topic Paper*, 2006 edn. London: DfES.

Eade, J., Peach, C. and Vamplew, T. (1996) 'Bangladeshis in Britain: The Encapsulated Community', in Peach C. (ed.) *Ethnicity in the 1991 Census*. London: HMSO, pp 150–60.

Ellis, L. and Thompson, R. (1989) 'Relating Religion, Crime, Arousal, and Boredom', *Sociology and Social Research*, 73(3): 132–39.

Farrall, S. and Calverley, A. (2006) *Understanding Desistance from Crime*. Milton Keynes: Open University Press.

Field, J. (2003) *Social Capital*. London: Routledge.

Gadd, D. (2006) 'The role of recognition in the desistance process', *Theoretical Criminology*, 10(2): 179–202.

Giordano, P. C., Cernkovich, S. A. and Rudolph, J. L. (2002) 'Gender, Crime and Desistance: Toward a Theory of Cognitive Transformation', *American Journal of Sociology*, 107(4): 990–1064.

Giordano, P., Longmore, M. A., Schroeder, R. D. and Sefferin, P. M. (2008) 'A life course perspective on spirituality and desistance from crime', *Criminology*, 46(1): 99–132.

Glaser, B. (1998) *Doing Grounded Theory: Issues & Discussion*. Mill Valley, CA: Sociology Press.

Glaser, B. and Straus A. (1980) *The Discovery of Grounded Theory: Strategies for Qualitative Research*. Chicago, IL: Aldine.

Laub, J. H. and Sampson, R. J. (2001) 'Understanding Desistance From Crime', in Tonry, M. H. and Norris, N. (eds) *Crime and Justice: An Annual Review of Research*, Vol. 28. Chicago, IL: University of Chicago Press, pp 1–78.

Maruna, S. (1997) 'Going Straight: Desistance From Crime and Life Narratives of Reform', *The Narrative Study of Lives*, 5: 59–93.

Maruna, S. (2001) *Making Good: How Ex-Convicts Reform and Rebuild Their Lives*. Washington, DC: American Psychological Association Books.

Maruna, S., Le Bel, T., Mitchell, N. and Naples, M. (2004) 'Pygmalion in the reintegration process: desistance from crime through the looking glass', *Psychology, Crime & Law*, 10(3): 271–81.

McNeill, F. (2003) 'Desistance-Focussed Probation Practice', in Chui, W. H. and Nellis, M. (eds) *Moving Probation Forward*. London: Pearson Education, pp 146–63.

McNeill, F. (2004) 'Desistance, Rehabilitation and Correctionalism: Developments and prospects in Scotland', *The Howard Journal of Criminal Justice*, 43(4): 420.

Parker, H. (1976) 'Boys Will be Men: Brief Adolescence in a Down-Town Neighbourhood', in Mungham, G. and Pearson, G. (eds) *Working Class Youth Culture*. London: Routledge.

Peach, C. (1998) 'South Asian and Caribbean Ethnic Minority Housing Choice in Britain', *Urban Studies*, 35(10): 1657–680.

Peach, C. (2006) 'South Asian migration and settlement in Great Britain, 1951–2001', *Contemporary South Asia*, 15(2): 133–46.

Phillips, D. (1998) 'Black Minority Ethnic Concentration, Segregation and Dispersal in Britain', *Urban Studies*, 35(10): 1681–702.

Piggott, G. (2004) *Census Profiles: Bangladeshis in London*, DMAG Briefing. London: Greater London Authority.

Platt, L. (2007) *Ethnicity and Poverty in the UK*. Bristol: Policy Press.

Putnam, R. D. (2000) *Bowling Alone: The Collapse and Revival of American Community*. New York, NY: Simon and Schuster.

Rumgay, J. (2004) 'Scripts for Safer Survival: Pathways Out of Female Crime', *The Howard Journal of Criminal Justice*, 43(4): 405–19.

Salgado-Pottier, R. (2008) 'The modern moral panic: the representation of British Bangladeshi and Pakistani youth in relation to violence and religion', *Anthropology Matters Journal* (online), 10(1): 1–17, accessed 27 November 2008, www.anthropologymatters.com/journal/2008-1/salgado-pottier_2008_modern.pdf.

Samad, Y. and Eade, J. (2003) *Community Perceptions of Forced Marriage*. London: Foreign and Commonwealth Office, Community Liason Unit.

Sampson, R. J. and Laub, J. H. (1993) *Crime in the Making: Pathways and Turning Points Through Life*. London: Harvard University Press.

Sampson, R. J. and Laub, J. H. (2004) 'Life-Course Desisters? Trajectories of Crime among Delinquent Boys Followed to Age 70', *Criminology*, 41(3): 555–92.

Shover, N. (1983) 'The Later Stages Of Ordinary Property Offender Careers', *Social Problems*, 31(2): 208–18.

Shover, N. (1985) *Aging Criminals*. London: Sage.

Weaver, B. and McNeill, F. (2007) *Giving Up Crime: Directions for Policy*, Policy report, Scottish Centre for Crime & Justice Research, (online), accessed 6 June 2008, www.sccjr.ac.uk/pubs/Giving-Up-Crime-Directions-for-Policy/35.

Primary sources

ONS (Office for National Statistics) (2007) Office for National Statistics (online), accessed 2007, www.statistics.gov.uk.

Chapter 8

Inside-out: transitions from prison to everyday life

A qualitative longitudinal approach[1]

Mechthild Bereswill

The social organisation of prison has been investigated from multiple perspectives and by different disciplines and scholars during the last decades. Currently, we find macro-theoretical views like the one by Loic Waquant (2008) who focuses his argumentation on the correspondence of changing welfare regimes with the changing role of prison in society at the fore. Waquant shows how the "criminal justice system acts in concordance with workfare to push its clientele onto the peripheral segments of the deskilled job market" (Waquant 2008: 25) and how incarceration is linked with the dynamics of the ghetto and "ethnoracial exclusion" (Waquant 2008: 27) in the US. Beside this analysis of "the novel functions" of the prison from the perspective of a political sociology (Waquant 2008: 33) we also find a criminological tradition of prison research that explores the changing social organisation of prisons from inside the institution itself, from the perspective of the inmates as well as from the prison officer, and analyses the ongoing privatisation of prisons (James *et al* 1997; Liebling 1992, 2005; Liebling and Prince 2001; Crewe 2009). The quality of life in prison is investigated and prison is seen as a complex system of social relations. Such research also leads to questions about the "Effects of Imprisonment" (Liebling and Maruna 2005) on the life and wellbeing of prisoners—a perspective that has been investigated and discussed consequently by social psychologist Hans Toch from the 1970s onwards (1975, 1977; Johnson and Toch 1982). Here, Gresham Sykes' (1958) concept of the "pains of imprisonment" has been taken up again, asking for the long-term consequences that incarceration has for the prisoner. Looking at these debates about incarceration, we find an important shift of perspective in relation to the authoritarian institution that prison is (and, following Sykes, will remain). Whereas abolitionists argued against any positive aspects of prison programmes and resumed that "nothing works", reformers tended to ask "What works?". According to Liebling and Maruna (2005) and relating to the work of Toch, the crucial question that shall lead our investigation of imprisonment is "What hurts"? (Liebling and Maruna 2005: 11). Drawing attention to the "pains of imprisonment" means focusing on the extraordinary experience of the loss of autonomy and the existential anxieties the human being has to cope with in everyday life in prison.

American sociologists such as Gresham Sykes (1958) and Erving Goffman (1961) were among the first researchers in the 1950s and 1960s to explore these processes from the perspective of the inmates. Sykes called the experience of imprisonment an "attack on the psyche", whilst Goffman spoke of the "mortification of the self" in total institutions. Both authors stressed the powerful effects of such institutional environments on the sense of self of their inmates. Imprisonment provokes a deep-seated crisis of both autonomy and identity as it thoroughly unsettles an individual's subjectivity. Since then, the structural functionalism of Sykes has been questioned, as has Goffman's role theoretical approach to the interplay of institutional and biographical processes. However, their insights on the powerful influence of prison and especially Sykes' psychosocial reflections on what he calls the "pains of imprisonment" (Sykes 1958/1999: 63ff) are still instructive for research on the experience of being imprisoned (cp. Liebling and Maruna 2005; Windzio 2006; Bereswill 2001; Johnson and Toch 1982; Toch 1975), but also for exploring the specific conflicts that accompany processes of resocialisation after being released from the closed environment of prison. In other words, successful or unsuccessful resocialisation, dynamics of desistance, and long-term processes of social integration are related to the influence that imprisonment has on the inmate's agency and capacities. At the same time—and in contrast to the approach of Goffman and Sykes who concentrated on the inmate's world inside prison—the experience of incarceration is intervening into biographical processes which allow very different patterns of coping with the extraordinary loss of autonomy and all the anxieties which the subject has to deal with. In consequence, transitions from prison and social integration are related to prison experience as this experience is shaped by the biographical self-constructions of the individual.

Such self-constructions can be reconstructed by exploring the biographical narratives of people who went through an incarceration and have to cope with the stressful experience of stepping in and out of the total institution. Here, a parallel to Shadd Maruna's (2001) work on desistance can be outlined: like desistance from crime, resocialisation from prison also has to be understood as a complex and conflict-ridden subjective process that cannot be limited to some objective issues which have to be accomplished by ex-prisoners. At the same time the tendency to reduce the scientific understanding of resocialisation to looking at relapse rates and asking for the employment and partnership status of ex-offenders is very dominant in criminological research. Even qualitative studies which draw attention to the experiences and access the contradicting self-interpretations of the individual very often miss the emotional depth and the latent meanings of the self-reports of their interviewees (cp. the critical discussions by Gadd and Farrall 2004 and Bereswill *et al* 2008: 30f.).

Such critical interrogations lead to another understanding of the transitional processes that characterise life in and after prison: resocialisation from prison is a complex psychosocial process in which the individual has to balance his or her inner conflicts and anxieties with the—very often contradictory—expectations and limitations of the social world. Coping with life after prison is part of an ongoing biographical process that is neither linear nor shaped by the cognitive or rational capacities of the subject only. Social integration is a dialectical dynamic between the integration of an individual into social contexts and the conflict-ridden appropriation of experiences by the unique subject's inner world. Following this theoretical assumption has methodical consequences as we need to reconstruct the—also unconscious—dimensions of conflict rather than the rationalisations or cognitive scripts that characterise the biographical narratives of someone. Such an approach has been developed in our own studies on the biographical processes of young males who have been incarcerated in juvenile detention centres in Germany during 1998–99. We had the extraordinary chance to follow these adolescent men after their release and to talk with them about their lives over years in a longitudinal research setting. Before presenting selected results from the study, the theoretical and methodical background of the research will be discussed.

The reconstruction of biographical processes—a conflict theoretical approach

Our biographical approach to social integration is part of the "Hanover Prison Studies" (Bereswill 1999, 2004; Bereswill *et al* 2008; Neuber 2009; Greve and Hosser 1998). Here, a group of sociologists and psychologists are engaged in a large-scale, longitudinal study of male adolescents during and after their incarceration in different juvenile detention centres.[2] In the qualitative part of this study, we conducted biographical interviews with 43 young men in three different juvenile detention centres in East and West Germany. In 30 cases we succeeded in meeting our interviewees after their release—or even their re-incarceration. And up to 2007, nearly nine years later, we interviewed 12 of them annually. These data allow us to reconstruct resocialisation processes in context of the life course and the biographical self-interpretation of our interviewees.

The main research questions of the studies can be summed up as follows: How do our interviewees cope with prison and how does prison shape their conflicts regarding resocialisation? How can we understand this in the context of the biographical experiences of these highly disadvantaged young men? In order to get a deeper understanding of the interrelationship of institutional and biographical dynamics, we analyse the self-interpretations of male adolescents in detail: looking back at their biographical conflicts before prison; investigating their accounts of surviving the pains of imprisonment; identifying continuing and changing patterns of biographical conflicts and process structures through time (Bereswill 1999, 2002, 2004; Bereswill *et al* 2008; Neuber 2009).

Qualitative longitudinal studies (Saldana, 2003; Farrall 2006) offer the rare opportunity to reconstruct social processes over a longer period of time. In the case of biographical studies this includes also the looking back to past experiences and we therefore gain data which are shaped by a complex temporality.

We can reconstruct the self-interpretations and biographical constructions the young interviewees present by telling their life stories *before* prison. These stories are shaped by the interview interaction and the research context (*in* prison or *after* prison). These data are obviously influenced by the different contexts and the research interaction over the years (Bereswill 2008). However, such narratives represent more than context-bound interactive constructions of the self. In contrast, we can identify repeated stories, familiar patterns of interaction over different interviews, and unsolved conflicts as well as unfulfilled wishes over the years. We also learn about transformations of such patterns and see how young adults change or try to change their lifestyles.

During the course of a longitudinal study we can reconstruct the biographical processes of people from the perspective of a near past and also a common future—we see the young men in their transitions to adulthood once a year and we talk about seeing each other again. The interlinked dynamics of the reproduction and the transformation of biographical conflicts can be investigated over time. These different dimensions of biographical temporality which are characteristic for a longitudinal perspective lead to general questions about biographical studies: How are experience, memories and the narrative related? This fundamental question can be answered from different methodological perspectives. Biography research mostly looks for sequential layers of experiences over time that can be identified by analysing different linguistic configurations in a given narrative (Rosenthal 1995; Dausien 1996).

In contrast to this methodological tradition we took up a psychoanalytical approach that allows for a multilayered exploration of biographical experiences. Expressions of individual subjectivity result from a two-fold, interlocking process. First of all, subjectivity is based on *inter*subjectivity. This means it rests on relations of mutual exchange between people. Such mutual exchange is not restricted to early mother-child relations. It is a lifelong process. Second, subjectivity is an expression of *intra*subjectivity. It also rests on the unique dynamic processes *within* the subject:

> In psychoanalytic terms, the subject is a complex and conflicted being. Conscious and unconscious identifications and introjections intersect with internalisations of extra-personal experiences gained in the outside world. This means internal and external conditions can overlap, but they can also be at odds with each other.
>
> (Bereswill and Ehlert, 1996: 25, translation: M. B.)

This means focusing on the conflict-ridden aspects of biographical processes which don't follow a sequential or chronological logic. Instead we focus on the conflicts and frictions which occur in the mutual relationship between the subject's inner world, including unconscious wishes and anxieties, and his or her unique perception of reality. From this psychodynamic inspired point of view, biographies are multi-layered processes, shaped by life-long conscious and unconscious conflicts that individuals experience with the different aspects of their social identities (Graf-Deserno and Deserno 1998: 43). Consequently, social roles are always submissive to or liable to be modified by the indvidual's own design (Adorno 1995: 22). But societal expectations are specific and not always subject to the individual's will. That means the young men in our study have to find compromises between their (unconscious) wishes and reality. This model of biographical subjectivity means looking for tensions, discontinuities and inconsistencies in people's biographical self-representations.

In the case of our specific study we also have to be aware of the fact that the narrators in this text are adolescents who can be described as "men coming into their own". Vera King (2002, 28f.) draws attention to the "virtual nature" of this developmental experience. She refers to a "*psychosocial realm of possibilities*", which entails "extensive psychic, cognitive, and social processes of separation, development and integration that are connected to letting go of childhood and achieving a gradual *individuation*" (King 2002, original emphasis).

Such a "psychosocial realm of possibilities" cannot exist without conflicts and tensions of various types. These are conflicts the adolescents experience and act out while at the same time coping with their own process of change and with the pressure to conform to their surroundings. The interplay between personal steps of development and social pressure shakes the biographical self concepts of young men and gives chances to transform their patterns of action. The strongly felt discrepancy between wishes and reality also induces something new—creativity and autonomy. Accordingly, King (2002) strongly points out the "origin of something new in adolescence". At the same time, she draws attention to the fact that the "psychosocial realm of possibilities" is not unlimited. The increase of autonomy, the gaining of more room to act and be creative in adolescence, is subject to specific situational conditions, to an objective "structure of chances" (King 2002: 32). Consequently adolescence is not a multi-optioned "realm" of creative transformation. It also has to be seen in terms of long-term social inequality.

As we see it, prison is one of several barriers to reintegration in such an individual's life course (Bereswill 1999: 15f.). Integration into society ends up being an obstacle course of overcoming social discrimination and marginalisation. In terms of societal expectations the life course of young prisoners seems to be an ongoing process of lacking social integration: lacking school-leaving qualifications, no or incomplete training, being unemployed, being homeless, suffering from unresolved conflicts in family, not being able to cope with early fatherhood, problems of addiction and debts—the life situation of young prisoners has not changed recently during the last years; such young prisoners are multiply distressed. The biographical process and the subjective conflicts about integration that the young men have to cope with are thus connected to their low objective chances of such integration.

In addition, apart from possibilities of social participation through activities such as education and work, social integration depends also on a personal network of active social relationships. Resocialisation turns out to be a complex interrelation between social chances of integration and participation on the one hand and, on the other, to inter-subjective relationships of acknowledgement and recognition between human beings.

When these features of adolescent development possibilities are associated with the basic effects of incarceration, further tensions emerge: imprisonment fundamentally provokes conflicts of autonomy. For adolescents and juveniles, this means that—given a total environment with rigid structures and authoritarian modes of contact—acute conflicts around autonomy are aggravated and at the same time, chances to solve such conflicts creatively are extremely restricted. In this perspective of the subjective processes of development as related to social structures of chance, incarceration interacts with adolescent biographies on two levels. First, imprisonment helps to shape their understanding of their "inner self" and their sense of who they are. Second, it has consequences for their social chances of integration,—bearing in mind that their incarceration is supposedly intended to prompt subsequent steps towards integration into work and education.

This argument is underlined by the fact that biographies of the young men in our sample share mostly one structural element. Their biographies are highly discontinuous. Their life courses are characterised by changing relations from a very early point in life, by having spent time in various different institutions, changing school very often, and so forth. This disruptive pattern is also manifested as changing and contrasting modes of emotional relations and attachment—a dynamic which in many cases is stopped by imprisonment because the closed environment does not allow the adolescents to run away nor does it allow the institution to throw them out. In consequence, for many of our interviewees prison offers a tempting environment of structure, as will be clear in the following.

"Inside I'm a different person than outside": incarceration as an ambivalent promise of change

Our findings will be presented in two stages: first, our findings related to the experience of being incarcerated will be summarised. An ambivalent image of the "pains of imprisonment" occurs. Second, three different patterns of biographical self-interpretations in context of coping with prison will be introduced. The two patterns which show the sharpest contrast will be exemplified by hermeneutic case studies and a case comparison. This shows how close biographical experiences of conflict and the institutional experience of being held tight in confinement are intertwined with each other.

The exploration of the relationship between internal and external dynamic processes involves methodological challenges. Biographical patterns of behaviour are investigated as patterns of conflict. And the deeper meaning of these conflicts is not immediately accessible to us. It has to be reconstructed by hermeneutic interpretation, including the latent or unconscious meaning (Bereswill 2007;

Lorenzer 1988; Leithäuser and Volmerg 1988). The following results are based on such reconstructions which have been done by combining different methods of analysing and interpreting qualitative data. The leading perspective was the one of a step-by-step case comparison by first looking for minimal and maximum contrasts in relation to coping with imprisonment. Along this first approach to the data which followed the procedure of an open coding of the narratives we found the first hints of how coping with prison corresponded with biographical experiences, resources and conflicts. Such biographical coping patterns will be discussed below. In addition to this, two biographical case studies will be discussed in detail. These case studies are based on very detailed sequential readings of passages of the biographical interviews with in-depth interpretations of passages we identified as irritating, non-understandable, affect-laden or exemplary for what we found to be central for the case in relation to our research questions. Writing up the case studies we always started by discussing what and how the narrator tells us about his experience of prison. The next step was to look for the correspondence of this narrative with the biographical self-construction we found in the biographical narrative. These steps of analysing and interpreting the complex stories of our interviewees have always been accompanied by reflecting the research relationship and the interaction in the interviews over the years.

We started each interview by asking the interviewee to tell us about his arrival there. The following quotation is taken from an interview with an incarcerated young man who recollects his arrival: "Oh my God, this is it. You either go mad or you break down or—I don't know—you fall into a coma". This statement expresses a fear that is created by the loss of autonomy entailed in the experience of incarceration. It illustrates what Gresham Sykes in 1958 called an "attack on the psyche". Incarceration creates crisis—ample evidence for this can be found in our interviews, even though not all participants express their fears as openly as the young man quoted here.

Clearly, the institutional intervention feels painful and is humiliating. From the point of view of many adolescents, the justice system constitutes an authoritarian provocation. They feel treated unfairly and are outraged at the everyday patronising which they cannot escape. Yet, at the same time, our interviews with young men show that their views of prison are not just negative, even after their release from prison. Of course, they all stress the painful limitations to which they must adjust. Nevertheless, they also describe positive learning processes connected with the hope for better integration into society. This contradiction is expressed in the following statement of a young man recently released from prison. He says: "Prison is a hole, but it was the best thing that could have happened to me".

In the closed institution, coercion happens among the inmates as well as between inmates and staff (Toch 1975 and 1992; Sim 1994; Bereswill 2001, 2002; Windzio 2006). At the same time, prison constitutes a place where changes take place: quitting the consumption of drugs, finishing school or an apprenticeship and the opportunity to reflect on one's life—these are central motives that are repeatedly talked about during incarceration—even after relapses. Despite the many contradictions entailed in prisoner work schemes, incarceration often provides these adolescent men with an opportunity to identify positively with the image of the male worker—an ideal that often collapses quickly after their release from prison. This is due on the one hand to the grave marginalisation of this group of young men in the labour market. On the other, the *internal identification* breaks down when the rigid structure of the institution has been left behind (Bereswill 2004). The rigid structural frame of the institution provides orientation and support. It raises the hopes for more internal structure: the young men are being taken by the hand and they thus feel better equipped to take their lives into their own hands.

For many young men this hope turns into disappointment after their release. Their newly found structure is fragile and finally collapses. The increase in their (potential) capabilities remains limited to the closed institution. Without the tight grip of the *controlling and care-taking* institution, it becomes difficult to take life into one's own hands. The following quotation provides a glimpse of this conflict:

> I liked it better inside because I had less (work) to do, I didn't need to go to the employment office all the time, I went to work and got my money—somehow it was easier inside.

Other cases also illustrate that the release from prison constitutes a threshold over which the young men stumble. The social marginalisation of most of the young men intensifies their individual problems with adjusting to the transition: How can they fulfill the socially still dominant ideal of the employed worker? Which alternative ideals of masculinity are available to them? How to balance conflicting wishes for independence, attachment and orientation? These conflicts that besiege the individual after his release now have to be dealt with in an open frame. In many cases, this frame entails administrative and organisational support—but the experience of the internal loss of structure is seldom addressed. This is illustrated in a description of someone who—looking back on his experience of release from prison—concludes, "inside I'm a different person from outside", and he adds shortly thereafter, "I had changed, but the others hadn't changed".

Very often the release is experienced as a severe disruption. The transition between the two experiential spaces is highly taxing. This dynamic is underlined by specific biographical constellations that has been discussed above: very often incarceration intervenes in biographies already *abundant with discontinuity*. In other words, we see biographical patterns that are characterised by dependency, lack of attachment and a high level of intervention from institutions. The young men's experiences of changing primary relationships, changing institutions and unstable modalities of relating and caretaking are reflected in orientations that drift between a desire to establish total independence and passive dependence on given structures. These patterns constitute the backdrop for the intervention of the closed or "total institution" (Goffman 1961; von Wolffersdorff *et al* 1996). The institution seems to promise structure, continuity and support—a hope that hardly ever materialises.

Biography, autonomy and coping with imprisonment

Our biographical, longitudinal interviews show *how* the institutional experience of incarceration and biographical patterns interlock. Different coping responses evolve corresponding to the various conflicts of identity and masculinity. In particular, our research uncovered three different biographical coping strategies in the interviews in our sample: autonomy-in-relation, rationalisation of conflict, and struggling for recognition (each of these themes is described briefly below but developed further in the following section).

Autonomy-in-relation

Only rarely do the young men experience their incarceration as an *internal* biographical turning point. Biographical crises tend to be connected with crises of relationships. Participants provided lively descriptions of their experiences with significant others. Social integration and the many obstacles connected with it are tied to a network of relationships. Autonomy and social bonds are closely intertwined. In these rare cases the young inmates respond in a self-reflexive way to the educational attitude of prison staff—which does not mean that desistance outside prison is a guaranteed. Instead it depends on how the self-reflexive dynamics which are triggered inside can be translated to the outside prison reality one has to cope with.

Rationalisation of conflict

More often, incarceration is experienced as an *external* biographical turning point. The narratives focus on formal changes: processes of achieving a qualification and finding a way out of delinquency are viewed as positive results of an inevitable adaptation to societal expectations. Conflicts are avoided and rarely talked about. Attachment to others is couched in material relationships of exchange. The ideal self of the young men is that of a cool, independent, rational winner, both in the legal or in the illegal realm. This image of the "real man" who is under control of everything is reinforced in prison subculture and severe individual crises like drug addiction or grave family dependencies are covered by an over determined version of being a reasonable young man, now on his straight and narrow.

Struggling for autonomy

The third and most frequent constellation entails the experience of incarceration being articulated as *continuing struggle for autonomy and withheld recognition*.

The influence of the prison is described as a grave intervention into one's personality—in the positive or the negative direction. For instance, one of our interviewees described his time in prison as his "last chance" and a chance he plans to make the most of; another rebelled against the unjust and authoritarian rules and regulations until he is withdrawn from every educational programme on offer. The common ground between the two is the experience of prison as powerful influence on one's own life—being mirrored in very polarised versions of adapting and resisting, versions of a lonesome autonomy that is repeatedly threatened by the outside world's power.

These patterns should not be seen as clearly defined typologies. Rather, they should be interpreted as an expression of the continuum that reflects the very different forms of autonomy conflict experienced by adolescents whereby the closed environment makes them even more acute and magnifies them as if they had been placed under a convex lens. In the following, a comparison is drawn between the two patterns that project the strongest and most contrasting images: imprisonment as an inner biographical turning point and imprisonment as a biographical continuum linked with an ongoing struggle for autonomy. Very clear differences are evident here in the ways that young adults perceive the disciplinary or educational aims of juvenile detention.

Imprisonment as an inner biographical turning point

FREDDY GROTE: ADOLESCENT CRISES AND UNPROCESSED GRIEF

> It's like, well, I would not say the wardens were father figures, but they're the grown ups around here, the ones who look after us, a bit like parents or guardians, well that's how I see it anyway.

The quote above is taken from the first set of interviews with Freddy Grote, first interviewed at the age of 21 in a prison in East Germany. He perceives his imprisonment as a form of disciplinary intervention in his life, feels protected and accepts the role of a child being raised by the state. Freddy speaks with respect when he talks about individual wardens and his training instructor, and has most to say about the people who are most important to him outside prison. They are his mother and his girlfriend, of whom he says "They give me strength. They keep picking me up and putting me back on my feet". This interview sequence is typical of Freddy's attitude while in prison. He feels supported, cared for and part of the relationship network in which he is caught up. He again sees himself as a child—he is taken care of and supported, but is also encouraged to hold out and see things through.

Everything Freddy has to say is shaped by his belief that he is actively changing his ways. He seems driven by a range of different motives. This includes working on his relationship with his girlfriend: Freddy enthusiastically describes the letters they exchange and how the process of clarifying things between them has intensified their relationship. Two further motives appear central to how Freddy deals with his imprisonment. He identifies closely with his job in a prison workshop and does body building exercises to stay fit. When talking about work he responds "What, before? Work? No, I did not work back then" and refers to his time as a member of a gang of young men who partied and used drugs. Now he emphasises the value of his work and the recognition it brings, "When others come along and say, Oh that's cool". Intensive exercise is also a way of dealing with his earlier use of party drugs, as he explains "Yeah, I was 58 kilos when I came in here and now I weigh 70. That's my goal, to build muscle". At the same time, Freddy distances himself sharply from the violent subculture among prison inmates and goes on to emphasise the difference between their fitness training routines and his own body building exercises.

Freddy's first interview on imprisonment focuses entirely on the change in his person. Particularly noteworthy is the fact that he believes his restricted circumstances in prison serve in fostering his autonomy—despite his belief that he need not have been sent to prison. For example, he criticises his sentence and sees it as unjust. He is convinced that he would have escaped delinquency even without a prison sentence, making all the more remarkable his positive reference to the disciplinary and educational role of prison and the relationships it offers. How can this constellation be better understood in biographical terms?

Freddy's review of his life focuses on one critical aspect. He repeatedly emphasises the contrast between a happy childhood and a disrupted adolescence. He describes his childhood as being in the care of people who were "always there". Apart from his mother, these reliable figures include his grandmother and his brother's biological father, whom he also calls father. He makes a point of adding that they had "a proper father-son relationship". The presence and attention of adults who assume different roles and responsibilities falls abruptly apart as first his grandmother dies and then, shortly afterwards, the father. His mother, who up to now had only had to take on some of the responsibility, is left behind with two sons aged 12 and 18. Freddy remembers the family not only becoming smaller, but their relationships changing as his mother's boyfriend joins them. The loss of the father strengthens the childrens' vehement rejection of this new man and his ideas on bringing up children. The relationship between Freddy and his mother also deteriorates as a result.

Along with his brother, Freddy flees the tensions at home, joins the hedonistic "techno" music scene and gets his first taste of freedom and youthful passion. He experiments with drugs and gets involved in joy-riding. According to Freddy, life suddenly had "a completely different meaning".

However, the heady goings-on with his "mates" are replaced by dates with his girlfriend long before he is sent to prison. Now, he feels, it is his girlfriend who helps him find "the true meaning of life", drawing an expressive parallel in which he equates the intensity of what he experienced with his "mates" with that of being in love.

Even a year after his release from prison, during a follow-up interview, Freddy emphasises the link between the change in his person and the change in his relationships. He summed up imprisonment in a positive light when he says, "It all came together somehow", and gives the impression of a relationship-focused, successful young man with ambitions that he strictly distances from his earlier days of hedonism. His rigidity points to the fact that his internal change process is far from complete. As opposed to the subject of imprisonment, Freddy no longer wanted to talk about his personal conflicts. He sees his delinquency and his drug consumption as a closed chapter and refused to take part in any further interviews for this research.

The interviews with Freddy give a deep insight into a crises of adolescence during which imprisonment is been experienced as a transitional space for changing oneself in relation to others. However, to follow this reading—which is very close to Freddy's own interpretation of prison—is problematic. In the case of Freddy, prison clearly gives him important impulses for change. But his appropriation of these impulses is embedded into his relations to significant others outside prison. Those relations also bridge his resocialisation conflicts after being released from prison.

Processing imprisonment as a biographical struggle for autonomy

LUKAS MAIER: CONFUSED REBELLION

For 18-year-old Lukas Maier, prison is a place of ongoing and ever-spiralling power struggles. At the start of the first interview, he describes himself as an incorrigible rebel who remains untouched by prison measures. He says "They've tried lots of different sanctions with me" and goes on to explain that he just happens to break the rules now and again and that is just the way it is. Then he says, defiantly, "If I want a smoke, I'll have a smoke. It's not exactly a crime. And if I want to sleep in, I'll sleep in".

Lukas's message that he is incorrigible is accompanied by an angry description of his numerous conflicts with those in authority, all of which he re-enacts by citing, for example, the war of words between himself and a teacher. His interview accounts contain long passages about sanctions that he finds both stupid and unfair. He argues with the wardens, regularly smokes cannabis and is subject to a variety of disciplinary measures: lock-up, solitary confinement, suspension from school and, finally, transfer to another institution. Lukas' accusation-filled anger at the "useless" measures applied in prison is bound up by disappointment. He feels he gets no recognition and is thus insulted and tries to cover it up by emphasising the division between the expectations and provisions of the prison system:

> I mean, they've shown me that I've got nothing more to look forward to, I can't work towards anything, so I won't, I do not want to work towards anything.

In his eyes, the institution has abandoned him. He believes that the tight thumbscrews applied in prison can no longer be released. Consequently, he tries to turn the rejection he feels into stubbornness: he "will not" do anything—an attitude he peppers with his own accusation-filled stories. His sustained anger at the institution of prison and its specific representatives clearly indicates how strongly tied he feels, but he is unable to do anything but criticise.

While being interviewed in prison, his attitude is one of provocative deviancy. The same applies to his accounts of his background, which involve a long chain of disciplinary measures and periods in institutions, and which nearly always end with him being thrown out. Despite this demonstrative presentation of his rebellious and uncontrollable nature, however, Lukas admits that prison also has a positive influence on his life: prison has brought him to his senses because he has given up his compulsive use of hard drugs. His head is clearer, although that also leads to conflict: he now knows what he, in his words, "has done" to his father. His relationship with his father is characterised by admiration, respect, fear and—most of all—guilt and shame. While in prison, Lukas has always believed that he was responsible for his father's recent heart attack and says: "Because I also knew what I'd done to my father. And that I'd embarrassed him in front of my relatives".

Lukas idealises his father in each and every interview: his father is his sole role model, he has made something of his life and deserves for his son to finally take responsibility for his own life—this is how in a series of interviews Lukas explains his father's accusation-filled expectations to himself and to his interviewer. His father, who emigrated to Germany from southern Europe in search of work, had actually abandoned two families—he had left the children from his first marriage and later left Lukas and his mother. Lukas blames his mother for the way he has turned out and accuses her of not having brought him up properly.

His father is seriously ill, lives alone and drinks—and gives his son long lectures on why he should stop smoking cannabis. Despite the apparent dependency-related and recognitional conflicts between father and son, Lukas assumes all the blame and does not openly rebel. Instead, he avoids the situation—both before and after imprisonment. Just as he did before going into prison, as soon as he is released he escapes to his father's home, quickly takes up with his old ways, commits further burglaries and consumes a range of different drugs.

Reading the passages in which Lukas talks about himself and his father, an image of an accusing, punishing and authoritarian father-son relationship comes to light—one glued together by shared identification with ethnicity, honour and masculinity. This dynamic interplay is illustrated in the self-accusations Lukas expresses in the first follow-up interview conducted six months after his release. When he talks of his experience directly after release, it is clear that on the inside he struggles hard with his father's interference in his life (even though on the outside he portrays it as entirely appropriate) seeing himself as unable to abide by his father's rules. The following passages illustrate the dynamics of these accounts, with Lukas telling of the hour-long lectures his father holds and his attempts to escape them:

> Always on at me, I have to change my ways, this and that, and at some point I've long got the message, and I think for longer than two or three hours, there comes a time when it's just a waste of time. And, well, I, er, think that's just how it was, because I was a coward.

Lukas is caught up in an angry, dependent and accusation-filled relationship with his father. Its basic structure is repeated in prison but with the difference that he is not entirely able to escape the lectures he receives from the people in there. Then there is the anger he feels towards his father but is unable to openly show or express. He releases it in prison, even at the risk of receiving tough sanctions in response. The idealisation of his father and the angry accusations towards juvenile detention are thus an expression of unsolved family breakdown conflict that manifests itself as an inner cement between father and son. This constellation does not break down over time. Lukas continues to idealise his father and throws insults around, calling himself irresponsible, the prison useless, "shitty", and says that if he really got going, let himself get all worked up, then "maybe the Walkman would fall apart or something, what do I know!? I hate, y' know, the law and everything, like".

After his release, Lukas' hermetic dependency on his father's recognition changes as the years go by. He meets a young woman who, like him, is from an immigrant family and comes, in Lukas' words, "from my country". He emphasizes how important the relationship is to him and how well he gets on with her parents. His relationships are in transition, he expands his personal relationship network. He also moves into his own flat. He is out of work, dreams of a career as a rapper and continues to consume large quantities of cannabis—an ambivalent image of the gradual waning of his desperate struggle for autonomy along with his continued sedating of those internal struggles.

If we had stopped interviewing Lukas one year after his release from prison the last picture we would have had would have been the above. Only during the following years we have been able to follow his step-by-step struggle to find his own way as a young man while not giving up his identification with his father. Year on year, he met his interviewer and talked again and again about his dreams, wishes, his partnership conflicts and the ongoing changes in his life. After some years of unemployment, Lukas started an apprenticeship within the same field of work as his father. Lukas is very proud about his ability to work, showed the interviewer photos of himself and his products and calls the researcher after having failed a practical examination, telling her that he, of course, will repeat this examination and not give up.

The longitudinal interviews with Lukas are an outstanding example of the intertwining dynamics of an institutional intervention and biographical conflicts which cannot be seen on the first glance as such. In his case prison is a provocation—to rebel and to struggle against authorities while being held tight, an experience that is extraordinary for someone who has been sent away again and again and at the same time accused for his deviant behaviour. After being released Lukas was able to separate from his father step by step and—in the long run—to take up his identification with work that is also related back to his father. His personal and social transition takes time and his reliable participation as interviewee in our research becomes part of this transitional process. Here, he can expose himself as a creative rebel and later on as a successful skilled worker, two self-constructions that mirror his struggle for acknowledgement by significant others but also by society.

Conclusion

The narratives of the young men we interviewed in and after prison give rich evidence of the fact that all the pains of imprisonment still exist and have to be integrated in the self-perception of every inmate inside the total institution. Therefore, the structural functionalism of Sykes seems to be more convincing as critical voices tell us. At the same time, this argument is limited to the momentary social situation *inside* prison. Exploring the long-term consequences of incarceration means integrating the prison experience into a perspective that allows the contextualisation of the extraordinary and conflict-ridden situation in the closed environment into the biographical processes *before*, *during* and *after* incarceration.

Combining a longitudinal research design and a conflict-theoretical analysis of biographical narratives we can reconstruct the interlocking of the institutional experience of incarceration and biographical patterns of appropriating such an intervention into ones life. This can be shown by discussing one of the pains of imprisonment from a biographical perspective: "the loss of autonomy" that is one of the strongest characteristics of the closed setting inside prison walls. Every participant of our study had to struggle with their extremely limited autonomy under the regime of the authoritarian institution. Analysing their ways of coping with this confrontation in the context of the biographical self-constructions of the young men brings to light the fact that this specific conflict of autonomy corresponds with serious autonomy struggles the young men went through *before* their incarceration and have to deal with *after* being released to the outside world. Imprisonment intensifies the adolescent dynamics of (conscious and unconscious) autonomy conflicts that socially marginalised young men have to accomplish under restricted circumstances of social integration. Our case studies evidence the fact that this dynamic is not limited to the psychosocial pains inside prison but is re-bound to past experiences and continues throughout the transition from inside to outside again.

What have we learnt about life after prison by such a research focus? A comparison of the two cases shows a differentiated and sometimes paradoxical image in terms of the effect of imprisonment through the eyes of the inmates.

Freddy Grote turns what he feels is an unfair punishment into some sort of self-discipline and initiates his own integration through his work and his partnership. He represents an exceptional case, the realm of the ideal in reintegration and puts his success down to the occupational training opportunities offered in prison, but also to his family and girlfriend. His is a case in which active learning relationships play the key role and, in institutional terms, develop without any great need for occupational integration work or social therapy resources. According to the questions in the introduction to this chapter, Freddy Grote shows that the conclusion "nothing works" does not cover his own interpretation of prison—from his perspective "something works"—prison is part of a restructuring process of family and partnership arrangements. Asking for "what hurts", we see how the narrator turns the shock of the loss of autonomy into a frame of reference of support and learning.

Compared with Freddy Grote's extraordinary affirmative attitude, Lucas Maier's relation to prison is highly ambivalent, divided and bound up with mixed feelings. On the one hand, imprisonment has sobered him up—something he sees as positive. On the other, he is completely fixated on the sanctioning, punishing side of prison. The sanctions he experiences strengthen his unresolved feelings of shame and his need for autonomy and recognition. The results are ongoing dissatisfaction and an angry attitude towards all programmes and reintegration activities in prison. In his case, discipline and education result in full-blown punishment and his rebellion. His search for intensive relationships and the need for autonomy comes to nothing. Only over the years of the longitudinal interviews do we learn to identify the deeper meaning of Lukas' prison rebellion that seems to enable him to move on in the direction of an own way of living without breaking off his relationship with his father. What seems a contrast on first glance—Lukas' self-construction as rebel and his later identification as a successful and skilled worker—can be understood as different ways of expressing his longing for autonomy and recognition: as someone who defends himself and fights for his ambitions. Prison, in this case, is a place of confrontation. Imprisonment does not lead to social integration. Instead, it leads to inner conflicts with dependency, autonomy and separation which Lukas needs his space and time to cope with. His case seems to prove that "nothing works" in prison as everything he could do or learn inside is not available for him because the institution excludes him step by step. Lukas Maier seems to turn all his pains of imprisonment into anger and rejection. Framing this pattern of conflict into his biographical narratives over the years we could draw a paradoxical conclusion: "What works?" in his case is the fact that "nothing works"—a dynamic that cannot be fully understood without understanding the biographical conflicts of Lukas Maier. However, this provocative argument is risky as it could be misunderstood as a plea for incarcerating young men. Instead of such a short-handed argument, the crucial question is why other institutions of the welfare state have been unable to hold those young men who end up in prison, like we also see in the life course of Lukas Maier.

The results of our study document the effects of imprisonment on the lives of male adolescents. How young men deal with these effects depends on their biographical resources to cope with conflicts—a potential that is deeply embedded into their social chances and their experiences with significant and generalised others who provide the ground for autonomy-in-relation. At the same time, young offenders who are sent to juvenile detention are multiple disadvantaged and very vulnerable adolescents who are not well equipped for coping with the pains of imprisonment that correspond with their ongoing conflicts of autonomy. These conflicts are aggravated after being released in part in response to the high demands of a resocialisation process.

In contrast to the biographical approach that is being suggested here, research on social integration after prison—as well as research on desistance—very often is still limited to statistical evidence or to the evaluation of selected programs of rehabilitation. To understand the successes as well as the failures of young offenders we need to understand their biographical self-construction and we have to ask for their experiences with the pains of imprisonment which include the painful transitions from outside to inside and back again. Resocialisation processes from prison need to be seen as complex psychosocial processes full of conflicts that have to be contained by an environment that can be characterised as holding tight. It also suggests the value of looking at how adolescents view their lives prior to incarceration, obtaining a better understanding of how they perceive imprisonment, and understanding how these views interact with other aspects of their lives.

Notes

1 In writing the final version of this chapter I was supported by the editors of the volume and an anonymous reader whom I thank very much for his/her helpful remarks and suggestions which supported my work. My thanks also to my colleague Anke Neuber—my arguments in this chapter are based on our discussions and team work in researching adolescence in prison for more than 10 years.

2 The studies are situated at the Criminological Research Institute of Lower Saxony (KFN) in Hannover, Germany (www.kfn.de) and received financial support from VolkswagenStiftung, Stiftung Deutsche Jugendmarke, Deutsche Forschungsgemeinschaft.

References

Adorno, Theodor W. (1955) 'Zum Verhältnis von Soziologie und Psychologie', in Adorno, Theodor W., *Aufsätze zur Gesellschaftstheorie und Methodologie*. Frankfurt am Main: Fischer, pp 7–62.

Bereswill, Mechthild (1999) *Gefängnis und Jugendbiographie. Qualitative Zugänge zu Jugend, Männlichkeitsentwürfen und Delinquenz. (JuSt-Bericht Nr. 4) KFN-Forschungsberichte Nr. 78.* Hannover: Kriminologisches Forschungsinstitut Niedersachsen.

Bereswill, Mechthild (2001) '"Die Schmerzen des Freiheitsentzugs" – Gefängniserfahrungen und Überlebensstrategien männlicher Jugendlicher und Heranwachsender', in Bereswill, Mechthild and Greve, Werner (eds) *Forschungsthema Strafvollzug*. BadenBaden: Interdisziplinäre Beiträge zur kriminologischen.

Bereswill, Mechthild (2002) 'Doing Violence, Concepts of Masculinity, and Biographical Subjectivity – Three Case Studies'. *KFN-Forschungsbericht Nr. 78*. Hannover: Kriminologisches Forschungsinstitut.

Bereswill, Mechthild (2004) 'Inside-Out: Resocialisation from prison as a biographical process. A longitudinal approach to the psychodynamics of imprisonment', *Journal of Social Work Practice. Psychotherapeutic approaches in health, welfare and the community*, 18(3), November: 315–36.

Bereswill, Mechthild (2007) 'Figthing Like a Wildcat. A Deep Hermeneutic Interpretation of the Jack Roller', *Theoretical Criminology*, 11(4): 469–84.

Bereswill, Mechthild (2008) 'Gender and Subjectivity in the Interview Situation: A Critical Discussion', *Psychoanalysis, Culture & Society*, 13: 316–24.

Bereswill, Mechthild, Koesling, Almut and Neuber, Anke (2008) *Umwege in Arbeit. Eine biographische Längsschnittstudie zu den Tätigkeitserfahrungen hafterfahrener junger Männer*. Baden Baden: Nomos.

Bereswill, Mechthild and Ehlert, Gudrun (1996) *Alleinreisende Frauen zwischen Selbst- und Welterfahrung*. Königstein/Taunus: Ulrike Helmer Verlag.

Crewe, Ben (2009) *The Prisoner Society. Power, Adaption and Social Life in an English Prison*. Oxford: Oxford University Press.

Dausien, Bettina (1996) *Biographie und Geschlecht. Zur biographischen Konstruktion sozialer Wirklichkeit in Frauenlebensgeschichten*. Bremen: Transcript.

Farrall, S. (2006) 'What is Qualitative Longitudinal Research?', LSE Methodology Institute, Papers in Social Research Methods, Qualitative Series, Paper 11. London: LSE Methodology Institute.

Gadd, David and Farrall, Stephen (2004) 'Criminal Careers, Desistance and Subjectivity: Intepreting Men's Narratives of Change', *Theoretical Criminology*, 8(2): 123–56.

Goffman, Erving (1961/1973) *Asyle. Über die soziale Situation psychiatrischer Patienten und anderer Insassen*. Frankfurt am Main: Surkamp.

Graf-Deserno, Susanne and Deserno, Heinrich (1998) *Entwicklungschancen in der Institution. Psychoanalytische Teamsupervision*. Frankfurt am Main: Fischer.

Greve, Werner and Daniela, Hosser (1998) 'Psychische und soziale Folgen einer Jugendstrafe: Forschungsstand und Desiderate', *Monatszeitschrift für Kriminologie und Strafrechtsreform*, 81: 83–103.

James, Adrian L., Bottomley, Keith, Liebling, Alison and Clare, Emma (1997) *Privatizing Prisons. Rethoric and Reality*. London: Sage.

Johnson, Robert and Toch, Hans (1982) *Pains of Imprisonment*. Beverly Hills, CA: Roxbury Press.

King, Vera (2002) *Die Entstehung des Neuen in der Adoleszenz*. Opladen: Leske und Budrich.

Leithäuser, Thomas and Volmerg, Birgit (1988) *Psychoanalyse in der Sozialforschung. Eine Einführung*. Opladen: Leske und Budrich.

Liebling, Alison (1992) *Suicide in Prison*. London: Routledge.

Liebling, Alison (2005) *Prisons and Their Moral Performances. A Study of Values, Quality and Prison Life*. Oxford: Oxford University Press.

Liebling, Alison and Maruna, Shadd (eds) (2005) *The Effects of Imprisonment*. Cullompton: Willan Publishing.

Liebling, Alison and Prince, David (2001) *The Prison Officer*. Cullompton: Willan Publishing.

Lorenzer, Alfred (1988) 'Tiefenhermeneutische Kulturanalyse', in König, Hans-Dieter (ed.) *Kulturanalysen. Psychoanalytische Studien zur Kultur*. Frankfurt am Main: Fischer, pp 11– 98.

Maruna, Shadd (2001) *Making Good*. Washington, DC: APA Press.

Neuber, Anke (2009) *Die Demonstration kein Opfer zu sein. Biographische Fallstudien zu Gewalt und Männlichkeitskonflikten. Interdisziplinäre Beiträge zur kriminologischen Forschung, Band 35*. Baden Baden: Nomos.

Rosenthal, Gabriele (1995) *Erlebte und erzählte Lebensgeschichte. Gestalt und Struktur biographischer Selbstbeschreibungen*. Frankfurt am Main and New York, NY: Campus.

Saldana, J. (2003) *Longitudinal Qualitative Research*. New York, NY: Alta Mira Press.

Sim, Joe (1994) 'Tougher than the rest? Men in Prison', in Newburn, Tim and Stanko, Elizabeth A. (eds) *Men, Masculinities, and Crime – Just Boys Doing Business?* London: Willan Publishing, pp 100–17.

Sykes, Gresham M. (1958/1999) *The Society of Captives. A Study of a Maximum Security Prison. Princeton*, NJ: Princeton Classic Editions.

Toch, Hans (1975) *Men in Crisis. Human Breakdowns in Prison*. Chicago, IL: Aldine.

Toch, Hans (1977) *Living in Prison. The ecology of survival*. New York, NY: The Free Press.

Toch, Hans (1992) *Violent Men: an Inquiry into the Psychology of Violence*. Washington, DC: Lexington Books.

Waquant, Loic (2008) 'The Place of Prison in the New Government of Poverty', in Frampton, Mary Louise, Lopez, Ian Haney and Simon, Jonathan (eds) *After the War on Crime: Race, Democracy and a New Reconstruction*. New York, NY: New York University Press, pp 23–36.

Windzio, Michael (2006) 'Is there a deterrent effect of pains of imprisonment? The impact of "social costs" of first incarceration on the hazard rate of recidivism', *Punishment & Society*, 8: 341–64.

von Wolffersdorff, Christian, Sprau-Kuhlen, Vera and Kersten, Joachim (1996) *Geschlossene Unterbringung. Kapitulation der Jugendhilfe?* Weinheim und Münche: Juventa.

Chapter 9

'I can't make my own future'

White-collar offenders' anticipation of release from prison[1]

Ben Hunter

A preoccupation with the future is a concern for us all, but perhaps nowhere is this more explicit than for those serving prison sentences. Using interview data, this chapter focuses on the existential aspects of white-collar offenders' prison experiences, with a particular focus on the future each had identified upon release. Some felt optimistic about life after prison, constituting themselves as made stronger by their experiences and as active participants in their change in self. This reflection was based on an understanding that they were still in control of their futures and that much was possible for them. Other prisoners felt change had been inflicted upon them by their prison sentence. They were unable to view any positives in a future in which their identity as offenders was already determined. Understanding that release from prison would force them to confront difficult decisions was to understand how they had changed.

Introduction

There is a nascent but growing interest in criminology for the insights that existentialist thought can provide for understanding crime and the experiences of offenders (see for example Lippens and Crewe 2009). The intention here is to build on this body of work by discussing the imprisonment experiences and the anticipation of release from prison of a small number of prisoners within the context of existentialist considerations of the future. Existence is highly personal and should not be generalised about or abstracted. The individual lives within a particular situation, their understanding of that situation informed by their own unique past and future project for their self. This chapter starts by outlining the relevant aspects of existentialist thought that might help us understand prisoners' experiences and the sociology that has made existentialist concepts its key concern. These concepts are then utilised in discussing the experiences of a group of prisoners convicted of white-collar offences, focusing on how offenders conceived of themselves and envisioned their lives after prison.

Existentialism and the future

The future constantly preoccupies us. We are inundated with questions concerning what we want to do, what we feel we must do and when we will do them. Such questions about our future are fundamental to our existence. Existentialism, as a 'style of philosophising' considers the challenges that existence presents us with (Macquarrie 1972: 14). These revolve around issues of meaning within our lives, our relationship to others, who we are and who we can become. Responding to these challenges is done through interaction with the world and reflection on the particular situations that are encountered and the emotions they provoke. These all provide important information that constantly challenges our sense of who we are. Even the most seemingly mundane of encounters have implications for what they 'say' about our life while particularly extreme experiences can have the impact of shattering our understanding of ourselves, forcing a realisation that change has taken place (Douglas 1984).

Existentialism – thinking about the future

The concerns and themes of existentialist thought are many and varied, as is entirely appropriate for a body of work that has as its focus no less a topic than the whole gamut of human existence. For the purposes of this chapter, and for reasons that should become apparent, the summary of existentialist thought presented here concentrates on the individual existent's relationship with and understanding of their future.

If we accept the notion that the only fixed property of human existence is change (Nietzsche 1968, 2004) then it is no exaggeration to say that the future is where one exists. At any given point in existence one is moving beyond who one currently is. That is, one is constantly becoming. It is not possible to try to understand who one is at this moment in terms of a fixed set of characteristics because such a moment, even as it is apprehended, is gone.

One's existence then, is constituted in who one can become and all the possibilities that entails. One must choose a particular future and therefore a particular self over all others. The way in which the present and past is interpreted is constituted by the future, by the specific goals that are of concern and the specific self project one wishes to realise. Therefore, it is the case, as Kotarba notes, that the question 'Who am I?' is, in part, answered by looking to the future rather than the past (Kotarba 1979: 358). By understanding who one can become and knowing something about the possibilities that are open to them the individual can understand who they are.

As much as existentialism emphasises freedom to choose however, it is not the case that literally any possibility is open. Whichever future is chosen for must be consistent with one's past, which is immutable (Sartre 1958; Heidegger 1962). Part of existence involves managing the tension between our past, present and future self. In this way, who we are now and who we may yet become are grounded in who we were. This is what Heidegger (1962: 373) means when he stresses '... I am as having been ...' and also as Sartre describes:

> ... the freedom which escapes toward the future can not give itself any past it likes according to its fancy ... It has to be its own past, and this past is irremediable ... If the past does not determine our actions, at least it is such that we can not take a new decision except *in terms of it*.
>
> (Sartre 1958: 517, original emphasis)

Who one was is therefore an important part of who one can be and although one is free to choose a future and a self, this must be done with a regard to who one was (see for example Maruna 2001; Maruna and Roy 2007). Maruna demonstrates this with his study of the 'redemption scripts' of offenders who had desisted from crime (Maruna 2001: 85–108). Desisters could not alter that fact that they had previously offended, but they could script their lives in such a way that a new 'law-abiding' persona came 'logically' out of their deviant past (Maruna 2001). In short then, the meaning placed upon the past is a function of who one is, which in turn, as we have seen, is informed by who one can be.

Existentialism and sociology

The explicitly sociological aspects of existentialist thought have been considered by a number of researchers. Such 'existential sociology'[2] has aimed to capture the complexity and diversity of human life through understanding how individuals experience their everyday worlds (see for example edited collections by Douglas and Johnson 1977; Kotarba and Fontana 1984; Kotarba and Johnson 2002). Existential sociology emphasises the essentially ambiguous nature of social existence that requires us to place our own meaning on what we encounter, making efforts to constitute ourselves in terms of our prevailing self conception and the discourses we invoke to justify our decisions (Fontana 1980).

Existential sociologists have claimed a less 'grim' view of human existence than that promulgated by existentialist thought more generally and associated with the dread of death and the meaningless nature of existence (Douglas 1984: 88–94).[3] Nevertheless, and as might be expected, the core concepts of existential sociology reflect wider existentialist concerns. Emotions are a vital part of human existence as they provide the drive to action (Clark 2002). The ideals and values individuals hold are important in orienting them to their world (Douglas 1984). However, central to human existence and interaction with the world is the sense of self, which all individuals hold but cannot necessarily rationalise, developed as a result of the need to negotiate the various situations that the individual will encounter in interacting with the world, i.e. in existing (Douglas 1984). It is through the sense of self that the individual comes to understand their place in the world and the options this offers to them. It situates them with reference to others and also with reference to their own past, present and future (Johnson and Kotarba 2002).

Social interaction is inevitably fraught with tension and difficulty as individuals discover their self-conception is to a greater or lesser extent at odds with the place in the world society assigns to them (Kotarba 1979: 359). This tension is not helped by the situationally dependent nature of the self. Particular locales and interactions emphasise different facets of the self, often leaving individuals unsure of their own self-identity (Kotarba 1979). It is the struggle to locate who we are that is a key aspect of existence as the self evolves through social encounters, and who one 'is' is constructed through interaction with others (Goffman 1963; Douglas 1977; Kotarba 1984). Consequently our sense of self is in part constituted in social encounters and will necessarily be reconstructed as one moves between social situations and social institutions (Ebaugh 1984, 1988).

This in turn means that the self is in a constant state of becoming[4] (Kotarba 1979; Fontana 1984). It develops constantly in response to the lived reality of its being in the world through an awareness of itself and the myriad encounters and novel situations that social life entails (Fontana 1984). Fundamental to the conceptualisation of the self then, is an understanding of how it reacts to the possibility of its own change. If an experience that suggests the possibility of change is perceived as something that can be easily coped with, possibly by accommodating it within the current conception of the self, then the individual is unlikely to feel a sense of ontological insecurity; the sense that one's very being is threatened (Yalom 1980). However, if the change is viewed as a threat, because the individual feels they lack the resources to cope then they are likely to experience the dread that is concomitant with their inner self – their very being – being put at risk (Douglas 1984). A situation that threatens change is likely to be an unsettling time as the individual's place in the world is suddenly less certain, the meaning they place on their existence in jeopardy. Previous and firmly held beliefs about 'who' one is may no longer apply, heralding confusion and a certain amount of 'ontological disorientation' (e.g. see Douglas 1984).

This necessarily brief summary of existential thought and its sociological implications highlights the relevant aspects of existence that can inform an understanding of prisoners' anticipation of the future. More substantial reviews of existentialism and its relation to sociology can be found elsewhere (Douglas 1977; Kotarba 1979, 1984; Fontana 1984; Lester 1984).

Existentialism and criminology

A concern with certain existential aspects of offending has long been implicit in some criminological work (e.g. Katz's 1988 focus on emotions; see also Morrison 1995; Crewe and Lippens 2009 chart the relationship between existential thought and criminology). However, it is only in the last few years that a consideration of the relationship between the core themes of existentialism – freedom, angst, becoming – and the lives of offenders has become explicit (see Farrall 2005,

2009; Farrall and Calverley 2006; Lippens and Crewe 2009). This chapter seeks to add to this work with an understanding of the experiences of a small number of prisoners convicted of a white-collar offence, defined here following Edelhertz as:

> An illegal act or series of illegal acts committed by non physical means and by concealment or guile, to obtain money or property, to avoid the loss of money or property, or to obtain business or personal advantage.
>
> (Edelhertz 1970: 3)

For all that the future is a preoccupation for every individual, it is an even more explicit and very relevant concern for prisoners. Considering what life will hold after prison is an issue that requires actual consideration, not a mere philosophical quandary. Existential aspects of imprisonment have been noted previously within criminology, although not always explicitly as existential. Prison has been cited as making life 'futureless' because the routines and disciplines of prison life focus on who a prisoner was (i.e. an offender) rather than who they can become (Meisenhelder 1985; Farrall and Calverley 2006). Further, Jose-Kampfer has noted the 'existential death' that imprisonment heralds, with prisoners going through stages of mourning for their previous life (Jose-Kampfer 1990). Certainly prisoners do think about their lives after prison and a feature of the few studies that have asked prisoners to think about life after prison is the anxiety expressed by prisoners who do not have concrete plans for release. Fears are expressed over where they will live, what they will do and how they 'start again' (Farrall and Calverley 2006: 74–75; Crawley and Sparks 2004 note similar anxieties amongst older prisoners). A part of such concerns is that prisoners frequently lack the resources to re-establish themselves once they leave prison (Petersilia 2003; Richards and Jones 2004). White-collar offenders who are serving prison sentences are not thought to suffer from the material concerns that preoccupy prisoners more generally however. They are assumed to enjoy financial resources and support networks that other offenders lack (Benson and Cullen 1988; Benson and Kerley 2001; Shover and Hochstetler 2006: 142–44).[5]

The argument goes that these resources will render unproblematic the transition from prison back into society and so it might be thought that any difficulty with such issues would not be a feature of their anticipation for the future. However, beyond these generalisations that ignore the great diversity in the demographic characteristics of white-collar offenders (Benson and Kerley 2001; Weisburd *et al* 2001) there is little *a priori* reason to think that white-collar offenders' experience of prison is particularly straightforward, notwithstanding the notion that they are particularly well placed to cope with the rigours of prison (Benson and Cullen 1988). There is even less reason to think they are immune to existential concerns over their future that prison may precipitate. The intention here then is to explore what was significant to white-collar offenders about their prison sentence in terms of their release. This is as a means of contributing not just to an understanding of a group of offenders whose prison experiences remain ambiguous, but also to highlight what an existential perspective can add to explorations of prison experiences more generally. It appears uncontroversial to expect that prisoners think about their future and their lives after prison and is therefore equally uncontroversial to consider prison within the context of a framework that makes the future an explicit topic of concern.

Methods

Data were gathered through semi-structured interviews with six white-collar offenders who were serving prison sentences of less than 18 months each. Offenders were identified through their prison files and contacted via letter outlining the study and asking them if they would like to participate in the research. Interviews were part of a wider project, which intended to follow up prisoners after their release. At the time of their interview, each prisoner had been in prison for at least six months. Interviews focused on prisoners' time in prison, what their plans were upon release and potential sources of help and hindrance to them in living the lives they wished to live and were coded to identify common themes in prisoners' experiences. Interviewees ranged in age from 40 to 61. Their offences included fraud, embezzlement, false accounting, forgery and customs and excise offences. Interviewees were not the corporate executives of white-collar crime myth, but more indicative of a general trend of white-collar offenders as rather 'normal', i.e. as having far more in common with the 'average' non-offender than other offenders (Benson and Kerley 2001; Weisburd *et al* 2001).[6] That is to say that white-collar offenders are noted as having very conventional aspirations and almost mundane lives, running small businesses (Croall 1989) to support modest lifestyles (Weisburd *et al* 2001).

Interviews with prisoners demonstrated that they had been considering what life after release would hold for them in some detail. Their thoughts of the future were variously about work, about social interactions, and about the general direction their lives would take once they had served their sentences. All these offenders recognised that they had changed in some way as a result of their convictions and their imprisonment. Three prisoners were rather optimistic about life after prison, the other three were less so. Little seemed to connect offenders who shared a particular outlook. The age of offenders did not tie them together and all spent similar amounts of time in prison. Two of the 'pessimists' and one of the 'optimists' admitted their offence. The others denied guilt. Offenders' views of their future therefore seem grounded more in their own subjective view on their personal futures and the relationship of their future to their past. There was no intention prior to analysis to group offenders and the decision to do so should not be taken to indicate the presence of particular 'types' of prisoner who shared a uniform prison experience. Rather, it merely reflects a convenient way of discussing broadly shared experiences that prisoners had.

Welcoming change; being and feeling 'in control'

For three prisoners, change was a positive experience, encapsulated by an altering in their outlook on life and a shift in perspective regarding who they were. These prisoners felt they had reached a new understanding of themselves and their life and this understanding was one they were happy with. Joel, convicted of insurance fraud in relation to his auction business, explains the shift in his priorities:

> I call it the egotistical side. The arrogant cocky side. And the more gentle side has come, I don't know, maybe it's age. Maybe it's the change, maybe there's a male version, I don't really worry about it, all I know is I prefer that. It's more peaceful. It's more tranquil and that's how I intend to live when I get out of here ... To give you a good answer, things that used to really matter to me before, cars, money, women, this, that, God knows what, holidays ... I'm not sure much of it matters to me any more, glad I did it, but it becomes a lot less important.

Convicted forger Mark was similarly positive. He identified himself as being more confident and self-assured as a result of his time in prison:

> Fucking horrible thing to say about that, but it is true, there's a lot of truth in [the notion that he was a 'better person' as a result of being in prison], I believe anyway. Yeah, because it can actually make you stronger. I think I'm a lot stronger person because of it and I'm more open minded, I suppose, as well. Not that I thought of myself as close minded before, but I probably am more open minded.

Julie, sentenced to 18 months in prison for embezzlement, had come to a similar realisation as a result of her experiences. She realised she wanted to be a different person to how she had perceived herself previously:

> So really, I've been very lucky. I mean luck isn't the word I'd like to use, you know it's suddenly realising, it's putting it all into perspective, putting my life back into perspective ... all [my husband] wants to do basically is look after me and instead of going for it and saying 'I don't need looking after' suddenly since I've been here I think 'yes I do', why not let him look after me ... And the boys [her adult sons] are the same you see, the boys are exactly the same and it's sort of protection instead of sort of going and saying 'I don't' ... 'yeh alright come on let's be protected' and that's learned me a big lesson, you know a big lesson being here. Really and it's done me good I shouldn't be saying that should I but I do, I feel so different since I've been here and I feel I'm going out a better person.

Joel, Mark and Julie therefore drew positives from the experiences they had undergone. This change in perspective was not to do with imprisonment or their offences *per se*. As Julie said:

> It's nothing to do with the crime. Whatever it was it's nothing to do with that; it's with me it's finding me again … And I think whatever happens I've got a new perspective on life; things aren't, material things aren't important any more, it's to do with … material things never have been actually, do you know what I mean?

Mark was similarly happy about how he had changed since his prison sentence began:

> *BH*: So are there any changes in you yourself do you think?
> *Mark*: A bit more confident, I think, more confident in myself, because you have to be fairly confident in here, otherwise you're going to get bullied. You've got to be fairly upfront. I've got more confidence. I won't probably take as much shit as I used to before. More self-assured, I suppose.

Offences and sentences were therefore conceived of as learning experiences. Joel, Mark and Julie identified themselves as 'better people' because of what they had gone through. It was not just that they were 'surviving' prison, or as Mark put it 'what doesn't kill me makes me stronger' however. They actively identified ways in which they were more capable and more happy with who they were. They acknowledged that they had changed, but this change was something they were active in embracing, taking it upon themselves. They could not deny that their lives had changed, nor the significance of their experiences in terms of what this meant for their futures but they could ensure that it was characterised as a positive experience. From their perspective, their experiences allowed their 'true selves' to emerge. Joel described:

> … there is a little voice inside me which always, was always fighting to try and speak, yes? Which was the other side of me, the quieter side of me, the bit of me that likes drawing, painting, likes relaxing, reading a bit of verse, reading a bit of history … Rather than the side that's always going 'ahhh, ahhh, ahhh, ahhh' [i.e. he was very active] all the time, yes?

This shift in perspective was directly related to how these offenders viewed their futures. There was for them uncertainty over what direction their lives would take. However, they responded to this uncertainty by identifying themselves as people who were well placed to cope. They thought about employment and their future, but not in definite terms, e.g. 'I want job x'. They were open to the possibilities that the future held. As Mark put it:

> So it's kind of like, I don't, in terms of employment, I don't have any real plans because I know when I get out there, something will turn up, something totally unexpected will almost certainly turn up and that will be the route I take.

Joel was similarly unconcerned about what he would do after his release:

> Delighted, I'd be quite happy to be a milkman. I don't care as long as I don't have this shit [the stress of his former auction business] to deal with.

Mark provided an interesting exposition on the future as unproblematic, characterising himself as someone who could cope come-what-may:

> *BH*: You say you feel a lot more confident [about your future].
> *Mark*: Yeah. I'm okay, because I can actually probably put myself to anything, I've got that ability. I'm okay. I'll be alright. I don't think anything in here, I think I've got to help myself. I don't think there's anything in prison that could help me that way.
> *BH*: How does that feel, knowing that it's all on you?
> *Mark*: It's alright. It's my life, it's always been up to me, hasn't it? At the end of the day, it's always up to each of us individually. I'm not going to blame them or blame that. So at the end it's down to me.
> *BH*: You're okay with the uncertainties of it?
> *Mark*: Yeah, it's exciting in a way.

These three reconstructed their pasts in a particular way that boded well for their future, reacting to the potential change in the self that their experiences threatened by identifying something positive within it. Although such reflections by these prisoners are on their present and related to their pasts, they are related to their individual futures. From an existential perspective, failing to identify any positives in the experience of conviction and imprisonment might be to accept a future self as irrevocably changed by circumstances over which they had little control. Instead they chose for themselves a future in which they would be happy and survive. This necessitated that they had gained from their experiences of arrest and imprisonment rather than losing something to them.

As noted above, the need to retell one's past has been linked to desistance from crime by Maruna (2001). To do this is to form a coherent narrative in which present change and a future in which one is a non-offender comes naturally out of the deviant past. This is a way of resolving the potential dissonance involved in 'choosing' to become a non-offender, grounded in the potentially problematic understanding that the offender was potentially free to choose not to offend at any time.

For Maruna's desisters, their deviant past was 'necessary' in order for them to become the person they 'really were'. For these white-collar offenders, reinterpreting the past was equally important for what it meant for attempts to move 'forward' with their lives. Their desires were expressed in rather straightforward terms; Mark's assertion that he'll be 'okay' and Joel's lack of concern as long as the stress of his former life was left behind for example. From this perspective they had fewer concerns over the future because the ability to satisfy their concerns was located within them.

By identifying such goals these three affirmed a commitment to their 'new' self and their future way of living. Because they had changed in a way that they felt in control of the future seemed less threatening. They could envision a future in which their way of living 'worked' and made them happy. Perhaps recognising that they could not return to the lives they had, they chose to reject those lives and make new futures for themselves. In these futures, their criminal pasts were, if not exactly an aid, not a hindrance because they formed the foundation for the experiences that had made them who they now were.

Unwelcome change; self as constituted by the future

For the other three offenders interviewed change was a less welcome experience. Andrew, Brian and Richard recognised they had changed, but this change was characterised as something that was inflicted upon them, as something that had 'happened' to them rather than being solicited. It marked a shift in who they were, but one that was unwelcome. This understanding of change was a result of the rather bleak future each envisioned for himself. For former accountant Brian, convicted of embezzlement, the source of such a shift was partially located in the unwelcome effects of the prison environment:

> It dawns on you that you're just a number again. You're just another con. It's weird … And there's no doubt it will change me as a person, being here. I can't go back, once I'm out of here, I just can't go back to being the old me again. You see too much in this sort of place. Your personality does change, you have to become a lot more self-sufficient shall we say. You can't trust what anyone says and you can't take things at face value. You've got to look after number one. It's a change of mindset completely. From being someone that's in an office Monday to Friday, nine to five, dull, boring accountant to this environment is a real culture shock.

Of more concern than the prison environment however was what the future held and in particular what would happen upon release from prison:

> *BH*: What's been the biggest change in your life since your conviction?
> *Brian*: I suppose the realisation that when I get out of here, it is not all a bed of roses. I've been in finance for fifteen, twenty years. I'm finished, I was forty years, I spent my fortieth birthday in here and I can't go back into working in finance. I've had it as far as that goes so I'll come out of here thinking

> I've got a big civil action against me, I've got no career to fall back on. I've got to start all over again. I think that's probably the biggest thing, the time to sit here and reflect and realise that, *that there's going to be some big changes when I get out*. (emphasis added)

Brian's concerns with employment were echoed by Andrew, convicted of fraud while working as a further education lecturer:

> What happens when I get out I don't know. I will be signing on the dole, that is the first thing I will do, *first time in my life* I will be signing on the dole and that is it. Every time I go for an interview for a job I will be telling them that I have got a criminal record and I have been to prison before. Straight away that is going to put the employer off me. But what choice have you got. Either lie and run the risk of breaching your licence and coming back or telling the truth and staying on the dole. So I have got a very bleak future to look forward to. (emphasis added)

Part of the worry regarding future employment was the feeling that not literally any job would be sufficient. Before prison Brian had enjoyed a particular lifestyle and wanted to live to those means again:

> But that's my dilemma, it's finding a job that pays reasonably well because I don't want to, I'd come to stack shelves at Tesco if I could do it but I know it won't pay the money so … which won't help me if I were to take a low paid job. It's not going to help because it's not going to pay the normal expenditure.

Andrew recognised the irony of needing a fraudulent CV to aid his search for 'honest' work:

> End of story you are stigmatised. So no matter what you do, no matter how you mask your CV … if you fill your CV in and fill the gaps, oh I was abroad working for a year and they find out you are not, you've falsified an application for employment. Fraud in itself. So what do you do be honest and put fraud on knowing you are not going to get the job or back to the cashier at Tesco's. It is just, there is no way around this now.

There was, therefore, the understanding that their futures held new – and unpleasant – experiences. As Andrew says, the experiences he anticipates will be those he encounters for the first time. Andrew and Brian felt they would have to do things they never had before and that this was a direct result of their convictions. These were not presented as 'possibilities' for what the future held. They were cited as certainties for what lay in wait after release. Viewing the future in this way led them to see their pasts as 'causing' that future. Conviction and imprisonment were shattering experiences that denied them any chance to live the lives they wished and be the selves they wished to be. As Brian said, the biggest change in his life is his concern with his future and what that holds for him. He is not constituted by his past, but by what he can become and this is curtailed by the fact he will have to start again. Within the context of a future where he has no options, his past was identified as negatively affecting him.

Richard, convicted of customs and excise offences did not have these employment concerns because the company he owned was being run in his absence and he would resume his place there upon leaving prison. However, he still had worries about his release:

> I have great reservations about going out and meeting people almost to a fear thing really but um, I get quite daunted having to you know, face people I've known before or, not meeting strangers because I have that anonymity of I don't have to tell them 'hi I'm a convict' but a guy I've had a pint in the pub before with or I might have chatted to or I might have done business with. I'm expecting there's going to be quite a bit of, you know 'don't have anything to do with him because he's a convict or a criminal' and that will happen because I've probably, I've done that myself in the past …

As Brian and Andrew had done, Richard was starting to envision his future. In that future he was 'an offender' and this necessitated making certain decisions on how to act. His family provided him with more information on what this new identity of his would mean:

> … I've already noticed they've [his family] started to release things to me that um, that I must handle now and it can be silly little things like you know well this person hasn't been in touch and your accountant said he won't act for people with criminal convictions and so I've started to experience the backlash of the fact that I've got a criminal conviction now but I'm sure it will manifest itself in a lot of other ways as well you know ... And that's quite worrying and things you know because I think there's no such thing as, I think it's the society we live in and I don't blame society but, you do the crime if you like and you've been found guilty and you pay your debt to society but *it never ends*, you know society will never let you forget that. (emphasis added)

For Richard, prison provided a cocoon from the rigours of life as a convicted offender. As the end of his sentence drew near and his family began to prepare him for his release he started to experience what his conviction would mean in terms of how he lived his life. Andrew expressed similar anxiety over life after prison, but in even more bleak terms:

> *Andrew*: I never perceived I could be on my arse as much as I am now. Never ever considered it. It was just, there is no future. There is no amicable future for me at all. Nothing. *I can't even make my own future …*

> *BH*: And you can't see any ways that you can cope with that?
> *Andrew*: No. There is nothing, it is desperate. Absolutely desperate. I think I am entering into a period of my life where I will be in and out of prison for the rest of my life now because *I can't get my life back.* (emphasis added)

For Andrew, the future as he saw it denied him any opportunity to be who he felt he was. He saw no way to constitute himself through his actions and to be the person he identified himself as.

Through a realisation of the (lack of) options awaiting them when they left prison, these three prisoners' awareness of who they 'were' or had become deepened. Each came to understand that in the future he would be 'an offender'; that is someone who had offended in the past. Some of them felt that one of the inevitable consequences of this was that they would have no option but to continue to commit crime. Who Andrew was (at the time of the interview) was constructed in terms of what options were available to him upon release, which he perceived as being few and far between:

> ... when I go out I have got two choices. I can become a check-out person or a cashier on a petrol station but then again because its fraud it is difficult to deal with anything to do with money, so you take that out of the equation there are very little jobs that you can do. So what have you got? They have left me with very little option except a life of crime. I have got to put my intelligence now to commit more crimes to keep the lifestyle I had without taking it away from me.

Andrew, Brian and Richard therefore realised that release from prison would be the catalyst for a range of experiences very different to any they had previously known. Anticipating being forced to live a certain way and the problems of being an ex-offender impacted on their sense of self as for them, the future was filled with new and negative experiences. The stigma of conviction and its associated travails; finding a job, forging (or not) a CV, disclosing a criminal past, the cessation of contact by friends and acquaintances all embodying how they had changed and the slim hopes they had of becoming again the people they had been.

Understanding who they could be helped them make sense of who they were 'now'. As they saw it, upon release from prison they would be ex-offenders and would have to live some portion of the rest of their lives in terms of this. A realisation that you have to make the decision as to whether or not to lie on a CV, as Andrew faces, is to realise you have changed. Future interactions have to accommodate this change.

For these three offenders, there was the concern that the life they had prior to their sentence was now unattainable. Their concerns were that they had been changed by their offences and incarceration prompted by the realisation that the world they knew shifted so that previously pertinent points of reference – former jobs, former acquaintances – were no longer viable. Heavy within this is the notion that a lifetime separates the person they were from the person they are now and emphasises the significance of their experience, underlining that life will now be different. In contrast to the first three offenders presented here, Brian, Andrew and Richard made no connection between the life they had led prior to their conviction and the one they would lead upon leaving prison. Brian's assertion that he 'can't go back' demonstrates a disconnection between various 'phases' of his life. Brian's view contrasts with those who were more optimistic about change who viewed their particular futures as naturally occurring out of their pasts, demonstrating a more coherent view of oneself, one not fractured by particular experiences.

In short, therefore, the place of these offenders in the world had changed without them wishing it to and, in this, their identity failed to fit with their sense of who they were (Fontana 1984). Knowledge of the challenges that faced them upon release was knowledge of who they could be, highlighting this change.

Discussion

All of the prisoners interviewed reported changing. It is the nature of that change that appears significant to them. Change that was perceived as being inflicted upon them was troubling compared to that which they felt they had negotiated for themselves. The two areas where offenders seemed to differ were on the amount of certainty they placed on their future and the understanding they had of themselves.

First, those who were optimistic about their futures were in some ways less certain over exactly what lay in store for them than the others who, although unhappy about what the future might hold, at least had an idea of how they would proceed, e.g. through presenting a fraudulent CV. The more optimistic offenders had set priorities for themselves that bordered on the vague, e.g. to 'be happy' but this ambiguity had the advantage of meaning goals might be achievable in a variety of ways. Contrast this with the very specific imperative Brian had to find a job that paid a certain amount. A great privilege, it seems, is to be placed on certainty when it comes to the future (Ebaugh 1984). Not knowing is perhaps thought to be worse than knowing something bad awaits. Contrast this with these accounts in which it was those offenders who 'knew' what their futures held who were less happy than those who were a little more uncertain. Those who had no definite plans and nothing certain they could identify constructed a self that had no concerns for the future. It seems an advantage of an uncertain future is that anything is possible.

The second contrast between these two groups of prisoners was the way in which they came to an understanding of a new self. The three who were rather sanguine about their futures had reacted to their situations by starting to construct a new self to frame their experiences. Joel and Julie actively rejected their past selves. From the perspective of their offending and imprisonment as learning experiences their futures seemed manageable. Conversely, those who were pessimistic about what the future held had had a new identity pushed upon them. Their place as 'an offender' had become a master status for them (e.g. Patrick and Bignall 1984). Their experiences were interpreted within the context of this status. It was not just that everything they were was related to being an offender. Everything they could be was similarly constructed with reference to this. Their past lives then became something that had been lost rather than something they rejected, taken away from them by conviction and imprisonment.

An existential analysis adds to an understanding of prisoners' experiences by noting the potential for angst that anticipating release from prison can prompt, grounded in the realisation that one has changed. What is specific to this analysis is how offenders' concerns for their future frame their understanding of their personal history. In focusing on white-collar offenders, a group typically fancied to have many advantages that stand them in good stead for resettlement, this study has shown that existential issues have no respect for the 'privileged' position of particular individuals. It is the case that those interviewed here were not 'elite' offenders but nor were they indicative of the prison population more generally. They might objectively be thought to be in possession of resources that would stand them in good stead in resettling. For example, they were not facing concerns over what they would live upon.

Concerns with establishing themselves and leading a 'normal' life were paramount for these offenders. Several of these prisoners worried that they would not be afforded the opportunity to return to lives that were previously imbued with normalcy. Absent within offenders accounts was a mention of involvement in what Maruna (2001: 99) terms generativity; the concern to make a contribution that benefits successive generations. Rather than expressing an interest in generative pursuits, offenders' worries were more focused on themselves and what they could do to benefit themselves after release. However, this is not unreasonable or surprising given that these offenders were looking to the future rather than the past and present, as were Maruna's interviewees.

More generally, the existential perspective employed here provides a way of framing the discourse with oneself that contact with the criminal justice system can prompt that has regard for the past that is unique to each prisoner. Specific to prison, which these accounts indicate, is that the reflection on the self over one's life that prison encourages is focused on what is yet to come. This is separate to the notion that prison time is 'futureless' (Meisenhelder 1985; Farrall and Calverley 2006). These prisoners could envision lives after prison, i.e. they had futures, but as a result of these futures interpreted their criminal pasts in rather different ways.

Highlighting the relationship between offenders' pasts and futures is in keeping with broader observations within criminology that offenders engage in efforts to maintain coherent narratives regarding their lives (Farrall 2005; Maruna 2001; Maruna and Roy 2007). It also demonstrates the existential imperative that past and present have regard for the future (Macquarrie 1972). An existential perspective directs us to attend to the highly personal nature of existence. There is little that is typical about our being in the world and because of this it is not easy (or desirable) to ignore the specific form of an individual's life. Although the above analysis has grouped offenders the particular details of their experience are unique to them.

It could perhaps be argued that the three who were somewhat pessimistic about their futures were being unnecessarily so. Equally, perhaps those who were optimistic everything would turn out 'okay' would have a rude awakening when they left prison. Indeed, it would be rather surprising if we discovered that all six of these prisoners had accurately divined their futures. The accuracy of their predictions is not the issue, though. These were individuals speaking in a concrete situation and armed with incomplete information about what life held for them. In other words, they were living as all people do. The anguish and elation they felt was a product of that situation, which was in turn a reflection of the futures they viewed for themselves. These prisoners' portrayals of their particular futures were influenced by what they *felt* about such futures.

In such futures all six of these offenders were different people to who they had once been. For the more pessimistic offenders the future was replete with stigma, humiliation and difficult choices. Those who were upbeat about the future were so because they knew they would make something of their lives and generally 'be okay'. However, both 'groups' had to realise that they could not return to their lives as they were. Identifying particular future selves impacted on their interpretation of the past. If we are to understand the lives of offenders it seems reasonable to start with how they understand themselves. Fears of stigma that will be suffered and denied opportunities or the more positive anticipation that all will 'turn out okay' say important things about the people who feel them. We might scoff at Mark's gung-ho optimism in characterising himself as the ultimate agent with his assertion that his future is 'all on him'. Equally, we might dismiss Andrew as being rather melodramatic for his claim that the only way he can succeed in living a 'normal' life is with a forged CV. Nevertheless, that is what they felt and because of these feelings came to a certain understanding about themselves. Feelings about the future are important aspects of existence for all individuals. This recognition of the fraught, incomplete nature of existence is crucial here and so perhaps it is this that an existential framework adds more than anything.

Notes

1 I would like to thank James Hardie-Bick, Ronnie Lippens, Suzanne Karstedt and the editors for their constructive comments during the development of this chapter.
2 Neither existentialism nor existential sociology represent unified positions on particular topics. Nevertheless, common threads are identifiable within each.
3 Douglas perhaps does his non-sociological fellows a disservice with this characterisation of their philosophy. Certainly existentialists have emphasised that existence has no intrinsic meaning other than that which we create for ourselves, that we are essentially

alone in the world and that we are free to act with no constraints upon us, not even those we choose for ourselves (Nietzsche's infamous assertion of the 'death of God', Sartre's insistence that we are alone). However, they also argue that this should be a cause for celebration, not despair. We are free to choose our own existence and create that which we wish to be. That we are alone in the world and free to constitute ourselves is better viewed as empowering than terrifying. In fact Douglas' comments about the shiny happy persona of existential sociology are somewhat undone by his fellow existential sociologist's assertion that humans '... tremble with terror at the tragic possibility of what the future has in store for them' (Fontana 1984: 175).

4 Becoming as an existential philosophy concern is slightly different to the way it is described in existential sociology. The writings of Nietzsche (2004) make becoming an inescapable and inevitable part of human existence. Existential sociologists do recognise this inevitability but link the constantly changing nature of the self more explicitly to social encounters. Existential philosophy has emphasised the fundamental importance of the individual with respect to *their* life. Existential sociology is concerned with how such importance is dealt with by concrete individuals leading individual lives (Fontana 1980).

5 Shover and Hochstetler actually draw upon an offender-based definition of white-collar crime, i.e. that which characterises a white-collar offender as being of a particular status within society and as opposed to an offence based definition, which identifies white-collar crime as a particular sort of offence, e.g. as presented in the Edelhertz definition in this chapter. Nevertheless, offence based studies of white-collar crime have noted a general difference between their samples and offenders more generally in terms of (amongst other things) material resources (Benson and Kerley 2001; Weisburd *et al* 2001: 24).

6 Definitional issues raise their head again here. Weisburd *et al* use an offence-based definition. Under an offender-based definition white-collar offenders are, by that definition, in possession of better resources and status than other offenders (and indeed, most people generally).

References

Benson, M. L. and Cullen, F. T. (1988) 'The special sensitivity of white-collar offenders to prison: A critique and research agenda', *Journal of Criminal Justice*, 16: 207–15.

Benson, M. L. and Kerley, K. R. (2001) 'Life course theory and white-collar crime', in Pontell, H. N. and Shichor, D. (eds) (2001) *Contemporary Issues in Crime and Criminal Justice: Essays in Honor* of *Gilbert Geis*. Upper Saddle River, NJ: Prentice Hall.

Clark, C. (2002) 'Taming the "brute being": Sociology reckons with emotionality', in Kotarba, J. A. and Johnson, J. M. (eds) *Postmodern Existential Sociology*. Oxford: Rowman and Littlefield.

Crawley, E. and Sparks, R. (2004) 'Older men in prison: Survival, coping and identity', in Liebling, A. and Maruna, S. (eds) *The Effects of Imprisonment*. Cullompton: Willan Publishing.

Crewe, D. and Lippens, R. (2009) 'Introduction. Existentialism: Freedom, being and crime', in Lippens, R. and Crewe, D. (eds) *Existentialist Criminology*. London: Routledge.

Croall, H. (1989) 'Who is the white-collar criminal?', *British Journal of Criminology*, 29: 157–74.

Douglas, J. D. (1977) 'Aspects of existential sociology', in Douglas, J. D. and Johnson, J. M. (eds) *Existential Sociology*. London: Cambridge University Press.

Douglas, J. D. (1984) 'The emergence, security and growth of the sense of self', in Kotarba, J. A. and Fontana, A. (eds) *The Existential Self in Society*. Chicago, IL: Chicago University Press.

Douglas, J. D. and Johnson, J. M. (eds) (1977) *Existential Sociology*. London: Cambridge University Press.

Ebaugh, H. R. F. (1984) 'Leaving the convent: The experience of role exit and self-transformation', in Kotarba, J. A. and Fontana, A. (eds) *The Existential Self in Society*. Chicago, IL: Chicago University Press.

Ebaugh, H. R. F. (1988) *Becoming an Ex: The Process of Role Exit*. Chicago, IL: Chicago University Press.

Edelhertz, H. (1970) *The Nature, Impact and Prosecution of White-Collar Crime*. Washington, DC: USGPO.

Farrall, S. (2005) 'On the existential aspects of desistance from crime', *Symbolic Interaction*, 28(3): 367–86.

Farrall, S. (2009) '"We just live day-to-day": A case study of life after release following wrongful conviction', in Lippens, R. and Crewe, D. (eds) *Existentialist Criminology*. London: Routledge.

Farrall, S. and Calverley, A. (2006) *Understanding Desistance from Crime: Theoretical Directions in Resettlement and Rehabilitation*. Glasgow: Open University Press.

Fontana, A. (1980) 'Toward a complex universe: Existential sociology', in Douglas, J., *Introduction to the Sociologies of Everyday Life*. Boston, MA: Allyn and Bacon.

Fontana, A. (1984) 'Introduction: Existential sociology and the self', in Kotarba, J.A. and Fontana, A. (eds) *The Existential Self in Society*. Chicago, IL: Chicago University Press.

Goffman, E. (1963) *Stigma*. Harmondsworth: Penguin Books.

Heidegger, M. (1962) *Being and Time*, translated by Macquarrie, J. and Robinson, E. New York, NY: Harper.

Johnson, J. M. and Kotarba, J. A. (2002) 'Postmodern existentialism', in Kotarba, J. A. and Johnson, J. M. (eds) *Postmodern Existential Sociology*. Oxford: Rowman and Littlefield.

Jose-Kampfer, C. (1990) 'Coming to terms with existential death: An analysis of women's adaptation to life in prison', *Social Justice*, 17(2): 110–25.

Katz, J. (1988) *Seductions of Crime: The Moral and Sensual Attractions of Doing Evil*. New York, NY: Basic Books.

Kotarba, J. A. (1979) 'Existential sociology', in McNall, S. (ed) *Theoretical Perspectives in Sociology*. New York, NY: St. Martin's Press.

Kotarba, J. A. (1984) 'A synthesis: The existential self in society', in Kotarba, J. A. and Fontana, A. (eds) *The Existential Self in Society*. Chicago, IL: University of Chicago Press.

Kotarba, J. A. and Fontana, A. (eds) (1984) *The Existential Self in Society*. Chicago, IL: Chicago University Press.

Kotarba, J. A. and Johnson, J. M. (eds) (2002) *Postmodern Existential Sociology*. Oxford: Rowman and Littlefield.

Lester, M. (1984) 'Self: Sociological portraits', in Kotarba, J. A. and Fontana, A. (eds) *The Existential Self in Society*. Chicago, IL: University of Chicago Press.

Lippens, R. and Crewe, D. (eds) (2009) *Existentialist Criminology*. London: Routledge.

Macquarrie, J. (1972) *Existentialism*. London: Penguin Books.

Maruna, S. (2001) *Making Good: How Ex-Offenders Reform and Reclaim Their Lives.* Washington, DC: American Psychological Association Books.

Maruna, S. and Roy, K. (2007) 'Amputation or reconstruction?: Notes on the concept of "knifing off" and desistance from crime', *Journal of Contemporary Criminal Justice*, 23(1): 104–24.

Meisenhelder, T. (1985) 'An essay on time and the phenomenology of imprisonment', *Deviant Behaviour*, 6(1): 39–56.

Morrison, W. (1995) *Theoretical Criminology: From Modernity to Post-Modernism.* London: Cavendish Publishing.

Nietzsche, F. W. (1968) *Twilight of the Idols and the Anti-Christ.* Originally published in 1889 and 1895, translated by Common, T. Harmondsworth: Penguin.

Nietzsche, F. W. (2004) *Ecce Homo: How One Becomes What One Is.* Originally published in 1908, translated by Hollingdale, R. J. London: Penguin.

Patrick, D. R. and Bignall, J. E. (1984) 'Creating the competent self: The case of the wheelchair runner', in Kotarba, J. A. and Fontana, A. (eds) *The Existential Self in Society.* Chicago, IL: University of Chicago Press.

Petersilia, J. (2003) *When Prisoners Come Home: Parole and Prisoner Re-entry.* Oxford: Oxford University Press.

Richards, S. C. and Jones, R. S. (2004) 'Beating the perpetual incarceration machine: Overcoming structural impediments to re-entry', in Maruna, S. and Immarigeon, R. (eds) *After Crime and Punishment: Pathways to Offender Reintegration.* Portland, OR: Willan Publishing.

Sartre, J. P. (1958) *Being and Nothingness: An Essay on Phenomenological Ontology.* Originally published in 1943, translated by Barnes, H. E. New York, NY: Philosophical Library.

Shover, N. and Hochstetler, A. (2006) *Choosing White-Collar Crime.* London: Cambridge University Press.

Weisburd, D., Waring, E. J. and Chayet, E. F. (2001) *White-Collar Crime and Criminal Careers.* Cambridge: Cambridge University Press.

Yalom, I. (1980) *Existential Psychotherapy.* New York, NY: Basic Books.

Chapter 10

Life after punishment for Nazi war criminals

Reputation, careers and normative climate in post-war Germany[1]

Susanne Karstedt

Life after punishment, reputation and transitional justice

On return to their communities from prison offenders are confronted both with the stereotype of being a 'criminal', and with a tarnished reputation among family, friends and neighbours. Stereotyping assigns them to a social category – that of a released prisoner – mostly independent of their personal characteristics or the specific nature of their offence, and thus defines in which ways they are received and treated beyond their immediate networks by agencies, employers and others, or what they are to expect in terms of such treatment. Reputations, in contrast are 'embedded in social relations, and as a consequence, reputation is connected to the forms of communication embedded within a community', as Gary Fine (2001: 3) defines them. Rather than being an opinion 'that one individual forms of another … [they are] shared, established image[s]'. Consequently, reputation can be managed and shaped by the individual, and addresses those whose opinion matters to her.

Sentenced offenders thus face a double task when entering into the process of desisting: they need to escape from and avoid being stereotyped as 'criminal', and simultaneously they have to re-establish their reputation as law and norm abiding, and as reliable and trustworthy individuals, or as someone who is steering clear from criminal friends, drugs and violence. The urgency, weight and demands that these two tasks pose to offenders on their road to desistance might differ widely. Hunter (2008) shows for high-level white collar offenders that all of them worried about their reputation within the networks of family, friends, professional colleagues and their communities. Re-entrance into these social circles caused huge worries and anxieties among these men, who had previously enjoyed high status, impeccable reputations and could muster a considerable amount of power. Low-status offenders and those whose offences were related to drug addiction encounter different problems in managing and shaping their reputation with significant others, however as Farrall and Calverley (2006; Calverley and Farrall 2011, forthcoming) show they are equally affected by anxieties and disappointment in the process of restoring and establishing their reputations after punishment.

Stereotypes and reputations of ex-offenders are of immediate consequence as they have the potential directly to shape their lives and outcomes of interaction (Fine 2001: 3). They are defined by the moral evaluation of offences and offenders in their social circles and wider society, and thus by the 'normative climate' predominant towards crime and offenders in general as well as towards specific crimes and offenders. Stereotypes and reputations are affected by status hierarchies and power, as well as by the normative boundaries that society on the whole or particular social networks establish, redefine and confirm in assigning these to offenders who re-enter after having served their sentences. Common public perceptions of crime and 'criminals' might be more decisive in stereotyping offenders than in establishing new and revised reputations, where personal encounters and networks might have a stronger impact, and make such perceptions more malleable. The normative climate in sub-groups and subcultures might well differ from overall moral censure. Nonetheless, common perceptions provide a level of 'normative conduciveness', as well as networks and groups provide 'structural conduciveness' (Fine 2001: 6) towards re-establishing reputations after punishment.

Usually, offenders re-enter society and networks with rather stable normative climates, where perceptions of offenders and offences are widely shared, and moral and normative boundaries are firmly established. Stereotypes of offenders and their reputations thus can be seen as 'functional' in confirming these boundaries and underpin social and normative cohesion. A very different and unique situation arises for transitional and societies which have gone through a process of transitional justice. Such transitions come with thorough and sweeping changes of perceptions of crime and justice, of offenders and offences, and they force societies and social groups to re-draw moral boundaries. Procedures of transitional justice ranging from international and national trials, lustration and screening to Truth and Reconciliation Commissions have a seminal role in this process (see Karstedt 2009).[2] In addressing the crimes and human rights abuses of the previous regime, they vindicate (previous) victims, and thoroughly strip perpetrators of the power that had been a precondition (and justification) for their crimes. Transitional justice re-draws moral and normative boundaries. Transitional societies are thus defined by structural landscapes of 'defeated' and 'defended' peoples and settings, with spaces for the defeated (the previously powerful) and the defended (the previous victims). The Germans after the Second World War, the Serbs in the conflict in Yugoslavia, and the Afrikaner population in South Africa represent the defeated (see Hagan and Kutnjak Ivkovic 2006).

Transitional justice in its widest sense as established by the UN definition (UNSC 2004) throws moral boundaries and stereotypes of crimes and criminals into disarray, and turns reputations upside-down. They establish new status hierarchies by criminalising those previously in power, who now find themselves and their actions defined as 'criminal', and they in particular impact on established reputations for a broad range of social groups. Leaders of state, high-ranking officials in the state bureaucracy, the police and military, as well as lower ranking bureaucrats, police officers and soldiers are likewise affected. If actions by those with high reputation and status are deemed 'criminal' and their actions are valuated as morally unacceptable the whole group is affected, and required to rethink the framework, conditions and evaluations that guided their actions. When those sentenced in transitional justice procedures return into society and their social circles the previously firm (moral) foundations on which reputations as shared and established images were built, have dissolved. The opinions of those who matter might have changed, gone underground or are only shared by a small number of like-minded people in closed and marginal circles.

Transitional justice certainly represents a unique and exceptional situation of reputational management for ex-offenders as well as for communities and society. However, with transitional justice spreading across the globe, and its resumption in the late 1980s in Latin America, as well as the establishment of International Criminal Tribunals and the International Criminal Court since the 1990s, numerous sentenced perpetrators have returned into their thoroughly changed societies, or are awaiting release. As desistance for this group is a matter of fact and circumstances, we nonetheless know very little about how they are received in their respective societies and social circles, or what type of careers they have embarked upon. Are they posing a danger to the fragile peace in transitional societies? Understanding these processes in transitional societies might be helpful in shedding new light on the life after punishment for 'normal' ex-offenders and stable societies, and it might be the exceptional and unique situation from which fresh thinking and insights can arise.

This chapter takes a historical approach, and explores the life after punishment for men (and one woman) who were sentenced for war crimes and crimes against humanity in post-war Germany after the Second World War, first under the auspices of the Allies (until 1949) and later in the Federal Republic of Germany. It is based on cases in West Germany omitting the East, and covers all hierarchical groups, from military leaders to professionals, bureaucrats and soldiers and concentration camp guards. Gleaned from secondary sources, the research follows their life after punishment, their release, careers and networks in post-war German society, which saw itself confronted with the legacy of war crimes and genocide.

The 'prisoners' dilemma'[3] of transitional justice

What is Charles Taylor, former President of Liberia going to do if he is sentenced in The Hague and ever released from prison? Where and how will he spend his life after having been released from an English prison, where he might serve his term? What kind of career would former President of Yugoslavia, Slobodan Milosevic have experienced, had he lived to receive a sentence from the International Criminal Tribunal for the former Yugoslavia (ICTY)? Would he have returned to his own country, and how would he have been received back home? What will happen to a number of less well known perpetrators, who have been sentenced to long years of imprisonment and life sentences by the ICTY for war crimes and genocide after having served in part or in full their sentences in Scandinavian, German and Dutch prisons? According to the laws and practices in these countries, early release is highly probable. Can we imagine Pinochet as an 'ex-offender' had he ever been sentenced and later released? Where are the members of the Argentinean Junta, who stood on trial during the 1990s? General Videla and several of his colleagues are back in their homes, but with a resumption of prosecution for the allegations against them looming.

When the ICTY was established in the 1990s nearly half a century after the International Military Tribunal in Nuremberg, the attention of the international community was naturally focused on bringing the perpetrators to trial for genocide, war crimes and severe human rights abuses (Hagan 2003). The drafters of the respective treaties and agreements, that established the ICTY and later the Rwandan tribunal, almost entirely neglected questions regarding the execution of sentences, where these should be served, and which national laws should apply to those who served their sentences in various prisons scattered across Western Europe. As van Zyl Smit (2002a, b, 2005) points out, sentencing guidelines did not exist, and it was equally left undecided which (national) laws and regulations should apply to the execution of the sentences. Accordingly, the foundations for executing international criminal sentences were suspiciously absent, as were any decisions as to the application of national laws. In fact, the contrast between the meticulous regulation of the prosecution and the trial, and the nearly total neglect of regulation for the execution of sentences could hardly have been more glaring. Most Western European countries, where some of the offenders sentenced by the ICTY serve their sentences provide for early release and review of sentences, even life sentences. Should these laws be applicable to those who had been sentenced for mass murder and genocide?

Furthermore, international criminal law yet has to incorporate the specific instrument that has a prominent place in national procedures of transitional justice: amnesties (Mallinder 2008). Amnesties are an integral part of transitional and post-conflict justice and have been widely used, with the South African Truth and Reconciliation Commission (TRC) as the most prominent contemporary example. Notwithstanding its many shortcomings, the TRC is deemed as one of the most successful amnesties in recent times, similar to the amnesty that was granted to the members of the Paris Commune in 1880, 10 years after the bloodshed of that event. In his history of post-war Europe, Tony Judt (2005: 61) argues that the political and economic recovery and success of the West European countries was mainly owed to sweeping amnesties for war criminals, collaborators and those involved in mass atrocities: 'without … collective amnesia Europe's astonishing post-war recovery would not have been possible'.

International criminal justice as well as transitional justice is riddled with a 'prisoners' dilemma', which simultaneously represents the reputational dilemma of transitional societies. It is hardly surprising that the problems of actually sentencing and subsequently reintegrating offenders into a thoroughly transformed political, social and normative climate were marginalised in the quest for justice on the one hand and strong tendencies towards collective amnesia on the other hand. Both tendencies decisively shape the ways in which the reputational problem of offenders as well as society is addressed (and solved). Whilst criminal trials provide the spectacle of individuals of highest reputation accused of heinous crimes, collective amnesia, and its counterpart, legal amnesties are conducive to containing the reputational damage done to groups and individuals; even if not condoning the crimes, they nonetheless spare perpetrators the stigma of long prison sentences and allow for generous policies of commuting sentences or early release.

Post-Second World War Europe and post-war Germany in particular provide a rich historical experience of the ways in which nations, societies, groups and individuals relate to a past of atrocities and 'unspeakable' memories and truths (Cohen 2009), and reputations are re-established and restored. Part of this collective experience, and embedded within is the experience of those who stood on trial for war crimes and crimes against humanity (genocide), and who were sentenced to the death penalty (which was often later commuted) or lifelong and long imprisonment. In Germany this group of (mostly) men comprised of a considerable number; more than half of the 6,500 perpetrators who stood on trial in (West) Germany were sentenced in the immediate post-war period (Karstedt 2008a; Rückerl 1984). This group, not the least due to the efforts of the Allies was highly visible as it included numerous high-ranking members of the military, political and administrative elites (Karstedt 1998). Their experiences of their trials, imprisonment and final release, as well as their life afterwards exemplify the ways in which reputations were (re)constructed, managed and shared by both offenders, their social circles, the media, politicians and the wider public. As many of them had been exemplary figures during the Nazi regime, they also shaped the ways in which other and minor, less implicated members of their groups and organisations re-defined their reputations. Thus, they had a role in the formation of collective memory as well as in the development of collective amnesia in post-war Germany.[4]

How were their reputations accepted, contested, or nested in subcultural and marginal domains (Fine 2001: 10)? What kind of career and life did they resume after they had been released, and in which ways did German post-war society react towards those who had been finally tried and sentenced for mass atrocities and been actively involved in the Holocaust? Did they silently and secretly blend into a slowly changing moral climate, were they openly defiant or visibly and publicly repentant? Which groups were actively involved in and campaigned for their release? Was there an undercurrent of secret and mutual understanding, and exchanges in small circles of like-minded people who had shared some of their lot? How were they integrated into a transforming moral and normative climate in (West) German society where many had been involved, were compromised, had been bystanders, or pretended never to have known anything, and finally had been victims?

This study seeks to answer these questions by exploring the lives after punishment for German perpetrators of genocide and war crimes, who were sentenced in the various trials conducted by the Allies (mainly the US) at Nuremberg between 1945 and 1949, by the British and later in the Federal Republic of Germany. Cases were collected from secondary sources for different groups, each representing a specific previous reputation, and the very social circles, significant others and larger organisations sharing and supporting it. The selection of cases is not exhaustive, and was mainly guided by the availability of information about their lives after punishment. Cases of the following groups are included (see Table 1 in the Appendix for information about cases included in this chapter):

- Members of the Nazi elite, who were tried at the International Military Tribunal in Nuremberg between 1945 and 1946, and in the follow-up trials in Nuremberg between 1946 and 1949.
- High-ranking members of the armed forces who were charged with war crimes and tried in one of the follow-up trials in Nuremberg (Trial of the High Command of the Army) and by the Allies in their respective theatres of war.
- High-ranking members of the state bureaucracy who were charged with crimes against the civilian population of the occupied countries, including the deportation of the Jewish population to death camps. Organisations include the Foreign Ministry and the Ministry of Justice, with separate follow-up trials in Nuremberg.
- Professionals, in particular doctors who had been involved in atrocities in concentration camps and had conducted the euthanasia programme, i.e. the mass murder of mentally and physically disabled persons. They were mainly tried in the so-called Doctors' Trials in Nuremberg.
- Members of the SS mostly directly involved in genocidal action. These were mainly sentenced in the 'Task Force Trials' conducted between 1947 and 1948 in Nuremberg, but also later in the Federal Republic of Germany.
- Concentration camp guards who were on a daily basis involved in genocidal action; they were tried in the Auschwitz Trial 1963–65 in Frankfurt and the Majdanek Trial 1975–81 in Duesseldorf.

Basically, the groups represent all hierarchical levels of the machinery of killing in the Nazi state. It is of decisive significance that the first four of these groups were tried in the immediate post-war situation, and hence could not only take advantage of the various amnesties, but also of the fact that their trials and their imprisonment took place in a historical period and within a collective that was still fully over-shadowed by the Nazi regime, the war and post-war experiences of the population. In contrast, the last group stood on trial and served their prison sentences in a social and normative environment and climate that was definitely changing toward a more clear and pervasive condemnation of the perpetrators, and the full acknowledgment of the Holocaust. I will first give an overview of these changes of public opinion and sentiment before turning to the groups and cases.

Reputations in a changing normative climate: legal procedures, moral assessment and public opinion in post-war German society

As Gary Fine (2001) points out reputations are shared and embedded in social relationships, and consequently they are as much shaped by these relationships as by the individual; 'reputations allow us to conceive of ourselves in particular ways' and as a consequence 'personal reputations directly affect how we come to see ourselves' (Fine 2001: 3). The reputations (and 'identities') that individuals 'are given channel the identities that we can select' (Fine 2001: 3). The normative and moral boundaries of the collective thus define the ways in which former prisoners perceive of themselves and their reputation. They confine and shape the actions ex-offenders take to (re)establish their reputation, and the changes they and significant others deem necessary in order to achieve this. When there are no pressures to accept responsibility and guilt, and to demonstrate 'signal changes' towards a new identity and reputation, then guilt and responsibility are seen differently, and the judicial procedure, the sentence as well as the time served in prison acquire a different meaning and significance. Even innocence may be claimed and maintained successfully, and become deeply engrained as part of one's self-perceptions and self-presentations.

In transitional societies reputations therefore are thoroughly contested in general public opinion, and divided between those who assign a negative reputation to the perpetrators in contrast to those groups who support a more positive image (see Theissen 2009). These divisions mainly coincide with the lines drawn between defended and defeated groups in post-conflict societies, where victims and perpetrators and all those, who cannot be counted into one of these two groups, are present. However, post-war Germany represents an extreme case among transitional societies, as the people of the perpetrators (the defeated) were mainly among themselves, and thus experienced a strong sense of collective fate (see Karstedt 1998, 2008a, 2010). Nonetheless, public opinion was considerably divided on the issue of bringing the perpetrators to justice, and remained so until the mid-1960s, when it finally started to turn towards uniformly accepting that genocide had been committed, and that those responsible and implicated were to be punished as criminals. However, during the immediate post-war period and until this turning point, the social groups and circles where sentenced and imprisoned war criminals turned to for support and after their final release, were seminal in managing the reputations of these ex-offenders. Exemplary for evolving gaps between public opinion and reputational support in confined social circles is the case of Albert Speer, 'Hitler's architect'. After his release from the Allied prison in Spandau in 1966, he returned into 'high' society, where he was embraced and generously accepted in addition to being courted by the media, at a time when the Eichmann and Auschwitz trials had already started to change public opinion considerably (see Reif 1978).

The group of perpetrators involved in crimes against humanity, genocide and mass killings, war crimes and atrocities is of course a special one. As their crimes are unique in their lives and lifetime, this sets them apart from other offenders. Their trials and imprisonment take place in a transitional moment when norms and morality are decisively shifting. As transitional societies decide whom to punish, whom to exonerate and how to treat returning ex-offenders they make decisions about reputations, and transitional justice assigns these reputations accordingly. This equally applies to criminal trials as well as to lustration procedures (Heimer and Stinchcombe 2009).

The process of shifting normative boundaries in a transitional situation is related to processes of 'othering' and 'saming' to use the same linguistic device of concept creation. Transitional justice implies that those who are the defended and the defeated change place – those who were defeated are now defended, and vice versa, and likewise those who are 'others' and 'same' are redefined. These processes refer to the interests and social organisations affecting the politics of reputation, which in transitional societies are intricately linked to the politics of dealing with the past (Frei 2003). Who is defined as 'same' and as a member of the group and can earn and share respective reputation, whose reputation is deemed too negative, tarnishing or dangerous to be proffered membership and support? Who can profit from wider public support and who has to turn to subcultural and marginal groups that resist moral and normative change? Which institutions and organisations act as 'reputational entrepreneurs' (Fine 2001: 12)? What is the role of communities who share the experience and a common fate with the perpetrator? The history of Germany (West) and its Nazi war criminals will shed light on the emerging patterns of the politics of reputation, and in which ways they affected their lives after punishment. As in contemporary procedures of transitional justice, criminal justice was combined with and linked to amnesties, and both shaped German public opinion for decades to come.

It is an often neglected and perhaps unduly censured fact that amnesties were an integral, though unplanned part of criminal justice and lustration in post-war Germany and Europe. In fact, in Germany, quite sweeping amnesties had already started during the occupation. In this process the Russians took a lead in their zone, while the Americans were most reluctant. However, young people were soon exempt from de-Nazification (lustration) procedures, and further amnesties were introduced on an ad-hoc basis when it had become obvious that de-Nazification was a nearly impossible task (Karstedt 2008a). The mixture of harsh justice and ad-hoc amnesties during the immediate post-war period under the auspices of the (Western) Allies shaped public opinion and assessment of the Nuremberg Tribunal, and also impacted on criminal justice policies and the prosecution of war crimes and genocide in (West) Germany itself.

After the foundation of the Federal Republic of Germany in 1949, the mood of the public turned to closing the books and putting the past at rest. First Chancellor Konrad Adenauer expressed this mood when publicly asking for a halt of further scrutinising the past of high-ranking officials and civil servants, but simultaneously embarking on a policy of reconciliation with the West and re-compensation for the state of Israel and the Jewish population. This attempt to 'draw a line' under the past resulted in the encouragement of networks of former high-ranking Nazi officials and SS officers to promote blanket amnesties and a general pardon, which was not realised because of the adamant opposition of the Americans and Chancellor Adenauer himself. However, those who had been ousted from office by de-Nazification were allowed to resume their offices (with the exception of high-ranking SS officers) or claim their pensions by an Act passed by the Federal Parliament in the early 1950s. This amounted to a blanket amnesty for all those who had undergone de-Nazification procedures. Other amnesties ensured indemnity for violence and killings at the very end of the war if the acts had been committed in the belief that they had been ordered as a duty, which again amounted to a blanket amnesty for atrocities and war crimes, which had peaked during the last months of the war. In 1952, the German government decided not to ratify the European Convention on Human Rights, which would have allowed the prosecution of atrocities that had been deemed legal during the Nazi regime. Thus many practices of repression of the Nazi regime were declared 'irrelevant' in terms of criminal prosecution. This decision was reversed by the government of Chancellor Willy Brandt in the 1960s, which paved the way to further prosecutions. But even in the 1960s, legal provisions amounting to a stealthy amnesty for atrocities were slipped in under the cover of other laws (see Friedrich 2007).

Most of the war criminals who had been sentenced before 1949 by the Allies (mainly by the Americans) were released after serving only a fraction of their sentences, with the exception of those who had been tried in the Nuremberg Tribunal, and were in custody of all four Allies in Spandau Prison in Berlin. After 1949, when the Federal Republic of Germany had been established and had abolished the death penalty in its constitution, appeals were directed towards the American High Command and US High Commissioner McCloy to pardon offenders sentenced to death, and to convert their sentences to life imprisonment. Many of them, as will be seen, left prison after serving between only two and four years.

Not surprisingly, German politicians and criminal justice officials were very reluctant to resume the prosecution of war criminals and those who had been involved in the Holocaust. In 1956, a major trial of the members of SS Task Forces (*Einsatzgruppen*) and Police Reserve Battalions indicted for war crimes and genocide in Poland and Russia went by without much notice from the public, the media or politicians. Amnesties were more or less completed by the mid-1950s, not only in Germany but also in the European countries that had been occupied by the Nazi regime (see Karstedt 2008a). However, at the beginning of the 1960s, a process of resuming prosecution of war criminals and those involved in the Holocaust started. This process was driven by three important trials: the 1961 Eichmann trial in Jerusalem, the 1963–65 Auschwitz trial, and the 1975–81 Majdanek trial, both of which took place in Germany. Preparations for resuming the prosecution of war criminals and those involved in mass killings had started in 1958 with the inauguration of the Central Office for the Investigation of National Socialist Crimes (*Zentrale Stelle der Landesjustizverwaltungen zur Aufklärung nationalsozialistischer Verbrechen*), which was very much owed to the relentless efforts of a handful of individuals. It had become evident in the trial (1956–58) of the so-called SS Task Forces (*Einsatzgruppen*), who were mainly responsible for the genocide in the East, that many of the most atrocious crimes had not been brought to justice and that a concerted effort to do so was necessary. At the same time other organisations sprang up worldwide with the purpose of bringing Nazi perpetrators to justice and of putting pressure on Germany, not the least in the communist German Democratic Republic.

Given the prominence of the initial (and international) military tribunals between 1945 and 1949, the whole process of transitional justice provided a framework in which the genocide of the European Jews could be cast as war crimes, and not as a crime sui generis, or a crime against humanity (see Olick 2005). It took more than another two decades until the term 'Holocaust' was widely used, and the Holocaust became to be perceived as a separate crime of an unimaginable scale (Alexander 2002). The fact that the Nuremberg Trials were set up as a Military Tribunal actually contributed to these perceptions, and consequently only the murder of the Jewish population outside of Germany was prosecuted there. Even those who had been convicted of crimes against humanity, as genocide was legally termed then, were in a position that they could define their offences as war crimes, committed in the course of military duty, and as such they could count on the sympathetic understanding of the public and social institutions, including the German Protestant Church, as I will show below. In communist East Germany, the resistance movement against fascism could claim for themselves and many others the 'myth of innocence' as Mary Fulbrook (1999) termed their claims of non-involvement.

The Nazi war criminals, who were released from prison between the early 1950s and mid-1960s started their lives after punishment in a legal climate that was shaped by ad hoc and stealthy amnesties after an initial phase of harsh justice, and by a reluctance to take responsibility for further national prosecution of perpetrators. The ensuing normative climate and public opinion consequently tended towards closing the books (though never unanimously, and continuously excluding the core of the Nazi leadership, see Karstedt 2008a), and condoning what was generally conceived of as war crimes. The near-total absence of victims and their families in post-war German certainly was conducive to these developments (Karstedt 2010).

Case studies of former Nazi war criminals and their lives after punishment

The Nazi elite

It had been the deliberate policy of the Allies to put the core leadership of the Nazi state on trial first, including the leadership of the armed forces, the economy, the Nazi bureaucracy and the media. Thus 24 men of highest status, rank and reputation stood on trial, representing their institutions and organisations, as well as their members of lower ranks. The majority were sentenced to death, three were acquitted, and of those who had received prison sentences four had a more public life after punishment. These four cases will be explored more in-depth: Albert Speer, Baldur von Schirach, Karl Dönitz, and Erich Raeder.

Albert Speer, who had established his reputation as 'Hitler's architect', had been sentenced to 20 years of imprisonment for his responsibility for organising forced labour, in particular of prisoners of war. He had been described by observers at the Nuremberg Trial as the 'Gentleman Nazi' which reportedly had helped him to secure a prison sentence rather than the death penalty. From the start of the trial he had accepted 'responsibility' as a member of the Nazi elite and government, though he always denied guilt. In his memoirs and 'Spandau: The Secret Diaries' (Speer 1969, 1975), which were most successful (international) bestsellers, he had honed this reputation and given particular insights into the inner circle of the Nazi elite around Hitler. He presented himself as a technocrat who had been charmed by Hitler, and who was not aware of the atrocities and genocide planned and executed by the regime. He certainly had been decisive in orchestrating forced labour during the last years of the war, for which he accepted responsibility but denied guilt. After having served the full term of 20 years and been released in 1966, his hugely successful memoirs and books provided him with a comfortable life, socially as well as financially.[5] His knowledge of Hitler's inner circle made him a sought-after interview partner for the media, his reputation and international contacts attracted the attention of leading international journalists and authors (Sereny 1996), and his reputation as an 'innocent technocrat' not only triggered a public debate on the links between (neutral) technology, totalitarian regimes and atrocities (see Reif 1978), but also provided him with a relatively untarnished reputation that paved his way into the conservative elites of the young republic. All this made him a kind of celebrity of his time.

However, his reputation was not uncontested as in the mid-1960s public opinion and in particular attitudes in the younger generation had changed, after the Eichmann trial in Jerusalem, and the Auschwitz Trials in Frankfurt (Karstedt 2008a). The crimes of the Holocaust were acknowledged as such, and the perpetrators indeed seen as criminals, even if they led unsuspicious lives. Former members of the Nazi regime were deemed unacceptable when they returned to high positions of similar level in the federal and state governments (Karstedt 2008a). In particular, the German student movement named, shamed and even attacked numerous individuals who were seen as implicated in the Nazi regime and its atrocities. Thus, the stereotype of perpetrators and consequently of sentenced offenders had changed. Speer himself admitted to his biographer Sereny that, on his release, he had not been aware to what extent public opinion had changed and public condemnation of Hitler and his regime had become to dominate the public realm (Sereny 1996: 157). However this did not impede Albert Speer to retain and establish the positive reputation within high-level social circles, that he had prepared through his publications, and that was supported and spread by the media – though contested by others (see the contributions in Reif 1978).

In contrast to highly visible Albert Speer, Baldur von Schirach preferred not to lead a public life after punishment. He had been the leader of the Nazi youth organisation, and later became governor of Vienna. He had been a member of the Nazi elite, with access to Hitler and his circles, however, his positions within the Nazi state had been less important and seminal. In his function as governor of Vienna he had been responsible for the deportation of 185,000 Austrian Jews, for which he was sentenced to 20 years' imprisonment at the Nuremberg Trials. He served his full sentence and after his release in 1966, he published his memoirs under the title 'I believed in Hitler' in 1967. He cast himself as a young and idealistic believer in the 'good causes' of the Nazi ideology, and denied ever having known about why and where he deported the Jewish population of Vienna and Austria, and having been (knowingly) involved in the implementation of the Holocaust. In his biography though he admitted to having been present at the infamous speech in which the Leader of the SS, Himmler, informed leading party members about the murder of the Jewish population of Europe (Sereny 1996: 396), however, he dated it nearly a year later in 1944 (rather than 1943). He led a low key life until his death in 1974.

Notwithstanding that Baldur von Schirach had been a well-known personality during the Nazi regime, he certainly was not a reputational entrepreneur like Albert Speer. His memoir and its title indeed expressed a common and shared fate as many adult Germans felt the same, and thus it should have appealed to many. However, in contrast to Albert Speer he did not meander around the truth (Sereny 1996), and his claim that he had not known anything about the Holocaust was much less credible after the Eichmann and Auschwitz trials, given his position in the Nazi hierarchy.[6] Besides shifts in public opinion that made him and his memoirs generally less acceptable to the media, his former position as leader of the Nazi youth organisation had left him without major networks of support, or smaller social circles where he might have had achieved some reputation. Any involvement of a high-ranking former member of the Nazi elite in youth policies or organisations was simply impossible.

The case of former Admiral Karl Dönitz demonstrates the importance of organisations and networks in the reputational management of their lives after punishment for these high-ranking members of the Nazi regime. Since 1943 he had been the commander of the Navy, and succeeded Hitler as chancellor during the last days of the Nazi regime in 1945. He was sentenced in Nuremberg to

10 years' imprisonment on charges of preparation of aggressive warfare and war crimes. A charge of criminal marine warfare had been dropped after US General Nimitz had conceded that he had issued similar commands to the US navy in the Pacific theatre. His sentence was contested from the very first moment, and he saw it as a miscarriage of justice as he indicated in an interview in the 1970s (Dönitz 1972). After his release in 1956, he wrote his memoirs 'My changeful life' (Dönitz 1968), which were modestly successful, and travelled the country first as speaker at meetings of veterans, and soon as speaker to the newly established Federal Army respectively its navy. As such, he led a semi-public life restricted to the smaller and professional, however never subcultural social circles of the previous and new army.

In contrast to both Speer and von Schirach his sentence was based on charges of war crimes committed in the course of warfare and not against civilians. This allowed him to cast himself as a dutiful soldier, and his prison sentence as term served as a prisoner of war of the Allies, a fate which many veterans shared and could identify with. Serving time as a prisoner of war was a duty that had to be accepted for losing the war, and this interpretation in particular cleared him from the stigma of a penal sentence and his imprisonment. Without doubt he himself believed in this, and his networks provided him with a shared reputational image thus confirming his view. His reputation among veterans thus emerged unscathed, and as it was embedded in more restricted social circles, it was also less contested. This was aided by the fact that public opinion in Germany at that time tended more to collective amnesia and negation of the crimes against humanity that had happened (see Karstedt 2008a). Consequently he was also acceptable to the newly established army.

His own accounts shed light on the mechanisms within these networks where his reputation was established and retained. In an interview in the 1970s (Dönitz 1972) he described that when travelling he was often approached by veterans and asked whether they might join his table, a wish willingly granted. He revelled in the community of soldiers that was still alive and nourished by shared memories. These shared memories confirmed the sense of a common fate and 'sameness', not as criminals but prisoners of war and more generally as soldiers. The sense of sameness was furthered by the fact that the lost war, and the transition, as well as (not accepted) transitional justice had functioned as a great equaliser, and put common soldiers and the former commander on an (nearly) equal footing. Karl Dönitz still embodied the values and norms of the military community, and as his crimes were ignored, his reputation remained fairly stable.

When rearmament started and the new Federal Army was finally established in 1955, difficult questions arose around the highly sensitive issues of integrating the commanders and experts of the previous army, and of linking to the military 'traditions' of its predecessor, the army of the Nazi state. Finally, these had been sentenced as war criminals in international and allied military courts, and the army had been involved in the most heinous crimes and mass murder.[7] Karl Dönitz presented himself as a reputable and respectable professional soldier, and with a reputation from which no damage to the national and international image of the newly founded army and its institutions was to be expected.

While Karl Dönitz became a semi-public figure, his predecessor Erich Raeder, who was released from prison a year earlier because of ill health, led a very reclusive life until his death in 1960. He had received a lifelong prison sentence at the Nuremberg Trial for charges of planning aggressive warfare and war crimes, however, his offences were deemed more grave than those of Doenitz. His autobiography 'My life' published after his release from prison, presented a very positive portrait of Hitler, but did not attract attention beyond the circles of the navy, and he never became a public figure.

The four cases of men who held highest offices during the Nazi regime, and were sentenced in a landmark and widely publicised trial in Germany, certainly started their lives after punishment with a more public reputation than many other sentenced war criminals. However, these cases demonstrate that reputations developed rather differently for members of the elite who had been sentenced at Nuremberg and had been witnessed standing in the dock by the majority of the German population (see Karstedt 1998). The time of their release and respective shifts in public opinion defined whether their reputations were contested or not. The cases in addition testify to the importance of professional networks and semi-public circles in establishing and maintaining a reputation that was oblivious of the charges and sentences meted out by the Allies. To the extent that they represented a common fate, they could offer a backdrop for processes of personal identification and thus their reputations could rub off on the many others: Speer for technocrats who had served the Nazi regime and orchestrated the Holocaust, Dönitz for soldiers. Even if their crimes and sentences were mainly ignored – in the 1950s more than in the following decade – there certainly existed limits as to a positive evaluation of Hitler (as e.g. by Raeder; see for public opinion Karstedt 2008a) and denial of knowledge of the Holocaust (as in the case of von Schirach). Both Speer and Dönitz were more cautious in their hindsight evaluation of the Nazi regime, the war and their own actions. Karl Dönitz could take full advantage of a network of veterans, and of the re-establishment of a military tradition which also enjoyed cautious international support. The time of his release in the mid-1950s proved to be advantageous as his reputation was less contested than it might have been at a later time.

The Nazi military and bureaucratic elite

The Nuremberg Trials were complemented by a series of 'follow-up trials' for 'Hitler's willing executioners' (Goldhagen 1996) at the highest levels of the army and the state bureaucracy, including the High Command of the Army, the Foreign Office and the Ministry of Justice. According to agreements between the Allies, military leaders were extradited to the countries where they had committed their crimes, or were tried by court martials of the Allies, mostly in the countries of their respective theatres of war. With the exception of military leaders, these men had been less visible as public figures than the defendants in the Nuremberg Tribunal, however they were often more directly implicated in the deportation of the Jewish population from the occupied countries, the (financial) exploitation of the population, forced labour and for orchestrating and leading atrocities against these peoples. They had drafted the 'laws' that gave the air of legality to their crimes, and had committed their offences from their desks, a type of perpetrator later to be personified by Eichmann. They had been indicted for war crimes against the civilian population, forced labour and other atrocities.

The military elite

Members of the High Command of the Army initially received considerable prison sentences, but none of them served a full term, and most of them were released after a fraction of their original sentences. They were released in the early 1950s by remission of their unserved sentences. They never returned to any position in the military, however they secured leading positions often in associations of the German industry, or in associations of veterans and repatriates, the latter being of particular political importance in post-war Germany. They settled back into a comfortable middle-class life and into positions of quite some influence and importance in the young democratic state, where their skills and leadership were obviously welcome. Their reputations emerged unscathed by their sentences and imprisonment, and remained uncontested within their professional and social life, where they again rose to high status. One of them, Georg-Hans Reinhardt, founded a prominent think-tank on military strategy, and became influential in shaping the first stages of rearmament, activities for which he was awarded with the Federal Cross of Merit in 1962.

The cases of two Generals Albert Kesselring and Hermann-Bernhard Ramcke stand out in several respects. Like Karl Dönitz, both had been well-known commanders during the war. Ramcke had stood on trial in France, charged with atrocities against the civilian population of Brest, and sentenced to five years of imprisonment in 1951. He was discharged soon after his sentence in recognition of his long pre-trial detention, and subsequently had a position in a German company. He published books on his experiences during the war. Albert Kesselring was tried by a British court martial in Venice as responsible commander for the shooting of 335 Italian citizens who had been taken hostage in retaliation for the murder of German police officers by the Italian resistance army. His initial death sentence was first commuted to lifelong imprisonment, and later to 21 years by the British government. After having been diagnosed with cancer he was released in an act of clemency by the Queen in 1952 (von Lingen 2009).

During his detention and imprisonment, Kesselring had become a relentless reputational entrepreneur, who directed from his prison cell support and activities of lawyers, university professors, and politicians. Surprisingly, a campaign for his release sprang up in Britain, which was led by Lord Hankey and military historian Basil Liddell Hart (von Lingen 2009: 160) and supported by high ranking politicians, including Churchill as well as military leaders.[8] The campaign was based on his reputation as an 'honest enemy', and not the least driven by the prospect of integrating Germany into the new Western alliance of NATO. As long as military leaders were imprisoned, the German public could hardly be persuaded to support the contentious issue of rearmament.

When still in prison, Kesselring had accepted the offer of becoming president of the largest association of veterans. After his release he embarked on public activities, and issued statements which not only should clear him from any involvement in war crimes, and exonerate him from any guilt, but which attempted to make his acts as commander in the Italian theatre appear as particularly honourable. This was not in line with the cautious diplomacy of the German government, and certainly transgressed what was acceptable to the British government and Italian citizens. In the ensuing diplomatic upheaval, he was summoned by the German government and ordered to refrain from further public statements, and never was involved in the planning for the new army. He did not become the public figure that he had envisioned for himself, and his reputation did not go uncontested. In his books, published during the 1950s, he never distanced himself from his crimes, nor did he dissociate himself from his loyalty to Hitler. The veterans association of which he was president soon lost influence, and was rendered to obscurity.

Ramcke had even gone further in exonerating and lauding the activities of the SS and its members in meetings of former SS members. He too was rebuked by the German government, and could retain a more subcultural reputation in marginal right-wing political and social circles of ex-Nazis. In 1959, he lost a libel suit against a well-known journalist, who had witnessed the atrocities in Brest as a soldier. At his funeral in 1968 representatives of the Federal army were present, including the Minister of Defence, which gave rise to a controversy in the national and international press.

Both men misjudged the normative and political climate when they tried to re-establish their reputation, not only claiming total innocence, but also expressing allegiance to the Nazi regime, and exonerating the SS. Even if the German public tended towards collective amnesia, this never included reversing their dis-allegiance from the Nazi leadership, or particularly the SS (Karstedt 2008a). Notwithstanding support from the community of former soldiers, the reputation even of high-ranking military leaders was not uncontested, in particular if they strived for public presence. Both Kesselring and Ramcke's public statements, and the ensuing diplomatic fall-out were brought to light and critically discussed in the emerging democratic landscape of the media.

The bureaucratic elite: diplomats, SS leaders and lawyers

The Nazi state had thoroughly changed the mechanisms and institutions of government. The SS and its institutions had gained influence and extended their collaboration with as well as their presence in a number of ministries, in particular those that were tasked with governing the occupied countries during the war. This affected the foreign ministry and the ministry of justice, and consequently a number of high-ranking SS officers who had held important positions in these ministries stood on trial in Nuremberg. Their prison sentences between 10 and 25 years reflect the severity of their crimes against the civilian population, including looting of financial and other assets of the Jewish population, organising forced labour in the German war industry and orchestrating atrocious police action.

The foreign minister Count Schwerin of Krosigk, who had received a prison sentence of 10 years for being responsible for actions dispossessing the Jewish population, but had served just two years, was the most public figure in this group. His former reputation helped him to embark on a post-war career as writer and publicist, though with his personal memoirs published in 1974, he never was as successful as Albert Speer. His moderate success and his uncontested reputation – he never was involved in any scandal – speak to the condoning public climate but as well to cautious management of his public persona.

The other four in this group never spent more than two years of their long sentences in prison, and were released in the early 1950s. As former SS officers they were barred from office in the public sector, however the private sector and German industry proved to be most receptive. Indeed, a network of former SS officers had established itself and channelled members into lucrative positions in the German industry (Herbert 1996). The fact that such a concentration of high powered positions cannot be found in any of the other groups speaks to the activities and efficiency of this network, which also covertly lobbied for a blanket amnesty. They cast themselves and were seen as technocrats of management and administration, with skills not to be ignored in rebuilding the German economy. They returned into their lives after punishment with a professional reputation which in the contemporary normative climate was not questioned at all. The fact that one of them (Hans Kehrl) could publish his memoirs with the title 'Crisis Manager in the Third Reich' in 1973 testifies to the reputational assets that white-washed these men of being guilty of heinous crimes, and the stigma of imprisonment, as well as to the common though not uncontested understanding of technology and management as 'morally neutral' of any purpose.

The lawyers in the ministry of justice who had orchestrated raids by the Gestapo (Secret Police) first in Germany, and later in the occupied countries, who had drafted the laws that stripped the Jewish population of Germany and Europe of all civil and human rights, and had introduced the death penalty for minor crimes, received prison sentences between five years and a life sentence for the secretary of state and acting minister of justice Franz Schlegelberger. None of them served more than three years of their terms. Only one of them (Wilhelm von Ammon) secured a position in the higher ranks of the administration, this time in the Lutheran Church of Bavaria (for the role of the Lutheran Church, see below), the others lived as pensioners, or worked as solicitors or in a private law school.

In the late 1950s their reputations became contested, as the media published scandalising reports on their activities during the Nazi regime and their lives after punishment. These men could not take advantage of professional and other networks, and thus their reputations became more vulnerable, even if none of them led a public life.

Professionals: doctors

The Doctors' Trial in Nuremberg from 1946 to 1947 uncovered the most gruesome details of the implication of the medical profession in genocide, mass murder and crimes against humanity. The doctors had either been involved in experimenting on concentration camp inmates in the most atrocious ways, leading to (calculated) death or (if the victims did survive) to lifelong suffering, or in the so-called Euthanasia Programme, where they had orchestrated and been responsible for the deaths of hundreds of thousands of mentally and physically disabled people. This group includes a woman, with their sentences ranging from 15 years to lifelong imprisonment. They served between four and seven years of their sentences, which had been commuted to shorter ones, and they all had left prison by 1954. Their lives after punishment demonstrate the obliviousness and total lack of recognition of the criminal nature of their actions by the medical profession as well as the overseeing (professional) bodies, and testify to the strength of professional networks.

Herta Oberheuser had conducted experiments in a concentration camp for women (Ravensbrück) in Germany. The only reason for her not being sentenced to death was that she had not been a member of the SS (from which she was barred because she was a woman), a fact usually deemed an aggravating circumstance by the court. Her prison sentence of 20 years was reduced to 10 years in 1951, and she was released in 1952, having served just five years of her sentence. After her release she was licensed as a medical general practitioner and worked in a village. When she was recognised by survivors from the camp, prosecution was resumed, but had to be suspended as the same offence could not be adjudicated twice. Her licence to work as a medical practitioner was revoked, against which she unsuccessfully appealed. At her trial she had frankly described her victims as 'guinea pigs', and how it had been necessary to keep distance from her prisoner patients. Her case in particular demonstrates that victims could have a decisive impact on the lives after punishment for perpetrators, and that absence respectively presence of victims in transitional societies is important in shaping the moral climate for returning ex-prisoners. The fact that the reputations of these perpetrators were mainly uncontested during the first two decades after the war, helped them to slip back into their professional lives easily, and that their networks were undisturbed in supporting them seems to be linked to the absence of victims in a number of ways (see Karstedt 2010).

Most perpetrators in this group testify to the impact of professional networks, as these secured one of them a position as director of a department in a hospital

(Wilhelm Beiglböck). The importance of these networks is even more obvious in the case of the doctor responsible for the whole programme of euthanasia (action T4), and as such for the death of hundreds of thousands of mentally and physically disabled people. He had escaped the Allies after the war, and had worked under a false identity as a doctor in the local government of a northern city. He was uncovered in 1959 and committed suicide in pre-trial detention in 1964. It soon became obvious that his professional networks had covered him and that his real identity was well known amongst many and high-ranking colleagues.

Members and commanders of SS task forces

The men who had been commanders and members of the SS Task Forces differ from the members of the Nazi elite in a number of ways. They were less visible at the time of their crimes, their trials attracted much less public attention, and consequently, their lives after punishment, and their perspectives on their past and present lives are much less documented than for the men who were tried at Nuremberg. Further, as the SS Task Forces had been ordered to execute the Holocaust behind the front lines of the German Army, these men were deeply implicated in the Holocaust in Eastern Europe, and many of them were literally mass murderers, or they had overseen the men who shot hundreds of thousands Jewish men, women and children (see Browning 1992; Goldhagen 1996). At the Nuremberg Task Force Trial, where mainly the commanders of task forces had been tried, many had received death sentences for the mass killings committed, several of which were subsequently converted into life sentences, of which they only served a fraction.

Among the cases in this group, three men had initially received the death penalty, and they actually served between six and 10 years in prison. Most of these men started their lives after punishment in the second half of the 1950s. Even if they had been less visible, or had worked in less high-level positions than members of the other groups, it is important to note that these commanders of SS units and other forces (e.g. the police) were predominantly educated men, and many of them came from a middle class background. Nearly all of them slipped back into middle-class lives, and secured new positions mainly in the private sector, as they were barred from their previous ones as members of the SS. The process of their early release, the networks and institutions that were seminal in supporting them and that later offered them positions, shed light on their prospective life after punishment, which they mainly led in the most inconspicuous way. The following biographies in particular demonstrate the role of the Lutheran Church as reputational entrepreneur in campaigns first for commuting the death sentences, and later for early release of these perpetrators.

Eugen Steimle had received the death penalty for mass murder of the Jewish population in the Soviet Union, one of his most atrocious crimes being the mass killing of 50 disabled children. The sentence was commuted to imprisonment of

20 years in 1951, of which he served only three years until he was released in 1954. After his release he became a teacher (for which he had trained) for history and civic studies at a gymnasium (grammar school) which was run by the Lutheran Church, i.e. in a faith-based school where the Lutheran Church was his employer. Ernst Biberstein had been a pastor of the Lutheran Church, and had risen in the church hierarchy before he joined the Nazi party and the SS. Because of his direct involvement in mass killings of more than 3,000 men, women and children he received a death sentence, which had been reduced to a life sentence in 1951. The Lutheran Church had been decisive in reducing the death sentence to life imprisonment, and they campaigned later for his final release in 1958. For a brief period he worked in the administration of the church, however he was dismissed, and the church never offered him a position again. He worked as a low-level employee until his retirement.

The Lutheran Church, represented by a bishop in a regional church, closely collaborated in a campaign for the release of Martin Sandberger with regional politicians, including the minister of justice, and members of the federal parliament, amongst them a highly renowned Social Democrat. Sandberger had been one of the leading figures in orchestrating the genocide in the Baltics and was responsible for the deaths of hundreds of thousands of victims. He came from a well-connected family of vicars and civil servants, which explains his high-level support within the protestant milieu of South-West Germany, and which helped him to secure a position as legal adviser in a major company after his release. In hindsight it is difficult to understand why the Lutheran Church raised its voice for sentenced perpetrators of genocide, however it was part of and added its moral weight to a broader consensus across the ideological and institutional spectrum that mirrored the general mood of the public. The Lutheran Church had a particular interest in acting as reputational entrepreneur for these men deeply implicated in mass murder. Some of them had been pastors, others active members of the church, and the Lutheran Church had a history of ardent anti-Semitism. Managing its own post-war reputation seemed to require exonerating others from the crimes committed. The Lutheran Church started to change this position at the end of the 1950s, and the dismissal of Biberstein testifies to internal conflicts which were to erupt publicly a few years later.

Concentration camp guards

The Auschwitz Trial in the first half of the 1960s, and a decade later the Majdanek trial were situated in a different normative landscape, and both contributed to its further change (Karstedt 2008a). Victims started to have a voice and a presence in criminal trials, which they had not had in the immediate post-war years. Suffering, although temporally more distant, was brought to the fore during this later period. Next, prosecutions had been resumed since the mid-1950s, following international pressure and national initiatives, often by small groups and individuals. Finally, public opinion started to change towards recognition of the crimes of the Holocaust. Indeed, the moral assessment of the Holocaust had started to change profoundly, and the defendants in the trials were confronted with a public that was ready to assign negative reputations to them. Because the trials started nearly 20 years after the war, all defendants had had a respectable life before punishment.

Hans Stark was sentenced for murdering prisoners in Auschwitz in the most atrocious ways. Since he was a minor at that time (under 18 years old) he was sentenced according to juvenile law to 10 years' imprisonment. Before the trial he had trained for and worked as a teacher in an agricultural school. Afterwards, he was barred from being a teacher, but worked in the chemical industry and developed pesticides of the kind that had been used in Auschwitz. Hermine Braunsteiner-Ryan was sentenced for torturing prisoners in the women's camp Ravensbrück in 1949, but released in 1950 after serving only a fraction of her three-year sentence. She emigrated with her husband, a US solider, to Canada, and in the mid-1960s prosecution for her involvement in the death camp of Majdanek started. In the trial she was sentenced to two life terms of imprisonment for mass killings involving children. She was pardoned in 1996 because of ill health. During her trial she never showed any signs of remorse or recognition of guilt, and tried to intimidate the victim witnesses.

Both cases demonstrate the ambiguous nature of change in public opinions, and new assessments of these offenders and their crimes. There seems to be a division between offenders, some being welcomed back into the fold, others denounced and excluded, the latter personified by Hermine Braunstein. Excerpts from the Auschwitz trial show that only one of them showed faint recognition of having done something wrong. As society was changing, the offenders who had all led respectable lives in the period after the Second World War and leading up to their trials, did not feel any pressure to morally re-assess their actions, and hardly could accept or even understand the disrepute into which the trial brought them.

Reputations, the transitional moment and the *longue durée* of normative change

The 'transitional moment' throws established reputations in disarray, and in particular the reputations of those who were sentenced in procedures of transitional justice. Sentenced war criminals in post-war Germany had to re-build their lives after punishment. They received the support of a wide range of networks, as well as from the public that tended towards collective amnesia during the first decades after the war. The ex-prisoners could relate to smaller social circles as well as the broader public in memories of a common fate, and they provided backdrops for personal identification for many others. They were welcomed back as 'same', not as 'others' who had been stigmatised by a criminal sentence and imprisonment. Though under very different conditions and in a contrasting environment, ex-prisoners in Northern Ireland seem to experience a similar situation of support and slow changes in their own as well as their public images and reputation (Shirlow and McEvoy 2008).

The fact that the Nazi war criminals could share their reputation within their more or less confined social groups, exempted them from confronting their crimes and guilt. They could claim innocence, or at least ignorance, and they shared these feelings with numerous others. Both high-ranking as well as less visible Nazi war criminals could take advantage of reputational entrepreneurs, who campaigned for their release and eased their way back into similar lives in the new democratic society. However, their reputations became increasingly contested as a younger generation embraced a different perspective on war crimes and the Holocaust. The lines that they could not transcend in their reputational claims were often blurred and thus misjudged by high-level ex-prisoners. They might have been misled by a most supportive climate in their own social circles that was not fully shared by the public. As much as their reputational claims were supported by the normative climate of collective amnesia and denial, there are hardly any indicators that these individuals actively and decisively shaped collective memories in post-war Germany. They did neither acquire a reputation of evil, at best of the controversial, nor did they achieve a reputation of total innocence in the long run. The normative change mainly affected them rather that they had an active part in it, though it cannot be excluded that their influence slowed down and impeded changes of the normative climate. On the other hand, their lives after punishment were vulnerable to changes, loss of reputation and public scandals that often hit them unexpectedly after they had confidently settled back into their lives. Transitional moments it seems have a *longue durée*, and transitional justice takes time. German history demonstrates that transitional and international criminal justice still need to solve 'prisoners' dilemmas'.

Notes

1 Earlier versions of this research were presented at the Seminar 'The Experiences of Specific Groups of Ex-Offenders' of the ESRC Seminar Series 'Life after Punishment', Keele University, 2007, at a seminar at Warwick University, 2008, at a conference 'Transitional Justice and Rule of Law' at the Flemish Academic Centre, Brussels, 2009, and at the American Bar Foundation 2010. I am grateful to Shadd Maruna, Richard Sparks, Stephen Farrall, Stephan Parmentier, Adam Czarnota, Martin Krygier and Nancy Adler for their comments. I am hugely indebted to Gary Fine whose work on 'Difficult Reputations' and guidance provided invaluable insights and conceptual frameworks. I owe particular gratitude to Matthias Koch, Faculty of Sociology, University of Bielefeld for his invaluable research support. Parts of this chapter were published in German (Karstedt 2008b).

2 I use the term 'transitional justice' in its broader sense and according to the United Nations Report of the Secretary General on transitional justice. Contemporary transitional justice is viewed as 'the full range of processes and mechanisms associated with a society's attempts to come to terms with the legacy of large-scale past abuses, in order to ensure accountability, serve justice and achieve reconciliation' (UNSC 2004: 4). Transitional justice thus includes criminal prosecution of offenders before national as well as international tribunals and courts, civil procedures to claim damages for victims,

lustration and vetting policies for collaborators and members of past regimes, amnesties for individuals or groups of perpetrators, as well as truth commissions. In the aftermath of the Second World War, all types of procedures (with the exception of truth commissions) were used in the European countries that had suffered from German occupation and in Germany itself. In its broadest sense transitional justice at this time comprised of national court and lustration procedures, as well as of international criminal justice and procedures conducted by the Allies in their respective theatres of war and areas of occupation (see also Karstedt 2010).

3 I owe this term to Nicola Lacey and the title of her book, *The Prisoners' Dilemma* (Lacey 2008).

4 See Fine (2001) on the relationship between reputation and the formation of collective memories.

5 During his years in Spandau Prison in Berlin, his family was supported by a fund to which high level industrialists and friends contributed (Sereny 1996).

6 It is still contested how many of the German population actually knew about the Holocaust, which took place nearly exclusively outside Germany, and what and how much they knew; see Silbermann and Stoffers 2000, and Johnson and Reuband 2005 for detailed analyses.

7 The extent of the involvement of the German Army in the Holocaust became publicly visible only in an exhibition on the German Army in the 1990s (*Wehrmachtsausstellung*). Only since the late 1970s the Federal Army stopped naming barracks and other sites after high-ranking commanders in Hitler's army, and started to rename some of these that were linked to the names of war criminals.

8 Unsurprisingly, Hartley Shawcross, who had led the British prosecution at the Nuremberg Tribunal, was in opposition (von Lingen 2009: 168).

References

Alexander, Jeffrey (2002) 'On the Social Construction of Moral Universals. The "Holocaust" from War Crime to Trauma Drama', *European Journal of Social Theory*, 5: 5–85.

Browning, Christopher (1992) *Ordinary Men: Police Battalion 101 and the Final Solution in Poland*. New York, NY: Harper Collins.

Calverley, Adam, and Farrall, Stephen (2011, forthcoming) 'The sensual dynamics of processes of personal reform: desistance from crime and the role of emotions', in Karstedt, S., Loader I. and Strang H. (eds) *Emotions, Crime and Justice*. Oxford: Hart Publishing.

Cohen, Stanley (2009) 'Unspeakable memories and Commensurable Laws', in Karstedt, S. (ed.) *Legal Institutions and Collective Memories*. Oxford: Hart Publishing, pp 27–37.

Dönitz, Karl (1968) *Mein wechselvolles Leben*. Goettingen: Musterschmidt.

Dönitz, Karl (1972) *Deutsche Strategie zur See im Zweiten Weltkrieg. Die Antworten des Grossadmirals auf 40 Fragen*. Frankfurt am Main: Bernardt & Graefe.

Farrall, Stephen and Calverley, Adam (2006) *Understanding Desistance From Crime*. London: Open University Press.

Fine, Gary Alan (2001) *Difficult Reputations. Collective Memories of the Evil, Inept and Controversial*. Chicago, IL and London: Chicago University Press.

Frei, Norbert (2003) *Vergangenheitspolitik. Die Anfaenge der Bundesrepublik und die NS-Vergangenheit*, 2nd edn. München: Deutscher Taschenbuch Verlag.

Friedrich, Joerg (2007) *Die kalte Amnestie. NS-Täter in der Bundesrepublik*. Berlin: List.

Fulbrook, Mary (1999) *German National Identity after the Holocaust*. Cambridge: Polity.

Goldhagen, Daniel J. (1996) *Hitler's Willing Executioners. Ordinary Germans and the Holocaust*. New York, NY: A. Knopf.

Hagan, John (2003) *Justice in the Balkans. Prosecuting War Crimes in the Hague Tribunal*. Chicago, IL and London: Chicago University Press.

Hagan, John and Kutnjak Ivkovic, Sanja (2006) 'War crimes, democracy and the rule of law in Belgrade, the former Yugoslavia and beyond', *The Annals of the American Academy of Political and Social Science*, 605: 129–51.

Heimer, Carol and Stinchcombe, Arthur (2009) 'Biographies, Legal Cases and Political Transitions', in Karstedt, S. (ed.) *Legal Institutions and Collective Memories*. Oxford: Hart Publishing, pp 281–313.

Herbert, Ulrich (1996) *Best. Biographische Studien über Radikalismus, Weltanschauung und Vernunft 1903–1989*. Bonn: Dietz Nachfolger.

Hunter, Ben (2008) 'Narratives of Change: Exploring Desistance from White-Collar Crime', PhD thesis, Keele University, Keele.

Johnson, Eric and Reuband, Karl-Heinz (2005) *What We Knew. Terror, Mass Murder and Everyday Life in Nazi Germany*. London: John Murray.

Judt, Tony (2005) *Postwar. A History of Europe since 1945*. London: William Heinemann.

Karstedt, Susanne (1998) 'Coming to Terms with the Past in Germany after 1945 and 1989: Public Judgments on Procedures and Justice', *Law and Policy*, 20: 15–56.

Karstedt, Susanne (2008a) 'The Nuremberg Tribunal and German Society: International Justice and Local Judgment in Post-Conflict Reconstruction', in Blumenthal, D. A. and McCormack, T. (eds) *The Legacy of Nuremberg. Civilising Influence or Institutionalised Vengeance?*, International Humanitarian Law Series, Vol. 20. Leiden: Koninklijke Brill, pp 13–35.

Karstedt, Susanne (2008b) 'Leben nach der Strafe: "Schließlich stellte ihn die Landeskirche ein". Verurteilte nationalsozialistische Kriegsverbrecher im Nachkriegsdeutschland' (*Life after Punishment: Sentenced war criminals in post-war Germany*), in Groenemeyer, A. and Wieseler, S. (eds) *Soziologie sozialer Probleme und sozialer Kontrolle*. Wiesbaden: VS Verlag für Sozialwissenschaften, pp 256–76.

Karstedt, Susanne (2009) 'Introduction', in Karstedt, S. (ed.) *Legal Institutions and Collective Memories*. Oxford: Hart Publishing, pp 1–24.

Karstedt, Susanne (2010) 'From Absence to Presence, from Silence to Voice: Victims in International and Transitional Justice since the Nuremberg Trials', *International Review of Victimology*, 17: 9–30.

Lacey, Nicola (2008) *The Prisoners' Dilemma. Political Economy and Punishment in Contemporary Democracies*. Cambridge: *Cambridge University Press*.

Mallinder, Louise (2008) *Amnesty, Human Rights and Political Transitions*. Oxford: Hart Publishing.

Olick, Jeffrey K. (2005) *In the House of the Hangman. The Agonies of German Defeat, 1943–1945*. Chicago, IL: University of Chicago Press.

Reif, Adelbert (ed.) (1978) *Albert Speer. Kontroversen um ein deutsches Phänomen*. Muenchen: Bernard & Graefe.

Rückerl, Adalbert (1984) *NS-Verbrechen vor Gericht*. Heidelberg: C. F. Mueller.

Sereny, Gitta (1996) *Albert Speer. His Battle with Truth*. New York, NY: Vintage.

Shirlow, Peter and McEvoy, Kieran (2008) *Beyond the Wire. Former Prisoners and Conflict Transformation in Northern Ireland*. London: Pluto Press.

Silbermann, Alphons and Stoffers, Manfred (2000) *Auschwitz: Nie davon gehört?* Berlin: Rowohlt.

Speer, Albert (1969) *Erinnerungen*. Berlin: Ullstein (published as 'Inside the Third Reich' in 1981).

Speer, Albert (1975) *Spandauer Tagebücher*. Berlin: Propylän (published as 'Spandau: The Secret Diaries' in 1977).

Theissen, Gunnar (2009) 'Common past, divided truth: The Truth and Reconciliation Commission in South African public opinion', in Karstedt, S. (ed) *Legal Institutions and Collective Memories*. Oxford: Hart Publishing, pp 101–34.

UNSC (United Nations Security Council) (2004) *The rule of law and transitional justice in conflict and post-conflict societies*, Report of the Secretary-General to the Security Council, 23 August 2004, S/2004/616. New York: United Nations Security Council.

van Zyl Smit, Dirk (2002a) 'Punishment and Human Rights in International Criminal Justice', *Human Rights Law Review*, 2: 1–17.

van Zyl Smit, Dirk (2002b) 'Sentencing and the International Criminal Court', Sentencing Observer, 1, June: 1–2.

van Zyl Smit, Dirk (2005) 'International Imprisonment', International and Comparative Law Quarterly, 54: 357–84.

von Lingen, Kerstin (2009) *Kesselring's Last Battle. War Crimes Trials and Cold War Politics, 1945–1960*. Lawrence, KS: University Press of Kansas.

Appendix

Table 1 Overview of Cases of Sentenced Nazi War Criminals 1946–1983

Name	*Position during the NS regime*	*Sentence*	*Sentence commuted*	*Release: year and reason for release*	*Term served (without internment)*	*Life after Punishment: position and activities*
Nuremberg International Military Tribunal (20 November 1945–1 October 1946)						
Dönitz, Karl	Naval officer; commander of the German Naval Forces in WWII from 1943–1945; successor of Hitler in May 1945	10 years imprisonment	/	1956 released after serving full term	10 years	Published his memoirs "My changeful life" in 1968, where he describes his role exclusively as a military one. In high demand as public speaker at meetings of veterans, and veterans' associations, also for the new Federal Army founded in 1955. Died on 24 December 1980.
Raeder, Erich	Naval Officer; from 1928 to 1943 Commander of the German Naval Forces	Life sentence	/	Released in September 1955 because of ill health	9 years	Published his memoirs, "My Life" after his release. Rare public appearances as speaker. Died in November 1960

(continued)

Table 1 (Cont'd)

Name	*Position during the NS regime*	*Sentence*	*Sentence commuted*	*Release: year and reason for release*	*Term served (without internment)*	*Life after Punishment: position and activities*
Von Schirach, Baldur	Leader of all NS Youth organisations. Since 1940 Governor of Vienna and Head of Youth Education. As Governor of Vienna responsible for the deportation of its Jewish population to concentration and death camps.	20 years	/	Released in October 1966 after serving full term.	20 years	In 1967, he published his memoirs "I believed in Hitler". He denied any knowledge of the genocide/mass murder of the Jews in his positions. Ran a bed and breakfast with his family, no public appearances, died in August 1974.
Speer, Albert	Was part of Hitler's inner circle. Since 1937 responsible for all buildings in the capital city of Berlin. Since 1942 Secretary for Armament and Munition, and as such responsible for the war economy and the deployment of forced labour.	20 years	/	September 1966 released after serving full term	20 years	Published several volumes of memoirs after his release until his death in 1981. Was a public figure with a strong presence in the media, and easily integrated into elites of West Germany. Attracted attention nationally and internationally as the "Gentleman-Nazi".

Nuremberg Trial against the High Command of the Army (30 December 1947–14 April 1949)						
Reinhardt, Georg-Hans	Colonel General of the Army and Commander-in-Chief of the Northern Army. Involved in war crimes in the Soviet Union	5 years		Early release in June 1952, remission of unserved sentence	3 years	Chairman of the Society for Military Affairs, a think tank, since 1954; author of numerous memoranda on military affairs and security for the Federal Government and the Federal Army of (West)Germany. He was awarded the Federal Cross of Merit for his services in 1962.
Other Military Tribunals against Members of the German Army conducted by the Allies						
Kesselring, Albert	Field Marshall of the German Army in Southern Europe, Africa and Italy. Responsible for the execution of 365 Italian hostages, and tried by a British Military Court in Venice	Death Sentence	Commuted to life sentence in 1947, to 21 years in 1948	Early release in 1952, remission of unserved sentence after having been diagnosed with cancer	5 years	From 1952–1960 chairman of the Association of Veterans. Between 1953 and 1955 publication of two volumes of memoirs “Soldier Until the Last Day”, and “Reflections on World War II”. He never distanced himself from his actions as commander or from his loyalty to Hitler.

(*continued*)

Table 1 (Cont'd)

Name	*Position during the NS regime*	*Sentence*	*Sentence commuted*	*Release: year and reason for release*	*Term served (without internment)*	*Life after Punishment: position and activities*
Ramcke, Hermann-Bernhard	Highly decorated as General of the Paratroopers, commander of the city of Brest (France) declared fortress in 1944. Involved in war crimes against the civilian population of Brest and tried by a French Military Court	5.5 years in 1951	Allowance for 57 months of pre-trial detention	Release in June 1951, remission of unserved sentence	3 months	After his release executive manager in an industrial enterprise; published in right-wing extremist journals and publishing houses. Speaker at meetings of former members of the SS Army. A company of the Federal Army as well as the Minister of Defence were present at his funeral in 1968
Nuremberg Trial against the Foreign Ministry (15 November 1947–11 April 1949)						
Kehrl, Hans	SS Brigade Leader in the Headquarters of the SS Directorate; Director of the Office for Armament, attached to the Executive Manager for Armament, Albert Speer (see above). In this position responsible for illegal transfer and looting of property in the course of Nazi resettlement policies	15 years	/	Released in February 1951, remission of unserved sentence	2 years	After his release business consultant and appointed to the Federal Commission of Inquiry into the Concentration of the German Economy in 1963. Published his memoirs "Crisis Manager in the Third Reich" in 1973. Died in 1984

Count Schwerin von Krosigk, Johann Ludwig	High level positions in the Treasury and Foreign Ministry. Minister in the last (acting) government of Karl Dönitz in May 1945; Foreign Minister. Responsible for the looting of Jewish property by the German fiscal administration and tax authorities.	10 years	Commuted to 10 years in January 1951 by US High Commissioner McCloy	Released in January 1951, remission of unserved sentence	2 years	After his release author, journalist and publicist. Published his memoirs "It happened in Germany" in 1951 followed by three volumes of "Personal Memories" in 1974. Died 1977.
Nuremberg Trial against the Ministry of Justice (Lawyers' Trial) (17 February–14 December 1947)						
Ammon, Wilhelm von	Judge, seconded to the Ministry of Justice. Responsible for drafting the orders that allowed for searches, seizures and arrests by the Gestapo without any legal foundation, mainly in the occupied countries. Participant in the preparatory meetings for the euthanasia programme.	10 years	Released January 1951, clemency petition from US High Commissioner McCloy	Released January 1951 by grant of pardon	3 years	From 1957 to 1970 Director of the regional administration of the Lutheran Church in the South of Germany; author of legal commentary on the Bavarian Canon Constitution. Died 1992.

(*continued*)

Table 1 (Cont'd)

Name	*Position during the NS regime*	*Sentence*	*Sentence commuted*	*Release: year and reason for release*	*Term served (without internment)*	*Life after Punishment: position and activities*
Schlegelberger, Franz	Secretary of State in the Ministry of Justice, and temporarily acting Minister of Justice. Responsible for the penal decree that provided for the death penalty for the destruction of published orders by the German occupying government in Poland. During his term in office the number of death sentences increased dramatically.	Life sentence	/	Early release in January 1951, allegedly unfit for detention	3 years	After his release immediately subjected to de-nazification procedures and classified as "exonerated". Received full pension as state secretary, which was subsequently revised. Unsuccessful attempts at bringing further charges against him. Died 1970.

Nuremberg Trial of Doctors (9 December 1946–20 August 1947)

Beiglböck, Wilhelm	Doctor/ internist in the Dachau concentration camp; responsible for human experiments on inmates by exposing them to life-threatening subnormal temperatures.	15 years	/	Early release in December 1951, remission of unserved sentence	4 years	After his release he was offered a position by a professor in the Medical School of a South German university, who had been a member of the Panel of Experts of the German Society for Internal Medicine. He supported him in securing a position as Head of the Department of Internal Medicine in a hospital in a North German city in 1952. Died 1963

(continued)

Table 1 (Cont'd)

Name	*Position during the NS regime*	*Sentence*	*Sentence commuted*	*Release: year and reason for release*	*Term served (without internment)*	*Life after Punishment: position and activities*
Oberheuser, Herta	Doctor in the concentration camp of Ravensbrück; responsible for life-threatening experiments on inmates with sulfonamide	20 years	Commuted to 10 years in January 1951 by US High Commissioner McCloy	April 1952 early release through remission of sentence	5 years	After her release licensed as medical general practitioner in a small town in Northern Germany, and in a sanatorium run by the Templars in the region. In 1956, she was recognised by a survivor of Ravensbrück, who reported her to the police. In 1958 her admission to medical practice was withdrawn, and she had to close her surgery. She was barred from practicing as medical doctor. Died 1978.

Trial of the Task Force Groups (15 September 1947–10 April 1948)

Biberstein, Ernst	Had been a pastor in the Lutheran Church; Senior SS Storm Unit Leader; until 1943 Commander of the Task Force No 6 of the Task Forces Group C deployed in Ukraine; responsible for the murder of 2,000 to 3,000 Jewish men, women and children.	Death Penalty	Commuted to life sentence in January 1951 by US High Commissioner McCloy	Early release in May 1958, remission of unserved sentence. Campaign for his release led by the regional Lutheran Church of North Germany	10 years	After his release he was offered a position in the administration of the Lutheran Church, from which he was dismissed at the beginning of the 1960s. Afterwards he worked in minor, low level positions as administrator.
Steimle, Eugen	SS Regiment Leader; Member of the Security Service and Commander of two Special Task Forces of the Security Service; responsible for genocide in the Soviet Union.	Death Penalty	Commuted to 20 years imprisonment in January 1951 by US High Commissioner McCloy	Early release in June 1954, remission of unserved sentence	6 years	After his release teacher for German, history and social and civic studies at a Lutheran grammar school from 1955–1975 in South Germany. Died 1987.

(continued)

Table 1 (Cont'd)

Name	*Position during the NS regime*	*Sentence*	*Sentence commuted*	*Release: year and reason for release*	*Term served (without internment)*	*Life after Punishment: position and activities*
Sandberger, Martin	SS Regiment Leader; commander of Task Force 1a; principal responsibility for the genocide in the Baltic states with more than a million of victims.	Death Penalty	Commuted to life sentence in January 1951 by US High Commissioner McCloy	Early release in May 1958, remission of unserved sentence. Supported by a campaign of numerous members of the South German establishment, amongst them a Minister of Justice of a southern German state, the Bishop of the regional Lutheran Church, and a renowned Social Democrat and Vice President of the Federal Parliament	10 years	After his release, his Church connections helped him to secure a position as legal adviser in a major company. Attempts at resuming prosecution were dismissed. Died 2010.

Auschwitz Trial in Frankfurt (1963–1965)						
Stark, Hans	Member of the Gestapo (Secret Police) in the camp; sentenced for "*murder in an unknown number of cases, at least 340*" according to the verdict of the Frankfurt Regional Court in August 1965.	10 years imprisonment; sentenced according to Juvenile Court Law as he was underage when committing his crimes	/	Early release in 1969, remission of unserved sentence	4 years	After his release he worked in the chemical industry, where he developed pesticides. Died 1991.
Majdanek Trial in Duesseldorf (1975–1981)						
Hermine Ryan nee Braunsteiner	Guard in the death/ concentration camps of Ravensbrück und Majdanek	Life sentence	/	Pardoned by the Prime Minster of North-Rhine - Westphalia and later Federal President, because of ill health.	15 years	Died 1999.

Index